Restoration Stage Comedies and Hollywood Remarriage Films

In *Restoration Stage Comedies and Hollywood Remarriage Films*, Elizabeth Kraft brings the canon of Restoration comedy into the conversation initiated by Stanley Cavell in his book *Pursuits of Happiness: The Hollywood Comedy of Remarriage*. Before there could be imagined remarriages of the sort Cavell documents, there had to be imagined marriages of equality. Such imagined marriages were first mapped out on the Restoration stage by witty pairs such as Harriet and Dorimant, Millamant and Mirabell, and Alithea and Harcourt who are precursors of the central couples in films such as *Bringing Up Baby*, *His Girl Friday*, and *The Lady Eve*. In considering the Restoration comedy canon in one-on-one discourse with the Hollywood remarriage comedy canon, Kraft demonstrates the indebtedness of the twentieth-century films to the Restoration dramatic texts and the philosophical richness of both canons as they explore the nature and significance of marriage as pursuit of moral perfectionism. This book will be of interest to specialists in Restoration drama and film scholars.

Elizabeth Kraft is Professor of English at the University of Georgia, USA.

British Literature in Context in the Long Eighteenth Century
Series Editors: Eugenia Zuroski Jenkins and Jack Lynch

This series aims to promote original scholarship on the intersection of British literature and history in the long eighteenth century, from the Restoration through the first generation of the Romantic era. Both "literature" and "history" are broadly conceived. Literature might include not only canonical novels, poems, and plays but also essays, life-writing, and belles lettres of all sorts, by both major and minor authors. History might include not only traditional political and social history but also the history of the book, the history of science, the history of religion, the history of scholarship, and the history of sexuality, as well as broader questions of historiography and periodization. The series editors invite proposals for both monographs and collections taking a wide range of approaches. Contributions may be interdisciplinary but should be grounded in sound historical research. All manuscripts should be written so as to be accessible to a wide audience while also making lasting contributions to the field.

For a full list of titles in this series, please visit www.routledge.com/series/ASHSER-2115

The French Language and British Literature, 1756–1830
Marcus Tomalin

Christopher Smart's English Lyrics
Translation in the eighteenth century
Rosalind Powell

British Sporting Literature and Culture in the Long Eighteenth Century
Sharon Harrow

British Women and the Intellectual World in the Long Eighteenth Century
Teresa Barnard

Bluestockings Now!
The evolution of a social role
Edited by Deborah Heller

Dangerous Women, Libertine Epicures, and the Rise of Sensibility, 1670–1730
Laura Linker

Gender and Space in British Literature, 1660–1820
Mona Narain and Karen Gevirtz

Graveyard Poetry
Religion, aesthetics and the mid-eighteenth-century poetic condition
Eric Parisot

Restoration Stage Comedies and Hollywood Remarriage Films

In conversation with Stanley Cavell

Elizabeth Kraft

Routledge
Taylor & Francis Group

LONDON AND NEW YORK

First published 2017 by Routledge

2 Park Square, Milton Park, Abingdon, Oxfordshire OX14 4RN

52 Vanderbilt Avenue, New York, NY 10017

Routledge is an imprint of the Taylor & Francis Group, an informa business

First issued in paperback 2019

Copyright © 2017 E. Kraft

The right of Elizabeth Kraft to be identified as author of this work has been asserted by her in accordance with sections 77 and 78 of the Copyright, Designs and Patents Act 1988.

All rights reserved. No part of this book may be reprinted or reproduced or utilised in any form or by any electronic, mechanical, or other means, now known or hereafter invented, including photocopying and recording, or in any information storage or retrieval system, without permission in writing from the publishers.

Notice:
Product or corporate names may be trademarks or registered trademarks, and are used only for identification and explanation without intent to infringe.

British Library Cataloguing in Publication Data
A catalogue record for this book is available from the British Library

Library of Congress Cataloging in Publication Data
Names: Kraft, Elizabeth, author.
Title: Restoration stage comedies and Hollywood remarriage films : in conversation with Stanley Cavell / by Elizabeth Kraft, University of Georgia.
Description: New York : Routledge, 2016. | Series: British literature in context in the long eighteenth century | Includes bibliographical references and index.
Identifiers: LCCN 2016017506| ISBN 9781472484581 (alk. paper) | ISBN 9781315605876 (ebk)
Subjects: LCSH: English drama—Restoration, 1660–1700—History and criticism. | English drama (Comedy)—History and criticism. | Screwball comedy films—United States—History and criticism. | Influence (Literary, artistic, etc.)
Classification: LCC PR698.C6 K73 2016 | DDC 822/.409—dc23
LC record available at https://lccn.loc.gov/2016017506

ISBN: 978-1-4724-8458-1 (hbk)
ISBN: 978-0-367-88205-1 (pbk)

Typeset in Sabon
by Book Now Ltd, London

Contents

	Acknowledgments	vi
	Prologue: The reason and the rhyme	1
1	Something from nothing: Marriage, conversation, and the tragicomic plot	24
2	The thin man of mode	50
3	Whippoorwills, gypsies, and fantasies of the night: Aphra Behn's *The Rover* and Frank Capra's *It Happened One Night*	76
4	Luck, be a lady: Aphra Behn, Preston Sturges, and the ethics of genre	99
5	Playing and not playing: William Wycherley's *The Country Wife* and Howard Hawks's *Bringing Up Baby*	126
6	Forgotten men: William Wycherley's *The Plain Dealer* and Gregory La Cava's *My Man Godfrey*	155
7	Provisos and reprieves: William Congreve's *The Way of the World* and Howard Hawks's *His Girl Friday*	181
8	Happily ever after? The awful truth about careless husbands	204
	Epilogue: Hope springs eternal	224
	Bibliography	235
	Index	247

Acknowledgments

I would like to express thanks to the University of Georgia's Study in a Second Discipline Fellowship which provided me the opportunity to study for the academic year of 2003–2004 with our excellent core and affiliated film faculty: Charles Eidsvick, Antje Ascheid, and, especially, my faculty sponsor and mentor, Richard Neupert (all of Drama and Film), Laura Mason (History), Doris Kadish (Romance Languages), Steven Grossvogel (Romance Languages), Karim Traore (Comparative Literature), and Joel Black (Comparative Literature), whom I also thank for first mentioning to me Stanley Cavell's book *Pursuits of Happiness*, which made all the difference.

I received a seed-money grant from the University of Georgia Research Foundation which enabled me to attend the "Stanley Cavell and Literary Criticism" conference held in Edinburgh in May 2008. My time at the conference in the presence of Professor Cavell and scholars working in the context of his philosophical engagement with literature was invaluable as I began to draft my book. A Willson Center Fellowship in the Spring of 2010 was instrumental in allowing me time to continue the writing process which was finally completed in the summer of 2013. Once my manuscript made it to readers, I began to incur further debts for comments and directions that led to revision and refinement. On this count, I am particularly grateful to Professor Richard Burt for an incisive critique that helped me hone my final argument. Two anonymous commentators also provided feedback and direction as did Jack Lynch and Eugenia Zuroski Jenkins, editors of the series British Literature in Context in the Long Eighteenth Century in which I'm most honored to be included.

I am, as always, grateful to the University of Georgia's English Department, my home department, which made it possible for me to teach the material in various ways, beginning in May of 2002 with an intensive three-week course on the Restoration courtship comedies and the Hollywood comedies of remarriage and ending with a full semester on the same topic, but an expanded canon, in the Fall of 2012. Along the way, thanks to generous course assignments and supportive department heads (Nelson Hilton, Douglas Anderson, Valerie Babb, and Michael Moran) and undergraduate coordinators (Roxanne Eberle, Anne Williams, Sujata Iyengar, and Aidan Wasley), I was also able to work with students on film genre, on Restoration comedy, and on the Hollywood canon in classes that didn't reveal—but that did contribute to—the analogy I was pursuing.

I imagine, in some ways, I will be engaged in conversations with students about this material for the remainder of my time as a professor, and students will continue to refine my thinking for years to come. To date, though, I do have student debt that I would like to acknowledge: I am very grateful to the students in my first Maymester course on the material (which was a magical experience for me) and to those in my most recent semester-long course (in which I received some of the best student work of my 30-year career as a college professor). Those two classes—one taught as I began my project and one as I drew it to a close—truly demonstrate the thorough integration of teaching and research at the University of Georgia. In no way could I or would I have begun this project without my students; in no way could I or would I have completed it without them.

I would like to express gratitude to Brad Bassler, my colleague in Philosophy, for including me on the committees of his students Susan Maples and David Hart whose work was defined by engagement with Cavell on an honors thesis and a PhD dissertation, respectively. The fine discussions in the defenses for those superb projects were inspiring to me as I began serious work on my own project. I also thank Dr. Patricia Hamilton for inviting me to Union University in Jackson, Tennessee, to deliver a presentation on this project for the faculty and students in the Spring of 2014 as I geared myself up for the final "push." I flew through a potential tornado on a tiny plane for the visit. It was frightening, but well worth it. Feedback from Dr. Hamilton and her colleagues instrumentally affected my revisions as I neared the end.

I owe a profound debt of gratitude to Ann Donahue of Ashgate Press for commissioning this project and for nurturing it for many years. I also want to thank her for taking on another role in the end as she copy-edited my final draft for presentation to Taylor and Francis after the sale of Ashgate. Ann is a multi-talented editor whose friendship I value and whose talents I admire. To my new editors, Liz Levine and Nicole Eno, who gamely took up the project, I am grateful for professionalism and care as my book proceeded to publication.

I would like to thank William F. Prokasy who, as Provost of the University of Georgia, instituted the Study in a Second Discipline program which acknowledges, supports, and values continued intellectual development of faculty members by encouraging interdisciplinary collaboration as well as individual growth. Hugh Ruppersburg, Distinguished Professor of English and Associate Dean of the Franklin College of Arts and Sciences, a long-time advocate of film studies and of interdisciplinary programs, was also supportive during my time as a "film student," as was the then-department head of Drama and Film, Stanley Longman.

Bill Free encouraged this project from the beginning. His enthusiasm and support early on were essential.

Finally, I want to note that although my book is subtitled "in conversation with Stanley Cavell," I was not in correspondence with the philosopher during my research of and writing on the topic. However, in the very beginning, I contacted him with a description of my interests. His response was generous and encouraging, though he expressed in that exchange, as he had in *Pursuits of Happiness*, reservations about the relationship between Restoration comedy and Hollywood remarriage films. I hope to have answered some of those reservations, but whether or not I have done so to his satisfaction, it was a privilege and a true intellectual pleasure to try.

Prologue
The reason and the rhyme

This book began with an analogy that has evolved into a thesis. In the beginning, I noted a certain stylistic similarity between the comedies of the Restoration stage and the comedies of 1930s Hollywood film. It seemed a coincidence worthy of remark and occasional pedagogical elaboration that two such different times, places, and cultures could sustain generic interest in the witty pair at the center of each genre and could relish the barrage of language characteristic of these repartee-laden dramatic worlds. The rapid-fire back and forth of Rosalind Russell and Cary Grant in *His Girl Friday* conveys the sort of heightened communication—attentiveness to nuance, repetition, double entendre, connotation, body language—one hears and imagines (and in good performances witnesses) in scenes between *The Man of Mode*'s Harriet and Dorimant or *The Way of the World*'s Millamant and Mirabell. It was the two genres' similar approach to dialogue, their obvious pleasure in the exchange of spoken words, that initially prompted my bringing them together in order to think about the kinds of dramatic energy and psychological (or philosophical) commitment necessary on the parts of writers, actors, characters, and audiences alike to fully realize the performative moment. Wit, far from being a superficial feature of each genre's style, is an essential component of each dramatic world. In addition, the couple at the center of each canonical text of Restoration comedy and Hollywood comedy alike epitomize the brilliance of the well-formulated phrase (the carefully constructed argument, the clever twist on words, the effortless redirection of topic) while also demonstrating the power of attentiveness and reciprocity—subjects far from superficial to the genres or to the ages in which the genres flourished. When I encountered the work of Stanley Cavell, I began to think more deeply about this analogy. Cavell has acknowledged that the back and forth of witty exchange in the Hollywood comedies of remarriage can take the form (as it does in Frank Capra's *It Happened One Night*) of "incessant bickering," but, of course, marriage itself "entails a certain willingness for bickering," as well as the recognition that there is a kind of "bickering that is itself a mark, not of bliss exactly, but . . . of caring."[1] Cavell calls this insight "a little parable of philosophy, or of philosophical criticism" (*PH*, 86). Further, he remarks, "the quarrels of romance and the tirades of matrimony, arguments of desire and of despair" are "[s]o essential . . . to the genre of remarriage that . . . [they] may be taken . . . to pose the problem: What does a happy marriage *sound* like?" (*PH*, 86). This central question is tied to (either as cause of the focus, as its effect, or a combination of both) certain features of the film industry unique to the times that produced the genre—the recent introduction of sound as well as the nature of the screen presences and individual strengths of talent possessed by the actors employed in what is known today as the "classical Hollywood" period:

> Since the sound of argument, of wrangling, of verbal battle, is the characteristic sound of these comedies—as if the screen had hardly been able to wait to burst into speech—an essential criterion for membership in that small set of actors who are featured in these films is the ability to bear up under this assault of words, to give as good as you get, where what is good must always, however strong, maintain its good spirits, a test of intellectual as well as of spiritual stamina, of what you might call "ear."
>
> (*PH*, 86)

With very little revision, the same comment could be made regarding the comedies of the Restoration stage, newly "hearing" the sounds of actual women's voices, newly seeing female characters embodied by actresses of distinct and vivid personalities—actresses capable of giving "as good as" they got, maintaining "good spirits," and demonstrating the stamina needed to attend and to respond, the stamina Cavell calls "ear." As Edward A. Langhans has noted, the apron or forestage of the Restoration theater "was ideal for plays where words were important" and "meant that new authors were encouraged to write plays that were highly verbal and full of wit."[2]

The similarity, it turns out, is no coincidence, for the Hollywood repertoire, as Joseph Roach has convincingly demonstrated regarding Hollywood's silent era, is the product of the "deep eighteenth century," an example of the "uneven developments and periodic returns" that characterize this "complicated three-dimensional period" which has yet to end.[3] Roach's study relates the influence of Elinor Glyn, whose fascination with the court life of the reign of Charles II was translated into her signatory creation of Hollywood "It" culture from the beginning of the industry's self-definition. The Hollywood actresses of my concern are a generation removed from those fashioned by Glyn (Gloria Swanson and Clara Bow), but they reflect her influence nonetheless in the sense of self that makes them equal to their male coleads. It is the equality of the pair in the heterosexual relationship that defines the remarriage comedies of the classical Hollywood period, equality first evidenced on the Restoration stage (which reflected the culture of the Restoration court as Elinor Glyn perceived and translated it for the American film audience).

My purpose in bringing these genres together in a close, extended study is to deepen, as it were, our understanding of the deep eighteenth century and to assert the pervasive influence of a canon of work (Restoration stage comedy) often relegated to the footnotes of literary history.

Both Restoration courtship comedies and Hollywood comedies of remarriage, significantly, were products of repertory systems: the two licensed theaters of the Restoration (the King's Company and the Duke's Company) and the five major and two "major minor" Hollywood studios (MGM, Warner Brothers, 20th-Century Fox, Paramount, RKO, Universal, and Columbia).[4] As a result, actors and actresses became important signifiers both on and off stage or screen. John Fawell's observation that "knowing how to use the recognizable actors who fell in a [Hollywood studio] director's way was crucial to the director's ability to create a film of great resonance" applies with equal force to the Restoration theater manager and the plays he staged, as well as the Restoration playwright, who, as Katharine Eisaman Maus has put it, "inevitably wrote with particular performers in mind" in order "to play upon the spectators' sense of the relationship between an actor's personality and the roles he was required to enact."[5] Maus also comments on the "unprecedented celebration of female personality" on the Restoration stage, a celebration, she notes, not particularly echoed in society at large, but one that did argue for a "polarity" rather than a "hierarchy" between the sexes—a feature also notable in the Hollywood comedies of remarriage (599; 612–13).

Being comedic genres, the Restoration plays and the Hollywood films share a preoccupation with the topic of marriage, and both genres are notable for configuring central couples who possess verbal equality. Neither genre disguises the sexual imbalance of power or politics in its time, but both, nevertheless, present the central couple as existing on an equal linguistic plane. It is tempting to argue in each case that the preoccupation with this kind of equality heralds a new social reality—the rise of the companionate marriage on the one hand and the emergence of gender equity in marriage and society at large on the other, but, of course, history does not sustain such a reading. Lawrence Stone's sense that the eighteenth century witnessed a profound shift toward love-based, companionate, marriage, the thesis of his 1977 study, *The Family, Sex, and Marriage in England: 1500–1800*, prompted many critiques and qualifications in a lively scholarly debate that has lasted well into the twenty-first century.[6] Indeed, Maus suggests that the Restoration witty pair were influences on the "urban upper- and upper-middle classes ... [in which] ideas about family life and the relations between the sexes were undergoing profound modification" toward acceptance of companionship or, in Maus's language, "polarity" in marriage.[7] More recently, however, Ruth Perry has insisted that what emerged from the discourse and practice of marriage in the late seventeenth and early eighteenth centuries might more accurately be called the "privatized marriage" in which the wife was "detached ... from her family of origin and from her pre-existing friendships and concerns in order to put her at the service of being a companion to her new husband."[8] Whereas love and mutual attraction clearly became important factors in the early modern literary construction of marriage, reality was, as always, mixed. Marriages for money, position, convenience, custom, and a host of other reasons were made in the seventeenth and eighteenth centuries despite the examples held forth in the plays and the novels of the time. And marriages continue to be contracted on mixed motives even to this day, just as literature and film continue to elevate love and compatibility as the ideal foundation of marital union. What is interesting about the genres at the center of my concern is neither their valuing of love and compatibility (although they do value such) nor the evidence they might provide for some new ideal of marital relations (although they do seem to present a fresh version of an old institution). Rather, the real interest of these genres is that they find the subject of courtship and marriage so fascinatingly nuanced, the couples so distinct and yet so similar, and the individuals in the couples so similar, although so fundamentally different from one another. Like any "genre," these two employ formulaic plots, characters, settings, and scenes, but each instance adds a stroke to the composite painting or slightly shifts the perspective to reveal a new angle from which to view the picture. Marriage, far from being something that can be summed up in a phrase or an ideology, seems in these genres, during the intense periods when they flourished, to be a subject of near inexhaustible possibility, although eventually, both reached what Rick Altman has called a "saturation point" and as genres ceased to interest writers, producers, and audiences alike.[9]

Phillip Harth has observed that "seventeenth-century Englishmen were endlessly intrigued by historical parallels. There was often a political dimension to this interest, but it was by no means the only one. Another dimension was supplied by the perennial fascination with historical coincidence."[10] I agree that such a fascination is "perennial." As Mark Twain is said to have said (although he did not), "history may not repeat itself, but it does rhyme," and it is partly the rhyme of the Restoration and the Hollywood comedies that I find fascinating and significant. I would like to assert a reason for the rhyme as well. The reason is not cultural, but generic. It is this book's assertion that the Restoration period provided the foundational texts of remarriage comedy: first, in works that imagined marriages of equality and ultimately, in the work of Colley Cibber, who wrote the very first remarriage comedy. His *Careless Husband* (an outgrowth of and a response to the preceding age's hard-edged courtship comedies) takes a specifically philosophical look at the ethos that prevailed on the Restoration comic stage and, in doing so, previews the themes and motifs that briefly come to dominate the Hollywood screen.

The audience to whom I am speaking in this book is one that is both fascinated by historical coincidence and skeptical that "coincidence" is the proper term for repetition of the sort found in Restoration stage comedies and classical Hollywood screen comedies. Both genres contribute to the formation of the modern human subject at two crucial moments in the history of western culture. The Restoration period, despite its name, does not mark the restoration of the social order overthrown during the English Civil War. Indeed, as Pat Gill has remarked, Restoration "comedies of manners serve as eloquent testimonies that the Restoration did not restore a past way of life."[11] Instead, the comedies interrogate the social order and evidence, at their heart, a thoroughgoing skepticism about the nature of individual knowledge and judgment in a world that has become in many ways unmoored. The emphasis on contractual relations in these plays echoes similar emphases that will define the political and philosophical thought of John Locke, whose works, significantly, were integral to the thinking of the American founding fathers. Film audiences of the 1930s, too, felt unmoored. Had the vision of equality and prosperity upon which America had been built failed? The economic collapse of 1929 called into question the exceptionalism upon which the still young democratic nation had prided itself. Who or what had betrayed the contract between the nation and its citizens?

Both genres, in other words, emerged and flourished at times in which their nations were attempting to rebuild and reformulate themselves after catastrophic and irreparable loss. Both cultures were characterized by doubt and uncertainty that sometimes rose to the level of philosophical skepticism, intellectual and spiritual climates that would seem inimical to the comic spirit. In fact, Cavell has equated the tragic plot with the triumph of skepticism—the refusal or the inability to love, to accept love, to understand, to communicate—and he has identified the Hollywood melodrama, the "melodrama of the unknown woman," as the genre that shadows the comedy of remarriage in that, for the woman at the center of its text, there is no answering voice, no affirming ear to triumph over doubt and despair. Similarly, the late seventeenth and early eighteenth centuries witnessed the brief flourishing of a new genre centered on a heroine, whose suffering, as in the Hollywood melodrama, demonstrated the pathos of powerlessness, the effects of emotional, psychological, or physical violence or neglect. The she-tragedy should properly be considered a shadow genre to the courtship comedies of the Restoration period as both are products of a world of contested authority and pervasive insecurity that is also offering new possibilities for individual happiness pursued independent of oppressive parental or familial direction and social control.

The question at the center of both genres is how does one forge society from individual desire? In that sense, the central couple in each genre becomes an allegory of societal formation rather than enabling an inquiry into the nature of marriage. Given that marriages and families form the building blocks of society, however, the distinction perhaps seems a moot one. Still, I think it is important to acknowledge that Cavell's readings of the film couples examine marriage not as an institution but as a conversation with potential for overcoming the skepticism that is the legacy of modern life—"modern" referring to the post-Cartesian world in which we search for truth rather than assume it. Richard Rorty expresses impatience with Cavell for insisting that we must go back to Descartes so that we won't "miss 'the truth of skepticism'": "that the human creature's basis in the world as a whole, its relation to the world as such, is not that of knowing, anyway not what we think of as knowing."[12] Rorty agrees with Cavell's sense of the importance of what is not to be missed, but he finds it tedious to invoke Descartes when Rousseau, Thoreau, Kierkegaard, Tolstoy, and Wittgenstein, also discussed by Cavell, take us further along the same path. The focus of Descartes (and Berkeley after him) on skepticism regarding the external world is not as interesting to Rorty as the focus of the later writers on skepticism regarding the moral world. Yet, Cavell's sense of the connection between the epistemological and the moral (and even the existential) is at the very heart of his philosophical vision—and extremely important to his work on film. In my epilogue, I will return to this point.

Some scholars have taken issue with Cavell's philosophical approach to the film comedies on feminist grounds. David R. Shumway objects that "Cavell's neglect of feminist film studies causes him to misunderstand the cultural work of the genre."[13] The readings presented in *Pursuits of Happiness*, Shumway complains, "mystify marriage by treating marriage as if it were an adulterous affair" (82). Although that characterization of the relationships at the center of the remarriage film comedies seems perverse (does Shumway truly mean that the attentiveness and reciprocity exhibited by the couples is somehow disallowed in marriage?), I take more seriously his formulation of the "cultural work" of the genre as "the affirmation of marriage in the face of the threat of a growing divorce rate and liberalized divorce laws" (82). Nevertheless, Shumway's desire to separate the affirmation of marriage from the investigation of its nature, its possibilities, its challenges, is not a helpful critique of Cavell's central point. Like all genres, the remarriage genre is conservative, but like many other long-lasting genres (the western, for example) the comedies of remarriage raise the possibility of social disintegration (divorce). In other words, the genre builds into its conventions the threat to the stability it wishes to shore up—and it takes that threat seriously and does not dismiss it lightly. If marriage is to survive the current challenges, the films ask, why and how is it to do so? And the why is as important as the how.

These are not the questions at the center of the Restoration canon, but related questions are. The central couple of the Restoration texts worry the various issues surrounding independence versus commitment. Why marry rather than maintain one's personal freedom? (Strangely, given the social realities of the times, this question is as important to the female as to the male.) Why exchange a comfortable present for an unknown future? Why subject oneself to restrictions of behavior? Why open oneself to the possibilities of hurt, betrayal, neglect, or abuse? What are the benefits? What are the costs?

What I offer my readers, whether you have picked this book up from an interest in Restoration comedy, a curiosity about Hollywood remarriage films, or an investment in the relationship between philosophy and literature (specifically as propounded by Stanley Cavell) is an exploration of this thesis: I propose that Restoration comedies, that is, the canonical comedies of the period, begin the discussion that is continued by Hollywood comedies of remarriage. Shakespearean romance is important to both genres, but not as an originating point of philosophical exploration. Shakespearean romance stimulates but does not reflect the pattern of philosophical engagement that is crucial to both Restoration courtship comedies and Hollywood comedies of remarriage. Both of the genres central to my project are trying to work out problems. They mean to entertain, and they do entertain, but both genres address audiences that also need, if not answers to current concerns, at least some discussion, reflection, fanciful elaboration, or just some reference to and cognizance of things on their minds. It is perhaps enough to note this fact in one genre, as Stanley Cavell has so eloquently done. But my sense is that we benefit from noting that the intense concern of audiences and genres was manifest in two such distinct periods in two such different places with such similar focal points and philosophical insights. Cavell himself places the films in conversation with a wide variety of texts in order to illustrate "the persistence of a family of articulations of the moral life in modern thought" from Shakespeare through Locke and Milton to Capra and Hawks, with roots that go back to the beginning of philosophy itself.[14] My aim is to place Restoration comedies in a conversation they have not yet been asked to join but one in which I believe they belong.

It is a regrettable fact that Restoration comedies are customarily dismissed, even today and even by scholars in the field, as the products of "debased taste" or of limited interest.[15] Although Stanley Cavell decided to exclude them from his study of remarriage comedy (after seriously considering their relevance), he did so from the sense that the typical conversation featured therein was not the sort of conversation that "leads to acknowledgment" (PH, 19). He did not indeed question their cultural or their aesthetic significance. Rather, he likened them to the plays of Noel Coward in terms of their aesthetic appeal, while seeing them, like Coward's plays, as being "forever stuck in an orbit around the foci of desire and contempt" (PH, 19). In the works that have defined the canon since the early twentieth century, however, one does find the same emphases on acknowledgment and forgiveness and a movement forward into uncharted (and therefore frightening) territory as one finds at the end of the Hollywood comedies of remarriage. Moreover, as with the films, at least as Cavell reads them, these negotiations take place in a world that "desires a foundation for our judgments" and "a universe where such a desire is not fulfilled by religion."[16] Both genres seek the possibility of certainty in a specific kind of marriage, the kind of marriage defined by the couple at the center of each genre.

Both Restoration courtship comedies—which feature the oft-invoked breeches scene—and Hollywood comedies of remarriage—which include an occasional comedic cross-dressing and persistent fashion ambiguity—feature couples who exhibit playfulness and fluidity in construction of their gendered roles. This playfulness and fluidity derive from, demonstrate, and fuel their fascination, and occasional exasperation, with one another. Think of *Bringing Up Baby*'s David Huxley (played by Cary Grant) pouting in a negligee he has "borrowed" from Susan Vance (Katharine Hepburn), or call to mind *The Man of Mode*'s Harriet, "acting" Dorimant (and Dorimant mimicking her). These are moments of transvestism, to be sure, and they are also moments that signify—in each case—the beginning of the "transvestite" character's dawning awareness of desire. After all, if imitation is the sincerest form of flattery, parody is the heart of sympathetic knowledge; in these genres, parodic behavior or cross-gendered mockery often signals the beginning of self-knowledge as well as an opening to the knowledge of the other. Because marriage is assumed to be the fundamental social unit during both eras, the examination of the institution on stage and screen necessarily involves meditations on state or nation. What kind of society will even allow (never mind nourish) marriages in which both partners find the fulfillment that can be experienced only in conversation with another (i.e., an Other) to whom one is attracted and with whom one remains forever intrigued? And, what sort of state or nation can we hope for if marriages involving that sort of fulfillment provide the base?

As indicated in my title and my previous remarks, the primary philosophical work with which I will be "in conversation" throughout the following chapters is Stanley Cavell's *Pursuits of Happiness* in which the philosopher defines and delineates the Hollywood comedy of remarriage film. Film and stage bear close association, of course, because of their narrative biases, a bias we see from the beginning of the history of stage drama. As film technology developed, however, various kinds of subjects were explored. It was not predetermined in any sense of the word that the emerging art form would take a narrative turn. Early film featured actualities (scenics or travelogues and topicals or news stories) as well as experimentation with abstraction and special effects, but "[f]rom the beginning, *fiction films* were also important."[17] And, eventually, they came to dominate the industry as "audiences seemed to prefer films with stories" (Thompson and Bordwell 1994, 31). That being the case, and producers being producers, directors being directors, and actors being actors, there were points of transference between stage and screen as the new medium craved scripts and performers to entice a new audience. This new audience, though, was redefined by the new artistic medium. Indeed, one major difference between stage and screen is in the role of the audience.

Cavell meditates upon this difference in the first chapter of his *The World Viewed: An Ontology of Film*, a chapter he entitles "An Autobiography of

Companions." As filmgoers, he posits, we attend in the company of select others or in the absence of those others (should we go to the movies alone). As a public activity, film going is a strangely private experience, and the circumstances of our viewing of a film at the theater will always define our experience of a given film—a fact that may have been more noticeable during the heyday of classical Hollywood films such as the ones I will examine, but one that is still true today. Think of the last three or four films you have seen in a movie theater. Without doubt, you will remember the people you were with along with the film itself. Think of any movie from your childhood movie-going experience or from your adolescent and early adulthood dating life, and you will inevitably remember the birthday, family outing, blind date, anniversary, regular Friday night date, etc., on which you saw the film. In Cavell's words:

> The events associated with movies are those of companionship or lack of companionship: the audience of a book is essentially solitary, one soul at a time; the audience of music and theater is essentially larger than your immediate acquaintance—a gathering of the city; the crowd at a movie comprises various pools of companions, or scattered souls with someone missing.[18]

Theater is a public space in which, to invoke Jürgen Habermas and Richard Sennett, meaningful encounters between strangers can take place without any need to reveal the intimate details of one's life.[19] In a movie theater, one is in a psychologically vulnerable state to begin with, and conversations with strangers may therefore be awkward. Cavell explains that film, like photography, works by excluding us from its world. In a sense, he explains, "a screen is a barrier. It screens me from the world it holds—that is, makes me invisible. And it screens that world from me—that is, screens its existence from me" (*WV*, 24). We are aware of our own invisibility to the actors on the screen, as well as the voyeuristic quality of our watching them unseen. In the theater, the opposite is true. We know we are visible to the actors on the stage, who, depending on the conventions of the play or the times, do or do not acknowledge us overtly during the performance, but who always come out to greet us in the end, accepting our applause even as they depended on our attentiveness during the performance itself. The experience of a play is exhibitionist rather than voyeuristic—the world created or imitated rather than the world viewed, so to speak. Cavell says of the camera that although it "has been praised for extending the senses; it may . . . deserve more praise for confining them, leaving room for thought" (*WV*, 24). Aristotle long ago defined the experience of theater as one that invokes and refines the emotions—or purges them. And as Habermas has noted, theater, like the art museum and the concert, afforded the bourgeoisie the opportunity to participate in the defining of cultural value: in these venues, "discussion became the medium through which people appropriated art."[20]

10 *Prologue*

A final distinction to be made between the theatrical and the filmic worlds has to do with what Erwin Panofsky early on identified as the difference between a character in a play and an actor on the screen. Characters such as Othello and Nora (Panofsky's examples) or Dorimant and Mirabell, say,

> are definite, substantial figures created by the playwright . . . [who] can be played well or badly, and . . . "interpreted" in one way or another; but . . . [who] most definitely exist, no matter who plays them or even whether they are played at all.
>
> (WV, 27)[21]

In film, however, "the character . . . lives and dies with the actor" (WV, 27). Remakes of Hollywood classics are always disappointing unless they are significantly transformed. *The Philadelphia Story*'s Tracy Lord will always be Katharine Hepburn, C. K. Dexter Haven will always be Cary Grant, Macaulay (Mike) Connor will always be Jimmy Stewart, but, thanks to *High Society*, their singing doppelgangers can be none other than Grace Kelly, Bing Crosby, and Frank Sinatra. Elaborating Panofsky's observation, Cavell phrases the distinction between actors on the stage and on the screen thus:

> An exemplary stage performance is one which, for a time, most fully creates a character. After Paul Scofield's performance in *King Lear*, we know who King Lear is, we have seen him in flesh. An exemplary screen performance is one in which, at a time, a star is born.
>
> (WV, 28)

Nearly three hundred years separate the periods that witnessed the flourishing of the two distinct, although surprisingly similar, genres at the heart of my study. Why such an intense, if brief, focus on marriage in the two periods? The short answer is that during both times society was in the process of undergoing radical and observable change. If we look at any period of human history, we will note in retrospect the developments, transformations, and modifications, in life and behavior, style and thought. Sometimes a decade (the 1960s in America, for example) seems to belong to one era in the beginning and quite another era in the end. But during most periods of history, I would imagine, change strikes those living at the time as incremental rather than sudden and pronounced. In 1660, that was far from the case. In that year, not only a form of government, but also a prevailing ideology, was simply exchanged for its opposite. A society dominated by Puritan politics and religious practice gave way to one controlled by aristocratic license. Even Samuel Pepys, who would eventually embrace, enjoy, and in many ways epitomize the cultural milieu of the Restoration, looked upon the changes with a measure of trepidation. In 1662, on the Sunday that marked the "last . . . that the Presbyterians are to preach, unless they read the new Common Prayer and renounce the Covenant," Pepys attended the farewell sermon of Dr. William Bates. Although he was himself an Anglican, he expressed his admiration for the sermon and the service. He concludes his diary entry thus:

> I hear most of the Presbyters took their leaves today. And the City is much dissatisfied with it. I pray God keep peace among us and make the Bishops careful of bringing in good men in their room, or else all will fly a-pieces; for bad ones will not down with the City.[22]

As Pepys suggests, Restoration-era London cared deeply about the nature and quality of public worship, but paradoxically during this time, a libertine spirit (in)famously prevailed. Commitment to libertinism is evidenced both by sexual behavior that was markedly less restrained than in other eras and by an intellectual freedom that subjected all conventional thought to reassessment and—potential—rejection or revision. Arranged marriage, the norm for the upper classes (with whom the literature under consideration is exclusively concerned) came under scrutiny along with all other societal practices, and the stage provided one venue for both the examination of that type of union and the performance of an interesting alternative: courtship defined by mutual attraction rather than parental negotiation. At the beginning of the 1930s in America, the prevailing spirit was duress brought on by the Great Depression—another cataclysmic and sudden event that shifted social as well as economic realities. With the election of Franklin Delano Roosevelt in November 1932, a new spirit of hopefulness seems to have taken hold. The campaign theme song, "Happy Days are Here Again," seems to have turned attention to "happiness" itself. Where and how do we expect to be happy? Screen comedy offered one answer in its depiction of remarriage.

These are different times and different places and different media to be sure, but there are similarities in all of these differences, the primary ones being the pair around which each kind of text is structured and the concept of marriage that lies at the heart of each genre. John Harrington Smith's *The Gay Couple in Restoration Comedy*—published perhaps significantly in 1948, not even a decade after the Hollywood comedy of remarriage had dominated the screen—identifies the special quality in the central couple of the Restoration's comic canon as a "sex antagonism" that coexists with sexual attraction.[23] The distinct wisdom of the dramatists who created or discovered this couple was, in Smith's view, to see that

> young people, while wanting love, may at the same instant not want it, and that love may be complicated by a kind of pride which has its basis in the individual's consciousness of his [or her] sex as well as his [or her] individuality.

(5)

Smith reminds us that the dramatists who first brought us the couple he terms the "gay lovers" were writing against the tradition of platonic love that had flourished in the court of Queen Henrietta Maria and King Charles I. This fashion was promoted by the Queen in particular to "elevate the tone of courtly love-making" (16). Smith points out that whereas the concept of platonic love is precisely the definition of heterosexual attraction the Restoration comic world seeks to depose, the heritage was an important one in that it taught the courtier playwrights to regard love as a game. The platonic love game, of course, offered aesthetic pleasure (in Smith's view, primarily for women), but its central concern was neither marriage nor sexual intercourse. Thomas d'Urfey's *Astree* was the rule book, as it were; the ideal platonic couple was destined to exist in a world of elaborate language and gesture, a world of romance for the sake of romance.

Smith's insistence that we see the comedies of the Restoration stage as, at least on one level, a response to the platonic love fad of the previous age was likely driven by the still-too-common tendency to dismiss the works as frivolous (at best) and noxious (at worst). That the period gave birth to the "gay couple" indicates to Smith—and I agree—that the age itself was profoundly concerned with both love and marriage. "It may be doubted," Smith eloquently opines,

> that any period ever took love more seriously than this one, or thought more seriously about marriage, the degree of its seriousness being measured by the misgivings with which young people in the plays become conscious of their attraction for each other, their struggles to escape the net, and, at the end, the mixture of anxiety and studied insouciance with which they accept the result.
>
> (76)

The only comparable period, in my view, is the age through which Smith himself had just lived—another brief, but intense period of concentration on serious love games played for the highest stake of all: happiness.

As Smith's discussion moves into the 1670s (the decade during which most of the texts centrally featured in my study were written and staged), he notes a shift in the dynamic that first defined the "gay couple," the gallant becoming notably more powerful in the "cynical comedies" of the mid-1670s to the mid-1680s. Susan Staves endorses and elaborates Smith's reading in her fine 1979 study of the Restoration stage, *Players' Scepters*. Staves notes in these plays an emphasis on "cuckolding, sexual intrigue without love, and antipathy to marriage" that she attributes to the serious debates about marriage that dominated the culture (not simply the stage) from 1670 on.[24] The "attacks on marriage" so common during this period were indicative of more than a wayward libertine impulse (137). The experience of the Civil War, the interregnum, and the Restoration raised questions regarding authorities of all kinds. The writers and thinkers of the time were engaged in a serious reorienting—retheorizing—of their world. Chief among the considerations, as Staves points out, was the role of natural impulse in not only directing but authorizing behavior. What natural need, really, was served by the institution of marriage? What authority underwrote that institution? These questions would dominate late seventeenth-century English culture, resulting in redefinitions of both state authority and the institution of marriage, in both cases shifting responsibility to the individuals who defined themselves in relationship to the state and who bound themselves in relation to one another. Staves concludes,

> the literature of the Restoration shows not only a variety of attempts to imagine nature without hierarchy and without obligation, but also finally some acceptance of the early modern image of man as so fundamentally good-natured and innocent that he is able to conform to law and to abide by conventional morality not only without divine help and without pain, but with pleasure. Such men no longer require the authority of a divinely appointed sovereign but may be trusted to form their own government and to decide under what circumstances the executive they have appointed should be relieved of that authority delegated to him.
> (314)

And they can also be trusted to decide whom to marry and under what conditions to stay married.

If the Restoration courtship comedies are written against the cultural tendency to idealize love, their filmic counterparts are written against the cultural myth (or fact) of widespread sexual anxiety, neuroses that, in the words of James Thurber, have relegated the American male to a "'sort of divine discontent,'" "'a separation of the physical and the psychic which causes the adult to remain in a state of suspended love, as if he were holding a goldfish bowl and had nowhere to put it.'" This passage from Thurber's *Is Sex Necessary?* is quoted by Maria DiBattista in her *Fast-Talking Dames*, a study of the actresses who dominated the screen in the 1930s and 1940s. Like Smith before her, speaking of the Restoration comic canon, DiBattista defines the central energy of the films she studies to be "sexual struggle."[25] She, therefore, finds in Thurber's "dyspeptic inquiry" and in his beleaguered response to demanding, desirous women a "prologue to the comic history of dames" (26, 25).

For Stanley Cavell, the real possibility of divorce as a solution to unhappiness in marriage was the essential social fact precipitating a generic meditation on the nature of marriage in the mid-1930s and early 1940s. Society's coerciveness propels many couples into marriages that do not work for one reason or another. In cultures that provide ready means for the dissolution of such marriages, partners are free to learn from their mistakes and make more suitable choices the next time around. What fascinates Cavell about the film genre he studies is the repeated motif of "remarriage": a couple choosing one another all over again for unions that they insist will be, in the words of *The Awful Truth*'s Lucy Warriner, "different but the same."

Although much more difficult to obtain than in the twentieth century, divorce was not impossible in late seventeenth-century England, and, short of divorce, there were options for couples who found themselves yoked together in discord. Gellert Spencer Alleman's 1942 University of Pennsylvania dissertation, *Matrimonial Law and the Materials of Restoration Comedy*, devotes an entire chapter to the various legal means by which marriages could be dissolved in the period, most of which figure in the dramatic texts of the time. The one means that is never mentioned on the Restoration stage, according to Alleman, is "jactitation of marriage," which is basically a declaration that no contract or no marriage ceremony ever took place. The ecclesiastical court granting such a suit would "silence forever the defendant who falsely claimed marriage."[26] Although, Alleman notes, jactitation "could solve some of the dramatic situations" (125), it is never invoked on the stage—not even in the case of clandestine or deceptive marriages that in actuality would have prompted that very solution. The dramatic repertoire, though, seems more interested in the nature of marriage than in the fact of marriage. In other words, as Paula Backscheider has put it, the drama of this period functions as literature always functions, not as a "reflection or portrayal of society but as a complex cultural event implicated in and generative of the cultural milieu."[27] Therefore, miserable couples in the plays are not generally given the luxury of begging the question; their relief comes only after the serious reflection on marriage demanded by other options: reconciliation, separation, annulment, and parliamentary divorce.[28]

Whereas unhappy marriages abound in the Restoration repertoire, the courtship comedies that I place in conversation with Hollywood comedies of remarriage center their emotional energies on the "gay couple" contemplating marriage. Nevertheless, it is true that the couple's witty dance toward the altar is orchestrated on a stage that also bears witness to the fact that marriage itself is no guarantor of happiness. There is every chance that any given couple may spend married life contriving opportunities to go their separate ways, whether legally or not. Thus, whereas divorce is not the social condition motivating the Restoration courtship comedy in the same way that it motivates the Hollywood comedy of remarriage, the desire for divorce is a reality acknowledged by the culture and by the texts. It is worth noting as well that the monarch, who could have availed himself of divorce when his consort failed to provide a legitimate heir to the throne, did not do so. And despite his many mistresses, by all accounts Charles II was a friend, lover, and companion to Catherine, his queen. This model of royal marriage—given the bloody precedent that won the monarch the right to divorce in the interest of the succession—had to have had an impact on the courtier-playwrights.

In both eras, a central pair of actors surprisingly tapped into a vein of inquiry that intrigued their audiences. Nell Gwyn and Charles Hart, Myrna Loy and William Powell were not attempting to inspire philosophical musings. But they did. In both cases, the woman was a revelation, but also in both cases the man recognized and responded to the revelation he saw. We have films to document the delightful chemistry between Loy and Powell, chemistry evident in their first scene together on film, even though in that film they were not paired as dramatic leads. Nineteen thirty-four's *Manhattan Melodrama* starred Clark Gable, who would also be Loy's costar in *Wife vs. Secretary* in 1936. He would be voted "King of the Movies" to Loy's "Queen" in 1937, in a newspaper poll advertised in Ed Sullivan's syndicated entertainment column in the *New York Daily News*.[29] There was some industry and popular persistence in the thirties, in other words, that linked Gable and Loy, but although he himself featured the couple in *Manhattan Melodrama*, W. S. Van Dyke saw a more interesting pairing in Powell and Loy. And he saw it the first time they were together on film, which was, in fact, the first time they met in *Manhattan Melodrama*.

The scene is a taxicab occupied by Jim Wade, newly elected District Attorney, played by William Powell. Jim was adopted as an orphan and reared along with another orphan boy named Blackie, now a gangster, played by Clark Gable. Powell enters the taxi planning to go home and get some sleep. As the door closes, Loy wedges herself into the cab, falling backwards against its startled, but always suave, occupant. Loy is Gable's "girl," Eleanor Packer, and her design in hijacking the cab is to take Jim to a speakeasy where Blackie will meet them for a congratulatory drink.

JIM. Pardon me, if I seem to intrude.
ELEANOR. Well, I made it. You almost got away from me.
JIM. I did, hey? Just who might you be?
ELEANOR. Don't be unpleasant. My taxi got in a jam, couldn't move an inch. I forced my way through the crowd. It's a wonder I have any clothes left. . . . It's your fault. I wasn't elected. Or was I?
JIM. What's the name of the game? I'd like to play too.

As she speaks, Loy looks into a hand mirror, righting her disheveled appearance, avoiding eye contact with her companion but clearly aware of him and his attentiveness. Powell is perched on the edge of his seat, turned toward Loy, never taking his eyes off her. His body leans forward as though pulled by her energy. She clearly controls the conversation through what will become a hallmark of comic dialogue of this period, that is, the screwball non sequitur. And, although he says the line with intended irony, Powell manages to convey the impression that he really would like to play whatever game she has in mind.

Jim's question prompts a bit of improvisation on Eleanor's part. What is her game? "Oh, just a simple little frame-up," she says, glancing at Jim. "I force my way into your car, tear my clothes and scream. After all, you have to protect your career, so you pay." "Well, that is a nice little game,"

Jim comments, no longer interested in playing. He turns away from her, and over her protests orders the taxi driver to stop. They scuffle a bit as Jim tries to open her door, until finally Eleanor exclaims, "Blackie sent me," thereby arresting Jim's attention and calming his nerves. He apologizes, but she, again not looking at him, merely smooths her skirt and says, "Nothing like a District Attorney to keep a girl in shape. You and I must have a good wrestle someday." Powell chuckles at this line. And I say Powell rather than Jim because the laugh seems to be coming from the actor as much as from the character. Powell's enjoyment and admiration of Loy are evident.

As Roger Bryant has observed, Loy "visibly relaxes as they chat" in this scene.[30] For the first time in the film, she seems "at home." The taxi becomes a bed as Powell tucks a lap robe around his and Loy's legs—and this action, although intimate, has no nuance of seduction. It is familiar, domestic, comfortable, as though the two have always known each other (another important characteristic of comedy-of-remarriage couples and one that is similarly and memorably enacted, interestingly enough, by Clark Gable with Claudette Colbert in *It Happened One Night*). At this point, Eleanor reciprocates Jim's attention and attentiveness, and she asks a question: Why isn't he corrupt like the rest of the world? "Why be a freak? Why don't you give in?" "That's a long, long story," Jim replies. "You might as well get started," she says, "we'll probably have a long, long wait for Blackie." Jim's uncharacteristically playful response is delivered with the tongue-in-cheekiness that will become Nick Charles's trademark: "Well, I was born at home because I wanted to be near mother at the time." It is Loy's (and our) turn to chuckle. Who knew Jim had a sense of humor? It took Eleanor, herself a rather serious character elsewhere in the film, to reveal that dimension of Jim's personality.

More to the point, Loy and Powell simply have fun together, and in all their films, that fun is evident and infectious. As Loy herself explained in retrospect, "from that very first scene [in *Manhattan Melodrama*], a curious thing passed between us, a feeling of rhythm, complete understanding, an instinct for how one could bring out the best in the other."[31] Even in the unrelentingly melodramatic *Evelyn Prentice* (1934), there is a scene in which the irrepressible chemistry between Powell and Loy threatens to disrupt the dour script. Loy speaks in a soft monotone throughout the movie, tamping down the lilt in her voice that was so much a part of her comic charm. She is, after all, a neglected wife—neglected by William Powell! The two are seldom together, and when they are, Powell is distracted and distant. Of course, Prentice does finally realize that his marriage is endangered by his devotion to work, and one scene finds him at home during the afternoon. He walks in on his wife and young daughter doing their calisthenics on the bedroom floor. He plops down with them for leg lifts and bicycle "rides," and the film nearly leaps into another genre.[32] It is as though Powell is happy to be doing something, anything, with Loy, in this film that requires him to be so unnaturally inattentive and her so strangely subdued.

W. S. Van Dyke was reading Dashiell Hammett's *The Thin Man* and the idea of making a film featuring romance between a man and his wife intrigued him. He insisted on casting Myrna Loy opposite William Powell in the film, and well before the five sequels were completed, Loy had gained a reputation as the "perfect wife"—a label that stuck, somewhat to her chagrin. As she remarked,

> I prefer Gore Vidal's description of my image, "the eternal good-sex woman-wife," which removes the puritanical connotation of perfect. What man would want a perfect wife, anyway? What made the *Thin Man* series work, what made it fun, was that we didn't attempt to hide the fact that sex is part of marriage.[33]

The fact is that Loy did have the ability to inhabit a screen marriage and make it look like fun. Never, however, not even in the first *Thin Man* film (which I will discuss at greater length in Chapter 3), does Loy give the impression that marriage is easy. It is a constant state of recommitment, perpetually endangered by forces external and internal. It is a supremely adult activity and requires both maturity and common sense, along with the opposite ability, that is, the childlike ability to play and invent and enjoy. It is not an easy thing to be in close companionship with the same person year after year after year. In *The Best Years of Our Lives* (1946), Loy is the middle-aged wife of a returning war hero. Their young adult daughter, worrying over her own marital challenges, accuses her parents of not being able to understand. It is as though she speaks for America to Hollywood's ideal wife: "How could you understand? You and dad never had any trouble." "We never had any trouble," Loy replies, looking at Fredric March, who plays her husband in this film: "How many times have I told you I hated you and believed it in my heart? How many times have you said you were sick and tired of me; that we were all washed up? How many times have we had to fall in love all over again?" Comedies of remarriage are built on this bit of wisdom first illustrated by the incomparable Myrna Loy and William Powell.

To document the stage chemistry between Gwyn and Hart in as much detail as we can describe the screen chemistry of Loy and Powell is not possible. Indeed, Nell Gwyn alone is often credited for the emergence of the "witty pair" or the "gay couple," and she played opposite other talented actors during the course of her relatively brief stage career. Elizabeth Howe states firmly that the success of the "phenomenon . . . [that] became a recurring element of comedy in this period" for the first time in English theatrical history was due "directly" to "the talent and popularity of a single actress, Nell Gwyn."[34] In 1665, the King's Company paired Gwyn with her lover Charles Hart as Mirida and Philador in James Howard's *All Mistaken*. This first "gay couple," with their witty exchanges, their antiplatonic approach to love, and their emphasis on clear provisos by which to govern their behavior toward one another, "contains," as Howe says, "the fundamental ingredients of what was to become the characteristic Restoration 'gay couple' mode" (67). One essential ingredient was missing, however. Mirida and Philador reject marriage, whereas the typical "gay couple" eventually moves toward commitment. It was John Dryden's Florimell and Celadon (developed for Gwyn and Hart in his *Secret Love*) who set the pattern for "all subsequent gay couples" (70). Howe concludes,

> the Hart–Gwyn style of lovers are in a new sense equals, each fighting to maintain his or her independence and to form an alliance which will not constrict and so stifle their love. The dramatist conceived the innovation, but the inspiration of his assertive heroine was Nell Gwyn and thus, albeit indirectly, she brought a new approach to comic love relationships between the sexes.
>
> (71)

Derek Parker demurs, however, that "it was when . . . [Gwyn] was teamed with Hart that she really began to make her mark. They were successful from the moment they first appeared together."[35]

Contemporary evidence bolsters the notion of something quite special in the Hart–Gwyn pairing. Samuel Pepys, who saw *All Mistaken* in 1667, found it "an ordinary play" except for the two actors. Pepys, an admirer of Nell Gwyn's looks and personality is nonetheless discriminating as to her true talent, which is abundantly on display in her role as Mirida:

> Nells and Hearts mad parts are most excellently done, but especially hers; which makes it a miracle to me to think how ill she doth any serious part, as the other day, just like a fool or a changeling; and in a mad part; doth beyond all imitation almost.[36]

The parts really are "madcap"—both Philidor and Mirida are sociopaths, with Philidor promising to marry multiple women and Mirida torturing her thin suitor by insisting that he gain weight and her fat suitor by insisting that he trim down. When Mirida enters the stage on which Philidor has been left by several of his irate mistresses, she announces herself to be fifteen years old and already to "have fool'd five several men." "My humour," she continues, "is to love no man but to / Have as many Love me as they please / Come Cut or Long tail."[37] Philidor is smitten, and immediately the two strike a bargain to love without marriage, sealing their provisos with a song rather than a kiss. We must assume that Philidor's assessment is shared by the audience (at least by Pepys, and no doubt others as well):

> Faith you and I sing very well; we
> Are alike in that too: I see either
> Nature or the Devil, some body, or something,
> Made thee and me for one another.
> (2.1.259–61)

Although their hijinks through the course of the play involve a lot of what we would call "slapstick," physical comedy rather than wit (the hallmark of the gay couple), the fact remains that the two "madcaps" outsmart everyone and have a lot of fun doing so. The play must have revealed the same sort of "chemistry" to the King's Company playwrights as *Manhattan Melodrama* revealed to Woody Van Dyke, for Howard cast the two again in *The English Monsieur* and Dryden wrote *Secret Love* especially for Gwyn and Hart. It was to be their greatest success and a triumph for Dryden as well.

Pepys saw *Secret Love* at one of its first performances on March 2, 1667. He took his wife, and King Charles and the Duke of York were also in the audience. Pepys notes that Dryden's play is "mightily commended for the regularity of it," but it was Gwyn's performance that overwhelmed him, prompting the highest praise:

> The truth is, there is a comical part done by Nell, which is Florimell, that I never can hope to see the like done again by man or woman. . . . So great performance of a comical part was never, I believe, in the world before as Nell doth this, both as a mad girle and then, most and best of all, when she comes in like a young gallant; and hath the motions and carriage of a spark the most that ever I saw any man have. It makes me, I confess, admire her.[38]

A few days later, Pepys attended a tragedy at the Duke's theater and saw Moll Davies (one of the King's mistresses) dance a jig in boy's clothes that, to his mind, surpassed Nell's dance at the end of *Secret Love*. Moll Davies seems to have been a particularly talented dancer, who excelled at erotic movements (once prompting both the Queen and Lady Castlemaine to leave a performance), but as Derek Wilson has remarked, "where Nell was spontaneous and witty, Moll was simply coarse."[39] And, if the promise of a titillating jig could pack a theater on occasion, it was comedic skill that would prove more (or at least as) intriguing to Pepys, prompting a return to the King's house to see *Secret Love* again on March 25. Once more, he is impressed with the "excellent play" and Nell in her "merry part, as cannot be better done in Nature I think."[40] Two months later, he sees the play again, noting that although he has "often seen" it (suggesting that he did not record each occasion), it

> pleases me infinitely, it being impossible, I think, ever to have the Queen's part, which is very good and passionate, and Floramell's part, which is the most Comicall that ever was made for woman, ever done better then they two are by young Marshall and Nelly.[41]

Whereas Myrna Loy was the "ideal wife," Nell Gwyn was, according to *The Manager's Notebook* published in the early years of the eighteenth century, the "complete mistress": "airy, fantastic and sprightly, she sang, danced, and was exactly made for acting light, showy characters, filling them up, as far as they went, most effectually."[42] Indeed, in *Secret Love*'s proviso scene, Florimell suggests that the trick to a happy marriage is to regard it as a perpetual courtship. When Celadon proposes, that "whereas the names of husband and wife hold forth nothing but clashing and cloying, and dullness and faintness in their signification, they shall be abolish'd for ever betwixt us," Florimell agrees, replying, "And instead of those, we will be married by the more agreeable names of Mistress and Gallant."[43] Nick and Nora Charles would certainly concur (5.1.531–35).

Restoration courtship comedies argue that courtship can be fun, and the central couple hopes (sometimes with less optimism than Florimell, sometimes with more) that marriage, despite all its challenges, will be the same. Hollywood comedies of remarriage make the same argument, presenting couples who must learn to court one another again and who do so in the hope that on reentering the married state they will not become mere husband and wife again. The following study brings these two genres into deep conversation with each other. I begin in Chapter 1 with a discussion of two tragicomic texts, one from each period: John Dryden's *Marriage à la Mode* and Ernst Lubitsch's *The Shop around the Corner*. These texts introduce themes that will be elaborated by the genres proper (i.e. the Restoration courtship comedy and the Hollywood comedy of remarriage), but they also include tragic or potentially tragic subplots that speak to the presence of a shadow genre in each period (the she-tragedy and the melodrama). It is important to remember throughout my discussion that both of the genres I treat acknowledge and make a space for the melancholia and the pathos—and even the tragedy—that could so very easily upset the comic resolutions privileged by the genres. Their dedication to this acknowledgment is largely responsible for the equivocal, although happy, endings of all the works under consideration.

Chapter 2 begins in earnest the paired-text analyses in which I focus on a play and a film (or, as in Chapter 4, a playwright and a director/auteur) in terms of specific shared emphases. I adopt this methodology from Cavell's example in his *Cities of Words*, wherein he pairs philosophical texts and film texts for discussions that enlighten readings of both. My methodology, like Cavell's, has its origins in the classroom where I have repeatedly (since 2002) attempted to follow out "a complete tuition for a given intuition" (to borrow Cavell's words).[44] In both teaching and writing, I have found that the pairing of texts yields "accents" in response to questions or problems they share. Other pairings, as Cavell notes of his own pairings in *Cities of Words*, are certainly valid and would yield new and different accents. The pairings I present are in response to concerns I want to address regarding the "moral thinking" in both sets of texts, thinking that is in each text best illuminated in juxtaposition with the other, although discussion will reveal discrete readings that can also stand alone. I am convinced that the Restoration canon stands to benefit especially from the pairings as the focus demands and rewards serious discussion about the moral implications of the kind of marriage and the sort of happiness privileged by both genres.

One further note: I have added two film texts to Cavell's canon, and I have not treated all the movies in his canon as companion pieces to the

Restoration texts. I find *The Thin Man* (1934) to be a remarriage comedy insofar, as noted above, as it illustrates the kind of marriage all remarriage couples pursue. Although Nick and Nora would never contemplate divorce, the topic is deeply encoded in the first *Thin Man* film, and the five sequels that followed (from 1936 to 1947) are themselves versions of "remarriage." *My Man Godfrey* (1936) is a clearer candidate for inclusion and pairs nicely with William Wycherley's *Plain Dealer*. Cavell may have excluded this text because of the confusion in terms of the woman with whom Godfrey is or should be in conversation. I feel it is an important film text because of its emphasis on the "creation of the man"—another reason Cavell may not have found it interesting, given his emphasis on the creation of the woman. Yet, the film responds to his categories of analysis, and in some ways answers feminist critiques of Cavell's philosophy. I exclude *The Philadelphia Story* and *Adam's Rib* as having no clear parallels in the Restoration that I believe would reveal accents in pairing. I would hope that others would supplement my readings if parallel texts occur to them. Finally, I offer a brief reflection on the shadow genres as they underwrite a recent remarriage comedy/melodrama based on an eighteenth-century poem that owes much to both Restoration comedy and she-tragedy: Charlie Kaufman's *Eternal Sunshine of the Spotless Mind* (2004).

Notes

1. Stanley Cavell, *Pursuits of Happiness: The Hollywood Comedy of Remarriage* (Cambridge, MA: Harvard University Press, 1984), 86, hereafter *PH*. Subsequent citations to this work are given parenthetically in the text.
2. Edward A. Langhans, "The Theatre," in *The Cambridge Companion to English Restoration Theatre*, ed. Deborah Payne Fisk (Cambridge: Cambridge University Press, 2000), 8.
3. Joseph Roach, *It* (Ann Arbor: University of Michigan Press, 2007), 13.
4. For descriptions of the King's and Duke's Companies with regard to repertory concerns such as plays and performers, see Robert D. Hume's excellent essay, "Theatres and Repertory," in *The Cambridge History of British Theatre*, ed. Peter Thomson, vol. 2, *1660–1895*, ed. Joseph Donohue (Cambridge: Cambridge University Press, 2004), 53–70, and Judith Milhous's equally fine "Theatre Companies and Regulation," published in the same volume, 108–25. *The London Stage*, of course, also contains valuable information. On the Hollywood studios, the classic study is Thomas Schatz's *The Genius of the System: Hollywood Filmmaking in the Studio Era* (New York: Henry Holt, 1988). Also of interest is John Fawell's *The Hidden Art of Hollywood: In Defense of the Studio Era Film* (Westport, CT: Greenwood Publishing, 2008).
5. Fawell, *The Hidden Art of Hollywood*, 134; Katharine Eisaman Maus, "'Playhouse Flesh and Blood': Sexual Ideology and the Restoration Actress," *ELH* 46, no. 4 (1979): 599.
6. Stone, *The Family, Sex, and Marriage in England: 1500–1800* (New York: Harper and Row, 1977).
7. Maus, "'Playhouse Flesh and Blood,'" 612.
8. Ruth Perry, *Novel Relations: The Transformation of Kinship in English Literature and Culture 1748–1818* (Cambridge: Cambridge University Press, 2004), 197.

Perry also provides a helpful summary of the critiques of Stone's work and the phrase "companionate marriage" (pp. 192–93nn6–8).
9. "When a genre reaches the saturation point," Altman observes, "studios must either abandon it, restrict it to 'B' productions, or handle it in a new way." *Film/Genre* (London: British Film Institute, 1999), 62.
10. Phillip Harth, "Political Interpretations of *Venice Preserv'd*," *Modern Philology* 85 (1988): 348.
11. Pat Gill, "Gender, Sexuality, and Marriage," in *The Cambridge Companion to English Restoration Theatre*, ed. Deborah Payne Fisk (Cambridge: Cambridge University Press, 2000), 192.
12. Richard Rorty, "From Epistemology to Romance: Cavell on Skepticism," *The Review of Metaphysics* 34, no. 4 (1981): 759. (Rorty quotes Cavell, *The Claim of Reason: Wittgenstein, Skepticism, Morality, and Tragedy* [Oxford: Oxford University Press, 1979], 241.)
13. David R. Shumway, *Modern Love: Romance, Intimacy, and the Marriage Crisis* (New York: NYU Press, 2003), 81.
14. Stanley Cavell, *Cities of Words: Pedagogical Letters on a Register of a Moral Life* (Cambridge, MA: Harvard University Press, 2005), 5, hereafter CW. Subsequent citations to this work are given parenthetically in the text.
15. For one recent example and for the phrase "debased taste," see Dustin Griffin, *Authorship in the Long Eighteenth Century* (Lanham, MD: Rowman and Littlefield/Newark, University of Delaware Press, 2014), 27.
16. These are Ludger H. Viefhues-Bailey's words summarizing Cavell's readings of Shakespearean tragedy in *Beyond the Philosopher's Fear: A Cavellian Reading of Gender, Origin and Religion in Modern Skepticism* (Aldershot: Ashgate, 2012), 46.
17. Kristen Thompson and David Bordwell, *Film History: An Introduction* (New York: McGraw-Hill, 1994), 21.
18. Stanley Cavell, *The World Viewed: Reflections on the Ontology of Film* (Cambridge, MA: Harvard University Press, 1971), 10, hereafter WV. Subsequent citations to this work are given parenthetically in the text.
19. Jürgen Habermas, *The Structural Transformation of the Public Sphere: An Inquiry into a Category of Bourgeois Society* (Cambridge, MA: MIT Press, 1991); Richard Sennett, *The Fall of Public Man* (Cambridge: Cambridge University Press, 1974).
20. Habermas, *Structural Transformation of the Public Sphere*, 40.
21. Cavell quotes Panofsky, "Style and Medium in the Moving Pictures," in *Film*, ed. Daniel Talbot (New York: Simon and Schuster, 1959), 28.
22. *The Diary of Samuel Pepys*, ed. R. C. Latham and W. Matthews (London: HarperCollins, 1995), 8: 166, 169. See Roach on Pepys's erotic experiences in church once "It" culture came to prevail (*It*, 71–72).
23. John Harrington Smith, *The Gay Couple in Restoration Comedy* (Cambridge, MA: Harvard University Press, 1948), 5. Smith's clinical phrasing reminds me of the psychological diagnosis *Bringing Up Baby*'s Susan Vance elicits and applies to David Huxley: "The love impulse in men very frequently reveals itself in terms of conflict."
24. Susan Staves, *Players' Scepters: Fictions of Authority in the Restoration* (Lincoln: University of Nebraska Press, 1979), 167. For her most complete view, see her final chapter (253–314), in which Staves traces the arguments about law and nature to their roots in Greek "sophism, Epicureanism, and other ... atheisms." "The effect of the Peloponnesian War on the sophists was ... not unlike the effect of the Civil War on Restoration skeptics and libertines," Staves opines (254).

25 Maria DiBattista, *Fast-Talking Dames* (New Haven, CT: Yale University Press, 2003), 26. DiBattista quotes Thurber, *Is Sex Necessary? Or, Why You Feel the Way You Do* (New York: Harper, 1929), 44.
26 Gellert Spencer Alleman, "Matrimonial Law and the Materials of Restoration Comedy" (PhD thesis, University of Pennsylvania, 1942), 125.
27 Paula Backscheider, "'Endless Aversion Rooted in the Soul': Divorce in the 1690–1730 Theater," *The Eighteenth Century* 37 (1996): 128n6.
28 See Robert D. Hume's discussion of the implication of "divorce" when mentioned in this dramatic repertoire in "Marital Discord in English Comedy from Dryden to Fielding," *Modern Philology* 74 (1977): 251.
29 James Kotsilibas-Davis and Myrna Loy, *Myrna Loy: Being and Becoming* (New York: Knopf, 1987), 146, and Emily W. Leider, *Myrna Loy: The Only Good Girl in Hollywood* (Berkeley: University of California Press, 2011), 166.
30 Roger Bryant, *William Powell: The Life and Films* (Jefferson, NC: McFarland, 2006), 6.
31 Kotsilibas-Davis and Loy, *Myrna Loy*, 88.
32 As Leider notes, it is the "one goofy scene" in a film that otherwise "submerged the comic gifts of the stars" (*Myrna Loy*, 136–37).
33 Kotsilibas-Davis and Loy, *Myrna Loy*, 91. For William Powell's "take" on Loy's "perfection" as consisting of beauty and glamor combined with a sense of humor, an even temper, and a refusal to "nag," see Kathrina Glitre, *Hollywood Romantic Comedy: States of the Union, 1934–65* (Manchester, UK: Manchester University Press, 2006), 85.
34 Elizabeth Howe, *The First English Actresses: Women and Drama, 1660–1700* (Cambridge: Cambridge University Press, 1992), 66–67.
35 Derek Parker, *Nell Gwyn* (Stroud, UK: Sutton, 2000), 48.
36 *Diary*, 8: 594.
37 James Howard, *All Mistaken, or, The Mad Couple, a Comedy* (London: H. Brugis, 1672), 2.1.256. Hereafter, all quotations from plays will be identified in the text by act, scene, and line numbers.
38 *Diary*, 8: 91.
39 Derek Wilson, *All the King's Women: Love, Sex, and Politics in the Life of Charles II* (London: Pimlico, 2004), 238. See also Pepys, *Diary*, 9: 219.
40 Pepys, *Diary*, 8: 129.
41 Pepys, *Diary*, 8: 235.
42 Quoted by Parker, *Nell Gwyn*, 49.
43 Dryden, *Secret Love, or The Maiden Queen*, in *The Works of John Dryden*, vol. ix, ed. John Loftis and Vinton A. Dearing (Berkeley and Los Angeles: University of California Press, 1966), 114–203.
44 Stanley Cavell, *Disowning Knowledge: In Seven Plays of Shakespeare*, rev. ed. (Cambridge: Cambridge University Press, 2003), 5.

1 Something from nothing
Marriage, conversation, and the tragicomic plot

John Milton's definition of "marriage" as a "meet and happy conversation" is central to both genres I treat. In *Pursuits of Happiness*, Stanley Cavell repeatedly invokes the famous definition from *Doctrine and Discipline of Divorce*, "a document" he "take[s] to have intimate implications in the comedy of remarriage" (*PH*, 58), and the concept of marriage as conversation drives his discussion throughout. The word *conversation*, indeed, appears sixty-seven times in Cavell's argument. And there are many more references to talk and exchange and speech and, of course, words. In fact, his introductory chapter is entitled "Words for a Conversation." Conversation, Cavell maintains and I agree, is central to marriage and central to the critical (philosophical and literary) enterprise.

Samuel Johnson noted of *Doctrine and Discipline of Divorce* that it was generated by personal circumstances and that it caused little stir in its own time—positive or negative—as "it was, I suppose," says Johnson, "thought more worthy of derision than of confutation."[1] With this view, it might seem Johnson is dismissing Milton's *Doctrine* out of hand, but "meet and happy conversation" obviously lies behind the *Rambler*'s definition of marriage as "the strictest type of perpetual friendship"[2] as well as Johnson's advice elsewhere that the "man of sense and education" marry "a suitable companion" specifically for the happiness offered by the exchange of ideas: "It was a miserable thing when the conversation could only be such as whether the mutton should be boiled or roasted and probably a dispute about that."[3] Well before Johnson wrote (and, indeed, funding what he wrote), the long eighteenth century's evolving ideal of marital equality was reflected in the witty pair of the Restoration stage, whose "meetness" for equal exchange was key to plot after plot of the comic repertoire.

"What does a happy marriage *sound* like?" asks Stanley Cavell (*PH*, 86). What does any kind of "conversation" sound like for that matter? How do we know when talk is "familiar discourse," "commerce," "intercourse," as opposed to "formal conference" or mere communication?[4] And do we care? Perhaps we are not as demanding as Lewis Carroll's Red Queen; maybe it suits us to "leave all the conversation to the pudding." But that was not the case during the Restoration—nor indeed throughout the entire (long) eighteenth century, at least through the lives of Johnson and Richardson and Austen. We can deduce as much from the high premium placed on repartee during the Restoration period and from the equally high value placed on wit and intelligence in the courtship and other social conversations that dominate volume 1 of Richardson's *Sir Charles Grandison* and, a bit later, the novels of one of Richardson's biggest fans, Jane Austen.[5] Indeed, Samuel Johnson so admired repartee that he found it a fault in Shakespeare's comedies that there was none: "In his comick scenes he is seldom very successful, when he engages his characters in reciprocations of smartness and contests of sarcasm."[6]

Of course, Johnson's blanket condemnation of Shakespeare's comedies in this regard seems odd in that *Much Ado about Nothing*, in many ways, can be seen as the urtext of the very thing he liked about comedy—witty repartee between a man and a woman. Beatrice and Benedick provide the soundtrack of the happy-to-be marriage, the meet conversation between two equals, two friends, who happen to also be in love with one another. They spar, yes. But their fight is not about hostility. It's about reciprocity and the astute awareness that reciprocity is a kind of fight—that is, a fight for the space to love another as an equal as well as a friction necessary to the continuance of the species, to allude to Stephen Greenblatt's famous discussion about the chafing wit of Shakespearean comedy.[7] "The world must be peopled," says Benedick, as he giddily reacts to the "knowledge" that Beatrice loves him and prepares to renounce his disdain for the married state: "when I said I would die a bachelor, I did not think I should live till I were married" (2.3.244–46).[8] What follows is a combative conversation typical of the pair, but invested now (or revealed to be invested now) with erotic tension and amorous desire:

BEATRICE: Against my will I am sent to bid you to come in to dinner.
BENEDICK: Fair Beatrice, I thank you for your pains.
BEATRICE: I took no more pains for those thanks than you take pains to thank me. If it had been painful, I would not have come.
BENEDICK: You take pleasure then in the message?
BEATRICE: Yea, just so much as you may take upon a knife's point and choke a daw withal. You have no stomach, signior. Fare you well. *She exits.*
BENEDICK: Ha! "Against my will I am sent to bid you come in to dinner." There's a double meaning in that. "I took no more pains for those thanks than you took pains to thank me." That's as much as to say, "Any pains that I take for you is as easy as thanks." If I do not take pity of her, I am a villain.

(2.3.249–64)

Whereas Johnson fails to cite Beatrice and Benedick as the exception that proves the rule with regard to Shakespeare, others have found in the couple, not only evidence of wit and vivacity, but also a reflection of the manners of the time, at least as those manners are represented in the courtesy tradition. Philip D. Collington reads this scene against *The Book of the Courtier*'s discussion of the "womanly *sprezzatura*" (i.e., "seemingly effortless beauty" or in the *Courtier*'s own words "'not-regarded pureness'") of a woman who does not overemphasize appearance or artificially manufacture beauty.[9] The *Book of the Courtier* emphasizes a natural attractiveness, not only as less threateningly deceptive than its opposite, but also—and importantly—as more communicative:

> Do you not see how much more grace a woman has who paints (if at all) so sparingly and so little that whoever sees her is uncertain whether she is painted or not; than another woman so plastered with it that she seems to have put a mask on her face and dares not laugh so as not to cause it to crack, and never changes color except in the morning when she dresses; and, then, for the rest of the entire day remains motionless like a wooden statue and shows herself only by torchlight . . . And how much more attractive than all the others is one (not ugly, I mean) who is plainly seen to have nothing on her face, it being neither too white nor too red, but has her own natural color, a bit pale, and tinged at times with an open blush from shame or other cause, with her hair artlessly unadorned and in disarray, with gestures simple and natural, without showing effort or care to be beautiful.[10]

The *Book of the Courtier*'s Count Ludovico, who opines the above, concludes his remarks on womanly *sprezzatura* by observing that "men are ever fearful of being deceived" (48), but as the words of the passage make clear, men are also eager for responsiveness. What kind of conversation can you have with one who is as motionless as a statue and whose expressions you cannot see?

The female half of the Restoration stage "gay couple" is, like Beatrice, defined by *sprezzatura*. George Etherege's Harriet in *The Man of Mode* impatiently dismisses Busy's effort to "set that curl in order," declaring "I will shake 'em all out of order" (3.1.2–3).[11] William Congreve's Millamant in *The Way of the World* is a bit fussier with her hair—pinning it up with "poetry" to make it, according to Mincing, "so pleasant . . . so pure and crips" (2.1.373–74).[12] But she wears "[her] own Face," apparently—as Mirabell provisions that she will "like" it "as long as [he] shall" (4.2.245–46). The rhythms of speech that characterize the dialogue between Beatrice and Benedick are also familiar to readers of Etherege, Wycherley, Behn, Dryden, and Congreve. These rhythms, like the *sprezzatura* of their speakers, have been traced to the *Book of the Courtier*'s Emilia—"gifted with such a lively wit and judgment . . . [that she] seemed the mistress of all, and all appeared to take on wisdom and worth from her"[13] and Gaspare, who is given to "antifeminist flights of fancy" which Emilia takes pleasure in combating.[14]

Indeed, as Collington points out, the "enumeration of the ideal lady's and gentleman's graces" in the *Book of the Courtier* serves as "a defensive posture by which the impossibility that the other could attain such ideals serves as a pretext for not falling in love" (286, 290). This defensive posture is exactly the kind of thing that the central pairs in both Restoration courtship comedies and Hollywood remarriage comedies will have to overcome. They will do so by, in Cavell's words, "learning to speak the same language"—a language they invent rather than one they inherit, a language of "extravagant expressiveness" that engenders in the audience "conviction that each of them is capable of, even craves, . . . the pleasure of their own company" (*PH*, 88).

The Book of the Courtier provided the "sound" of a certain kind of marital conversation—one replicated first in Shakespeare's Beatrice and Benedick, then in the Restoration witty pair, and then again in the central couple of the Hollywood remarriage comedy. In many ways, however, *The Book of the Courtier* ran against models provided elsewhere in the courtesy tradition of the age that followed its appearance. Advice given to women, in particular, was not geared toward raillery or wit. When Restoration conduct books treat female comportment in conversation, they do not portray the models by which Harriet, Hellena from Behn's *Rover*, Millamant, and their sisters-in-wit act and speak. Richard Allestree's *The Ladies Calling* (1673) recommends a "Meekness of the Understanding . . . [that] consists in a pliableness to conviction."[15] "To the *Men* you are to have a *Behaviour* which may secure you without offending them," Lord Halifax tells his daughter, behavior that denotes "a way of Living that may prevent all corse *Railleries* or *unmannerly Freedoms*," placing the onus for polite conversation squarely on her shoulders with no hint of obligation on the man's part.[16] D. R. M. Wilkinson reflects that, in general, "the conduct implicitly advocated in the plays, no less than the manners, differs radically from the ideals of conduct in courtesy books," an observation that would seem to apply with special force to the women of the Restoration stage.[17]

Advice to men in the courtesy books could be downright cynical as we see in Francis Osborne's popular *Advice to a Son* (1656–58). Although this work strikes Wilkinson as closest of all seventeenth-century conduct books to the behavior and attitudes evidenced on the Restoration stage, it does not represent the pleasures anticipatorily modeled in the witty pair. Osborne, who regards marriage as "a Trap set for Flies," "a Clog fastened to the Neck of Liberty by the juggling Hand of *Policy*,"[18] sees so little pleasure to be had in such a union that he recommends his son pay attention first and foremost to the "true extent of *her Estate*," for the "Yoke of Marriage had need be lined with the richest stuff, and softest outward conveniencies, else it will gall your Neck and Heart, so, as you shall take little comfort in the Vertue, Beauty, Birth, *&c.* of her to whom you are coupled" (35–36). In Osborne's view, the sound of a marriage that begins with "whining *Love*" proceeds to "unhappy, dismal and clamorous" jealousy at best (38, 34) and "Misery" and "Beggery" at worst (38).

Certainly, the gay couple of the Restoration stage holds "whining love" in every bit as much aversion as Osborne does, but although it is true that the witty pair of Restoration comedy approach marriage skeptically, they do not descend to Osborne's level of cynicism. The precarious balance they achieve between hope for happiness and awareness of potential disappointment is a rare and precious thing. They are not blinded by romantic fantasy, or depressed by the realities they see all around them—the cuckolded husbands; the desperate wives; the sad and lonely condition of a woman trapped in a loveless, sexless marriage; the brutal fact of spousal abuse condoned by the mores of the times; the fear of faithlessness and betrayal that haunts even the most powerful of husbands. This pair tries to strike a new chord, and they play to the tune of Shakespeare's Beatrice and Benedick. They offer models of conduct not so much for emulation but more for philosophical speculation. What does such a couple stand for? What kind of world produces this pair? What sort of society will grow from their union? What sort of culture can sustain their conversation?

I have already noted the importance of Nell Gwyn and Charles Hart to the emergence of the witty pair on the Restoration stage. Generic experiments, however, were of equal significance in terms of the kinds of questions explored by the dynamic central couple. Three years prior to the first stage appearance of Gwyn and Hart, the Duke's Company, under the leadership of William Davenant, had already begun the serious stage treatment of courtship and marriage as a philosophical problem. Davenant, as manager of the Duke's Company, had been given by King Charles II exclusive rights to ten of Shakespeare's plays. One of the first uses that Davenant made of his privilege was to combine plot and character elements of *Measure for Measure* and *Much Ado about Nothing* into a new play called *The Law Against Lovers*, which appeared on the stage in 1662. It was not a smash hit, but Pepys found it "'a good play and well performed'" and Jacques Thierry and Will Schellincks, two visitors from Holland, thought it the best play they saw in England during their stay in 1661–62. Another commentator was less pleased, writing "that Davenant had merely cobbled together 'two good Playes to make one bad.'"[19]

Of course, it was Beatrice and Benedick that Davenant lifted from *Much Ado* for his *Law Against Lovers*. And they engage in a "merry war" in which, as John F. Cox says, "their initial disdain of matrimony and professed antipathy to each other [does] not quite [conceal] a growing mutual attraction" (8). According to Cox, Davenant brought his pre-Commonwealth memories of the popularity of Beatrice and Benedick to bear on his decision to reshape Shakespeare's *Measure for Measure*. He may have known firsthand that "Charles I in his personal copy of Shakespeare's Second folio, altered . . . [*Much Ado about Nothing*'s] . . . title [to Beatrice and Benedick] proclaiming his own interest in the witty lovers rather than their romantic opposites."[20] This couple had appealed to the earlier age, but Davenant seems to have felt that the current generation would require a more intensified version. As Cox points out,

> despite the parallels between the Beatrice-Benedick relationship in Davenant's play and Shakespeare's, Davenant borrowed little more than a hundred lines of actual dialogue from *Much Ado*. In *The Law Against Lovers* the repartee between Beatrice and Benedick is often harsher than in *Much Ado*, and Davenant accommodated his audience's taste for the salacious with much more bawdy dialogue than in Shakespeare's play.[21]

Alterations notwithstanding, Davenant seems to be responding to or creating—or, to a degree, both—the desire of his audience to hear the talk of a couple like Beatrice and Benedick. One of the great discoveries of the Restoration stage may have been that, as J. L. Styan puts it, "at bottom it is diverting to hear two attractive young people jeering at love when all the time we know that some sort of sexual chemistry will prove stronger than their clever tongues."[22] But it is also true that the talk itself is part of the chemistry—the words part of the attraction, the back-and-forth linguistic challenging of one another this kind of couple's foreplay (and not only symbolically, but literally). And, of course, it is quite interesting to read in Cavell almost the very same observation regarding the couple at the center of Hollywood remarriage comedies: "Talking together is for us the pair's essential way of being together" (*PH*, 146). It is their pleasure and, most especially, it is ours.

The Law Against Lovers goes beyond a mere reflection of the audience's taste, although clearly, as Katherine West Scheil has argued persuasively, pleasing the audience was as important to Davenant, as it would be to any theater manager.[23] There is something rather profound in the change he makes to the Beatrice–Benedick story, something that may indicate that the gay couple, who evolved from this pair, is performing a more serious social function (or at least a different social function) than we generally understand. The "gay couple," the "glittering lovers," the brilliant pair, who represent the essence of wit and sophistication, are usually read as eclipsing all other couples, whose "conversation" is pedestrian, plodding, predictable. Perhaps, though, they are ensuring that others' conversations (whatever their level of interest to the outside "listener") be allowed to take place.

In Davenant's play, Beatrice and Benedick fight Angelo so that Claudio and Julietta can love freely. Claudio and Julietta are not special; they just love one another and have expressed that love physically (in another sense of the word "conversation") prior to a formal marriage. For this act, as in *Measure for Measure*, Claudio is condemned to die by Angelo (put in office by the more lenient Duke, who has let law slide in favor of generosity and understanding). Benedick and Beatrice do not agree on much, but they do agree that Angelo "rules with a Rod in's hand instead of a Scepter, / Like a Country School-Master in a Church" and that his "Design" "against the liberty of Lovers" may ensure that his "rule ... last until the end of the world; / For there will be no next Generation."[24] In dedication to generation and to love, Beatrice and Benedick join forces. They do admit their love for one another eventually, but the "scheme" that brings them together in Davenant's play is not (as in Shakespeare's) a trick. It is, instead, a joint commitment to love, generation, and—indeed—conversation. Beatrice, in a moment of despair, pillories this ideal as talk that will lead to disgrace for women:

> yes, may she
> Who henceforth listens to your sighing Sex,
> Have her Ass-ears in publick bor'd, as Love's
> Known Slave, and wear for Pendants Morrice-Bells
> As his fantastick Fool.
> (4.1.378–82)

But in the end they agree to keep talking, and their last exchange reveals why:

BEATRICE: Take heed! Our quarrel will begin again
    And th'end of this long Treaty will but bring
    The war home to your own doors.
BENEDICK: I'll venture. 'Tis but providing good store of Cradles for Barracadoes to line my Chamber.
(5.1.633–37)

John Harrington Smith notes "the mixture of anxiety and studied insouciance" with which the gay couple of the Restoration stage accepts the idea of marriage.[25] Stanley Cavell notes as much about the central couple in Hollywood comedies of remarriage; the embrace that closes many of those comedies, he remarks, is less an embrace of pure happiness than one "betokening uncertainty" (*PH*, 160). That Shakespeare's Beatrice and Benedick are the model for both couples and that they reflect or echo the tonal register of Castiglione's *Book of the Courtier* is no coincidence. After all, both genres posit a social hierarchy dominated by an inimitable couple, whose uniqueness paradoxically ratifies and clarifies the existence of the world they inhabit.

As Michael Werth Gelber has noted, "at no point during the Restoration ... was *The Book of the Courtier* completely unknown or entirely neglected."[26] He is particularly interested in the Castiglionian echoes in the "courtly bias" evident in the criticism of John Dryden (28). Although it is true, as Gelber says, that "Dryden never refers either to *The Courtier* or to Castiglione by name," we do know that his friend William Walsh recommended that he read the book (28; 264n20). We see the influence of the *Book of the Courtier* in Walsh's *Dialogue Concerning Women, Being a Defence of the Female Sex*, published in 1691 with an introduction by Dryden, in which he praises the "*air of Gallantry*" that suffuses the work, likening Walsh to Ariosto, who also praises women.[27] Dryden calls himself the "*Servant*" of women and claims that he has "*never drawn . . . [his] Pen against them*," not only because he loves them, but because "*in this Age, and at this time particularly, . . . I find more Heroines than Heroes*" ([ix]).

Walsh's *Defence* is organized as a dialogue, or a debate, between Misogynes and Philogynes. Misogynes, who thinks "the Conversation of Women . . . ridiculous" (6) begins by conceding that marriage is necessary:

> The *Propagation* of Mankind being the only way to preserve it from Extinction; and the Copulation with Women being the only means that Nature has ordain'd to that end; there is no doubt but all Commonwealths ought to give any reasonable Encouragement to it; I have therefore always admir'd the Wisdom of those Governments that incited, or compelled their Subjects to marry, as a thing so much more necessary to Mankind in general, than pleasing to any one in particular, but that a man shou'd, out of a meer act of Judgment, run after Women, that he shou'd find delight in their company, is so very extraordinary, that the wise men of old thought it hardly possible, otherwise they had had no need of making such severe Laws to force 'em to it, as they did.
> (8–9)

To choose to keep company with women "only for the benefit of their Conversation," says Misogynes, is the same as choosing "rather to eat Jays and Parrots, than Woodcocks and Partridges, because the Feathers of the former make the finer show" (10). He levels the typical misogynistic charges against women—frivolity, vanity—and creates a genealogy of wise misogynists to which he himself belongs: Solomon, Euripides, Simonides, Lucian, St. Chrysostom, and Juvenal. Misogynes admits there are "Women of Understanding" (31), but they are perhaps even less pleasant than those without. The "Prudent Woman" irritates "all the World with her Management"; the "Politician" annoys by "making her deep Observations upon every-days News"; the "Learned Woman" talks "Nonsense in four or five several Languages" (31). After citing Jael, Clytemnestra, and Medea as examples of violent women, Misogynes rests his case.

Of course, his case is a satire on his position, as Philogynes points out: "I no more believe you a hater of Women, for the Invective you have made against 'em, than I believe *Erasmus* a lover of Folly, for the Encomium he has writ upon it" (47–48). Can Misogynes present stronger evidence? If so, Philogynes will yield additional time. Misogynes declines, and Philogynes begins his praise of women. Like his opponent, Philogynes offers a genealogy of women-lovers (including Solomon whom Misogynes had placed in his camp). In the course of this genealogy, he also provides an alternate rationale for conversing with the opposite sex. Aristotle, Philogynes points out, "made himself a Slave to his Mistress" from "Reason," not "Passion": "He said Love was not only upon the account of Copulation but Philosophy; and commands his Wise-man to be in Love, before he bids him meddle with the Commonwealth" (52). Marriage encourages a cultivated intelligence, for "in a Husband" women "propose a Man whose Conversation shall be agreeable as well as his Person; and who shall have wit to entertain 'em, as well as wisdom to direct 'em" (69–70).

Interestingly, Philogynes ends his argument with praise of three English monarchs, beginning with Boadicia, who

> at a time when the *Britains* groan'd under the Servitude of the *Romans* . . . arose, and by her Courage, as well as Eloquence, inspired her dispirited Countrey-Men with a Resolution of throwing off that Yoke which was grown [too] intolerable to be born.
> (127)

It was Elizabeth I, however, who presided over the country when it achieved "the greatest Glory our Nation cou'd ever boast": "It was in the time of Queen *Elizabeth* that this Island arrived at that pitch of greatness, to which it had been ascending for several Ages, and from which it has been declining 'till very lately ever since" (128). His final praise—and the longest of the three celebrations—is for the reigning monarch, whom he celebrates as a leader and as a wife:

> We have even in our own Time, and our own Countrey, a Princess who has Govern'd to their general satisfaction, a People the most curious to pry into the faults of their Governours, of any People under the Sun. A Princess, who though she never shew'd any fondness of Vain-Glory, or Authority, yet when the necessity of the Kingdom called her to the Helm, Managed Affairs with that dexterity which is very rarely found in those who are the most ambitious of Command.
> (129–30)

Put in sole charge of the country while William was at war, Mary governed with "prudence" (131) and "Courage" (132). Yet, she "grudge[d] her self that Authority, which she ow'd to the absence of a Husband whom she loved so much better than that" (132). Mary's devotion to William and to her country garners Philogynes's highest praise.

Constructions of the ideal kind of marriage as well as formulations of the ideal government were evolving—and interrelated—concepts during the late seventeenth century. The general trajectory followed by each "institution" can be described as a journey toward a cultural model that provides for greater personal fulfillment for those in the relationship or "conversation," to employ the term I have been using. This is not to say that great inequities are resolved by century's end. Far from it. It is to say, however, that the late seventeenth century turned to a series of explorations in prose, drama, and poetry to elaborate new ways of living together in society. John Dryden's works consistently revolve around this theme, employing the metaphor of marriage to explore the general theme of social union in the wake of the English Civil War, the ensuing interregnum, and the unsteady Restoration. In *Absalom and Achitophel*, Dryden articulates a political philosophy that in effect marries "divine right" political philosophy with the Lockean view (articulated in *Two Treatises of Government*) that the king rules at the people's will and by their consent. The narrator of the poem chastises the people of Israel (England) for presuming to "make Heirs for Monarks, and for God decree."[28] A people who overthrow a legitimate king open themselves to tyranny:

> What shall we think! can People give away,
> Both for themselves and Sons, their Native sway?
> Then they are left Defensless to the Sword
> Of each unbounded Arbitrary lord:
> And Laws are vain, by which we Right enjoy,
> If Kings unquestion'd can those laws destroy.
> Yet if the Crowd be Judge of fit and Just,
> And Kings are only Officers in trust,
> Then this resuming Cov'nant was declar'd
> When Kings were made, or is for ever bar'd.
> (759–68)

The king is the image of God (792), and his legitimate right to name his successor is likened (somewhat paradoxically) by the narrator to the Fall of Man:

> If those who gave the Scepter could not tie
> By their own deed, their own Posterity,
> How then could *Adam* bind his future Race?
> How could his forfeit on mankind take place?
> Or how could heavenly Justice damn us all,
> Who nere consented to our Fathers fall?
> (769–74)

Our private rights depend on the divine right of the monarch, who serves the fallen world as a protector and a guardian—not in anything he or she does so much as in the nature of authority he or she reflects—the authority of God.

Dryden's conclusion, however, grants the opposing view and pursues a rational defense of monarchy. Even if we say, for the sake of argument that "the People Kings can make" (795), is it "Prudent . . . a setled

Throne ... [to] shake"? (796). Changing the foundations of a state "is work for Rebels"; reason demands "mend[ing]" flaws, not rending and rebuilding from scratch (806, 808). In granting the idea that the people do have the power to "make" the monarch, and that in their own interest they refrain from rebellion against a sitting king, Dryden reflects both Locke's and Hobbes's more secular view of kingship—a view that will come to dominate after 1689. It is not, however, the view that Dryden himself would finally endorse. To him, the ascension of James II to the throne was a remarriage between England and her true religion. Dryden's famous conversions from Puritan to Anglican to Catholic were judged harshly in his own time, less so in ours as he suffered a great deal for his final religion when the times dictated another divorce for the country and its first form of Christianity. In *The Hind and the Panther*, one can hear the echoes of *Absalom and Achitophel*'s political philosophy as the Hind defends the Roman Catholic elevation of tradition over individual interpretation:

> What weight of antient witness can prevail
> If private reason hold the publick scale?
> But, gratious God, how well dost thou provide
> For erring judgments an unerring Guide![29]

The warring Protestant sects (including Anglicanism or "the *Panther*, sure the noblest next the *Hind*" [1.327])—to say nothing of "the jarring *Jews*" (2.317)—are ample proof that "no written laws can be so plain, so pure, / But wit may gloss, and malice may obscure" (2.318–19). The early Christian emphasis on teaching, not writing, is called as witness to the preference of oral tradition—as are Paul's "*darkly writ*" texts (2.346). The Church alone can interpret correctly, "for discord cannot end without a last appeal" (2.369).

In his prefatory remarks, Dryden charts the progress of *The Hind and the Panther* as a movement from the "general Characters and Narration" of part one to the "Dispute ... concerning Church Authority" of part two, to the "Domestick Conversation" between the Hind and the Panther of part three (122). In part three, we are more aware than in the other sections of the poem of the gendering of the female hind and the male panther. And the hind dominates the discussion that continues throughout the night and ends with the two retiring to their (still separate) but peaceful beds. Given that Dryden figures, in the ironic and somewhat crude voice of the Panther, the coming of Protestantism to England as a "Devorcing from the *Church* to wed ... [a] Dame" (3.205), this gentle ending anticipates a reconciliation or remarriage as the dawn approaches. By the time Dryden wrote his dedication to Walsh's *Defence of the Female Sex*, of course, this public vision was again a fantasy. Privately, however, Dryden remained reconciled and empowered by this reconciliation, at least in terms of his own voice, if not his political standing.

For Dryden, all writing, as Gelber has brilliantly demonstrated regarding Dryden's criticism, is concerned with both the "just," or "judgment and . . . the objective imitation of the external world"[30] and the "lively" or "imagination. . . [and] the subordination of the external world to the faculty that contemplates it" (12). The just resides primarily in structure or form; the lively in language. To emphasize the just over the lively is to "produce . . . only the cold and lifeless excesses of French classicism" (14). The goal of all writing—and of Dryden as a writer—is to synthesize the two faculties, to reflect the truth and to give pleasure. Gelber describes Dryden's critical development as a three-stage process. Beginning as a courtier poet, Dryden becomes a practical critic (providing the tools for reading his own works in prefaces and essays—primarily devoted to the drama), and finally he evolves into a man of letters writing in his "own voice, or at least the one which suits him best" (32). The description provided by Gelber of Dryden's final achievement links him, in my mind, with ordinary language philosophy and prefigures the relationship between Stanley Cavell and literary studies:

> In reading Dryden for pleasure, we ought also profit from what we read. . . . His central critical principles are of enduring importance. No other English critic so well demonstrates that broadly classical values in literature promote and do not detract from grandeur. No other demonstrates so well the interconnections between sound criticism and great literature; and the demonstration by him is all the more impressive since he was simultaneously both poet and critic. And no other critic demonstrates so well that—in literature as in criticism, in criticism as in life—the need is always to combine somehow the restraints of judgment and the flights of the imagination.
>
> (255)

To read Dryden's criticism, Gelber says, is to read the story of his life—what he thinks, what he notices, what he has learned—and to take pleasure with him in the language with which he expresses his ideas, observations, and thoughts. A Cavellian definition of criticism, if ever there was one.

In *Pursuits of Happiness*, Cavell describes his treatment of the film comedies as motivated by "the right to take an interest in . . . [his] own experience" (*PH*, 12). In the very first sentence of the book, he asserts that "each of the seven chapters that follow contains an account of *my experience* of a film made in Hollywood between 1934 and 1949" (*PH*, 1, my emphasis). A few pages later, he elaborates as follows:

> To take an interest in an object is to take an interest in one's experience of the object, so that to examine and defend my interest in these films is to examine and defend my interest in my own experience, in the moments and passages of my life I have spent with them. This in turn means, for me, defending the process of criticism, so far as criticism is thought of, as I think of it, as a natural extension of conversation.
>
> (*PH*, 7)

Cavell believes, as Toril Moi has explained, that "questions of expression and experience lie at the very heart of philosophy," and, therefore, "criticism—the act of accounting for one's experience of a work of art—can be [indeed must be, it would seem] philosophy"[31] Of course, not all literary criticism *is* an account of one's experience with the work in question. Indeed, as Richard Eldridge and Bernard Rhie have noted,

> literary theory, ... at the very historical moment Cavell was emerging on the philosophical scene, believed it was putting "the human" behind it ... in favor of more objective and less human-subject-centered study of the linguistic and material-cultural conditions of the production and reception of texts.[32]

Indeed, the notion of "the human" in the humanities has been suspect for quite some time—as though to claim to be human were to deny humanity to everyone else. Or, as though to take an interest in one's own experience is to assume that the experiences of others are somehow invalid, unimportant, inessential—even to those others. But, Cavell's approach to criticism, like Dryden's, is so rooted in the experiential it does not, indeed cannot, make such universal claims. All Cavell can do is explain as clearly as possible his own experience of the objects under consideration, modeling a *kind* of engagement that he invites us to try for ourselves, but never suggesting that *his* engagement is the *only* engagement possible, his responses the only responses, his insights the only insights.

Interestingly, in his most famous critical comment, *Essay of Dramatic Poesy*, Dryden follows the very same process. He begins the work with an epistle dedicatory to Lord Bathurst in which he recounts the very circumstances of composition: "This essay ... served as an amusement to me in the Country, when the violence of the last Plague had driven me from the Town."[33] The theaters also being closed due to the plague, Dryden says he "was engag'd in these kind of thoughts with the same delight with which men think upon their absent Mistresses" (3). He also seems to think of his essay as an ongoing conversation with Bathurst—especially on the virtue of writing plays in rhyme (and the ease of eschewing rhyme, despite the merits of verse). And he admits that at the present time "my judgment ... [is] a little alter'd" from the opinions he seems to endorse in the essay, "but whither [sic] for the better or the worse, I know not" (3). Still, he acknowledges, all of what he says in the essay is "problematical" (3)—matter for debate. Indeed, the very structure of the essay is dialectical with Crites, Neander, Eugenius, and Lisideius offering their various opinions as to the merits of ancient and modern, French and English playwrights and dramatic practices; and although it is customary to see Neander as Dryden's spokesman in the essay, the critic presents himself as one interested in the exchange of ideas—to advocate his own position or "to be better taught," "to yield on ... honourable terms" (5).

Two general and related aims, though, do underwrite Dryden's *Essay*: first, to draw Bathurst back into the conversation (to "awaken in [him] ... the desire of writing something ... which might be an honour to our Age and Country") and second, to "*vindicate the honour of our* English *writers from the censure of those who unjustly prefer the* French *before them*" (5). As such, Dryden's goal is to highlight the excellencies of the English stage as opposed to the French stage, and in doing so he is led to celebrate the "*Drama* of our own invention"—the tragicomedy. Lisideius attacks the form as "absurd": "here a course of mirth, there another of sadness and passion; a third of honour and a Duel: Thus in two hours and a half we run through all the fits of *Bedlam*" (35). But Neander counters with the commonsensical observation that we experience life in this mixed fashion—so why not art? Lisideius complains that we cannot recover our emotional equilibrium quickly enough to pass from "a Scene of great passion and concernment ... to another of mirth and humour, and to enjoy it with any relish" (46), but is that true? Neander thinks the process quite natural, even aesthetically pleasing: "Does not the eye pass from an unpleasant object to a pleasant in a much shorter time then is requir'd to this? and does not the unpleasantness of the first commend the beauty of the latter?" (46)

J. Douglas Canfield has described the "ideology" of the tragicomic plot as "a reaffirmation of feudal aristocratic values, portrayed as under stress by challenges from bourgeois parvenus, libertine lovers, and ambitious statesmen; from ethical nominalists, political pragmatists, and metaphysical atheists."[34] In that sense, the question of marriage central to those plots takes on larger significance. In these texts and in the comedies that form the heart of my study, as well as in the Hollywood genre to which I am comparing the Restoration comedies, the concern with marriage is a concern with community. In other words, indeed, in Cavell's words, the comedies are focused on the question of the "perfected human community" with "marriage as our best emblem of this eventual community" (*PH*, 152). This meditation on the "perfected human community" based on marriages of equality and conversation is not a realistic depiction of social conditions, but an ideal that in each genre is acknowledged to be fragile, difficult, and frightening. Because each genre conceives itself in terms of another related genre, one that chronicles the failure to attain the marriage that makes the perfected dream a possibility, I think it instructive to look at two examples of the tragicomic plot: John Dryden's *Marriage à la Mode* and Ernst Lubitsch's *The Shop around the Corner*. The comic plot in each of these texts fits the generic template of the Restoration courtship comedy and the Hollywood comedy of remarriage. But the comic plots do not stand alone. They are imbedded in relationship to a tragic or near-tragic plot, a shadow that lies behind or hovers over the action and the world inhabited by the characters. And each of these texts addresses directly the circumstance responsible for the need to rebuild, to question certainties, to find a way to transcend doubt,

38   *Something from nothing*

skepticism, and instability: the legitimacy of kingship and succession (and marriage as the synecdoche of the larger social order) for the Restoration, and the economic crisis that has upended society and social relations (and affected marriage as well, both in reality and as a symbol of social union) for the 1930s.

Dryden's *Marriage à la Mode* begins with the question that Stanley Cavell finds at the center of the later genre of remarriage Hollywood comedies: why is it necessary or desirable for married couples to remain constant to one another? In *Marriage à la Mode*, the question is not framed as a question about divorce, but as a question about fidelity:

> *Why should a foolish Marriage Vow*
> *Which long ago was made,*
> *Oblige us to each other now*
> *When Passion is decay'd?*
>   (1.1.4–7)[35]

Doralice, in a once-happy marriage of passion with Rhodophil, finds herself wondering what underwrites marriage now that "*the Pleasure is fled*"; after all, "*'Twas Pleasure first made it an Oath*," she sings (1.1.9–10). Her husband describes their situation in similar (although less tuneful) terms: "At last, we arriv'd at that point, that there was nothing left in us to make us new to one another" (1.1.151–52). He is contemplating an affair with the giddy Melantha as his wife contemplates a dalliance with Melantha's handsome betrothed, Palamede.

As Laura J. Rosenthal points out, this couple's dilemma is not simply a desire for "libertine indulgence." Instead it represents "an historically specific exploration . . . of what, in this post-revolutionary, post-divine-right, and post-absolutist world, still prevents infidelity."[36] Indeed, in the end, the couples discuss an arrangement that would allow both men to enjoy both women and vice versa. Rosenthal describes the moment as "an extraordinary" one: "while Restoration comedy teems with cuckolding plots, rarely do the characters pause and ask outright what would really be wrong with adulterous sex, especially if all parties agreed" (18). Rosenthal and I differ slightly on the answer to that question as the couples determine it—or I should say the men determine it, for they are the ones who decide. In debating the question "what if both women want the same man?" (or, in Rhodophil's words, "both long for the standing Dish?"), Palamede first proposes drawing lots and then demurs: "And yet that would not do neither; for they would both be wishing for the longest cut" (5.1.356–5). Rosenthal concludes that "prevention of female comparison" keeps the couples from wife swapping (19). I think the conclusion, however, is a bit more complex, hinging not on jealousy but on true insight into the essence of "remarriage." The play is frank about the fact that marriage is a relationship of familiarity and security—one that eventually will render ineffective certain stimulants to the appetite. Rhodophil reveals one strategy he used before neglecting Doralice to pursue Melantha—a strategy no longer effective:

> I have taken such pains to enjoy thee, *Doralice*, that I have fanci'd thee all the fine women in the Town, to help me out. But now there's none left for me to think on, my imagination is quite jaded. Thou art a Wife, and thou wilt be a Wife, and I can make thee another no longer.
>
> (3.1.79–84)

Nor can difficulty be an aid to marriage, although it does serve courtship fairly well, as Palamede notes: "I find that with taking all this pains for . . . [Melantha] I begin to like her" (5.1.224–25). Rhodophil, too, says to Doralice that if she could "make my enjoying thee but a little less easie or a little more unlawful, thou shouldst see what a Termagent Lover I would prove" (3.1.77–79). But, of course, that is impossible in marriage.

Doralice reveals that as a wife she suffers primarily from neglect rather than decayed appetite. In a soliloquy (which, conventionally, we take to be her sincere thoughts), Doralice bewails the "pretty time we Women have on't, to be made Widows, while we are marri'd" (3.1.86–87):

> Our husbands think it reasonable to complain, that we are the same, and the same to them, when we have more reason to complain, that they are not the same to us. Because they cannot feed on one dish, therefore we must be starv'd.
>
> (3.1.87–91)

"Sameness" is the very essence of marriage; indeed, Cavell notes that marriage is fundamentally a "willingness for repetition" (*PH*, 126) and to renounce this willingness is to invalidate the marriage. But it is also true that difference whets the appetite. A key question for the Hollywood genre is how to achieve a remarriage that is different but the same as the original marriage. It is also a question at the heart of the low plot of *Marriage à la Mode*.

Jealousy would seem to be one answer (and this will be the answer as well in Leo McCarey's *The Awful Truth*, which ends with a long seductive exchange between Cary Grant and Irene Dunne about things being "different but the same"). Rhodophil challenges Palamede: "Why would you have seduc'd my wife?" And Palamede counters in high dudgeon: "Why would you have debauch'd my Mistris? (5.1.298–99). They draw swords, only to be interrupted by Doralice, who asks them why they would "cut another's throats for nothing?" Both men are perplexed by the word "nothing." "How for nothing?" asks Palamede. "He courts the woman I must marry." And Rhodophil, too, answers: "And he courts you whom I have marri'd." But to Doralice the cause still seems minor, null: "You can neither of you be jealous of what you love not." Rhodophil answers, philosophically,

"Faith I am jealous, and that make me partly suspect that I love you better then I thought" (5.1.315–21). Doralice again proffers an alternative interpretation, dismissing Rhodophil's comment with "Pish! a mere jealousie of honour," but he insists, "Gad I'm afraid there's something else in't" (5.1.322–23). The near affair has opened Rhodophil's eyes, revealed himself to himself. His rival has awakened him to the fact that there are depths to his partner he has yet to have explored. As Rhodophil says to Doralice; "*Palamede* has wit, and if he loves you, there's something more in ye then I have found, some rich Mine, for ought I know, that I have not yet discover'd" (5.1.523–26). Palamede responds to the novel notion: "'Slife, what's this? here's an argument for me to love *Melantha*; for he has lov'd her, and he has wit too, and for ought I know, there may be a Mine. But if there be, I am resolved to dig for it" (5.1.371–74). Suddenly these very familiar women seem "terra incognita" to the men once more. Palamede uses this metaphor for the allure of the masquerade in which the thorough disguise disallows all prior knowledge; the man in pursuit of a woman at a masquerade is like a "bold discoverer [who] leaps ashoar and takes his lot" (4.1.141–42). Here, however, the metaphor is substantively different. The discovery is of buried treasure or hidden ores. And it requires plumbing the depths, not simply invading the surface.

This moment of insight notwithstanding, the comic plot of *Marriage à la Mode* ends on a tentative note. Doralice will not assure Rhodophil that she has been faithful to him, and although we know she has been we have also witnessed her promise "to venture to be . . . [Palamede's] second Wife" should she outlive Rhodophil and he outlive Melantha (5.1.283–84). And, although Rhodophil's renewed interest in his wife seems sincere enough at this point, Doralice reserves the right to pursue revenge with Palamede should her husband prove again neglectful and unfaithful. Although the more serious "high" plot ends with both the legitimation and the marriage of true lovers Leonidas and Palmyra, it, too, contains a caveat in the unfulfilled and unrequited passion of Amalthea, this play's "unknown woman," to use Cavell's term—the one who must sacrifice her own happiness for the happiness of the one she loves. As she tells Leonidas, she expects the remainder of her life to be spent mostly in "pray'rs for you" and the rest in "mourning my unworthiness" (5.1.525–26). She is the shadow figure that haunts the ideal of marriage as conversation—a figure who will be developed at large later in the Restoration's she-tragedies and in Hollywood melodramas such as *Now, Voyager* and *Stella Dallas*.

But even without the presence of the unknown woman, *Marriage à la Mode* highlights the tentativeness of stability—both domestic and national—and leaves us with the uneasy feeling that will be the hallmark of the two genres at the heart of my study. In this case, as in the case of *The Shop around the Corner*, the uneasiness is a direct effect of the split-plot dramatic structure, a structure that underwrites, despite its erasure, the more fully comic worlds of the Restoration courtship comedy and the

Hollywood remarriage comedy. As Jason Denman has argued, Dryden's play is "engaged in a vital skeptical debate about the relationship between temporality and human institutions" and as such demonstrates "the difficulty of constructing the temporal fictions that underlie univocal assertions of meaning."[37] Certainly, the difficulty of joining the two plots of the play is highlighted by the perfunctory way in which Rhodophil and Melantha, in particular, interact with the characters of the heroic plot. But Denman goes further to illustrate that the play is, in fact, informed by a "figural pattern" that links the "spheres of erotic and political activity," showing that in both domains stability "depends on the extraordinarily difficult task of creating moments of simultaneity" (1–2): "The low plot's tendency to interrupt assignations and deny sexual satisfaction undercuts the suspensions of time required to establish a modicum of political stability in the high plot; at the same time, the high plot is itself reflexive and overtly reliant on contrivance" (2). Simultaneity, when it is achieved, is done so only by suspending time.

In the high plot, the suspension exists in the mutual memory of life away from court shared by Leonidas and Palmyra in Act 2. Leonidas notes that in court (in public life, that is), there are few hours for "privacy, and Love," whereas "in Cottages, . . . Love has all the day." Palmyra agrees, the days actually seem shorter now that they are living in Polydamas's court; the sun itself seems to shine "faint and dimly" and "not half so long": "But, Oh! when every day was yours and mine, / How early up! what haste he made to shine!" (2.1.414, 407, 415–18). Their love has blossomed in a "green space," as Cavell would likely note; achieving that state of reciprocity and mutuality that will occupy these lovers through the course of the play—and in the end is made possible only by the intervention of others who legitimize their royal identities and facilitate their recognition, both in the sense of being recognized as a royal pair with a joint claim to the throne but also in the sense of recognizing one another. Amalthea has to identify Palmyra for Leonidas at the masquerade in Act 4; as Denman argues, although Leonidas claims he would recognize her anywhere, he does not do so until Amalthea points her out. Amalthea's words are telling: "Like Love's Dark-Lantern, I direct his steps, / And yet he sees not that which gives him light" (4.2.16–17). Further, the royal marriage is arranged and announced so hastily that, again as Denman notes, we cannot fail to see that timing will continue to be at issue, as it is for the characters of the comic plot. Those couples or would-be couples find erotic simultaneity very difficult to achieve. Denman, indeed, highlights the fact that the culmination of this theme is the "imperfect enjoyment" song that is sung at the masquerade.[38] Repartee also suffers in this play, interestingly enough. Palamede speaks in clichés with Doralice, rendering their dialogue less-than-sparkling. He does manage to inflect his speeches to Melantha with enough French to successfully court her (in a sense, those two learn to speak the same language—a trait we'll notice in the witty pairs of later texts). Melantha, however, is most successful with repartee on her own

(3.1.246–58) as she imagines both sides of a conversation with Rhodophil. As Denman observes, "If every encounter she has, whether with Rhodophil or Palamede or one noble or another, feels rushed and ill-timed, this encounter suggests that simultaneity is most easily found with oneself" (11). Like the pastoral memories of Leonidas and Palmyra, Melantha's most fulfilling moment (a masturbatory, "less than dignified moment," as Denman says [12]) is one that exists outside the parameters of the play's action and the society that is represented. It is not fully integrated and, as such, again draws attention to the tentativeness of stable relations, both political and personal, in the world of *Marriage à la Mode*.

Ernst Lubitsch defined the style of the 1930s sex comedy just as Dryden defined the style of the late seventeenth-century sex comedy. That both were so articulate and aware of what they were doing is a fact we must not lose sight of. Lubitsch understands, as Leo Braudy points out, "the thinness of the social fabric, the ease with which it is learned, and the insubstantial claim to respect that those who manipulate its forms truly deserve."[39] But "his love for the visible world . . . its frauds and its infinite details" is also everywhere evident (73). Braudy explains the "Lubitsch touch" as a philosophical as much as a stylistic phenomenon:

> In Lubitsch's directorial style, the actor's sense of "business," the way in which he uses the psychosocial valence of objects and gestures to build up a recognizable character, is turned into a device to signal irony and distance rather than one to induce empathy and connection. Here is the real importance of the Lubitsch touch, with its frequent Freudian overtone of revealing previously hidden motivations, the sexual story, by an adroit piece of business or a focus on a significant object. The Lubitsch touch signals to the audience that the old interpreter is at it again, letting us in on a privileged perspective, embracing the audience as a co-conspirator of interpretation, an accomplice in the director's and the camera's knowingness.
>
> (72)

Like Dryden, Lubitsch was concerned with the topic of marriage and like Dryden he tended to explore that topic in a split-plot or tragicomic narrative, first in the silent film *The Marriage Circle* (1924) and later in the Paramount "talkie," *The Shop around the Corner* (1940).[40]

The silent film revolves around two married couples, one tragically mismatched and, the other blissfully happy. As noted by Alan Jacobson, who incidentally also calls this film a "screwball comedy of manners," the film ultimately leaves the "viewer . . . wondering whether marriage is really more than a security measure for modern civilization."[41] And, if so, in what sense? Jacobson regards the fact that "Lubitsch inspires this deep and revolutionary . . . question" a signal source of admiration and cause for praise. *The Shop around the Corner*'s investment in the same question is perhaps

Something from nothing 43

masked by the fact that the two couples under consideration are of different generations. Furthermore, the happy couple is not together on screen as a happy couple except in a brief concluding moment that strikes a romantic chord loud enough to obscure the many notes of discord heard throughout the film itself. What does a happy marriage sound like? It is really difficult to say from the evidence Lubitsch provides. But, again, there seems to be a commitment at the heart of the skeptical script to honor the impulses that drive us toward the institution, if not to celebrate the institution itself.

That marriage exists despite overwhelming evidence that it does not lead to happiness is emphasized in the details of *The Shop around the Corner*, from the middle-aged Matuscheks' union doomed by infidelity (which itself seems to have been the product of neglect) to the youthful, romantic Klara's choice of reading material on the evening that she is to meet the "friend" with whom she has been corresponding. *Anna Karenina* indeed mirrors the Matuschek marriage almost exactly, except that Mr. Matuschek, rather than his wife, is driven to the point of suicide and would have been successful but for the fortunate return of errand boy Pepi. And although the film, unlike the Restoration play, does not set the pursuit of happiness within the larger context of state affairs, it does reference the issue of "governance" as it pertains in the hierarchy of the shop.

A spirit of nihilism hovers over the world of the "screwball" comedy as prefigured in Lubitsch's *Shop*. In fact, the film highlights the concept of nothing. Vadish, the store troublemaker, makes "something" out of the office gossip about Mrs. Matuschek's possible facelift, gossip the shopgirls insist is "nothing." More interestingly, the word "nothing" is associated with dictatorial leadership, evidenced by Miss Novak's bemoaning of the effect that Mr. Kralik's leadership style has had on her: "When I first came into this shop, I was full of life and enthusiasm. Now I'm nothing. You've taken my personality away. You're a dictator; that's what you are!" Kralik, in turn, experiences the tyranny of a "boss [who] doesn't have to give . . . a reason" for firing an employee. Mr. Matuschek dismisses Kralik, and Kralik dismisses the situation as "nothing unusual [as] it happens every day; people get fired all the time."

The film's meditation on inner and outer—secret motivation and public behavior—echoes a central trope of Restoration comedy, which also worries about secret loves, clandestine meetings, broken vows, and empty words. As is usual with Lubitsch, common objects are invested with symbolic meaning—the gimmicky cigarette boxes that play "Ochi Chernye" cheaply invoke the potential tragedy of falling in love, the "romance," as Klara lamely puts it, of "moonlight and cigarettes and music." The practical wallet, on the other hand, is twice linked with lasting love and value. Kralik tells Miss Novak that her secret suitor would much prefer a wallet to a cigarette box. "On one side, he has your latest letter; on the other side, a picture of you. When he opens it there you are, and that's all the music he wants." Pirovitch, helping his friend, tells Klara the same thing: "On one side, a picture of my wife; and on the other side, my little baby. When I open it, it says 'Papa' and not 'Ochi Chernye.'"

The letter, however, is the single most important object in the film. It is through letters that Klara and Kralik fall in love, anonymously. And their letters are eroticized from the beginning. With so many letters in envelopes, so many letters in boxes, so many letters in wallets, it does not take a Luce Irigaray to point out the sexual symbolism. But, whereas Irigaray bemoans the fact that women are just envelopes always to contain, never to be enveloped, Lubitsch does not gender the object. The letter—and its envelope and its box—are fetishized by both the man and the women, by both "dear friends." The negative sexual alternative is the one spoken to Kralik by Klara twice: "After all, I'm working under you." It is an anonymous letter, too, that informs Mr. Matuschek that his wife is having an affair with one of his employees. In that case, the correspondence is answered not in writing, but in action—very nearly tragic action, the result of disillusionment as much as sexual jealousy: "Twenty-two years we've been married. Twenty-two years I was proud of my wife. Well, she just didn't want to grow old with me."

Disillusionment is a real possibility for Kralik and Klara as well. Indeed, Kralik suffers momentary disillusionment outside the restaurant where he was to meet his "friend," when Pirovitch, looking through the front window for a girl and a carnation, reports: "If you don't like Miss Novak, I can tell you right now you won't like that girl, because it *is* Miss Novak." Kralik had originally asked Pirovitch to deliver a letter to his date explaining that he would not meet her that evening (having been fired by Mr. Matuschek, he felt too demoralized), but upon hearing her identity, he reacts to the six months of teasing and unpleasantness that had characterized his working relationship with Miss Novak rather than the fact that, as Pirovitch points out, "she wrote those letters." Both Kralik and Pirovitch leave, but soon Kralik returns. He does not wear the red carnation that would identify him as "friend" to Klara, but he does talk to her, provoking a series of insults and jibes and returning them as well.

Still, Kralik is clearly meditating on the strange difference between the inner and the outer—the letters Miss Novak writes as opposed to the things she says. If only they could see the "inner truth," he says, they would both be surprised. Klara denies it: if she were to see inside him, she knows what she would find: "Instead of a heart, a handbag; instead of a soul, a suitcase; instead of an intellect, a cigarette lighter which doesn't work." Kralik declares this sentiment an "interesting mixture of poetry and meanness" and warns her that her behavior (and her red hands) will destine her to be an "old maid." She retaliates by calling him bowlegged and a "little insignificant clerk." Although not the "inner stuff" of letters, the two have managed to penetrate beneath the surface, each wounding the other in half-conscious articulation of deepest insecurities and private fears.

Mr. Matuschek's attempted suicide paves the way for Kralik's transformation from "little insignificant clerk" to "manager," thereby providing him a degree of confidence he had been lacking heretofore, confidence that allows him to listen to Miss Novak more carefully and less emotionally. When Klara tells him that the illness she suffers after being stood up is psychological, Kralik responds dismissively: "As long as it's only psychological, you won't . . . " She interrupts: "Only psychological! Mr. Kralik, it's true we're in the same room, but we're not in the same planet." His eyes soften appreciatively: "Miss Novak, although I'm the victim of your remark, I can't help admiring the exquisite way you have of expressing yourself." There is still some of the old wry edge to his punning conclusion—"you certainly know how to put a man in his planet"—but from this point until the end of the film, we see Kralik's growing carefulness with and attentiveness to Miss Novak. Although this particular scene concludes with his comment that "there isn't much more I can say except that I wish you a Merry Christmas," the conversation between this pair has only begun.

The relationship culminates in the stockroom on Christmas eve. In the course of the clever and moving denouement, the characters transform the nothing of their relationship into a something. As Klara wraps the wallet she has purchased for her soon-to-be fiancé, Kralik, says to her, "Want to see something?" He pulls out a box and opens it to reveal a jeweled—"pretty near" diamond—necklace. Klara is dazzled, but the conversation nevertheless drifts toward their old antagonism. When it does so, Klara says "I'd like to be friends with you" and admits to having had even stronger feelings—to "falling for" Kralik—in her early days at Matuschek and Company:

> All my knowledge came from books. And I'd just finished a novel about a glamorous, French actress from the Comédie Française. When she wanted to rouse a man's interest, she would treat him like a dog. But instead of licking my hand, you barked! See I didn't realize the difference between this glamorous lady and me was that she was with the Comédie Française and I was with Matuschek and Company.

"Maybe," says Klara, "we'll both be engaged Monday morning. Or, in my case, it *might* happen." "I can tell you it *will* happen," says Kralik. As if in response to Klara's admitted love for fiction, Kralik begins to improvise a narrative about her "friend," whom Kralik says he has met—"you shouldn't have told him who I am"—and who "didn't believe it when you told him I meant nothing to you." This creation of Kralik's imagination, Mr. Popkin, is certainly disillusioning for Klara. This Popkin is depressed, overweight, unemployed, and bald, but it is his materialism—his concern with her salary and bonus and potential raise—that upsets her most. Could the inner man and the outer man be so different? The answer, of course, is no. When Kralik puts the carnation in his buttonhole and tells her to "take your key and open post office box 237 and take me out of my envelope and kiss me," once more Klara finds herself "psychologically confused," but not so confused that she neglects to ask Kralik to prove he is not bowlegged. With the lifting of his pants, and the kiss that follows, we see the coming together of inner, outer, appearance, and reality for both Klara and Kralik.

Their story, however, is just one of the stories in *The Shop around the Corner*, as the opening title makes clear: "This is the story of Matuschek and Company, Mr Matuschek and the people who work for him." And Mr. Matuschek, too, is the recipient of a letter that clarifies things for him at the end of the film. His employees have sent a Christmas tree to his hospital room, accompanied by "a little note," which he read "over and over" (as Klara and Kralik have read the letters from "dear friend"). The phrase that has touched him is their hoping he would "be coming back home soon." "You're right," he tells them; "this is my home. This is where I've spent most of my life." Although his realization prompts a softer, more caring managerial style—and generous Christmas bonuses—the fact should not be lost on the viewer that his devotion to his shop has contributed to the deterioration of his marriage.

A merchant's life is the exchange of goods for money, with the ideal being as Kralik puts it, "an empty, bare-looking shop with nothing in it" but a register full of cash—$9,654.75, to be precise (as this genre always is with regard to money). When Matuschek exclaims "that's the biggest day since '28" he articulates the reality in which the Hollywood comedy is produced and the economic uncertainty that threatens to reduce all to nothing with nothing to show for it. Hollywood comedies of remarriage generally do not address the Depression directly, but economic anxieties mark the canon and map themselves on the view of marriage articulated within the individual films. In *The Shop around the Corner*, we are left wondering if the "home," the shop, can nurture or sustain a marriage—and, if so, what kind of marriage? Can we imagine Klara, like Mrs. Pirovitch, at home with the babies? Or can we see her as a Mrs. Matuschek on the end of the phone, ordering her husband's employees around, and speaking to a husband, who plans to grow old with her but not to be young with her? We hope not, but the film offers no guarantee.

If the shop is a "home" and employees "family," what is a "marriage"?[42] How does marriage answer the demands of a capitalist society? And if it does not, and if in the grand scheme of things—power and money and cultural progress—marriage is nothing, why and how do people keep insisting that it is something, and not only something but a something that is better than the nothing of a full cash register and a depleted inventory? Allegorically, Lubitsch's concern is the same concern evidenced in Dryden's *Marriage à la Mode*, for the court society built on dynastic marriages and concentration of wealth and power within the aristocracy is no less inimical to attentive conversation than the world of competitive capitalism. The coercive pressures and pleasures derived from acceptance at court are the same as those derived from a full cash register and an empty inventory, at least as the texts under consideration present them. Both texts regard such pleasures with the extreme skepticism that underwrites the (potentially) tragic plot of each play and that threatens the comic plots as well. Overcoming this skepticism, for Doralice and Rhodophil and for Klara and Kralik, requires forgiveness, attentiveness, and the belief that their future can be both different from their past and the same.

Notes

1 "Milton," ed. Stephen Fix, in *Samuel Johnson: The Lives of the Poets*, vol. 21 of *The Yale Edition of the Works of Samuel Johnson*, ed. John H. Middendorf (New Haven, CT: Yale University Press, 2010), 124.
2 *Rambler*, no. 18, May 19, 1750, in *Samuel Johnson: The Rambler*, ed. W. J. Bate and Albrecht J. Strauss, vol. 3 of *The Yale Edition of the Works of Samuel Johnson*, ed. John H. Middendorf (New Haven, CT: Yale University Press, 1969), 103.
3 Recorded by James Boswell, in *Life of Johnson*, ed. R. W. Chapman and J. D. Fleeman (Oxford: Oxford's World Classics, 1980), 445.
4 From Johnson's *Dictionary of the English Language*, 2 vols. (London: W. Strahan, 1755), s.v. conversation.
5 See Caroline Gonda, who notes "*Grandison*'s close fidelity to the everyday, the mundane, the conversational," as a "congenial" model for later women novelists, Austen included. *Reading Daughters' Fictions 1709–1834: Novels and Society from Manley to Edgeworth* (Cambridge: Cambridge University Press, 1996), 101.
6 Preface to *Johnson on Shakespeare*, ed. Arthur Sherbo, vols. 7–8 of *The Yale Edition of the Works of Samuel Johnson* (New Haven, CT: Yale University Press, 1968), 7: 72.
7 Greenblatt, "Fiction and Friction," in his *Shakespearean Negotiations: The Circulation of Social Energy in Renaissance England* (Berkeley: University of California Press, 1988), 66–93.
8 Quotations from *Much Ado About Nothing* are from the edition available on the Folger Digital Texts website, http://www.folgerdigitaltexts.org/, which is licensed under a Creative Commons Attribution, the terms of which are available at http://creativecommons.org/licenses/by-nc/3.0/deed.en_US. No changes have been made to the text, which is cited by act, scene, and line.
9 Collington, "'Stuffed with All Honourable Virtues': *Much Ado about Nothing* and *The Book of the Courtier*," *Studies in Philology* 103 (2006): 291.
10 Baldesar Castiglione, *The Book of the Courtier*, ed. Daniel Javitch, trans. Charles S. Singleton (New York: Norton Critical Edition, 2002), 48.
11 George Etherege, *The Man of Mode; or Sir Fopling Flutter* (1676), in *The Plays of Sir George Etherege*, edited by Michael Cordner, 209–333 (Cambridge: Cambridge University Press, 1982).
12 William Congreve, *The Way of the World* (1700), in *The Complete Plays of William Congreve*, edited by Herbert Davis, 386–479 (Chicago: University of Chicago Press, 1967).
13 Castiglione, *Book of the Courtier*, 12.
14 Collington, "'Stuffed with All Honourable Virtues,'" 285. Collington notes that Mary Augusta Scott was the first to suggest that Beatrice and Benedick were modeled on Emilia and Gaspare in her "*Book of the Courtyer*: A Possible Source of Benedick and Beatrice," *PMLA* 16 (1901): 475–502.

48 *Something from nothing*

15 Allestree, *The Ladies Calling, in Two Parts*, Oxford, 1673), 30.
16 George Savile, Marquis of Halifax, *The Lady's New-Year Gift: Or Advice to a Daughter*, 2nd ed. (London: Matt. Gillyflower and James Partridge, 1688), 102–103.
17 Wilkinson, *Comedy of Habit: An Essay on the Use of Courtesy Literature in a Study of Restoration Comic Drama* (Leiden: Universitaire Pers, 1964), 6.
18 Osborne, *Advice to a Son, in Two Parts*, in *The Works of Francis Osborn* [sic] *Esq.* (London, 1689), 28, 33.
19 John F. Cox, introduction to *Much Ado about Nothing*, ed. John F. Cox, Shakespeare in Production (Cambridge: Cambridge University Press, 1997), 8–9, and Pepys, *Diary*, 3: 32.
20 See Anne Barton, introduction to *Much Ado about Nothing*, ed. Anne Barton, *The Riverside Shakespeare*, 2nd ed. (Boston: Houghton Mifflin, 1997), 374.
21 Cox, introduction to *Much Ado*, 8.
22 Styan, *Restoration Comedy in Performance* (Cambridge: Cambridge University Press, 1986), 189.
23 Schiel, "Sir William Davenant's Use of Shakespeare in *The Law against Lovers* (1662)," *Philological Quarterly* 76 (1997): 369.
24 William Davenant, *The Law against Lovers* 1673 (London: Cornmarket Press, 1970), 3.1.151–52, 157–60.
25 Smith, *The Gay Couple in Restoration Comedy* (Cambridge, MA: Harvard University Press, 1948), 76.
26 Gelber, *The Just and the Lively: The Literary Criticism of John Dryden* (Manchester, UK: Manchester University Press, 1999), 264n22.
27 Dryden, preface to *A Dialogue Concerning Women, Being a Defence of the Sex Written to Eugenia*, by [William Walsh] (London: R. Bently, 1691), [v].
28 *Absalom and Achitophel*, in *The Works of John Dryden*, ed. Alan Roper and H. T. Swedenberg, vol. 2 *Poems, 1681–1684*, ed. H. T. Swedenberg (Berkeley: University of California Press, 1972): 758, hereafter cited in text by line number.
29 *The Hind and the Panther*, in *The Works of John Dryden*, ed. Alan Roper and H. T. Swedenberg, vol. 3, *Poems 1685–1692*, ed. Earl Miner and Vinton A. Dearing (Berkeley: University of California Press, 1969), part 1, lines 62–65, hereafter cited in text by part and line number. The preface will be cited by page number.
30 Gelber, *Just and the Lively*, 12.
31 Toril Moi, "The Adventure of Reading: Cavell and Beauvoir," in *Stanley Cavell and Literary Studies: Consequences of Skepticism*, ed. Richard Eldridge and Bernard Rhie (New York: Continuum, 2011), 21.
32 Eldridge and Rhie, introduction to *Stanley Cavell and Literary Studies*, 4.
33 Dryden, "An Essay of Dramatick Poesie," in *The Works of John Dryden*, ed. Alan Roper and H. T. Swedenberg, vol. 17, *Prose 1668–1691*, ed. Samuel H. Monk and A. E. Wallace Mauer, (Berkeley and Los Angeles: University of California Press, 1972), 3.
34 Canfield, "The Ideology of Restoration Tragicomedy," *ELH* 51 (1984): 448.
35 Dryden, *Marriage à la Mode*, in *The Works of John Dryden*, ed. Alan Roper and H. T. Swedenberg, vol. 11, *Plays*, ed. John Loftis, David Stuart Rhodes, and Vinton A. Dearing (Berkeley and Los Angeles: University of California Press, 1978). References are to act, scene, and line numbers.
36 Rosenthal, "'All Injury's Forgot': Restoration Sex Comedy and National Amnesia," *Comparative Drama* 42, no. 1 (2008): 8.
37 Denman, "'Too Hasty to Stay': Erotic and Political Timing in *Marriage à la Mode*" *Restoration* 32, no. 2 (2008): 1–2.
38 "'Too Hasty to Stay,'" 2.
39 Braudy, *Native Informant: Essays on Film, Fiction, and Popular Culture* (Oxford: Oxford University Press, 1991), 73.

40 *The Marriage Circle*, directed by Ernst Lubitsch. 1924; *The Shop around the Corner*, directed by Ernst Lubitsch. 1940, MGM (Burbank, CA: Warner Home Video, 2002), DVD.
41 Jacobson, "The Great Marriage Debate of 1924: Lubitsch's Masterful Silent on DVD," *Bright Lights Film Journal,* April 30, 2004. http://brightlightsfilm.com/the-great-marriage-debate-of-1924-lubitschs-masterful-silent-on-dvd/., 2010.
42 For a very interesting discussion of the communal (corporate) significance of the 1990s update of *The Shop around the Corner*, Nora Ephron's *You've Got Mail*, see Jerome Christensen, "*Critical Response II:* Taking It to the Next Level: *You've Got Mail,* Havholm and Sandifer," *Critical Inquiry*, 30 no. 1 (2003): 198–215.

2 The thin man of mode

I want to begin this chapter with a note on genre and canon—two topics that have been implicit in my argument all along. Before embarking on the paired-text analyses that form the core of my study, however, I need to make a few things explicit in terms of the assumptions underlying my comments regarding both genre and canon. Stanley Cavell's *Pursuits of Happiness* meticulously and thoroughly establishes the generic features by which the "film comedy of remarriage" can be identified. Not all 1930s film comedies fit the bill—and, despite frequent allusions to the genre in reviews of more recent romantic comedies, no official addition to the canon has been recorded that has been accepted by Cavell himself. As he is the one who identified and described the genre for the purposes of philosophical investigation, his authority must be noted, although in *Pursuits of Happiness*, he often invites us to challenge his own readings of the films as remarriage comedies. Does it matter, for instance, that there is no "green space" in *His Girl Friday*? Or does the absence of the father, who is on the side of the daughter's desire, disqualify *Bringing Up Baby* as a candidate for generic inclusion? Cavell explains that to his mind the answer is no on both counts—but he leaves to the reader the option of resisting and rejecting his principles of inclusion.

The Restoration genre that I have described as the "courtship comedy" has not been defined or defended as such elsewhere. Indeed, most of the plays I include (the ones written by men, anyway) were influentially classified as comedies of manners by George H. Nettleton and Arthur E. Case, who produced, in 1939, a long-dominant anthology in the field. It was reissued thirty years later with a fuller apparatus by George Winchester Stone Jr., but that edition was not revised according to classification or canon.[1] This anthology presented the "comedy of manners" as "sophisticated, intellectualized comedy" characterized by moral ambivalence and the presence of witty lovers who spoke sparkling dialogue.[2] These plays were generally focused on the question of marriage, often featuring satiric treatment of arranged, or dynastic, marriage, in particular. They also typically validated the marriage of mutual affection, which was "well rooted in the culture," in their view.[3] The Nettleton, Case, and Stone anthology persisted virtually unchallenged until the 2001 publication of *The Broadview Anthology of Restoration and Early Eighteenth-Century Drama*, under the general editorship of J. Douglas Canfield. Responding to widespread dissatisfaction in the field with the labels under which Restoration and eighteenth-century drama had been studied for years (labels deriving primarily from Nettleton, Case, and Stone), Canfield attempted a new generic mapping that eschewed the term "manners" altogether. *The Man of Mode*, *The Rover*, and *The Way of the World* were denominated "social comedies"; *The Country Wife* was termed a "subversive comedy"; and *The Luckey Chance* was categorized as a "corrective satire." The concise version of the anthology is the dominant classroom text today, but the generic categories employed in the Broadview edition have not caught on. Although "comedy of manners" is seldom heard these days, none of the other terms has replaced it, in whole or in part.[4]

My construction of the "Restoration courtship comedy" was the result of two factors: the predominant classroom favorites plus my sense (a back formation, I suppose) that certain of these texts paired effectively with the remarriage comedies (and a few additional classical Hollywood comedies). "Courtship" is meant to stand in relationship to "remarriage." I hasten to add that there is a body of material in the Restoration and eighteenth-century dramatic repertoire that would constitute the genre "Restoration Marriage Play." Four of these works (Thomas Otway's *Soldier's Fortune*, Nathaniel Lee's *Princess of Cleves*, John Dryden's *Amphitryon; or the Two Sosias*; and Thomas Southerne's *Wives' Excuse; or Cuckolds Make Themselves*) were edited by Michael Cordner and published in an anthology for the Oxford World's Classics series. In an appended comprehensive list, Cordner provides a fuller canon of works "written between 1660 and the very early eighteenth century, in which at least one major plot centres on a marriage in disarray."[5] Several of my "courtship comedies" appear in the list: *The Country Wife*, *The Plain Dealer*, *The Luckey Chance*, and *The Way of the World* (along with the Cibber and Vanbrugh plays I discuss as participating in the evolution of the first remarriage comedy). But Cordner defined his genre as characterized by at least one major plot with a marriage in disarray, and I define mine by the inclusion of at least one witty pair of courting lovers, lovers described by Brian Corman as "sympathetic characters," who are "worldly and sophisticated" and whose "oft-praised exchanges of wit, exchanges again treasured by audiences today, are central to their courtships."[6] Corman's significant phrase "exchanges again treasured by audiences today" speaks to the relatively recent recuperation of this material for readers, students, and scholars.

It seems worth noting in a more than passing way that the Restoration plays became available for classroom study during the same decade that witnessed the rise of the Hollywood comedy of remarriage. I am not arguing cause and effect in any specific terms, but it does seem relevant to note that the emergence of one dramatic form (the Hollywood comedies of remarriage) happened at the same time as the reemergence of another

(Restoration comedies of manners). And it seems significant, as well, that the selection of "comedy of manners" in Nettleton, Case, and Stone is, at five texts, the longest in the anthology, with other "genres" being represented by one or two texts until the last section, "laughing comedy," which has three. Although my genre may have seemed to me as I was pursuing this project to be a back formation, it may actually represent the recognition of influence on the scriptwriters and directors, who were participating in a comic tradition long overlooked and newly significant. In other words, that the courting couples of Restoration comedy bear such resemblance to the witty couples of Hollywood films of the 1930s may not be a coincidence at all. This congruence is evidence of what Joseph Roach has called the "long but spastic revolution" spawned by the "culturally prescient texts and discourses" as well as the "prolific performances and behaviors" of the Restoration stage.[7]

The connection between the courtship comedies of the Restoration stage and the Hollywood remarriage comedies has seldom been explored at much length. One exception is an article by Oliver Tilley in which he responds to a casual comparison of the genres made by Pauline Kael in 1982, in reference to *Bringing Up Baby*, by systematically contrasting the genres in order to debunk the idea. His concentration on superficial differences is not enough to convince me. I maintain that the extended meditation on marriage offered by the individual members of each genre links the bodies of work both philosophically and aesthetically.[8] In one way or another, it must be significant that after a performance (and even reading) gap of half a century, Restoration comedy was reintroduced into the dramatic repertoire and literary canon in stage performances that predate the emergence of the "screwball" Hollywood film by a mere decade. Beginning in 1914 and 1915, a few Restoration comedies were presented by semiprofessional theatrical societies (the Stage Society and the Phoenix Society) in very limited runs (two performances was the norm for the Phoenix Society—significantly founded by Montague Summers, who is also responsible for the first full edition of the works of Aphra Behn). For around a decade, these performances gradually helped form a taste in the place of the distaste that had prevailed, an interest in the place of the horror typical of the post-Macaulay reader and potential theatergoer. Finally, as Peter Holland explains, the stage was set for success:

> In 1924, Nigel Playfair directed Congreve's *The Way of the World* at the Lyric Theatre, Hammersmith, with Edith Evans as Millamant. Through her performance Congreve's dramatic language was suddenly revalued and the critic James Agate could judge the play "the greatest prose comedy in the English language." Agate, calling [Charles] Lamb's defense of the drama as artificial "a world of mischief," recognized that the play had a startling reality, "as real as any canvas of old Hogarth or modern page of Zola."[9]

To some degree and too quickly, Holland goes on to say, the discovery of the Restoration comedy's "distinct style . . . modulated into the assumption that style was the only quality the plays had" (644). Still, the best productions, see "the pain, cynicism and anxiety behind the style, recognizing that the dramatic style mirrors a set of social forms needed to protect vulnerable individuals" (645). Edith Evans herself saw style not as an end in itself but as a vehicle for "tak[ing] . . . audience[s] to the centre of . . . [the plays'] meaning and experience"[10] (248).

To film scholar Edward Berkowitz, it seems clear that "the screwball form went back to Restoration comedy" and shared with the earlier form the emphasis on "situation-driven wit" rather than vaudevillian "physical slapstick."[11] He cites Robert Sklar's view that "screwball pictures were comedies of manners."[12] And like the first comedies of manners, these films examine the social order without, finally, disrupting it, although in the process they give "audiences a whole new vision of social style, a different image of how to be a person."[13] Sklar observes that "there is no question but that . . . [screwball films] made their contribution to cultural change, just by repeating over and over again how attractive it was to be a person who liked to have fun" (188).

Further supporting the notion of a close relationship between these genres and the likelihood that the remarriage film is, in fact, self-consciously based on the Restoration courtship comedy are a number of shared traits or features that go beyond the focus on the very similar witty pairs. Like the comedies of remarriage, the Restoration courtship comedies are generally driven by the heroine's desire; so in that sense they derive from "Old Comedy" in which the obstacle to marriage is not posed by an older man, a "senex figure" (*PH*, 1), but instead is focused on the heroine, "who may hold the key to the successful conclusion of the plot" (*PH*, 1). Although most of the plays do feature an older relative who attempts to control the young woman's choices, that relative does not pose a real problem for the heroine. Indeed, the true obstacles in her path are her own reservations about marriage, her uncertainty that the institution is malleable enough to insure her happiness, that it will offer both herself and her husband the freedom of self-expression necessary to true conversation. We will see perhaps the best example in *The Man of Mode*'s Harriet, but this internal conflict features decidedly in all of the Restoration texts. Produced in an age and primarily for an audience to whom dynastic marriage was a fact of life, these plays are actually quite odd in their insistence on the agency of the man and woman.[14]

Further, both genres, although emphasizing wit, are deeply influenced by the comedy of humors. Corman notes that although "wit versus humor . . . [is] central to the [theoretical] debate about comedy throughout the period," the actual practice (even of theorists who strongly took one side or the other) was to feature both characters of wit—with whom we sympathize and who make us think—and humors characters—static characters who are ridiculed and who serve as negative examples—in any given comic plot.[15] The same can be said of the comedies of remarriage that feature the inevitable cast of zanies, whose false wit, pretense, eccentricity, or buffoonery provide the backdrop for the true wit and style and specialness of the central couple.

The seriousness of intent behind the comic plot is also something shared by these genres. The plays are not simply about manners; they are thought-provoking, particularly on the question of marriage, its nature, its purpose, its problems. Stanley Cavell has argued that the films' focus on marriage is actually a concern with the pursuit of happiness through moral perfectionism. The plays, as well, participate in this conversation. The primary obligation of moral perfectionism, as Cavell explains it, is to make ourselves intelligible to ourselves. Each of us is "on a journey"; each "human self [is] confined by itself [and] aspiring toward itself" (CW, 26). Each of us seeks an "other" to whom we can express ourselves, can voice the intelligibility we discover. This friend, indeed, may be the goal or the instigator or the co-traveler of the self's journey, but whatever the case the friend is essential: "Only perfectionism," says Cavell, "places so absolute a value on this relationship" (CW, 27). And marriage (in its phases of courtship and remarriage) is "an allegory . . . of what philosophers since Aristotle have thought about under the title of friendship, what it is that gives value to personal relations" (CW, 15).

Perfectionism insists that

> the moral life is not constituted solely by consideration of isolated judgments of striking moral and political problems but is a life whose texture is a weave of cares and commitments in which one is bound to become lost and to need the friendly and credible words of others in order to find one's way, in which at any time a choice may present itself . . . in pondering which you will have to decide whose view of you is most valuable to you.
>
> (CW, 16)

Moments such as these are central to film comedies of remarriage, as Cavell has argued and as I shall elaborate. They are moments featured, too, in the stage comedies of manners, none more decidedly than in the Restoration text that forms a focus of this chapter.

Finally, both genres emerged after the introduction of a new element of production—the actress to the Restoration stage, sound to the Hollywood screen. Innovation in each case seemed to demand a re-examination of the standard comic plot of courtship and/or seduction. The presence of actresses for the first time on the English stage encouraged playwrights to broaden engagement with the female experience, especially in comic plots that conventionally portray love and courtship. No competent critic, to be sure, would question Shakespeare's ability to present nuanced female characters with complex motivations and deep desires. As discussed in the previous chapter, *Much Ado*'s Beatrice seems a prototype for the Restoration comic heroine. *As You Like It*'s Rosalind and *Twelfth Night*'s Viola may not match her in terms of witty repartee with the objects of their desires, but with regard to self-direction, they seem equally clear ancestresses to the willful, unconventional Harriets, Hellenas, and Millamants of the seventeenth-century stage. Still, a play such as Etherege's *Man of Mode* with its spectrum of female "types" and personalities suggests an unprecedented fascination with the lives and emotions of women. Although Harriet will be the focus of my concern with "moral perfectionism," the other female characters are essential to such a reading as they illustrate the coercive pressures and socio-psychological limitations that define women's lives in a rigidly patriarchal society. Like their counterparts in the films of remarriage, the heroines of Restoration courtship comedy demand the right to pursue happiness and take upon themselves the responsibility of articulating clearly, to themselves as well as others, the exact form that happiness must take.

I will return to Harriet's pursuit of happiness; first, however, I wish to mention briefly that the introduction of sound technology to film may have had as much, if not more, to do with the emergence of the remarriage comic plot than the changing social status of women and marriage in the 1930s. With a static microphone requiring actors to gather around tables or other surfaces that could hold vases of flowers or other displays in which equipment could be concealed, the comic films of the 1930s featured long sections of dialogue. Men and women who have a history together necessarily have more to say to one another than does a courting couple. And the way they talk is different, too. The kind of dialogue that makes a viewer want to hear more must suggest a history from which we are excluded and to which we long to be privy. The couple's talk must be intriguing as the "payoff" for watching them and listening to them is not to be the gratification of their overcoming obstacles to betrothal but the gratification of witnessing their reinvestment in and the reinvigoration of a relationship that exists already. Although the relationship (the marriage, usually) in such films is on the point of extinction, the movie demonstrates that the couple must stay together (or reunite) precisely because they still have so much to say to each other. For this kind of script to convince, the woman must talk as much as (sometimes more than) the man. As I will discuss below, Nick and Nora Charles are somewhat atypical of the genre as it is not their relationship but Nick's identity as a detective that must be "remarried"; nevertheless, their first private on-screen exchange illustrates beautifully the ongoing conversation that defines the central pair of the remarriage comedy film:

NICK: Sit down, Su*gah* . . . Leo?
LEO: Yes, sir?
NICK: [*Mumbles and gestures.*]
LEO: Right. Two cocktails.

56   *The thin man of mode*

NORA: Pretty girl. [*Referring to Dorothy Wynant to whom Nick had been talking at the bar before Nora arrived.*]
NICK: Yes, she's a very nice type.
NORA: You've got types?
NICK: Only you, darling. Lanky brunettes with wicked jaws.
LEO [*serving the drinks*]: Compliments for this evening.
NORA [*to Nick*]: Who is she?
NICK: Darling, I was hoping I wouldn't have to answer that.
NORA: Come on.
NICK: Well, Dorothy is really my daughter. You see, it was spring in Venice, and I was so young . . . . I didn't know what I was doing. We're all like that on my father's side.
NORA: By the way, how is your father's side?
NICK: Oh, it's much better, and yours?
NORA: Say, how many drinks have you had?
NICK: This will make six martinis.
NORA: All right! Will you bring me five more martinis, Leo, and line them up right here?
LEO: Yes, ma'am.[16]

Typical of the remarriage comedy genre is the interest taken by the man and woman in each other and their desire for a continuing conversation that exists on a plane they alone inhabit. In this exchange, Nora begins in a register that could signify sexual jealousy in another woman, but, as James Harvey has observed in commentary on a scene in the film in which she discovers Nick and Dorothy in an even more compromising stance than the conversation at the bar, Nora "can't or won't react conventionally" to situational evidence.[17] She would disappoint us, the viewers, if she did; for, after all, from the beginning of the film, as Harvey remarks, we have a "clear sense of how impossible it would be for Nick, even temporarily, to prefer a Dorothy to a Nora" (125). Further, in the "martini" exchange above, it is clear that Nora wants to be on a level with Nick as they talk. She has to catch up, in other words, and the expression on his face when she orders the five drinks suggests how much her determination pleases and amuses her husband.

There is a sense of mutual fascination in both the couple of the Hollywood remarriage comedy and the pair in the Restoration courtship comedy. On screen, we see the alert responsiveness of the actor or actress as his or her counterpart speaks—facial expression and body language that attest expectation of surprise, delight, or challenge. In the plays, we have indication of a similar attentiveness—Harriet's "acting" of Dorimant; Dorimant's willingness to adopt the name of "Courtage" and improvise a role at her direction for her entertainment, comments made in asides that reveal to the audience what emotions have been stirred by the other. The genres are very similar in their sense of the central couple's special dedication to lives of deliberate choice—not so much, as Cavell puts it, a choice of "what they ought to do"

Table 2.1 Features of Hollywood remarriage films and Restoration courtship plays

Hollywood remarriage films	Restoration courtship plays
1 The woman is never a mother	1 The woman is always an heiress
2 The woman's father is on the side of her desire	2 The woman's guardian is an impediment to her desire
3 Narrative opens in a city but moves to the "green space" of the country	3 Narrative is set in the city; the country is outmoded, old-fashioned, a trap for the woman
4 Principal man and woman share—even seem to invent—their own language	4 Ditto
5 The genre is preoccupied with "news"	5 The genre is preoccupied with "scandal"
6 The woman demands to be educated	6 Ditto
7 The genre seriously engages with the idea of social contract	7 Ditto
8 The chief moral danger faced by the central pair (and the genre itself) is smugness or elitism	8 Ditto, libertinism notwithstanding

as a choice of "how they shall live their lives, what kind of persons they aspire to be" (*CW*, 11). For all their similarities, though, there are differences; in Table 2.1, I list features of both genres—some contrastive, some comparative—which I will then elaborate through a focus on *The Man of Mode* and *The Thin Man*. Cavell, of course, is the source of the generic descriptors for the remarriage comedies listed in the left column. I posit parallel observations for the courtship comedies in the right column.

Nora Charles is in many ways atypical of the comedy of remarriage women, but in terms of the general template, she can be said to be prototypical as well—at least in the first two films before "little Nickie" makes an appearance. (Asta, although clearly a child-substitute, does not make Nora a mother; animals are often featured in the comedies of remarriage. Indeed, Asta, whose real name was Skippy, made quite a career in the genre, appearing in *The Awful Truth* and *Bringing Up Baby* as well as two of the *Thin Man* films.) In *Pursuits of Happiness*, Cavell explains that the significance of the couple's childlessness is twofold. First, "the absence of children . . . purifies the discussion of marriage," as well as the fact of divorce on which the plots depend (*PH*, 58). "The direct implication," Cavell astutely observes, "is that while marriage may remain the authorization for having children, children are not an authentication of marriage" (*PH*, 58). The second benefit conferred by the absence of children is that the couple themselves can engage in childlike behavior—playfulness and fun. The genre, in a sense, "turn[s] the tables on time, making marriage the arena and the discovery of innocence" (*PH*, 60).

The Thin Man, like all comedies of remarriage, emphasizes the sheer joy the couple takes in being together. Yes, they spend their time amongst thugs, cheats, criminals, and murderers, but they themselves live in a bubble of childlike joy. Nick's constant inebriation has been the subject of staid critical commentary, but to me such piousness is not pertinent (indeed it is a bit impertinent), for from the beginning, drink is clearly a metaphor for freedom from responsibility. The two are on holiday, after all, and even when Nick is persuaded to take on a sleuthing case, he and Nora continue to banter and tease like children, illustrating what Cavell describes as a common trait of the remarriage comedy genre: the couple's invention of a shared childhood.

In fact, patterns of visual and verbal allusion in the film suggest that Nick and Nora go back even further. The Christmas morning scene in which Nick shoots balloons off the tree with the air rifle Nora has given him ends with him curled in a fetal position, his boyish reaction to having broken a window. A scene late in the film, during which the two (alternately sitting in one another's lap) discuss the dinner party at which the murderer will be revealed, includes the following exchange:

NICK: Where were you on October fifth, nineteen hundred and two?
NORA: I was just a gleam in my father's eye!

Here we have a prefetal Nora to complement the earlier fetal Nick. These two have known each other always—even before they were born.

In *The Thin Man*, the childless, childlike couple exists in a world of stylized melodrama peopled with violent criminals, who act with hysterical impulse out of what seem to be almost primal urges, to say nothing of the Wynant family, with whom the plot of the film is primarily concerned. Clyde Wynant is divorced from his wife, Mimi, involved in a tempestuous relationship with his "secretary," Julia Wolf, and estranged from his son Gilbert, who is fascinated with modern psychological aberrations, presumably because he is seeking answers for his own troubled existence (he diagnoses himself as having a "mother fixation"). Clyde Wynant remains close to his daughter Dorothy, who, as the film opens, appears in her father's workshop with a young man, Tommy, to whom she is engaged. "Show her that there is such a thing as a happy marriage," says Clyde Wynant as his daughter and her fiancé depart. It is not Tommy who will do so, of course, but the Charleses.

As necessary as childlessness is to the couple of the remarriage film comedy is the woman's fortune to the stage courtship comedy—for perhaps the opposite reason. Whereas the film couple's childlessness purifies the genre's treatment of marriage by eliminating (or at least sublimating) one of the culture's key assumptions about the institution, the stage comedies' construction of the central couple tacitly admits that wealth adds to the young woman's allure. It is indeed the primary reason the man turns his thoughts to marriage at all as it is the last place he expects to find pleasure. But as *The Man of Mode*'s Dorimant illustrates, a fortune alone is not enough to tempt him. When Nan the orange-woman teases him with news that "there is a young gentlewoman, lately come to town with her mother, that is so taken with you" (1.1.48–50), his thoughts turn first to her appearance—"Is she handsome?" (1.1.51) When in reply the orange-woman emphasizes Harriet's "hugeous fortune" (1.1.53), Dorimant is put off:

> This fine woman, I'll lay my life is some awkward, ill-fashioned country toad, who, not having above four dozen of black hairs on her head, has adorned her baldness with a large white fruz, that she may look sparkishly in the forefront of the King's box at an old play.
>
> (1.1.56–61)[18]

When Medley appears to confirm Nan's report of Harriet's beauty and wealth, Dorimant's next question is "Has she wit?" (1.1.156). Medley answers that question—"more than usual in her sex, and as much malice" (1.1.157–58)—and completes the portrait in a way that entices Dorimant: "she's as wild as you would wish her, and has a demureness in her looks that makes it so surprising" (1.1.158–60). This combination of modesty (that is, decorousness) and wildness (or willfulness) will be consistent in the female half of the witty pair, and it is an apt description of the woman of the remarriage film comedies as well.

Harriet, of course, has been brought to London by her mother to marry Young Bellair. Her own expectations of marriage are fairly low it seems from her comment to Busy that she thinks she "might be brought to endure him, and that is all a reasonable woman should expect in a husband" (3.1.53–5). For all her cynicism, though, Harriet does seem to want more. At least, she objects to being "paid down by a covetous parent for a purchase" and vows, as she "need[s] no land" herself, she will "lay [herself] . . . out all in love" (3.1.74–6). When she and Dorimant meet for the first time in the Mall, the metaphorical register remains focused on material wealth, but wealth "to be won" at play rather than bought at market (3.3.86–7). If the insight of the film comedies is that marriage is about the couple apart from the family they produce, the insight of the stage comedies is that marriage is about the couple apart from the families whose fortunes they join.

Invoking Northrop Frye, Cavell associates remarriage comedies with Old Comedy that "puts particular stress on the heroine, who may hold the key to the plot, who may be disguised as a boy, and who may undergo something like death and restoration," as opposed to New Comedy that "stresses the young man's efforts to overcome obstacles posed by an older man . . . to his winning of the woman of his choice" (*PH*, 1). The comedies of remarriage, in fact, often feature a father who is on the side of his daughter's desire and who enables the fulfillment of that desire by teaching his daughter to recognize her own needs and encouraging her to pursue her own happiness. *The Thin Man* does not fully explore this generic theme, although the melodramatic Wynant story is founded on such a relationship between father and daughter. Perhaps more significantly, Nick and Nora's freedom to enjoy one another's company, the leisure they have to "play," is funded by her father's fortune, which Nick apparently manages at little cost of time or effort. Nora is an heiress; yet she encourages Nick to resume his life as a detective despite the wealth that makes such work unnecessary. Her reasons for doing so are driven by curiosity, a desire to know. She wants to know Nick more thoroughly (she asks Face, one of the criminals whom Nick invites to their Christmas party, if Nick was a good detective. "I wouldn't know," replies Face. "That time he caught me was an accident. I led with my right.") And she wants to know about life itself, not the life of privilege that she has always lived, but the grittier, harsher facts of life. Nick is her access to knowledge of these things.

Harriet, similarly, has an independent fortune of some sort. The details are cryptic, but the following exchange, as the plot winds its way to conclusion, suggests that Harriet's deceased father (or, perhaps, grandfather) has left her with a considerable measure of independence:

HARRIET: Were my fortune in your power—
LADY WOODVILL: Your person is.
HARRIET: Could I be disobedient I might take it out of yours and put it into his.
LADY WOODVILL: 'Tis that you would be at, you would marry this Dorimant.
HARRIET: I cannot deny it! I would, and never will marry any other man.
(5.2.368–75)

In this sense, *The Man of Mode* shares with the film comedies of remarriage a relationship to Old Comedy. Guardians do present obstacles, but in most cases, they are obstacles that the female half of the witty pair overcomes. In the end, Harriet reveals that she will not marry without Lady Woodvill's consent; her sense of duty will not allow it. That resolution in itself is enough to "melt my heart," Lady Woodvill says later (5.2.379–80); she has become reconciled to the union, promising to receive Dorimant at her country estate in the near future: "If his occasions bring him that way, I have now so good an opinion of him, he shall be welcome" (5.2.466–68).

Although, typical of her genre, Harriet despises the country, Dorimant's willingness to "make a journey into the country" for her sake is a clear sign of his sincerity (5.2.161). In Restoration courtship comedies, the country does not represent the Shakespearean green space of romance and possibility; instead it is the domain of the unfashionable and the unsophisticated. When asked by Young Bellair if she is "in love," Harriet replies "Yes, with this dear town, to that degree, I can scarce endure the country in landscapes and in hangings" (3.1.11–12). In fact, she has promised her mother to marry Young Bellair (with whom in the conversation quoted above she plots disobedience) for the sole purpose of "get[ting] her [mother] up to London" (3.1.42). For London, not the country, is the place where one can pursue love and happiness. It is no coincidence that the obstacle to Harriet's romance is her mother, Lady *Wood*vill; nor is it insignificant that the member of the older generation who connives to support young love (particularly that between Emilia and Young Bellair) is Lady *Town*ley. In the Restoration courtship comedy, London is what the "green world" (often Connecticut) is to the Hollywood comedy of remarriage: "a place in which perspective and renewal are to be achieved" (*PH*, 49). It is the place where the older generation yields to the younger—not in defeat but in reconciliation.

Both genres tend to invoke the myth of Eden, and the garden is clearly referenced in the remarriage comedies' emphasis on the rural retreat as a place for the reawakening of sexual desire and the discovery of self through "the acknowledgement of desire" (*PH*, 56). In Restoration comedies such allusions also abound. *The Man of Mode*'s Dorimant, for example, is "a devil . . . [who] has something of the angel yet undefaced in him, which makes him . . . charming and agreeable" (2.2.17–19).[19] For Mrs. Loveit, yielding to the desire awakened by Dorimant does not lead to self-knowledge. For Bellinda arguably it does, but both in the end are expelled from Eden, as it were. Of course, Dorimant tells each woman that he has renounced her but temporarily due to his need to "repair the ruins of my estate, that needs it—" (5.2.327–28). Because the play has not emphasized this financial need until this point, we might assume (as both Mrs. Loveit and Bellinda seem to) that Dorimant is simply mouthing platitudes "tender of my honor, though . . . cruel to my love" in Bellinda's estimation and meant to make "my grief hang lighter on my soul . . . [though] I shall never more be happy," in Mrs. Loveit's words (5.2.324–25; 329–31). Harriet is less diplomatic; indeed it is she who in the end sends her erstwhile rivals into exile:

HARRIET [*to Mrs. Loveit*]: Mr. Dorimant has been your God Almighty long enough, 'tis time to think of another—
MRS. LOVEIT: Jeered by her! I will lock myself up in my house, and never see the world again.
HARRIET: A nunnery is the more fashionable place for such a retreat, and has been the fatal consequence of many a *belle passion*.

(5.2.434–41)

Still, Harriet too must leave London, at least temporarily. Although Dorimant attends her, she still finds the prospect less than appealing: "Methinks I hear the hateful noise of rooks already—kaw, kaw, kaw—there's music in the worst cry in London! 'My dill and cucumbers to pickle'" (5.2.480–83). The marriage may take place in the country, but the final image, as well as the concluding dance, reveals that London will remain the place of the consummation of the marriage and the fulfillment that will define "remarriage."

In *The Thin Man*, California (from which the couple has come to New York in the beginning of the film and to which they return in the end) could be construed as the green space in which the romance between Nick and

Nora has flourished prior to the film's narrative. But the film seems more like a Restoration courtship comedy in its privileging of the city as the place in which desire is (re)awakened and happiness pursued. This reading may seem rather perverse in that the events in which Nick and Nora participate involve three murders as well as adultery, theft, and blackmail. But they, like Harriet and Dorimant, exist in a fallen world redeemed by love. In Nick and Nora's case, that love also involves Nick's rediscovery of his own identity—his acceptance of the unique abilities that he has sublimated, perhaps at some cost to his sense of self, in the state of marriage. As prescribed by the institution or, at least, by custom, he is required as head of household to manage the interests of his deceased father-in-law. Although several scenes in *The Thin Man* feature Nick and Nora in the conjugal space of their hotel bedroom, a space of conversation, adventure, and mutual tenderness, it is not until the final scene of the film that sex itself is implied. Nick and Nora retire to the sleeper car of the train on which they are traveling back to California, Nick having successfully caught the murderer of Clyde Wynant. Nora announces that Asta is to sleep on the top bunk with her tonight. Nick begs to differ: "Oh, yeah?" And the final shot shows Asta alone in the bunk Nora had claimed, covering his eyes with his paws.

In both *The Man of Mode* and *The Thin Man*, the male lead is introduced in scenes that not only emphasize his love of language but also demonstrate the dearth of conversational partners in the world he inhabits. Nick Charles's insouciant banter with bartenders and waiters is fast-paced, witty, and elegantly phrased—but, although they listen, they do so with dazed expressions of incomprehension or confusion as Nick waxes eloquent on the subject, in the following case, mixing drinks, at hand: "You see, the important thing is the rhythm. You should always have rhythm in your shaking. A Manhattan you shake to a foxtrot. A Bronx to a two-step time. A dry martini you always shake to waltzes."

When Dorothy and Tommy join him at the bar, Nick's lighthearted whimsy is replaced by a prosaic matter-of-factness, although somewhat slowly as he is prepared to flirt with Dorothy when she first approaches him. Once Dorothy reveals her concern about her father's whereabouts, the conversation descends into a series of questions and answers, and Nick's joviality is replaced by a kind of weariness. It will be some time before Nick accepts the responsibility of finding Clyde Wynant. At this point, he is sure the absent-minded professor has merely lost track of time. And he himself seems to be becoming bored with the topic when Nora and Asta make their dramatic entrance into the bar, lifting the mood for Nick and the audience alike.

As Kay Young puts it in analysis of this scene, "with the arrival of a worthy partner, a dialogue can begin."[20] Before Nora sprawls into the room, dragged by an overeager Asta, "Nick is ultimately alone . . . in the company of fawning bartenders and sweet ingenues" (265). He is performing, talking dialogue, not fully engaged. "Women and children, first, boys," Nora says as she is lifted from the floor. "Is she asking to be rescued or to be left alone?" Young muses (265). Nick does neither. Instead, he starts a conversation: "What is the score, anyway?" Young has described the typical pattern of a Nick and Nora exchange: She sets up the joke, he "designs his own fun in response," she finds the pun and "turns over the joke to her benefit. They both therefore 'score'" (267). When Nick introduces his wife to Tommy, her remark is a performance for Nick in which she seems less to have recovered her self-composure than to have never lost it in the first place: "Tommy, I don't usually look like this; I've been Christmas shopping!" James Harvey notes Nick's "delighted recognition" of Nora's "aplomb" here and the couple's mutual enjoyment throughout the film of the other's ability to stumble, recover, and triumph: "Their humorous, slightly sardonic appreciation of one another is never sharper . . . than when the other's poise is being tested or severely shaken in some way."[21]

In comedies of remarriage, Cavell has observed, the man

> must show that he is not attempting to command but that he is able to wish, and consequently to make a fool of himself. This enables the woman to awake to her desire again, giving herself rather than the apple, and enables the man to recognize and accept this gift. This changing is the forgoing or forgetting of that past state and its impasse of vengefulness, a forgoing symbolized by the initial loss of virginity.
>
> (PH, 32)

The Man of Mode's Harriet articulates the same principle. When Dorimant hesitates to speak of his love because "the company may take notice how passionately I make advances of love! and how disdainfully you receive 'em," Harriet rebukes him: "When your love's grown strong enough to make you bear being laughed at, I'll give you leave to trouble me with it. Till when pray forbear, sir" (4.1.192–97). Insistence on one's public dignity is incompatible with love, its awakening or its reawakening, as both genres realize. *Marriage à la Mode*'s Rhodophil is a prime example of one who has allowed public ridicule to interrupt the pleasures of conversation that marriage offers.[22] Having married Doralice for love, and having enjoyed her company for

> a whole half year, double the natural term of any Mistress, and think in my conscience I could have held out another quarter; but then the World began to laugh at me, and a certain shame of being out of fashion seized me.

The result? As noted in the previous chapter, and worth repeating as leading to a central insight of both genres, Rhodophil despairingly concludes:

"At last, we arriv'd at that point that there was nothing left in us to make us new to one another" (1.1.147–52). Being always "new to one another" requires an attentiveness to self and other that these genres understand to be both physical and verbal. Nick and Nora's joking exchanges, as Young has observed, are "a joint production . . . a conversation . . . [as well] as a physical creation designed between the team."[23] Their bodies often mirror each other (as in the martini scene which has them "leaning their heads into their hands, then lowering their hands to signal the end of the fantasied reverie" [267]). Similarly, Harriet and Dorimant are attuned to one another's bodies. That Harriet is smitten is evident to the orange-woman who reports to Dorimant: "she told me twenty things you said . . . and acted with head and with her body so like you" (1.1.70–2). Dorimant, likewise, mimics Harriet as he teases her about her desire for admiration:

> I observed how you were pleased when the fops cried "She's handsome, very handsome, by God she is," and whispered aloud your name—the thousand several forms you put your face into; then, to make yourself more agreeable, how wantonly you played with your head, flung back your locks, and looked smilingly over your shoulder at 'em.
> (3.3.107–14)

Harriet's rejoinder is equally critical—but also equally flattering—as she, like Dorimant, reveals her close study: "I do not go begging the men's as you do the ladies' good liking with a sly softness in your looks and a gentle slowness in your bows as you pass by 'em" (3.3.115–18). As they mimic and tease and parody one another, they enter the realm of jokiness that signals the acknowledgment of desire. As in the remarriage film comedy, such a realm inevitably recalls the garden of Eden. A few lines after Harriet "acts" Dorimant, her mother observes, he "has a tongue . . . would tempt the angels to a second fall" (3.3.136–37).

In Eden, such a fall was the consequence of desire for all kinds of knowledge, and a thirst for experience is also at the heart of each genre. The woman, in particular, seeks education. In the texts under consideration in this chapter, Harriet demands knowledge about London and Nora about "detecting." Emphasis on knowledge, information, experience is also signaled in each genre by a focus on "news"—gossip and scandal in the courtship comedies, newspapers in the remarriage comedies. The couple in each genre, however, cannot be satisfied by newspaper accounts (in *The Thin Man*, as in other remarriage texts, these are notoriously, even comically, inaccurate) or by cabals. The male half of the witty pair especially finds gossip tedious at best and threatening at worst (as we will see in *The Way of the World*). That Dorimant is a part of the fashionable crowd is without question, and that this crowd shares a penchant for language and wit is also clear. Lisa Berglund, in fact, has noted that all of the characters who "matter" in *The Man of Mode* are the ones who can function at a highly sophisticated linguistic level. She points to their fondness, in particular, for extended metaphor.[24] Still, I think it significant that Medley—the true impresario of the town set—recognizes in Dorimant the need for someone with "a genius . . . worthy of yourself" (1.1.264–65). Medley believes Bellinda to be such a partner, but Dorimant's silence at Medley's proclamation suggests otherwise. Like Young Bellair for Harriet, Bellinda is a match, but no match for Dorimant. Her inventiveness in arranging an assignation and manipulating Mrs. Loveit is entertaining to Dorimant, and it is important, I think, that after their tryst, they speak to one another in rhyme. As Dorimant begins to vow, "by all the joys I have had, and those you keep in store—," Bellinda interrupts him, "you'll do for me what you never did before" (4.2.23–26). But Harriet goes further to demonstrate that it is she, not Bellinda, who speaks Dorimant's native tongue. She does not rely on an extempore exercise in poetic dialogue. She reveals instead that her mind is furnished with the poems Dorimant incessantly quotes:

DORIMANT: "Music so softens and disarms the mind—"
HARRIET: "That not one arrow does resistance find."

(5.2.101–102)

Dorimant's private habit of quoting snatches of poetry that no one in the play prior to this scene even acknowledges has here elicited the perfect response from the one person in the play with whom he can have a true conversation.

Of course, Harriet and Dorimant's final exchange, the last conversation we witness between them, seems to indicate that each has retreated into a private world to which the other has no access and is not welcome. Such seems especially true of Harriet, who has ceased to speak in her native language and has begun to squawk like a bird. *The Thin Man*'s Nick and Nora, on the other hand, seem to grow increasingly close during the course of their adventure, and this closeness is signaled by a language that is theirs alone. In an exchange that precedes and precipitates the script's climactic dinner discovery of the murderer, the couple shares an odd mispronunciation of the word "suspect." Used as a noun, the word is pronounced, first by Nick ("I'm going to give a party and invite all the sus-PECTs") and then by Nora ("the sus-PECTS? Why, they won't come"), with the emphasis on the second syllable. Opposite Harriet and Dorimant, as their story draws to a (temporary) close, this couple seems to have one voice—although one that seems oddly confused about its native language.

Still, another crucial scene suggests that, like Harriet and Dorimant, Nick and Nora have moments of inscrutability, even to one another. Harvey's description of the air rifle scene is worth quoting in full:

> Someone has given Nick Charles an air rifle. He is lying in pajamas and robe on a couch in his hotel suite and shooting at the balls on the Christmas tree. Nora sits nearby in a fur coat—another Christmas present—and watches him dispassionately. This short, wordless scene is one of the high points of *The Thin Man* and one of the great moments of thirties movie comedy. In some ways it's a conventional scene. Its basic components are both banal and "cute": the grown-up hero behaves like a mischievous boy in front of his "mom" of a wife, who is disapproving but indulgent. What saves the scene from such archness? It *reminds* us of those banalities, but it doesn't convey them. For one thing, William Powell is so far from being or suggesting a boy that he can act like one and make such behavior seem like an essay in stylish (and rather cold) craziness rather than a move toward ingratiation. We can believe that this Nick Charles—who in general "plays" quite convincingly—might want to shoot the decorations off a Christmas tree. But we can never believe that he might think of such behavior as appealing or try to charm us with it, as another sort of actor might do in such a scene. Powell is at such an enormous distance from the thing he's mimicking here that he achieves a pure and controlled preposterousness . . . .
>
> And the close-ups of Loy looking at him are stunning ones: her beauty in this sequence seems almost hallucinatory. Yet her face is in some final way unreadable. The countenance she turns on her cut-up husband here is a deadpan one. It expresses nothing so clear as disapproval or sarcasm or even ruefulness. It suggests, rather, some kind of ultimate female resignation—so deep as to cast only the slightest shadow across her face.[25]
>
> (123)

Important to both genres is the sense that each of the couple has a separate, fully realized inner life and identity. And in each text of each genre there will be a moment funded by that inner life and identity—witnessed but not shared by the other.

Perhaps the reason for the insistence on individual integrity has to do with the genres' preoccupation with social contract. Both *The Thin Man* and *The Man of Mode* have prompted critical commentary that invokes Thomas Hobbes. Steven Marcus observes that all of Dashiell Hammett's novels, including the one on which Van Dyke's film is based, are set in a Hobbesian universe in which people experience life as a state of war, full of danger, uncertainty, and fear.[26] Young has described Nick and Nora as "bemused together in . . . a world of corruption";[27] the state itself, represented by Sergeant Guild, is ineffectual in curbing that corruption without the help of private detectives or stool pigeons like Nunheim. Contractual talk between the low plot characters demonstrates the instability of the social order. Promises are made and broken with dizzying (and dangerous) speed. Julia Wolf, Wynant's girlfriend, exploits his trust to steal from him. Mimi, Wynant's ex-wife, thinking she has discovered evidence that Wynant has murdered Wolf, hides that evidence clearly intending blackmail.

Jorgenson, Mimi's new husband, has another wife he has neglected to mention. Nunheim, the stool pigeon, cheats on his girlfriend. He also blackmails the real murderer of Julia Wolf, demanding more and more money until he himself is finally shot. Most interestingly, given the cast of petty criminals, molls, and thugs in this film, it is Macauley, Wynant's lawyer, who in the end is revealed to have murdered Wynant, Wolf, and Nunheim. In fact, Macauley's deadpan duplicity is a sadder commentary on the state of the world than the desperate criminality of the gangsters, as Nick's special rapport with them would suggest. Tanner, Face, and others whom Nick has pursued and "sent up" in the past greet him in the present as a trusted friend, for the contract under which detective and criminal operate is not only understood by both, but is beneficial to both. Tanner, for example, learns a trade while incarcerated in Sing Sing. Nick's trustworthiness in this contractual relationship is nowhere better demonstrated than in his refusal to press charges against Morelli for shooting him. When Guild presses him to do so, Nick dismisses the idea: "Maybe it was an accident."

The world depicted in *The Man of Mode* is less criminally inclined, but is in many ways more morally corrupt than that of *The Thin Man*. The subplot involving Bellinda—with its calculated duplicities and casual cruelties—is tawdrier than any aspect of *The Thin Man*, a fact underscored visually in the stage directions for the beginning of Act 4, scene 2. Set in Dorimant's lodgings, the scene begins with Handy alone on stage, taking care of the dirty sheets. J. L. Styan says of the directives: "The playwright indicates the cynicism of the moment by offering a glimpse of Handy '*tying up linen*,' a dry perspective on the commonplace event this cold affair has been."[28] This coldness, however, is less a character flaw in Dorimant than a survival tactic in the world he defines and dominates. As David Roberts has noted, "Dorimant is as much philosopher as philanderer, given to summarising the textbook of Restoration libertinism, Thomas Hobbes's *Leviathan* of 1650."[29] Dorimant explains his friendship with Young Bellair, for example, as based on the mutual benefits it confers on each of them: "It makes the women think the better of his understanding, and judge more favorably of my reputation; it makes him pass upon some for a man of very good sense, and I upon others for a very civil person" (1.1.467–71).

Dorimant's relationships with Bellinda and Mrs. Loveit are no less driven by the desire for mutual benefit, although each woman eventually realizes that her interest has been ill served by the contract she has entered. Pert charges Dorimant with breaking an "oath and covenant" (2.2.9–10) to which Mrs. Loveit bound him:

> I'll lay my life there's not an article but he has broken, talked to the vizards i'the pit, waited upon the ladies from the boxes to their coaches, gone behind the scenes and fawned upon those little insignificant creatures, the players; 'tis impossible for a man of his inconstant temper to forbear I'm sure.
>
> (2.2.11–16)

Although Mrs. Loveit defends Dorimant in response to Pert's accusations, she changes her tune soon enough, eventually wishing she "had made a contract to be a witch when first I entertained this greater devil!" (2.2.299–300). Bellinda, likewise, tries to bind Dorimant by a promise, although she has even more proof than Loveit of his "ill nature" and more reason to "think that . . . [he] may be . . . faithless, and unkind" (2.2.309; 311–12). She makes him vow that he will "never see Loveit more but in public places" (4.2.32–33), and within the hour she finds herself "betrayed indeed": "h'has broke his word, and I love a man that does not care for me" (5.1.79–81).

Dorimant articulates several times his credo that words spoken in love are not binding. Harriet, too, resists romantic vows, refusing to make promises to or to accept promises from Dorimant. The protection of pleasure seems as much a motive for her as skepticism: "I hate to promise! what we do then is expected from us, and wants much of the welcome it finds, when it surprises" (5.2.174–77). Yet it is Harriet who initiates the one binding contract in the play: her contract with Young Bellair to "never marry" each another (3.1.89). And it is Harriet who will, if anyone can, teach Dorimant that words spoken to her are binding and therefore must be chosen carefully. As the play draws to its conclusion, she continues to discourage vows, but she also continues to listen and respond to the only man she will even consider marrying. Yet, although their love is important to the city (the polis, as Cavell has discussed), their courtship must continue in a "green world." Harriet is well aware that "all beyond High Park's a desert" to Dorimant (5.2.164–65), and, although she too loves the town, she is also aware of the coercive pressures of fashionable life that impose clichés and prevent the true conversation of beings who understand themselves and who are intelligible to one another. So she demands that Dorimant not "turn fanatic" in love by promising to "renounce all the joys I have in friendship and in wine, [and] sacrifice to you all the interest I have in other women," but to merely "neglect these a while and make a journey into the country" (5.2.156–61). Dorimant, still under the influence of town values and habits, again goes to the extreme: "To be with you, I could live there and never send one thought to London" (5.2.162–63). Harriet reserves judgment but is willing to continue the conversation: "When I hear you talk thus in Hampshire, I shall begin to think there may be some little truth enlarged upon" (5.2.171–74).

Emphasis on social contract in the genres does not suggest that to the plays and films marriages (or other relations) are cold arrangements designed to stave off the dangers of a rapacious Hobbesian world. Although each genre recognizes that such a world could come to be, each also holds out the central couple as a redemptive model for a better kind of conversation in a world designed not just for human safety, but for human happiness—a Lockean rather than a Hobbesian world, as Cavell argues. Both Locke's notion of social contract and Milton's definition of marriage are born, Cavell maintains, of the revolutionary insight . . . that fundamental public institutions held to be sacred, beyond human judgment (the divine right of kings to rule; the sacrament of marriage), are human interpretations of constructions which, whether devised by God or by man, are meant for human benefit . . . and when that benefit is lost, a given dispensation of such institutions (of marriage, of an entire government) may be rejected and dissolved.

(CW, 51–52)

It is no coincidence that Locke's insistence that the people consent to the government that rules them is born of the world that saw the witty pair dominate the stage. Although these couples insist on mutual consent, it is particularly important that the woman demands that her voice be heard. She knows (and we know) that custom and law will define her as "the governed" in the state of marriage. It is a state in which she expects (and works to assure) a provision of happiness.

The seemingly unique purchase the central couple has on this happiness can lend them an air of smugness, as each genre illustrates. Harriet's jeering attitude toward Mrs. Loveit teeters precariously on the verge of meanness and a skilled actress such as Elizabeth Barry, who early played the role of Dorimant's cast mistress, could win the audience's sympathy as Harriet enjoys her triumph. Dorimant, too, seems overly confident that he can keep all options open as he assures both Bellinda and Loveit that his neglect will be temporary. To her credit, Bellinda turns away in disdain. Loveit as usual leaves in a passion that both indicts and rewards Dorimant's behavior. Only the winsomeness of the final exchange between the witty pair undercuts the self-satisfaction each demonstrates in exchanges with others as the play draws to a close. We recognize, especially in Harriet's imitation of the raucous crow cry, that this couple is taking a risk. Leaving the fashionable world with its predictable forms and codes and its engaging pleasures and distractions, they will have to invent for themselves ways of talking and being together that constitute the kind of marriage sought by many, but attained by very few.

Nick and Nora are presented as one couple of that few who enjoy such a marriage. Dashiell Hammett himself found the couple "insufferably smug."[30] The film couple is so engaging, however, that we as viewers are unlikely to note the smugness, but it is there. In the party scene, for example, both Nick and Nora circulate amongst their guests with sardonic amusement, stopping occasionally to exchange a few jokes with each other, answering the conversations of others with comments that seem more like personal meditations or punchlines than true responses. "Hey Nick! I think your wife's great," says one drunken guest. "Thanks," says Nick. "I wanted you to see her, [*turning and muttering*] and I wanted her to see you!" A reporter, who has crashed the party, seeking information about the murder of Julia Wolf, asks Nora: "Listen, isn't he working on a case?" Nora responds: "Sure.

He's working on a case of Scotch. Pitch in and help." From time to time, Asta appears at an interior door; he surveys the increasing chaos, and turns away, not exactly disapproving, but above it all nonetheless. At the end of the scene, as the revelers drunkenly sing "O Christmas Tree," Nora "takes it all in at a quick glance and walks over to Nick."[31] The camera moves in for a "big closeup of the two" as Nick looks at Nora, "amused." The scene ends with Nora's remark: "I love you Nickie 'cause you know such lovely people." Nora's tone and facial expression register an emotion composed in equal measure of awe and delight; we feel there is a distinct possibility that she really does find the crowd lovely in its own way. As Harvey notes, "We believe her: she values . . . [Nick]—and so do we—partly because he is surrounded in this way, by an alien world."[32]

That "alien world" in which Nick and Nora shine, however, is also a world that presents the dangers that stand poised to infect and destroy their happy marriage—or any happy marriage. Infidelity abounds in the low plot; Nick and Nora seem immune, but there are always temptations, as the film acknowledges. And there are other more serious dangers. Nick's identity as the film begins has been redefined by marriage. He was a detective; now he manages his wife's money. We are not inclined to see him as a version of Chris Jorgenson, but the comparison could be made. Marriage and domestication, the film suggests, can be risky for both men and women as the sense of individuality and independent "being in the world" are blunted by pressures of daily living—financial pressures, in particular, whether those pressures come from too little money (as in the case of Mimi and Chris) or too much (as in the case of Wynant and Julia Wolf). Unlike the low-plot characters, who are often difficult to distinguish, Nick and Nora both have very distinct personalities. Nora especially seems skilled at pulling back and reminding Nick of her separate identity when necessary. When her husband sends her off to Grant's tomb as he and Guild pursue Nunheim, Nora does a little of her own "detective work," discovering that Jorgenson has disappeared. The fact is a red herring in the plot, but the scene is important as it reveals, once more, the nature of Nick and Nora's relationship. In particular, we see that as Nick regains his footing as a detective, his delight in conversation with Nora seems to grow:

NICK: How'd you like Grant's tomb?
NORA [*on the other end of the telephone, wrinkling her nose*]: It's lovely. I'm having a copy made for you.

Nick, on his end, throws back his head and laughs, then asks: "What have you got, baby?" And they are once again a team.

Still, each text acknowledges that conformity is a real danger in the worlds depicted, and each does so in the same way in titles whose eponymous paradox deliberately points toward the fundamental likeness of the male lead and his dramatic foil. George Etherege's 1676 play, *The Man of*

Mode; or Sir Fopling Flutter, is centered on Dorimant, who is indeed a man of fashion, but not a man ruled by fashion. Or is he? John Dryden's epilogue teases out the implication of the title:

> Yet none Sir Fopling him, or him, can call;
> He's knight o'th'shire and represents ye all.
> From each he meets, he culls whate'er he can
> Legion's his name, a people in a man.
> His bulky form gathers as it goes,
> And, rolling o'er you, like a snowball grows.
> (ll. 15–20)

The epilogue turns Sir Fopling himself into the mirror, whose absence he bemoans in Act 4. As mirror, Sir Fopling reflects not only the gentlemen in the audience, but he also captures something of the other male characters in the play. In 1722, John Dennis remembered "very well" the first reception of this play: "it was generally believed to be an agreeable Representation of the Persons of Condition of both Sexes, both in Court and in Town; and . . . all the world was charm'd with Dorimant."[33]

Dorimant shares with Fopling an investment in language that both conveys his private psychology and reflects the values of his culture. He is given to quoting snatches of poetry, musing aloud to himself, and drawing others into conversations and situations that he (for the most part) controls.[34] Some of that control is due, of course, to Dorimant's social standing. Many of those to whom he speaks in the first act are his social inferiors, his servants, and vendors whom he patronizes. But much of Dorimant's power resides in his facility with language, his thorough command of the idiom of his time. In fact, although Fopling does not represent a sexual threat to Dorimant, he is positioned to upstage him in terms of style and éclat—a situation that often occurs in production and one that the text itself emphasizes in two ways. We "meet" Fopling, as we do Harriet, first through report. As Dorimant completes his morning ritual, he declines Handy's offer of "essence of orange" and says disdainfully: "I will smell as I do today, no offense to the ladies' noses" (1.1.362–63). He continues in this posture for one additional comment to his friends, Medley and Young Bellair: "That a man's excellency should lie in neatly tying of a ribbon, or a cravat! how careful's nature in furnishing the world with necessary coxcombs!" (1.1.385–89) But he quickly drops this pose of indifference when Young Bellair compliments his appearance. He preens, "You will make me have an opinion of my genius" (1.1.394–95). When Medley mentions that "a great critic . . . in these matters [has] lately arrived piping hot from Paris" (1.1.396–97), Dorimant's preening turns to pique: "He is . . . the pattern of modern foppery" (1.1.402–403), and he quickly decides to embroil Fopling in his own scheme to jilt Loveit. He will charge Loveit with infidelity and point to Fopling as his rival.

Although his friends follow his lead in approving the scheme, Dorimant's later jealousy, as well the town's approbation of Fopling, indicates that the rivalry is authentic. Late in the play, Dorimant engages in a conversation with the fop in which he mimics and mirrors his gestures as he and Harriet have done earlier. For all his ludicrousness, Fopling does represent a rival attraction, a choice that Dorimant could make as opposed to the decision he does make—or the person he could be as opposed to the person he is. Robert B. Heilman sees Sir Fopling as a foil who highlights Dorimant's failings: "[Fopling's] innocuous vanity contrasts with the self-aggrandizing sexual machinations of Dorimant. He is neither calculating nor aggressive, as Dorimant is. On the stage he can be played very sympathetically and can steal the show."[35] Indeed, one of the more recent and celebrated stage Foplings, Rory Kinnear, commented in a 2007 interview with Vanessa Thorpe that "when the play first came out in 1676 its title was changed for a while to Sir Fopling Flutter, because the character had gone down so well."[36] Although Kinnear is mistaken about the first performances in which Thomas Betterton's Dorimant held sway, his comment is an accurate description of slightly later productions in which actors such as Henry Woodward or Colley Cibber did indeed "go down well." Susan Staves quotes Thomas Davies's description of Henry Woodward, "one of the handful of actors who specialized in fop roles":

> His person was so regularly formed, and his look so serious and composed, that an indifferent observer would have supposed that his talents were adapted to characters of the serious cast; to the real fine gentleman, to the man of graceful deportment and elegant demeanor, rather than to the affector of gaiety, the brisk fop, and pert coxcomb.[37]

But, it was his verbal delivery, rather than his appearance, that marked him a fop: "The moment he spoke, a certain ludicrous air laid hold of his features, and every muscle of his face ranged itself on the side of levity. The very tones of his voice inspired comic ideas."[38]

Staves also makes the point that the fops "are intended to represent normative behavior . . . [as] is . . . indicated by the recurrent rumors that particular stage fops represented particular men."[39] Emma Katherine Atwood argues against this interpretation of the fop's normativity (a stance taken by Staves, Heilman, and Richard Brown in the 1980s), instead reading the character as one who "queers time" rather than gender and whose relationship with the temporal "can be read as a social choice to move into the margins of normative society."[40] Atwood's sharp distinction between "fop time" (atemporal, presentist, late) and "rake time" (hyperaware, precise, punctual) is demonstrated in the contrast between Sir Fopling (who, at one point [4.1.488–92] cannot distinguish night from day) and Dorimant, whose attention to time is crucial to his sexual success. Clearly, in my reading of the *Man of Mode*, Dorimant is the central concern and Fopling poses no threat to him with regard to his pursuit of Harriet. But the fop does demonstrate an imperviousness to opinion and ridicule that suggests a self-understanding Dorimant himself has yet to attain. Dorimant, however, may soon be the object of town derision. Following Harriet to Hampshire (and we recall that Fopling ludicrously calls his servant John Trot by that name), Dorimant will resign some of his control over the fashionable world, but more importantly, he will reject, in pursuit of happiness, some of the control the fashionable world has over him.

About midway through *The Thin Man*, Nick Charles is informed that the reported suicide of murder suspect Clyde Wynant was "phoney." Nick mutters, "Yeah, I thought so. From now on they're going to think every thin man with white hair is Wynant." When Wynant is finally found, his corpse is at first mistaken for that of a fat man because of oversized clothes that lie beside a body burnt beyond recognition. Although Wynant is *The Thin Man*'s thin man, the following appropriation of the phrase in the title of the film sequels (five in all) effectively transfers the description to Nick himself, and indeed suggests that in the collective mind of movie audiences Nick, or at least William Powell, was always "the thin man." Wynant does not share qualities with Nick in the same manner that Fopling resembles Dorimant, but he and the melodramatic world in which he lives do stand for, as Cavell has argued, "the rejection, or negation, of marriage" and the remarriage genre (*CW*, 109). In this world, "frozen in meaning, resistant to change or exchange," the traumas of the past "are compulsively active in the present" (*CW*, 109). There is no room for spontaneity or playfulness. And although the drive toward conformity seems less dangerous to Nick than to Dorimant, the former copes with a similar strategy as he moves through the world of thugs and cops and floozies. Like Dorimant, Nick asserts his separateness in private language—jokes, snatches of song ("for tomorrow may bring sorrow, so tonight let us be gay"), quips, barbs, and asides that are apparently Nick's way of remaining apart from the crowd while he is in its midst. That Dorimant and he have the same strategy of avoiding the "mode" on the one hand and melodrama on the other is significant. They may seem to be talking to no one in particular when they burst into verse or song, but they know what they mean and they mean what they say—a fact that distinguishes them from the crowd and announces their readiness for conversation when the right partner comes into the room.

Notes

Thanks to Kevin Gladney for the title of this chapter, which I use by permission granted long ago. I hope he remembers.

1 They pick up the term from John Palmer's 1913 study entitled *The Comedy of Manners* (London: G. Bell and Sons), although they depart from his (now thoroughly discredited) central thesis that the comedies of the Restoration reflected and celebrated the manners of the times.
2 Stone, "Comedy of Manners," *British Dramatists from Dryden to Sheridan*, ed. George H. Nettleton and Arthur E. Case, rev. ed. by George Winchester Stone Jr. (Carbondale: Southern Illinois University Press, 1975), 149.

3 Nettleton, Case, and Stone, *British Dramatists*, 151. Cf. P. F. Vernon's discussion of both the Platonic and the Protestant traditions as contributing factors to the ideal of romantic love in "Marriage of Convenience and the Mode of Restoration Comedy," *Essays in Criticism* 12 (1962): 370–87.
4 Both Richard Bevis and Robert D. Hume have reflected on the ways anthologies and pedagogical demands shape literary history, with pertinent comments on the dominant canon of Restoration comedy. See Bevis, "Canon, Pedagogy, Prospectus: Redesigning 'Restoration and Eighteenth-Century English Drama,'" *Comparative Drama* 31, no. 1 (1997): 178–91; and Hume, "Construction and Legitimation in Literary History," *The Review of English Studies*, New Series 56 (2005): 632–61.
5 Cordner, ed. *Four Restoration Marriage Plays* (Oxford: Oxford World's Classics, 1995), lix.
6 Corman, "Comedy," in *The Cambridge Companion to Restoration Theatre*, ed. Deborah Payne Fisk (Cambridge: Cambridge University Press, 2000), 59.
7 Roach, *It*, 13.
8 Oliver Tilley, "American Movies' 'Closest Equivalent to Restoration Comedy'" *Kinema: A Journal for Film and Audiovisual Media* (Fall 2009): http://www.kinema.uwaterloo.ca/article.php?id=460&feature. For a more considered discussion of genre that factors in (although modifies) Cavellian principles, see Timothy Gould's essay, "Comedy," in the *Oxford Handbook of Philosophy and Literature*, ed. Richard Thomas Eldridge (Oxford: Oxford Handbooks Online, 2009), 95–116.
9 Peter Holland, "Restoration Drama in the Twentieth Century," in *The Continuum Companion to Twentieth-Century Theatre*, ed. Colin Chambers (London: Continuum, 2002), 644. J. L. Styan, too, notes the eye-opening revelation of Edith Evans's Millamant in *Restoration Comedy*, 95.
10 Styan, *Restoration Comedy*, 248.
11 Edward D. Berkowitz, *Mass Appeal: The Formative Age of Movies, Radio, and TV* (Cambridge: Cambridge University Press, 2010), 61.
12 Berkowitz, *Mass Appeal*, 61, citing Sklar's *Movie-Made America: A Cultural History of America Movies*, rev. ed. (New York: Vintage Books, 1994), 187–88.
13 Sklar, *Movie-Made America*, 187.
14 Canfield even mentions the "fantasy of no-fault divorce" in his introduction to *The Broadview Anthology of Restoration and Early Eighteenth-Century Drama*, ed. J. Douglas Canfield (Peterborough, Ontario: Broadview Press, 2001), xvi.
15 Corman, "Comedy," 52–53.
16 *The Thin Man*, directed by W. S. Van Dyke (1934; Burbank, CA: Warner Home Video, 2005), DVD.
17 James Harvey, *Romantic Comedy in Hollywood: From Lubitsch to Sturges* (New York: Alfred Knopf, 1987), 124.
18 George Etherege, *The Man of Mode; or Sir Fopling Flutter* (1676), in *the Plays of Sir George Etherege*, ed. Michael Cordner (Cambridge: Cambridge University Press, 1982). References are to act, scene, and line numbers.
19 For a discussion of this imagery as it participates in a tradition of representation in the late seventeenth century, see Nancy Rosenfeld, *The Human Satan in Seventeenth-Century English Literature: From Milton to Rochester* (Aldershot, UK, and Burlington, VT: Ashgate, 2008), 147–68.
20 Young, "Hollywood 1934: Inventing Romantic Comedy," in *Look Who's Laughing: Gender and Comedy*, ed. Gail Finney, Studies in Humor and Gender 1 (Langhorne, PA: Gordon and Breach Science Publishers, 1994), 265.
21 Harvey, *Romantic Comedy in Hollywood*, 124.
22 John Dryden, *Marriage à la Mode*, in *The Works of John Dryden*, ed. Alan Roper

and H. T. Swedenberg, vol. 11, ed. John Loftis, David Stuart Rhodes, and Vinton A. Dearing (Berkeley and Los Angeles: University of California Press, 1978). References are to act, scene, and line numbers.
23 Young, "Hollywood 1934," 267.
24 Berglund, "The Language of the Libertines: Subversive Morality in *The Man of Mode*," *Studies in English Literature, 1500–1900* 30, no. 3 (1990): 371.
25 *Romantic Comedy in Hollywood*, 123.
26 Marcus, introduction to *The Continental Op*, by Dashiell Hammett (New York: Vintage, 1974): xxiii; xxvi. I'm quoting, however, from the *American Masters* episode on Hammett on which Marcus contributed comments, including his oft-quoted linking of Hammett to Hobbes. *Dashiell Hammett: Detective, Writer*, directed by Joshua Waletzky (New York: Winstar TV and Video, 1999), DVD.
27 Young, "Hollywood 1934," 264.
28 Styan, *Restoration Comedy*, 162.
29 Roberts, *Thomas Betterton: The Greatest Actor of the Restoration Stage* (Cambridge: Cambridge University Press, 2010), 56.
30 Qtd. by Dennis Dooley, *Dashiell Hammett* (New York: Frederick Ungar, 1984), 118.
31 Albert Hackett and Frances Goodrich, *The Thin Man* (1934). Screenplays for You https://sfy.ru/?script=thin_man_1934. Description of the action in this scene is taken from the script as reproduced on this website. It accurately describes the scene as filmed.
32 Harvey, *Romantic Comedy in Hollywood*, 130.
33 Qtd. in *The London Stage*, pt. 1 (1660–1700), March, 11 1676, from "A Defense of *Sir Fopling Fluttter*" in *The Critical Works of John Dennis*, ed. Edward Niles Hooker, vol. 2, *1711–1729* (Baltimore: Johns Hopkins University Press, 1943), 2: 248.
34 Roberts makes the interesting observation that indoors, Dorimant is in control but "out in the open spaces of the Mall, he falls victim to counterplots which dent his heroic self-assurance" (*Thomas Betterton*, 56).
35 Heilman, "Some Fops and Versions of Foppery," *ELH* 49, no. 2 (1982): 383.
36 Vanessa Thorpe, "My Unforgettable Father, Roy," *The Observer*, February 11, 2007. http://www.guardian.co.uk/artanddesign/2007/feb/11/art.vanessathorpe
37 Thomas Davies, *Memoirs of the Life of Garrick*, vol. 1 (London, 1780), 265, qtd. in Susan Staves, "A Few Kind Words for the Fop," *Studies in English Literature* 22 (1982): 416.
38 Qtd. in Staves, "A Few Kind Words," 416.
39 Staves, "A Few Kind Words," 418.
40 Atwood, "Fashionably Late: Queer Temporality and the Restoration Fop," *Comparative Drama* 47, no. 1 (2013): 85; 100. See also Richard Brown, "The Fops in Cibber's Comedies," *Essays in Literature* 9 (1982): 31–41.

3 Whippoorwills, gypsies, and fantasies of the night
Aphra Behn's *The Rover* and Frank Capra's *It Happened One Night*

In my exploration of the analogy between remarriage film comedy and Restoration courtship comedy, I pair texts in order to explore various facets of the central relationship. As Cavell has noted of his own pairings of philosophical texts and films, other combinations would be possible, and "each . . . would yield its own accents" (*CW*, 15). The reasons for my choices may strike some as arbitrary, but (again like Cavell) I have tested them in the classroom over the period of a decade in five slightly different courses (different due to the deletion from course to course of texts and contexts that I deemed ultimately unhelpful or even distracting). Although the combination of *It Happened One Night* and *The Rover* is one that I thought initially would not sustain itself, it proved early on evocative to students in an almost Jungian fashion. Walls and water, in particular, function in both texts as central symbols of the key relationship. Kings hover in and around the action of the texts, as does the threat (and sometimes more) of violence against women. Both narratives begin with female rebellion against paternal (and fraternal in the case of *The Rover*) control; both explore the possibility of women charting their own courses in love, and both figure such charting as an actual journey.

Not coincidentally, given the central theme of each work, both *The Rover* and *It Happened One Night* are set in worlds that are distorted, that invert the norms one expects of the times in which they occur, especially for the women of those times. The setting of *The Rover* is carnival time, so Hellena's assertiveness is allowable; although her high spirits provoke comment (her sister Florinda cautions "prithee, be not so wild" and her brother refers to her as a "Wild Cat" [1.1.36; 136]), they do not occasion condemnation.[1] On her "journey," Hellena can wander the streets of Naples disguised as a gypsy or a boy; she can be flirtatious and extravagant in her speech and behavior because carnival gives her license she would not otherwise take. She will never be a nun (as her brother intends her to be) but she will be good (indeed "too good for this world," as Willmore notes at the beginning of *The Second Part of the Rover* after she has died and left him to return to the rakish ways he temporarily forsook for his marriage). In *The Rover*, Hellena is actually quite madcap, almost closer to *Bringing Up*

Baby's Susan Vance than to the spoiled, rich, overprotected Ellen Andrews (Claudette Colbert's character in *It Happened One Night*) to whom I am comparing her. But there is an important affinity between Hellena and Ellen. Ellen has also led a rather nun-like existence. And in the topsy-turvy world she enters, the world of "Night Bus" (the name of the short story on which the film is based), Ellen too finds herself experiencing and enjoying a rare freedom. She tells Peter Warne that she's usually surrounded by bodyguards, servants, keepers of various kinds and always has been. "Would you believe it?" she exclaims as they eat breakfast the morning after the first of three sleepovers in an autocamp, "This is the first time I've ever been alone with a man. It's a wonder I'm not panic-stricken!" "You're doing alright," he replies sardonically.[2]

A witty, capable, and heretofore (over)protected woman on her own for the first time in a nocturnal world of strange intrigues and intriguing strangers is part of the complex charm of both *The Rover* and *It Happened One Night*. Hellena and Ellen seem somehow above and beyond the danger of the dangerous territory each explores. Perils clearly abound for others in these texts, and the literal and figurative darkness of each setting makes this fact clear in both works. Florinda is nearly raped twice; Angellica falls victim to emotions that are unreciprocated and that prompt violent outbursts of anger.[3] Political instability is hinted at in *The Rover*'s temporal setting and in the fact that Willmore and his English pals are roving cavaliers, their sovereign still "Lord of the wat'ry Element," not yet restored to his "rightful" throne (1.2.62). In *It Happened One Night*, much of the violence is economic. Scenes of dispossessed travelers form the backdrop to the love story. A woman on the bus faints, and her distraught son explains that they "haven't ate nothing since yesterday." When Peter asks, "what happened to your money?" the boy wails: "Ma spent it all on the tickets. We didn't know it was going to be so much." Times are difficult, and Capra's film acknowledges that fact, just as Behn's play pays homage to the recent troubles many in her audience would remember all too well. "Hellena" and "Ellen" are variants of the name that derives from the Greek word for "light" or "torch." In their respective nights, each of them does in a profound sense light the way, illuminate a path out of the darkness of their era or their day, as it were.

What has caused the darkness to fall in each narrative is a crisis of state: in *The Rover*, Civil War, regicide, and political/religious revolution; in *It Happened One Night*, as I've said already, the Great Depression and the resulting dislocations and privations visited upon the average American worker. If the contrast between these two situations seems stark—one being overtly political and the other, overtly economic—the contrast between the ideologies of the two authors in response to their darkened worlds might be said to be even more pronounced, that of night and day, perhaps. Behn the bawdy royalist would seem to have little in common with Capra the sentimental populist, but as it happens and as these texts reveal, the two shared values that define the ideal vision that leads Hellena and Ellen to the light. First, and perhaps most surprisingly, each text endorses an antimaterialistic ethic, refusing to allow monetary value to define worth. Each text posits, in opposition to materialism of this sort, a salvific return to their own, idealized (if not blatantly fictional) notions of traditional society. Both play and film proffer blithely patriarchal utopian visions despite the implicit challenges to patriarchal ideology encoded, and even acknowledged, in each text. Both include, and then try to erase, markers of ethnicity and race that problematize their visions. And, finally, both rely on the strength, articulateness, and clear-sightedness of their central female characters. It is true that both texts may seem to try to weaken, silence, and blind their central female characters in the end. But the woman (Hellena/Ellen) has perceived so much. Do we really believe the wool can be pulled over her eyes or stuffed in her mouth once she has seen what she has seen and come to know what she has come to know?

The answer, of course, is no. Each text convinces us of the intelligence and wit of the central female character, but that is not to say that she will necessarily acknowledge all she sees or say all she thinks. In fact, each text emphasizes a certain restraint in the woman, an acceptance as well as a transgression of boundaries and rules. Cavell entitles his *Pursuits of Happiness* chapter on *It Happened One Night*, "Knowledge as Transgression." He explains in the opening sentence that

> if it is inevitable that the human conceive itself in opposition to God; and as debarred from a knowledge of the world as it is in itself; and as chained away, incomprehensibly, maddeningly, from the possibility of a happy world, a peaceable kingdom; then it is inevitable that the human conceive itself as limited.
>
> (PH, 73)

But what does it mean to be limited and does limitation necessarily imply lack of some sort? "In either case," he concludes, "it [such a conception] portrays being human as being inherently subject to the fate of transgression, to commandments and prohibitions that are to be obeyed and that therefore *can* be disobeyed" (PH, 74). Although Cavell begins this discussion in the realm of God/man relations (a realm invoked by the first transgression of knowledge in Genesis), he quickly moves to the "social plane," noting that human boundaries confine our lives in much more immediate and noticeable ways than the limitations that prevent our attaining a God's-eye view of the world. Indeed in two matters in particular, "human societies have been most anxious to limit": "the capacity to relate oneself to the world by knowledge and the capacity to relate oneself to others by marriage" (PH, 74). He continues: "We seem to understand these capacities for relation as constitutive of what we understand by human society, since we attribute to them, if unchecked, the power to destroy the social realm" (PH, 74).

Of course, his reading of Capra's film text is a meditation on the limits of knowledge and the barriers to marriage. Rather than chafing at the limits and the barriers, this film demonstrates their profound significance in the pursuit of happiness and moral perfectionism. For one thing, we understand ourselves as "subject to law and as bringers of the law"—and, as such, we rely on reason to set boundaries that circumscribe our behaviors and enable us to recognize ourselves as part of a world, a society (*PH*, 77). Ellen Andrews rejects rule and law in the beginning, escaping from her father, pursuing a course of her own, until she meets Peter, with whom (under whose tutelage, but also in conjunction with his own education) she begins to learn to live within boundaries, to respect barriers such as the "Walls of Jericho" or the rule that one must not "gold dig" when accepting a ride from a stranger or the necessity of living within one's means. There are times she knows and Peter must learn that transgression is necessary for the formation of community, for marriage (and remarriage) to take place. Barriers, although necessary, can represent narcissism, self-enclosure, and isolation, after a point.

Cavell spends a good bit of time on Peter's perplexing behavior following Ellie's transgression of the Walls of Jericho in the second of their autocamp sleepovers. The couple has been talking to one another across the barrier, so to speak, at Ellen's instigation. She wants to know if Peter has ever been in love. Hasn't he ever thought about it? she asks. He replies, in a kind of reverie:

> Sure—sure, I've thought about it. Who hasn't? . . . I've even been sucker enough to make plans. I saw an island in the Pacific once. Never been able to forget it. That's where I'd like to take her. But she'd have to be the sort of a girl who'd jump in the surf with me—and love it as much as I did. You know, those nights when you and the moon and the water all become one—and you feel that you're part of something big and marvelous.

As he continues to smoke and fantasize about "someone who's real," "a girl who was hungry for those things," Ellen is clearly moved; she has recognized her own desire in Peter's dreamy monologue, and the result is a crossing of the barrier that has kept them apart for so long. Peter, however, is unprepared; instead of welcoming her, he tells her to return to her side of the barrier—which she does in order to cry herself to sleep.

Peter's problem, in Cavell's words, is "having to put together his perception of the woman with his imagination of her" (*PH*, 100), and he cannot do that without reshaping the narrative he has been writing. His "scoop" of the story of Ellen Andrews's "mad flight to happiness" has suddenly become his own story: "I met her on a bus coming from Miami. I've been with her every minute. I'm in love with her." This story is true, but as much cannot be said for the excuse Peter gives himself (and his editor) for leaving

Ellie asleep in the autocamp while he rushes to New York to sell the story to his editor for the $1,000 he feels necessary to respond to her "transgression." "A guy can't propose to a gal without a cent in the world, can he?" is nothing more than a "cover story," and one that it is just as well he has no chance to tell Ellie. For, after all, what the couple really needs is a divorce in order to make remarriage possible. Peter's is a self-absorbed action that precipitates an estrangement from Ellie, a necessary disruption of the intimacy they have established on the road, an intimacy founded on "narcissism" and one which "must be ruptured in order that an intimacy of difference or reciprocity supervene" (*PH*, 103). Peter has to learn that "you cannot achieve reciprocity with the one in view by telling your story to the whole rest of the world" (*PH*, 109). You cannot "transcend" the barrier. Instead, you must live from "within your connection with others, forgoing the wish for a place outside from which to view and direct your fate" (*PH*, 109). You must acknowledge the existence, the reality, of the one on the other side of the barrier, and you must allow yourself to be acknowledged in return.

From Cavell's analysis of *It Happened One Night*, key concepts emerge that are helpful to an analysis of *The Rover*. First is the linkage of knowledge and desire and the notion that pursuit of each will involve both transgression and the creation and acceptance of barriers, breaking rules as well as embracing intrinsic (as opposed to imposed) laws. Second, there is the doubleness of fantasy/reality and the need to merge split perception of the other (the woman in particular) into an acceptance of the whole in all of her complexity. Third, there is the implication that from the central couple a new social order will emerge, one founded on better principles than the old order, one that offers more reliable paths to happiness, one that does not take itself for granted as it knows dissolution is always possible. That violence is central to each text is an important feature signifying, on its most basic level, the disruption or rupture necessary for both marriage (the breaking of the hymenal barrier) and remarriage (divorce and re-union). Violence indicates as well that attention must be paid, alertness is necessary. Sometimes it takes a sock in the nose or a gun pointed to one's chest to bring this point home. But the central lesson of each couple can be stated thus: for one's own good and the good of one's society, one cannot go about the business of living without questioning, without a healthy skepticism. To do so is to live half asleep, partially aware, nearly unconscious, mostly dead. To live and love (which is, according to these texts, the only way to truly live), one has to take an interest, first, in one's own life, and, then, in the life of another (*PH*, 12). Language (conversation) provides the means for the couple at the texts' center to do just that. Genre and its conventions (film/drama, screen/stage) offer such means to the viewer as well.

Hellena announces her determination to seek love and knowledge at the outset of Behn's play. She begins by quizzing Florinda about "Don Belvile." When her sister chastises her, Hellena explicitly says, "I wou'd fain know as much as you" (1.1.4):

'Tis true, I never was a Lover yet—but I begin to have a shrew'd guess, what 'tis to be so, and fancy it very pretty to sigh, and sing, and blush, and wish, and dream and wish, and long and wish to see the Man, and when I do look pale and tremble, just as you did when my Brother brought home the fine English Colonel to see you.

(1.1.9–13)

Moreover, she encourages Florinda in Florinda's resistance to the "unjust Commands" of their father regarding his plans to marry her to "Rich Old Don Vincentio." "Now hang me," Hellena exclaims heartily, "if I don't love thee for that dear disobedience" (1.1.17; 22–23). And she goes further, embracing transgression—"I love mischief strangely"—and pursuit of happiness: "I'm resolv'd to provide my self this Carnival, if there be ere a handsome proper fellow of my humour above ground" (1.1.23–24; 33–35). Of course, she tempers her language as she, Florinda, and Valeria set off to the street party in masquerade, vowing to "be as mad as the rest, and take all Innocent freedomes" (1.1.163–64), but clearly the donning of disguise, the rejection of authority (as Callis implies, Don Pedro would disapprove), the refusal of barriers (Don Pedro has also placed Hellena under Callis's guard), and the headstrong determination to have her own way define this young woman as a transgressor at least on the level of Ellen Andrews. Hellena does not jump off a yacht to escape control and follow her own desires, but that is no doubt only because she is not on a yacht. She wants to move freely in pursuit of love and knowledge, and like Ellie, she arranges to do so in the only way she can.

Yet, there is a boundary that Hellena will not cross without license; she will give Willmore "leave to love" her, but not "leave to lye with" her (1.2.188–89) unless "Himen and his Priest, say amen to't" (5.1.417). The alternative is to behave "upse Gipsie" in earnest. Indeed, Willmore proposes to "turn Gipsie, and become a left-handed bride-groom, to have the pleasure of working that great Miracle of making a Maid a Mother" (5.1.432; 426–28), but Hellena knows that the result for her will be "a cradle full of noise and mischief, with a pack of repentance at my back," as well as a life of weaving "Incle" (or "linen thread") in the manner of true gypsy women, who have to support themselves by selling trinkets and crafts (5.1.430–32; 432n). To be a left-handed bridegroom is to keep a mistress.[4] It is a ridiculous proposal to make to the daughter of a "noble family," but Willmore does not know Hellena's identity when he proffers such a union. Moreover, as a potential fate for Hellena, that of becoming a mistress is hinted by other details in the text. Indeed, as Nancy Copeland, Stephen Szilagyi, and Julie Nash have all pointed out, one of Behn's primary objectives in *The Rover* is to "minimize the difference between the status of the virgin and the whore."[5]

Angellica, a courtesan (or the equivalent of a kept mistress), is a second partner to Willmore, perhaps in some ways a more equal match than Hellena. The trajectory of her narrative features surrender to love followed by descent into madness and violence, a transformation, although certainly not one to be celebrated. Angellica's relationship with Wilmore serves to expose the violent, coercive forces that define and defy the pursuit of happiness, especially for women. That this more sinister narrative is meant as commentary on the main plot and the central couple is clear from Thomas Killigrew's *Thomaso*, the source play from which Behn drew several plotlines. There is no female ingénue in Killigrew's two-part comedy, nor does his title character either seek or find himself sought by a witty young woman, as Behn's Willmore puts it, "so of one Humour" as his own (5.1.445). Thomaso has a complex sexual/romantic history that includes having "taken the maidenhead" of the courtesan Paulina seven years before the play's opening as well as pursuit of the Spanish General's former mistress, Angellica (on much the same terms as we see in Willmore's pursuit of his Angellica), and ultimate union with the play's virtuous young woman, Serulina (the equivalent of Florinda, whom Thomaso, like Belville, rescued at the Siege of Pamplona).[6] And although the character "Hellena" does not appear in *Thomaso*, her name does. Killigrew's Hellena, however, is "an old decayed Curtezan, that hopes to be restored to 15."[7] In his first conversation with Angellica, Thomaso proclaims, "Faith, 'tis a very ill woman (if she be handsome) that will not make a good whore" (2.4.112–13)—a sentiment that speaks, as Jones DeRitter has argued, to *Thomaso*'s "self-congratulatory fantasy" of cavalier male sexual entitlement.[8] Behn's play, as DeRitter observes, critiques that fantasy by satirizing "sex roles and sexual politics" (84).

Thomaso demonstrates what Alfred Harbage long ago summarized as Killigrew's tendency to divide women into angels and whores "'with the latter class subdivided into good courtesans and bad courtesans'" (qtd. by DeRitter, 87). His Angellica is the "good courtesan," who is grateful for Thomaso's seduction as it liberates her from a mercenary attitude toward sex and teaches her to love. Behn, as DeRitter aptly points out, will have none of that. Her Angellica too allows herself to be seduced in the interest of transcending a merely commercial approach to love, but she finds herself trapped in the language and assumptions of mercenary exchange. Her anger, however, does not proceed from her own limitations. It is a justified anger at Willmore's inability to reciprocate a love he has cajoled from her. She may have been foolish, as Moretta suggests, to believe "such a swaggerer" (3.1.153), but such foolishness, such vulnerability, is necessary in love. Even Hellena flares up and flaunts out when Willmore's language or behavior displeases her. Even she is afraid from time to time that she will be, to borrow language from the remarriage comedy genre, "taken for a sucker." She is not so different from Angellica in that regard. She differs only in that, in the end, her emotional risk results in marriage. Behn's Angellica finds herself in a melodrama because the man she loves abandons her; Hellena remains in a comedy because the man she loves reciprocates that love. Furthermore, both Angellica and Hellena, who compete for narrative/stage dominance in *The Rover*, epitomize what Thomas A. King has described as the Restoration actress's ability to present both herself (lower class, accessible, sexualized) and the character she typically played (upper class—often aristocratic—desirable, but chaste). In King's view, the Restoration actress's wit consists in the *"interactive dualism"* she exploited: "The actress neither became her character onstage nor stayed herself: the tension she maintained between the two produced the erotic dynamic of the Restoration stage."[9]

The angel/harlot doubleness may not be as evident in *It Happened One Night* (it will be much more central to the next film text I discuss, *The Lady Eve,* in which Jean will tell Hopsy "the best ones [women] aren't as good as you probably think they are, and the bad ones aren't as bad, not nearly as bad"). Nonetheless, it is several times alluded to in the autocamp scenes, along with other alternate sexual choices or identities. I suspect, for example, it may be no coincidence that the first autocamp is Dykes (in the short story, it is "Dakes").[10] I think it is an interesting progression from that camp where Ellie and Peter are considered married, to the second in which they are suspected of unmarried cohabitation and condemned as a result, to the third where their marriage, although attested by a license, is joyfully questioned, presumably because of their open affection for one another. More significant, however, is the way the film calls attention to the actress as actress. Cavell has argued that the "comedies of remarriage ... have a way of ... harping on the identity of the real women cast in each of these films ... by way of some doubling or splitting of her projected presence" (*PH*, 64). In the case of this film, the newspaper photographs of "Ellen Andrews" alert our attention to the split between public and private, "the split or doubling between what happens during the day and what happens at night, which amounts to a split or doubling between reality and something else" (*PH*, 64). Cavell calls that "something else" "dreaming," but there are other possibilities—some attractive, some not—of lives to be led; personalities to develop; sexual possibilities to explore, to embrace, or to reject—"realities," in other words, that could have been but for other realities (which, in fact, are fantasies) that came to be, at least on stage or screen.

Claudette Colbert's screen performance acknowledges such a split or doubling. Ellen has at least two distinct and conflicting personalities—cynical, suspicious, and arrogant, on the one hand, and fun-loving, cheerful, childlike, and kind, on the other. Colbert distinguishes these versions of Ellen (which are too wildly distinct to be seen as "moods") by modulating the register of her voice. The cynical, suspicious, arrogant Ellen speaks in a voice that is almost an octave lower than the fun-loving, cheerful, childlike Ellen. There is a third voice, about halfway between the two, that Colbert uses once or twice, most significantly in the scene in which Ellen crosses the "Walls of Jericho" to ask Peter to take her with him to his dream island. This voice is sincere, soft, and vulnerable (she also uses it in the confessional scene with her father). It is the voice in which she articulates her true desires, when she finally comes to understand what those desires are. Cavell states:

If we do not equate knowledge with the results of science but understand it as the capacity to put one's experience and the world into words, to use language, then the will to knowledge and the will to marriage may be seen to require analogous limitations in order to perform their work of social constitution, limitations that combat their tendencies to privacy or their fantasies of privacy.

(*PH*, 74)

Both marriage and language require an encounter with an Other, someone not us, who prevents our retreat into narcissism by "facing us with that reciprocity and exchange apart from which separate human individuals cannot acquire the force so much as to name themselves" (*PH*, 74). Probably the most important shared motif in the texts under consideration is what I think of as the naming moment. It is in this moment in each text that the authors find a way of expressing just what is so special about the love relationship central to their stories, what sets it apart from the other relationships in the texts, what makes it an ethical and erotic ideal worth pursuing for characters and viewers alike.

By the time the "naming moment" arrives in *It Happened One Night*, Peter has saved Ellie from a number of scrapes (including rescuing her from the unwanted attentions of a particularly obnoxious traveling salesman named Shapely, played by character actor Roscoe Karns). Despite a bit of pique at some of his strategies, Ellie has begun to accept grudgingly Peter's various gestures of help, and she has just discovered his motive for doing so. He knows who she is; he's read about her escape in a newspaper; he has already referred to her as "Miss Andrews" (strangely, actually, as he well knows she is Mrs. Westley). His most common name for her, however, is "brat." She has referred to him as "young man" up to this point, trading on her class status. In the first autocamp, she learns *what* he is—that is, what he does for a living—for he has explained that he wishes to accompany her to New York in order to write a story about her adventurous escape and reunion, a story he hopes will reestablish him at the newspaper from which he was fired the day before.

After weighing her options, Ellie accepts Peter's extra pair of pajamas and settles warily into her bed on the other side of the "Walls of Jericho." There, as the camera focuses on her face, she looks toward the blanket and asks, "What's your name? Who are you?" The answer Peter gives is telling: "I am the whip-poor-will that cries in the night. I am the soft morning breeze that caresses your lovely face." He is an embodiment of her dreams of freedom, her fantasies of romance, her longing for another life than the one she knows. The fact that she asks his name is as significant as the answer he gives. In doing so, she indicates her willingness to forge a relationship, her acceptance of their joint journey, with adventures along the way neither can predict, to a destination neither quite knows. But it is also significant that she insists on his real name: "Peter Warne," he says. "I don't like it."

"Don't let it bother you. You're giving it back in the morning." But by then it will be too late. The couple is already married—and well on their way to divorce and remarriage. For the woman, the "*warne*ing" cannot be rejected. She has already gone too far, erred on the side of the recklessness that Peter represents, not the caution that he would advise.

I would argue that the naming moment in *The Rover* bears exactly the same meaning. That Willmore is a cad and a rake, a womanizer, who will stop at nothing to gain conquest and who acts just about as badly as any character in Restoration drama if not a good deal worse, does not detract from the sincerity of his love for Hellena—a sincerity signified in the naming moment that comes at the end of the play. This exchange is briefer than the parallel scene in *It Happened One Night*. After all, Willmore and Hellena have been exploring their fantasies and dreams of romantic escape for nearly five acts. Invoking or employing gypsies, rovers, adventures at sea, confinement in a nunnery, scaling walls and kidnapping, cross-dressing, spying, and so on, these potential lovers have imaginatively embarked on many journeys to explore their desires for freedom and adventure. At the end of the play, however, they set forth in reality on the journey that will begin with their marriage. And the brief but telling exchange sums up eloquently the significance of their union. Willmore, not able to persuade Hellena to "Weave a true loves knot" outside of marriage, yields, saying "I adore thy Humour and will marry thee, . . . it must be a bargain" (5.1.443; 444–46). The union agreed upon, he wonders, "is it not fit we shou'd know each others Names" (5.1.449–50). Hellena agrees, and asks in turn, "I beseech ye your Name" (5.1.455). "I am call'd *Robert the Constant*," he tells her. "I am call'd *Hellena the Inconstant*," she replies (5.1.456; 461). In a sense, they exchange characters and, in doing so, acknowledge the fundamental change that will occur in each of them as a result of their union. Willmore is constant, apparently, during the course of his brief marriage; Hellena does embrace change (she dies because she travels with her husband on a dangerous sea voyage). The naming moment in *The Rover*, as in *It Happened One Night*, is a testament to the belief that love changes people. Peter Warne is a blustering drunk when we first meet him, and Ellen Andrews is a disgruntled, whining brat; Willmore is a lascivious, violent sexual predator, and Hellena is a willful, headstrong girl. What seems to interest both Capra and Behn is the way such ordinary obnoxious individuals are transformed by love into remarkable halves of remarkable couples, who together—momentarily anyway—convince us that their charm, wit, and grace are enough to transform the world as well. And in both texts, the world does cry out for transformation. *It Happened One Night*'s landscape is peopled with predators, victims of poverty, charlatans of various sorts. There are wealthy people—such as Andrews—whose money protects him from the sufferings of the rest of the population and whose power commands attention and action that others (such as Peter Warne) can experience in fantasy only. Indeed, as Christopher Beach has argued, *It Happened One Night* offers "an extended commentary on the structure of social class in Depression-era America."[11] Citing other significant analyses of the film (works by Joseph McBride, Elizabeth Kendall, and, in particular, Rita Barnard and Barbara Ching),[12] Beach convincingly demonstrates that Capra's film text foregrounds class in a way not called for by the source material and one that significantly contributed to the film's "appeal . . . to American audiences of the mid-1930s."[13] Peter Warne, man of the people, supplants King Westley, "the embodiment of social privilege and pretension" (74), a "lounge lizard" (220) in Barnard and Ching's formulation, representative of an old, dissipated order that needs replacing by a man who knows how to "stretch a dollar."[14]

Lawrence Levine remarks that Capra "had grave doubts about, and criticisms of, large-scale corporate enterprise . . . [and in] most of his Depression films, he found ways to reproach powerful capitalists for their values and their actions."[15] "Nevertheless," Levine continues, "Capra's films seem to imply that the problems Americans faced were due less to imperfections in the system than to human fallibility: to madness, irrationality, selfishness, greed." Levine argues that the remedy Capra inevitably proposes is a return to "traditional values and lifestyles," a remedy that demands, among other things, that "women of independence, power, and dignity" be "transform[ed] into traditional feminine roles."[16] It was Capra himself who likened *It Happened One Night* to *The Taming of the Shrew*.[17] But just what kind of taming does Ellie receive from Peter? Coppélia Kahn reads Shakespeare's play as a critique of "*male attitudes towards women*," a "farcical representation of the psychological realities of marriage in Elizabethan England, in which the husband's will constantly, silently, and invisibly, through custom and conformity, suppressed the wife's."[18] Katherine's strength and will force us to see the male drive for dominance as "a childish dream of omnipotence" (89) somewhat akin to Peter's expertise as dunker, piggybacker, and hitchhiker or Andrews's heavily funded pursuit of his daughter, who, despite the reward and the publicity, would not be found until she was ready to be found.

Kahn sees *The Taming of the Shrew* as presenting, like all of Shakespeare's comedies, "the triumph of love" that renews society through the young couple's "ardor and mutual tolerance" (97). Although Levine's observation regarding Capra's investment in "traditional feminine roles" might accurately describe the women in later films (*Mr. Smith Goes to Washington, Meet John Doe*, and, certainly, *It's a Wonderful Life*), the observation is less just with regard to the depiction of Ellen Andrews. Like Kate, Ellen is transgressive, but her acts of rebellion are not so much tamed as they are redirected. Her outburst on the yacht (turning over her father's lunch tray, diving into the water to escape his control) is an act of self-determination. At that point, her sense of her own path to happiness is skewed. When she recognizes the nature of her desire (Peter) she again transgresses boundaries in pursuit of that desire. The same headstrong longing for happiness that led to her initial escape drives Ellen to her final assertion of will (this time, with her father's blessing and aid—but not, by any means, his control).

The Ellen Andrews first encountered by Peter Warne on the night bus is locked in her own version of herself. Her wealth confers, to her mind, a set of undeniable privileges. Peter Warne, who is poor but undaunted, has no particular regard for class status as he clearly demonstrates when he forces Ellen to share her seat at the back of the bus with him. Ellen turns from him, and she remains cool and haughty the next morning as they stand in the bus station waiting for the journey to continue. Ellen smokes a cigarette while Peter stands at some distance contemplating her. As he does so, a man emerges from the shadows behind Ellen, grabs her suitcase, and runs away. Peter reacts immediately, giving chase as Ellen first registers alarm at Peter's sudden rush toward her (as she seems to assume) and then appears relieved and somewhat bored, as he runs past her. When Peter returns, he announces, winded and apologetic, "he got away. I suddenly found myself in the middle of the brush, and not a sign of the skunk." Ellen raises her eyebrows and without even looking at Peter, says, in her loftiest, most cultivated tone, "I don't know what you're raving about, young man. And furthermore, I'm not interested." "Maybe you'll be interested to know your bag's gone," Peter says in the "hard" tone mandated by the script.[19]

Like Colbert, Clark Gable uses vocal register to suggest dimensions of personality and potentialities of existence in the character of Peter Warne. His tone can signify a jaded sense of life's possibilities, a wearied acceptance of its perennial disappointments, and an oddly optimistic openness to the possibility of meaningful interaction with others—conversation, that is. Peter loves language; indeed, as the film begins, he is being fired from his job at a New York newspaper for writing a column in "free verse," "Greek" to his editor. Once aboard the night bus, Peter engages the driver in talk centered, significantly enough, on a bundle of newspapers stacked on a seat at the back of the vehicle. The conversation begins with a simple request as Peter says, "pleasantly," as the script directs, "If you'll be good enough to remove those newspapers, I'll have a seat."[20] When he receives no response, he picks up the bundle of papers and throws it out of the window, prompting the driver to shout "pugnaciously," "Hey! Wait a minute!" Peter seems to sense an opportunity for a conversation of sorts. The script describes him as "turn[ing] and glanc[ing] at the driver with a quizzical look in his eyes." As Gable plays the scene, "quizzical" is manifest in his characteristic half grin and cocked eyebrow, the actor's signature way of indicating willingness to proceed in whatever the encounter offers.

The driver's opening gambit—"What do you think you're doing?"—might seem unpromising, but Peter is willing to engage. He first feigns ignorance ("huh?") and when the driver elaborates ("The papers! The papers! What's the idea of throwin' 'em out?"), Peter waxes eloquent:

Oh—the papers—That's a long story, my friend. You see, I never did like the idea of sitting on newspapers. I did it once and all the headlines came off on my white pants. On the level, it actually happened. Nobody bought a paper that day. They just followed me all over town and read the news off the seat of my pants.

In the script, the driver is to respond from his own grounded reality: "What're you gonna do about the papers? Somebody's gotta pick 'em up." But the film wisely understands this moment as a rhetorical, not an ideological, conflict. So the driver fires back with a cliché: "Fresh guy, huh! What you need is a good sock on the nose." Peter again seizes the moment as an improvisational challenge, saying with a lilt in his voice that seems as much indebted to the sheer joy he takes in talking as to his half-inebriated state, "Listen, partner. You may not like my nose. But I do. I always wear it out in the open where if anyone was to take a sock they could do it." From this point the conversation quickly deteriorates. "Oh yeah?" the driver says. Peter's response is judgmental, an effort to encourage the driver to try a bit harder in this combat: "Now, that's a brilliant answer. Why didn't I think of it? Our conversation could've been over long ago." "Oh, yeah?" the driver says again. Peter counters: "You keep that up, we're not going to get anywhere." The driver says, yet again: "Oh, yeah?" And Peter, conceding, responds, "You got me. Yeah!" His disappointment is temporary, however, as a more appropriate conversational partner has boarded the bus. She seems dour and uncommunicative at first, but somehow Peter seems to know he has met his match, and he indicates as much in the peculiar way of this film comedy—by testing her reaction to proper English grammatical construction. He may throw in a "lady" as a gesture to his populism, but he will not end a sentence with a preposition: "Excuse me, Lady, but that upon which you sit is mine." Whereas his use of the language had reduced the driver to an "oh yeah," Ellie immediately understands and contests Peter's claim.

Later, Ellie's own correct usage of an adverbial modifier ("it seems to me you are doing excellently without any assistance") will prompt a mocking jibe from Oscar "one-on-the-side" Shapely, but she and Peter, even when at odds with one another, speak the same language with careful—even loving—attention to its "rules," its levels of discourse, its possibilities for discrimination and social stratification, as well as unification and transcendence of boundaries. That is not to say that they are free from linguistic pretentiousness and snobbery. Peter has genuine skills and talents, but he prides himself on his so-called expertise in matters of doughnut dunking, piggybacking, and hitchhiking—subjects complete, in his own mind, with specialized vocabulary and ideological significance. Interestingly, Ellie acknowledges Peter's proficiency in the matter of doughnut dunking. As Cavell eloquently argues, the trajectory of the film's narrative is concerned with Ellie's coming to accept the provisions Peter provides. Although later she resists the raw carrots he procures, she is enthusiastically appreciative of the egg, doughnut, and coffee breakfast he sets before her in the first autocamp, and she eagerly learns from him the dunking technique that will keep her doughnut from "get[ting] soft and fall[ing] off" into her coffee. She challenges him, however, on the presumption that underlies his disdain of her definition of piggybacking. Granted, she is mistaken in that definition, but she is also right to challenge his "I never knew a rich man yet who could piggy-back ride." "You're prejudiced," she says, almost sadly. Peter had evoked a fond memory by carrying her across the stream, the first fond thought she has had of her father since she dove off his yacht in Miami. Peter's disdainful squelching of this nostalgic impulse toward emotional reconciliation is, as Ellie implies, a class-based gesture of contempt, but it is also a challenge to her to define herself as something other than her father's daughter. The next time Peter offers to "instruct" her, Ellie teaches a lesson of her own. Having patiently, if skeptically, watched as Peter tries to hitch a ride using his perfected tripartite system, Ellie hikes up her skirt, extends her leg, and brings a car to a screeching halt, proving "once and for all that the limb is mightier than the thumb." Once in the car, Peter scowls and snarls, "why didn't you take off all your clothes; you could've stopped forty cars." "I'll remember that when we need forty cars," Ellie chirps, happy in her triumph, certainly, but also, I believe, satisfied in having successfully shifted the discourse from class to gender, from her father to herself, from the things she does not know to those she does.

The class tensions evident in *It Happened One Night* differ substantially from those that inform *The Rover*, although Behn's play is more complicated than most Restoration comedies in its treatment of wealth. Usually, the key issue will be estate and dowry—and certainly the latter is at stake in that Florinda has a fortune to bestow. Interestingly, Belville seems unconcerned (as does Florinda herself) that the fortune may be reduced if Hellena refuses the convent (which she does in the end). Only Hellena mentions that fact— and when she does so it is to dismiss its importance as she tells Florinda "lay aside your hopes of my Fortune by my being a Devote" (1.1.43–44). Enough is enough, she seems to say, and the play does not interrogate that position (as, for example, *The Way of the World*, will do). Indeed, Wilmore's diatribe against the "marriage market" as well as the play's easy renunciation of the portended Florinda/Don Antonio match draw attention away from the power of fathers and brothers to the overarching question that was central to Killigrew's *Thomaso* and that Behn retains in her adaptation: How can the wealth of the roving cavaliers be repaired, if not restored? The answer, in both *Thomaso* and *The Rover, Part 1*, is through marriage and family alliances with wealthy foreigners from Roman Catholic countries— Spain and Italy, respectively.

Given the circumstances in which, first, *Thomaso* and, later, *The Rover* initially appeared, the focus on foreign alliance is understandable. In *Thomaso*, written in 1654, we see attitudes toward wealth that are based on precapitalist assumptions about social organization that *The Rover* retains. The king and the aristocrats (the cavaliers) are impoverished; Roundheads or Parliamentarians have money. If in *It Happened One Night*, the upper crust must learn accountability and responsibility from the less well-to-do, in *The Rover*, the aristocracy, dislocated and dispossessed by what we might call the emergent middle class, has nothing to teach the less wellborn about money. The lesson Blunt needs to learn has to do with class. Written in and for a precapitalist society, Behn's play (and her society) cannot be expected to reflect values of hard work and fiscal responsibility. Indeed, luxury itself is not at issue, and will not be for almost a century. Money and fortune do drive the plot of *The Rover* in as significant as way as in *It Happened One Night*, but the "lesson" is focused not so much on attitudes toward spending as on who has a right to the world's resources—capital being one, although certainly not the most important, of these resources.

The terms that are operative in Behn's economy are "prodigality" and "avarice." And although the first can be a problem, it is the second that causes most concern. For one thing, avarice can lead to disloyalty and disloyalty can impede justice. What disloyalty? The disloyalty of landed gentry, who made peace with the Cromwellians rather than forfeit their lands and estates. And how impede justice? By interfering with the restoration of the Stuart court (in the play's narrative present) or with the Stuart succession (in the present during which the play was written and produced). Ned Blunt is "treasurer" for the roving cavaliers, an elder brother who has retained his wealth during the interregnum ("I thank my Stars, I had more Grace than to forfeit my Estate by Cavaliering" 1.2.46–47). Blunt may be serving as a double agent (a spy) in that he is overtly supporting the Protectorate and the Commonwealth, while keeping company with roving (and fighting) cavaliers and also managing their money. If not a spy, he is at least playing some kind of double game, as he himself admits when Belvile wonders why his "following the court" is allowed by the Commonwealth. Blunt replies, "they know I follow it to do it no good, unless they pick a hole in my Coat for lending you Money now and then, which is a greater Crime to my Conscience. . . than to the Commonwealth" (1.2.50–53). The cavaliers are easy enough in his company, as his buffoonery and naiveté mark him ready enough to be gulled by both them and Lucetta. At the end of the play, he is ridiculously garbed in a "*Spanish* habit," clothed as one "of a Nation I abominate" (5.1.519; 515). Belvile responds that the outfit actually makes him "look en Cavalier" (5.1.525), but the transformation is not convincing—for neither Blunt nor his class nor his "*Conventickling*" co-religionists are the answer (or, at least not Behn's answer) to the world's problems, to the rebuilding of community (Epilogue, 5).

If nothing else, Blunt's attitude toward love marks him as inadequate. Waxing eloquent (inasmuch as he can) over his "mistress," Blunt provokes Willmore to ask "Dost know her Name?" "Her name?" Blunt answers, "what care I for Names?" (2.1.42–43). Nor can he carry on a conversation:

"pox on't, that I had but some fine things to say to her" (3.2.4–5). Instead, he resorts to his usual "'adsheartlikins!" and finds himself very soon in the sewer. Not that conversation could have dissuaded Lucetta from her purpose to rob him. But a taste for witty exchange might have prevented Blunt from misunderstanding so radically the nature of her interest in him. It is such a taste that redeems Willmore and such a taste that, Behn suggests, may redeem the world.

Both DeRitter and Szilagyi have read Willmore as a satire on cavalier excess and have emphasized Behn's Angellica, in particular, as negative commentary on the casual sexism of *Thomaso* and the Stuart court. Szilagyi indeed reads Angellica as the "body politic," whose "yearning for fidelity" has "been betrayed" and whose anger should be read as an admonition to the King and the nation "that not even love is a transcendent sovereign power when the body politic has become defined by financial contract."[21] DeRitter also finds that in Willmore "Behn works to expose the disruptive aspects of rakish behavior," but he goes on to say that in the play Behn wishes to provide her English sisters with a possible solution to the problem"—Hellena.[22] For DeRitter, Hellena's significance is that she is "willing to use the rake's tools against him" (91). To my mind, her significance is that she is an alert, aware, responsive, and responsible conversationalist, who is looking for the right person to talk to and recognizes him, despite his manifold shortcomings, when she hears him.

Hellena's wit and love of language is emphasized early on. Her speech is inventive, imaginative, exuberant, and exciting. Even talking to Florinda, she is given to cascading rhythmic flourishes as when she describes being in love as "to sigh, and sing, and blush, and wish, and dream and wish, and long and wish to see the Man" (1.1.10–12) or when she asks her sister the following:

> prithee tell me, what dost thou see about me that is unfit for Love—have I not a World of Youth? a humour gay? a Beauty passable? a Vigour desirable? Well Shap't? clean limb'd? sweet breath'd? and sense enough to know how all these ought to be employ'd to the best advantage; yes, I do and will.
>
> (1.1.38–43)

Angellica's "voice," in contrast, has altogether a different register. In her second speech in the play (uttered in response to the news that Willmore, Frederick, and Belville have been admiring her beauty, but laughing at her price), Angellica offers clear demarcation of the emotions that drive her: "I'm not displeas'd with their rallying; their wonder feeds my vanity, and he that wishes but to buy, gives me more Pride, than he that gives my Price, can make my pleasure" (2.1.115–17). Her knowledge of men and her confidence in her own imperviousness to love lead her to declaim, "Inconstancy's the sin of all Mankind, therefore, I'm resolv'd that nothing but Gold, shall charm my heart" (2.1.128–30). Her self-assurance will be a challenge to the impecunious Willmore, who will overcome her with his verbal virtuosity and a surprising self-confidence of his own.

Hellena also has a ready imagination and a gift for description that she employs in her sister's behalf later in Act 1, Scene 1. The young women have been joined by their brother, Don Pedro, who has come to inquire about Florinda's meeting with Don Vincentio, the man her father wishes her to marry. Florinda, in love with Belvile, of course resists this match and begs her brother to intervene with their father to save her from what she sees as little better than slavery. Against her aversion, however, Don Pedro posits Don Vincentio's wealth (and Belvile's poverty); the two quarrel until Hellena interrupts to take her sister's part, speaking to and for Florinda more effectively than Florinda can speak for herself. Hellena's theme is Don Vincentio's physical repulsiveness, and she draws out every weapon in her arsenal to impress on her brother the cruelty of such a match. Florinda is fair and European, and Don Vincentio is swarthy and bred in the Indies. Further, the old man is likely to be too stingy to employ a valet after he is married; therefore, it will fall to Florinda "to uncase his feeble Carcass" (1.1.103), before he goes to bed. Once there, he starts to snore before Florinda can join him in "his foul sheets" (1.1.101). As Hellena noted earlier, Don Vincentio "may perhaps increase her Bags [wealth], but not her Family" (1.1.83). Nevertheless, once married Florinda can have no other mate: "And this Man you must kiss, nay you must kiss none but him, too—and nuzel through his Beard to find his Lips.—And this you must submit to for Threescore years, and all for a Joynture" (1.1.113–15). It would be better, she continues, for Don Pedro to consign their sister to work at the hospital for "Lazers and Cripples" than to marry her to Don Vincentio (1.1.120–21).

As previously mentioned, Don Pedro orders Callis to "watch this Wild Cat" (1.1.136) and place her under lock and key for the duration of Carnival. "At Lent," he avers, "she shall begin her everlasting Pennance in a Monastery" (1.1.127–28). Hellena asserts "I had rather be a Nun than be oblig'd to Marry as you wou'd have me" (1.1.129–30). Don Pedro counters: "Do not fear the blessing of that choice—You shall be a Nun" (1.1.131). Hellena has another view of her future—and her right to choose both it and the "*Saint*" with whom she will spend it (1.1.134). And as for spending Carnival in a locked room, Hellena has no intention of doing that, either. It is easy enough for her to persuade Florinda, who is eager to see Belvile. And Callis has a "Youthful itch of going myself" (1.1.170). Costumes are already on their way; Don Pedro is unlikely to find out as he is "gone already"; Callis agrees to "attend, and watch us," in the manner of a chaperone; and Hellena's confinement is over before it begins (1.1.173–74).

It is in her exchanges with Willmore, however, that Hellena reveals her attentiveness, her presentness, her aliveness to the moment and to the person with whom she speaks (one who is as alive, as "real"—to borrow

Peter Warne's word—as she herself is). In their first conversation, one hears the rhythms of chiastic exchange—the coming together, moving apart—of true conversation. Hellena begins the dialogue with an antagonism that also speaks recognition: "Have a care how you venture with me Sir, lest I pick your Pocket, which will more vex your *English* humour, than an *Italian* Fortune will please you" (1.2.127–29). Willmore ignores the antagonism (it is part of her gypsy masquerade, after all) and acknowledges the instant sympathy between them: "How the Devil cam'st thou to know my Countrey and Humour?" (1.2.130–31). She continues playfully insulting him (marking his forward impudence; saying it does not displease her) and he responds by forthright admission of her insight, quickly followed by a sexual innuendo to take the discourse to another level: "but cannot you divine what other things of more value I have about me, that I would . . . willingly part with[?]" (1.2.136–37). She capitalizes on this opening, talking of his heart rather than his libido, and he responds by adopting the language of romance, agreeing that it is his heart he'd like to part with, but mentioning his long period of sexual deprivation: "I am come from Sea, Child, and Venus not being propitious to me in her own Element: I have a world of Love in store" (1.2.145–46). Here is another similarity, which Hellena reveals. She too has been deprived and may be deprived forever, if she takes "a Foolish Vow" (1.2.148). In the dialogue that follows, the two continue to flirt, exploring the dimensions of their mutual desire, and establishing both the nature of the "game" and the stakes for which they play.

Hellena makes it clear that she will be a loving subject as well as an object of love; "when I begin," she tells Willmore, "I fancy I shall love like any thing" (1.2.180–81). Her goal in their first conversation, however, seems primarily to determine the zest of Willmore's appetite. She teases him with news of her virginity, hints of her sojourn in the nunnery, references to the possibility that under her mask he might discover a face that does not please him (knowing full well that it will). When she finally works him up to the pitch of admitting his impatience, she closes the dialogue by revealing to him that she understands the difference between love and lust. He declares they are the same, and the difference between the two similar characters and the terms for which they weigh amorous combat are set.[23]

Once more I note that Cavell has said of the film comedies of remarriage that they ask and answer the question: "What does a happy marriage sound like?" These two texts, with their attention to contrastive conversational tones, seem particularly interested in that question. And both also illustrate what a happy marriage does *not* sound like—it does not involve yelling and blustering as in Ellie and Peter's "plumber's daughter" improvisation nor does it involve the histrionics and anger of Angellica's reaction to Willmore. That is not to say a happy marriage is all harmony. There are disagreements that forward self-knowledge and knowledge of the other. Hellena, discovering that Willmore despite his "swearing" is with Angellica, bristles at first and then says, "How this unconstant humour makes me love him! . . . I'l

[sic] do something to vex him for this" (4.1.281; 285). And she proceeds, in disguise as a boy, to tease Willmore with news of yet another mistress. Once he realizes that he is talking to his "little Gipsie," Willmore too adjusts his discourse: "Egad if I do not fit thee for this, hang me" (4.2.403; 406). Their understanding of one another allows their conversation to proceed on a level unrecognized (heard, but unheard) by Angellica and—although the topic is infidelity and dishonesty (and we will see the same sort of "conversation" in *The Awful Truth*)—somehow, through the course of the scene, Willmore and Hellena reach an understanding, whereas Angellica continues to demand vows and promises she knows Willmore cannot keep. Asked to swear he will never marry his "Errant Gipsie" (4.1.419), Willmore says to Angellica:

> If it were possible I should ever be inclin'd to marry, it shou'd be some kind young Sinner, one that has generosity enough to give a favour handsomely to one that can ask it discreetly, one that has Wit enough to Manage an intrigue of Love.
>
> (4.2.450–54)

And, of course, he is admitting as much to Hellena, as well.

By the end of the play, the two lovers have the support of the entire company. Hellena tells her brother that she has determined that "the Three hundred thousand Crowns my Uncle left me . . . will be better laid out in Love than in Religion" (5.1.493–95), and she puts her resolution to a vote: "let most voyces carry it, for Heaven or the Captain!" (5.1.496–97). And "All *cry*": "A Captain! A Captain!" (5.1.498). Her brother begrudgingly agrees: "take her—I shall now be free from fears of her Honour, guard it you now, if you can. I have been a slave to't long enough" (5.1.581–84). Willmore's response is telling. Casually, he says: "I am of a nation that are of opinion that a woman's honor is not worth guarding when she has a mind to part with it" (5.1.504–05). And Hellena endorses this view: "Well said Captain!" (5.1.506). The exchange draws attention to the particularly English nature of this proposed marriage, one that recognizes the woman's desire as well as the man's, one that proposes an equality between husband and wife that hearkens back to Milton's notion of "a meet and happy conversation" and that looks forward to Johnson's and Wollstonecraft's definition of marriage as "perpetual friendship." Although the ideal, of course, will be far from universally embraced and even further from universally realized, it is nonetheless an ideal posited in the relationship between Willmore and Hellena.

Finally, I think it worth noting, in the interest of bolstering my sense that these texts truly offer a philosophical/moral commentary on courtship and the nature of marriage (as well as divorce and remarriage), that the controlling metaphors of both *The Rover* and *It Happened One Night* are biblical images. The film's famous "Walls of Jericho" is obviously a dominant image and clearly functions as a metaphor for a virginity or a chastity that has yet to surrender but that is under siege in a way. *The Rover* also invokes siege and conquest and links battle to sexual knowledge. Florinda falls in love with Belville at the Siege of Pamplona because he protects her from the "Licensed Lust" (1.1.67) of the victorious soldiers, whose prerogative of rape and pillage is unquestioned by Florinda, as much as she appreciates not having fallen victim to their rights of conquest. The biblical metaphor that to my mind underwrites the action of the text, however, is spoken by Willmore. Unlike the "Walls of Jericho," which appear three times in Capra's text, this reference is briefly articulated. But it takes place during the initial conversation between Willmore and Hellena, and the narrative invoked provides the template for *The Rover*'s plots and subplots.

In his attempt to seduce the gypsy Hellena, Willmore claims biblical authority: "the Old Law had no Curse (to a Woman) like dying a Maid: witness *Jephtha*'s daughter" (1.2.166–67). Hellena is familiar with the story, but for her it requires explication. "A very good text, this, if well handled," she remarks, going on to gloss the reference thus, "I perceive, Father Captain, you wou'd impose no severe penance on her who were inclin'd to Console her self, before she took orders" (1.2.168–70). The penance for Jephthah's daughter is, of course, severe. Jephthah, "a mighty man of valour" and "the son of a harlot" (Judg. 11:1) is cast out of his father's home by his legitimate half siblings, who despise his birth. Later, however, they need his military prowess, and they appeal to him for aid. He is understandably unsympathetic: "Did not ye hate me, and expel me out of my father's house? and why are ye come unto me now when ye are in distress?" (Judg. 11:7). The answer, of course, is that they need his skill in war; in exchange, they promise that should he win the battle against the Ammonites, he shall become their leader and reign over them in Gilead. This promise of more than restitution is quite enough to spur Jephthah into battle, but his confidence seems a bit low as he not only implores the aid of God, but also makes an extraordinary promise: "Jephthah vowed a vow unto the Lord, and said, If thou shalt without fail deliver the children of Ammon into mine hands, Then it shall be, that whatsoever cometh forth of the doors of my house to meet me, when I return in peace from the children of Ammon, shall surely be the Lord's, and I will offer it up for a burnt offering" (Judg. 11:30–31). A vow to God is binding, so when, after a victorious battle, Jephthah returns home and is greeted upon arrival by his daughter, who "came out to meet him with timbrels and with dances" (Judg. 11:34), he realizes she must be sacrificed. Poignantly, the text underscores the father's agony: "And she was his only child; beside her he had neither son nor daughter" (Judg. 11:34):

> And it came to pass, when he saw her, that he rent his clothes, and said, Alas, my daughter! thou hast brought me very low, and thou art one of them that trouble me: for I have opened my mouth unto the Lord, and I cannot go back.
>
> (Judg. 11:35)

His daughter agrees:

> My father, *if* thou hast opened thy mouth unto the Lord do to me according to that which hath proceeded out of thy mouth; forasmuch as the Lord hath taken vengeance for thee of thine enemies, *even* of the children of Ammon.
>
> (Judg. 11:36)

She asks for one thing only: "let me alone two months, that I may go up and down upon the mountains, and bewail my virginity" (Judg. 11:37). Of course, he did so, and "at the end of two months, . . . she returned unto her father, who did with her *according* to his vow which he had vowed" (Judg. 11:39). Fancifully, Hellena seems to suggest that those two months could, even should, have been spent in ways other than bewailing, for what greater penance could be required of Jephthah's daughter than the one she was already committed to undergo? But the text will not support that reading, for we are told definitively "she knew no man." Further, her fate is presented as an emblematic feminine tragedy: "And it was a custom in Israel, that the daughters of Israel went yearly to lament the daughter of Jephthah the Gileadite four days in a year" (Judg. 11:39–40). As Jephthah's daughter bewailed her virginity before she died; the daughters of Israel bemoaned a fate they would wish to avoid—not sacrificial death, but, as Willmore says, "dying a Maid" (1.2.167).[24]

That it is a tragedy in a woman's life to have lived and died without having experienced sexual love is the lesson Jephthah's daughter has to teach. It is one Hellena embraces, and one that Ellen Andrews, too, illustrates. It is she, after all, who pulls aside the hymenal Walls of Jericho; like Hellena, she recognizes and expresses her longing "to love, and be beloved" (5.1.471–72): "I love you, Peter. Nothing else matters. We can run away. Everything will take care of itself." Both works underscore and validate the woman's desire by the end-of-text interrogation of masculine authority's use of money to control women. Hellena's fortune may be her own, but it has come to her through an uncle and has been directed, along with her desire, toward the "holy intent of becoming a Nun" (5.1.491)—in other words, to, like Jephthah's daughter, sacrifice her virginity for the love of God. Andrews's $10,000 reward to keep Ellie from Westley, Peter's flight to earn $1,000 to legitimize his proposal, Andrews's buyout of Westley for $100,000, all seem to be versions of masculine posturing equating money with power and control over women. By the end of each text, the male comes to recognize that neither his worth nor the worth of the woman he loves is to be understood in such terms. After all, it is Peter's bill for $11.63 and Willmore's recognition that Hellena is a "bargain" that "both the *Indies* shall not buy from me" (5.1.446; 444) that prove value and worth, and in doing so transform fantasies of the night into dreams of a new day.

Notes

1 Aphra Behn, *The Rover* (1677), in *The Works of Aphra Behn*, ed. Janet Todd, vol. 5, *The Plays, 1671–1677*, ed. Janet Todd (Columbus: Ohio State University Press, 1996). References are to act, scene, and line numbers.
2 *It Happened One Night*, directed by Frank Capra (1934; Culver City, CA: Columbia Classics, 1999), DVD.
3 On the motif of rape in Behn's play, see Anita Pacheco's "Rape and the Female Subject in Aphra Behn's *The Rover*," *ELH* 65, no. 2 (1998): 323–45. Whereas Pacheco reads Willmore's sexual aggression as evidence and critique of Restoration libertine culture, James Evans has recently argued that the casting of William Smith as Willmore suggests that "the character was conceived to emphasize his comic dimension as a flawed, yet still desirable partner for Hellena." See his "Teaching Willmore," in *ABO: Interactive Journal for Women and the Arts, 1649–1830* 4, no. 1 (2014): 2.
4 Gordon Williams, *A Dictionary of Sexual Language and Imagery in Shakespearean and Stuart Literature* (London: The Athlone Press, 1994), s.v. "left," 797.
5 Szilagyi, "The Sexual Politics of Behn's *Rover*: After Patriarchy," *Studies in Philology* 95 (1998): 435–55; 447; Copeland, "'Once a Whore and Ever': Whore and Virgin in *The Rover* and Its Antecedents," *Restoration* 16 (1992): 20–27; Nash, "'The Sight on't Would Beget a Strong Desire': Visual Pleasure in Aphra Behn's *The Rover*," *Restoration* 18 (1994): 77–87.
6 Interestingly, although *Thomaso* was never performed, Killigrew did draw up a cast list for an all-female production in which the 14-year-old Nell Gwyn was to play the courtesan, Paulina. See [George Villiers], *Plays, Poems, and Miscellaneous Writings Associated With George Villiers, Second Duke of Buckingham*, ed. Robert D. Hume and Harold Love (Oxford, Oxford University Press, 2007), 1:17–18; and Charles Beauclerk, *Nell Gwyn: Mistress to a King* (New York, Grove Press, 2006), 73.
7 Killigrew, *Thomaso, Or, The Wanderer, A Comedy* (London: J. M. for Henry Herringman, 1663), "*Dramatis Personae.*"
8 DeRitter, "The Gypsy, *The Rover*, and the Wanderer: Aphra Behn's Revision of Thomas Killigrew," *Restoration* 10 (1986): 84.
9 King, "'As if (She) Were Made on Purpose to Put the Whole World into Good Humour': Reconstructing the First English Actresses," *The Drama Review* 36 (1992): 92.
10 There could be any number of reasons for the change and its seeming (although, perhaps, pejorative) reference to lesbianism. The writers could be thumbing their noses at the censors (as post-Hays code writers often did), they could be paying homage to someone with the actual last name "Dykes" or "Dyke" (Woody Van Dyke, perhaps?), or they could simply think the name sounds better or more realistic than "Dakes." Another possibility is that a prop person misunderstood the direction for the sign and wrote Dykes instead of Dakes—what does it matter, anyway? Although any and all possibilities exist, I am inclined to read the film's revision to the source story as the industry's silent witness within a heteronormative text to a diversity it cannot overtly reflect (similar to the moment in *Bringing Up Baby* when Cary Grant, dressed in a negligee, makes a leap while saying he's gone "gay all of a sudden").
11 Beach, *Class, Language, and American Film Comedy* (Cambridge: Cambridge University Press, 2002), 71.
12 McBride, *Frank Capra: The Catastrophe of Success* (New York: Simon and Schuster, 1992); Kendall, *The Runaway Bride: Hollywood Romantic Comedy of the 1930s* (New York: Knopf, 1990); Barnard and Ching, "From Screwballs to

98 *Whippoorwills, gypsies, and fantasies of the night*

Cheeseballs: Comic Narrative and Ideology in Capra and Reiner," *New Orleans Review* 17, no. 3 (1990): 52–59.
13 Beach, *Class, Language, and American Film*, 71.
14 Beach, *Class, Language, and American Film*, 74.
15 Levine, "Frank Capra's America: Part Four, Pessimism in Capra's Cultural Politics," *Journal for MultiMedia History* 2 (1999): http://www.albany.edu/jmmh/vol2no1/Levine4.html.
16 Levine, "Frank Capra's America: Part Three, Capra's Fundamental Values," *Journal for MultiMedia History* 2 (1999): http://www.albany.edu/jmmh/vol2no1/Levine3.html.
17 See Linda Mizejewski, *It Happened One Night*, Wiley-Blackwell Studies in Film and Television (Oxford: Blackwell, 2010), 10, 18.
18 Kahn, "'The Taming of the Shrew': Shakespeare's Mirror of Marriage," *Modern Language Studies* 5 (1975): 89, 94. For an alternative view that the play reflected rather than parodied values of Shakespeare's age, see Lynda E. Boose, "Scolding Brides and Bridling Scolds: Taming the Woman's Unruly Member," *Shakespeare Quarterly* 42, no. 2 (1991): 179–213; and Emily Detmer, "Civilizing Subordination: Domestic Violence and the *Taming of the Shrew*," *Shakespeare Quarterly* 48, no. 3 (1997): 273–94.
19 Robert Riskin, Shooting draft for *It Happened One Night*, based on a story by Samuel Hopkins Adams, 1934. http://www.dailyscript.com/index.html.
20 Riskin, Shooting draft for *It Happened One Night*.
21 Szilagyi, "Sexual Politics," 455.
22 DeRitter, "The Gypsy," 91.
23 I am borrowing from my rendition of this exchange between Hellena and Willmore in "Ethics, Politics and Heterosexual Desire in Aphra Behn's *The Rover*," *Essays in Theatre / Études thétrâles*, 19, no. 2 (2001): 111–25.
24 For the range of eighteenth-century interpretations of this text (from deists to Anglican clergymen to librettists), see Susan Staves, "Jeptha's Vow Reconsidered," *Huntington Library Quarterly* 71 (2008): 651–69. See also Debora Kuller Shuger, *The Renaissance Bible: Scholarship, Sacrifice, and Subjectivity* (Berkeley and Los Angeles: University of California Press, 1998), 128–66.

4   Luck, be a lady
Aphra Behn, Preston Sturges, and the ethics of genre

As suggested by the brief focus on elitism in Chapter 2 and the reference to sexual violence in Chapter 3, there are some uncomfortable facts about the two genres at the center of my study. To those already noted, this chapter will add a third: textual evidence of the underlying racial and ethnic prejudices at the heart of the respective cultures. For some critics, one or both of these genres have been in a sense spoiled by these disturbing facts, at least in terms of enjoyment, appreciation, and praise. To be sure, the plays and films have generated plenty of valuable deconstructive critique pointing out their exploitation of women, their blinkered or destructive treatment of ethnic others, and their ideological elitism. A focus on class conflict in particular has generated important analyses of work by Aphra Behn and Preston Sturges, the focus of this chapter. In his discussion of Behn's Tory comedies of the Exclusion crisis (*The Second Part of the Rover*, *The City Heiress*, and *The Roundheads*), for example, Robert Markley points out the way the playwright structures political and class antagonisms through sexual ideologies that privilege the license (for both men and women) of cavalier libertinism. He notes that Behn idealizes the "freedom of exile" and exile itself as a domain of "loyalty and generosity" and perpetual courtship in contrast to the repressiveness and "moneygrubbing" of Puritan (and Whig) rule, as well as the bourgeois notion of marriage that proves particularly repressive for women's desires.[1] Sturges, too, highlights class difference only to deny it in the end (in both *Sullivan's Travels* and in *The Lady Eve*), as Eric Schocket has argued in a particularly interesting essay on the literary and filmic strategy of investigating the problems of the poor in America through "class transvestism." Such portrayals, he says, merely translate "class conflict into class difference and then into cultural difference," effectually silencing "revolutionary" ideas by containing them "within a rhetoric of pluralism."[2]

These are valuable critiques, to be sure, but they do leave one wondering why, given their blindnesses, these texts should command our attention at all today. Some, maybe even most, would answer that it is valuable to examine the artifacts of the past for what they tell us about the deep-seated prejudices of our cultural productions—and to hold accountable the institutions (the aristocracy, Hollywood, the patriarchal assumptions and coercions of both) for encoding, enforcing, and exacerbating those prejudices. Such examination is no doubt valuable, but to my mind it is not the job of "literary criticism" to point out the deficiencies of the works it brings to attention. I find that Stanley Cavell has articulated my own sense of the job of criticism, and as this book is so fully indebted to him on other scores I will use his language to state my view. I had formed the same opinion prior to reading Cavell, but I had never articulated it in my own words, perhaps from a failure to see the need, perhaps from a shyness born of early training in which "appreciation" was frowned on because it could be and often was so stridently expressed as to negate commentary, analysis, and evaluation.

For Cavell, and for me, the task of criticism begins with individual aesthetic pleasure so intense that it demands that the critic/philosopher bring "pressure and questioning" to the work of art in order to explain, and even justify, that pleasure.[3] If the work will "bear up" under this pressure, then the critic and the reader of criticism can come to agreement that it "warrant[s] praise"; it deserves our attention and commands our appreciation (*Philosophy*, 70; 82). When Cavell (whose work is grounded in the intersection of literature and philosophy) is discussing Shakespeare or Thoreau or Emerson or James, he is unlikely to meet the kind of opposition that requires such justification. But there will always be those (it seems) who will deny classical Hollywood films the status of art. The same can be said of Restoration comedies. The texts in both canons are widely recognized as having a certain importance in the history of their genres; lasting artistic value on the order of Shakespeare is consensus more difficultly accorded any text in either canon. Although I believe Cavell has made powerful cases for most of the films I discuss in this book, his appreciation of their presentation of marriage as remarriage has been challenged by scholar-critics, who place themselves squarely in the field of film studies and who are as reluctant to open space for philosophy as philosophy (by Cavell's account) is to embrace literary and other aesthetic questions. As for Restoration comedy, few if any but specialists pay it much mind, and as noted earlier even those who do value the aesthetic achievement of the period tend to shy away from putting moral/ethical pressure on the plays. They seem to assume without question that a body of work so focused on sexual matters has little interest in the higher, more ennobling, aspects of human existence. I hope that it is already evident that the plays will bear a good bit of pressure with regard to their ethical/moral as well as their aesthetic significance. In this chapter, I will go further to suggest that although they, like the Hollywood comedies of remarriage, bear witness to the presence of the troubling injustices of their times and, also like the films, the plays seldom resist the injustices they record, some members of each genre allow certain uglinesses of their times to trouble their comic plots to a notable degree. That they do so is a fact that in itself deserves our praise. Aphra Behn and Preston Sturges are the two authors who take it on themselves to pause over inequities that other writers, and that they themselves in other works, paper over.[4]

What does it mean to pause over, to reflect on, racial and ethnic prejudices in a comic genre? Comedy, after all, trades in stereotypes. Are pausing and reflecting tantamount to reinforcing, to reinflicting, the harm such stereotypes have done? In *Philosophy the Day after Tomorrow*, Cavell tacitly addresses that question with a focus on a Fred Astaire dance number in Vincente Minnelli's 1953 film *The Bandwagon*. The sequence is, broadly speaking, about Astaire's character, a "song-and-dance man whose star has faded in Hollywood . . . returning apprehensively to New York to try a comeback on Broadway" (21). He goes into an arcade and attempts to engage with several machines and people to no avail, when he trips over the feet of an individual, who at the time would have been called, a "shoeshine boy" (despite the fact that he is a grown man). This "shoeshine boy" is black, but the nomenclature had less to do with race than station. As evidence, I point to Ellie Andrews's summoning of the vendor on the night bus in *It Happened One Night*. "Say, boy!" she calls. When he comes into the frame, we see a white man, who appears to be at least her own age, if not a good bit older. But, although some white men might be "boys" in 1953, it's safe to say that many more black men in America during that time would be called "boy" due to the inequity in social and racial status that was encoded in American society. It is, therefore, all the more remarkable that in Minnelli's film Astaire's encounter with the "shoeshine man" results in "a dance of identity" (*Philosophy*, 73). The black man invites Astaire onto the shoeshine stand, while Astaire sings a song to which the beat of the black man's shoe brushes provides the rhythm. The shoeshine man then dances or "moves in some enhanced shuffle completely around the stand, . . . tracing a circle around Astaire" as if enclosing him in a space of shamanistic magic (*Philosophy*, 75).[5] Astaire responds by leaping over the head of the shoeshine man and dancing a frenzied, feverish, "lunging and reeling" sequence as he repeats the words "'Shoe shine; shine on my shoes; I've got a shoe shine; a shoe shine'" (*Philosophy*, 75). In the end, Astaire has rediscovered his dance and his voice (his language) through the medium of the black man who serves (as does Bo Jangles in the blackface number in *Swing Time*) to allow Astaire both to pay tribute to and to appropriate black culture.

Of course, appropriation is the very source of the discomfort we have in witnessing this scene, and it led at least one critic to include this sequence in a study of white America's prohibiting full equality to African Americans by the plundering of black culture and talent. Cavell objects on the grounds of close analysis of the scene, which he convincingly describes (with illustrative stills) as "specifically . . . about this painful and potentially deadly irony of the white praise of a black culture whose very terms of praise it has appropriated" (*Philosophy*, 69). At the end of the dance, in fact, Astaire departs from the black man, holding out his hands in a gesture of longing or "beckoning" (*Philosophy*, 81). Admittedly, the image is one of pathos, and Cavell acknowledges as much. He goes on to ask, however, how that makes Astaire so different from ourselves that we dismiss the gesture as empty or judge the character (or even the actor) as insincere? After all, "his parting gesture declares that he alone cannot alter the conditions of injustice . . . and he has for himself gone on record as declaring his willingness for change, creating . . . a moment of change," as Cavell reads the scene (*Philosophy*, 81).

Therefore, the dance deserves praise and can be read, itself, as a tribute of praise to black dancing. But the paradox remains. To praise black dancing in the way he does is for Astaire to engage in appropriation, to be sure, but, even worse, it is also to indulge in "self-praise" and self-celebration at the expense of the other (the black man ends the scene on his knees, after all) (*Philosophy*, 81). Yet for all of this discomfort, Cavell insists on praising the dance: "Not everything has happened in the Arcade, but something has; it is my judgment that enough has happened there to warrant our consent to the justice of it, that it is good enough to warrant praise" (*Philosophy*, 82). His assessment leads to a further question, however. Why not be content with his own personal pleasure in the dance, his own personal conviction that it speaks to matters of justice in ways that do not compromise its aesthetic appeal? And that is the key question for the critic. Cavell's answer is the critic's answer. It won't do to rest content with the idea of individual and idiosyncratic pleasure because that is "in fact not the way the experience comes to" him or to any critic (*Philosophy*, 82). The pleasure is culturally determined and culturally significant. It is the critic's job to articulate the pleasure—not shutting down discourse or denying disagreement, but assuming the experience has meaning for all of us as a shared part of our cultural experience. "If I am to possess my own experience," Cavell concludes, "I cannot afford to cede it to my culture as my culture stands. I must find ways to insist upon it, if I find it unheard, ways to let the culture confront itself in me" (*Philosophy*, 82)

It is seldom in either the Restoration courtship or the Hollywood remarriage genre that the uncomfortable contradictions at the heart of each culture become central to the aesthetic experience in the way they do in Fred Astaire's dance. In fact, they are usually passing moments. On the screen, these contradictions manifest in the presence of black extras, such as the extras in *The Thin Man* and *It Happened One Night*, who portray workers on trains and in bus stations selling coffee and giving directions to the restrooms. On the stage, they appear in references to Jews that we recognize as part of what James Thompson has referred to as the "casual, throwaway anti-Semitism" of the early modern age.[6] Sometimes, the passing moments don't pass quickly enough to prevent our wincing as they occur. I think of two moments in *His Girl Friday* that include casually dismissive references to blacks in America—the significance of the death of a "colored" policeman to an upcoming election due to the importance of the "colored vote," and a joke involving the birth of a "pickaninny" in the backseat of a police car.[7] A similarly wince-inducing moment occurs in Behn's *Rover* when Frederick complains that women "will out-trick a Broker or a Jew" (1.2.257). It doesn't necessarily make it better that, as Peggy Thompson points out, the allusion in Behn's play alerts us to the economic stakes of courtship in this play. Most significantly, "economic motives" surround the betrothal of Florinda. She is "implicitly link[ed] with the thief, Lucetta," whose treatment of Blunt fuels a "free floating misogyny" that ultimately infects all the male characters, as demonstrated in their eagerness to attack and rape Florinda.[8] In other words, it doesn't really make it morally or ethically acceptable that *The Rover*'s casual reference to a tricky Jew is merely a means of addressing the real concern of the play: the mistreatment of women (or that the casual use of demeaning racial language in *His Girl Friday* is an avenue to concerns about class and justice and corruption among members of the white population of the film and, implicitly, of America at the time). On the contrary, these casual references are all the more troubling because they indicate a comfort with the injustice that underwrites the derisive language, even in scripts largely focused on questions of justice. In fairness, though, it must be noted that Hildy's remark on the "colored vote" is stated as a matter of fact, much as we would (and do) refer to voting blocs today in political and journalistic analysis. Oppressed minorities do, after all, have a right, a reason, and an obligation to vote as their interests dictate, and it behooves politicians to know that fact. "Pickaninny," the dismissive, demeaning word, is spoken by "Staircase Sam," already pegged as a moral lightweight in an earlier scene that shows him lurking beside the window of the press room in order to look up women's dresses as they climb the steps across the hall. And Behn, interestingly, says "Broker *or* a Jew" (my emphasis) when, as Frank Felsenstein has argued, typical "anti-Jewish prejudice" of the time made "it convenient to label *all* brokers and [stock] jobbers as Jews" (my emphasis).[9]

Still, it generally takes such delicate parsing to absolve the comedies of the Restoration stage and the films of classical Hollywood from charges of participation in "the extensive undergrowth" (to borrow Felsenstein's phrase) of anti-Semitism on the one hand and racism on the other (1). That makes it all the more interesting when prejudice becomes a featured part of a play or film text, as it does in *The Second Part of the Rover*[10] by Aphra Behn and *Sullivan's Travels*,[11] by Preston Sturges. And although neither of these texts fits into the genres at the center of this study, their treatment of stereotyping *as* stereotyping establishes the presence of a self-consciousness in each author/auteur that is important for analysis of those of their works that do make a significant contribution to generic meditations on marriage and moral perfectionism. This self-consciousness is brought to attention in highly theatrical moments that serve as scenes of cultural and generic self-interrogation in a way similar to the Fred Astaire dance number analyzed by Cavell—and not least because these moments are intended to (and do, in my case) produce reactions of aesthetic pleasure and satisfaction.

It is admittedly shocking to hear or read the language with which Behn's Fetherfool announces to his compatriots, Willmore and Beaumond, the "strangest news" that two heiresses have come to Madrid (where *The Second Part of the Rover* is set):

> Whe Lieutenant *Shift* here, tells us of two Monsters arriv'd from *Mexico*, Jews of vast fortunes, with an old Jew Uncle their Guardian; they are worth a hundred thousand pounds a piece,—Marcy upon's whe 'tis a sum able to purchase all *Flanders* again from his most Christian Majesty.
>
> (1.1.169–73)

Willmore's response indicates that he assumes that "monster" is an epithet indicating Fetherfool's xenophobia (of either Jews or Mexicans or both), for he laughs, "Ha, ha, ha, Monsters" (1.1.174). Willmore has just arrived in Madrid with Blunt and Fetherfool, but Beaumond, having been there awhile and having heard of these heiresses already, confirms their "monstrosity": "He tells you truth *Willmore*" (1.1.175). Interestingly enough (although their physicality will soon be revealed), Fetherfool continues to harp on the women's religion saying that even though he's a Justice of the Peace "and they be Jews" he would still marry one of the heiresses for her fortune (1.1.180). Indeed, he and Blunt have already concocted this plan (Blunt chastises Fetherfool for "declar[ing] our design" [1.1.182]). It is at this point that Beaumond explicitly outlines the problems any suitor will face (and makes it clear that those problems have nothing to do with religion or nationality): "One of them is so little, and so deform'd, 'tis thought she is not capable of Marriage; and the other is so huge an overgrown Gyant, no man dares venture on her" (1.1.184–86). Willmore is now intrigued, although his next remark reflects his continued moral befuddlement: "Prithee let's go see 'em; what do they pay for going in?" (1.1.187). He clearly thinks they are come to Madrid to entertain, like the "freaks" on exhibit at home in England every summer at Bartholomew Fair.[12] But Fetherfool sets him straight: "I'de have you know they are Monsters of Quality" (1.1.188). All of this discussion, from the worry over physical mating to the notion of entertainment of a freak-show variety to the plan of Fetherfool and Blunt to win the Jewish guardian's approval and marry the women, treats the "monsters" as objects to be enjoyed, appropriated, claimed. Then, suddenly, the most surprising information of all is shared, information that radically shifts our perspective from how the other characters feel about the "monsters" to how the "monsters" feel about them. Lieutenant Shift tells Willmore, "The Gyant, Sir, is in love with me, the Dwarf with Ensign *Hunt*" (1.1.191–92). And the love, we find, is reciprocated.

It's interesting to track Willmore's responses in this initial scene, for they must in a sense model the expected reactions of Behn's audience. First he laughs at Fetherfool's description of outsiders as "monsters," then, once their physical natures are revealed, assumes a bit of Smithfield entertainment is waiting in the wings, and then, before audience members can wipe the smirks off their faces at Fetherfool's phrase "Monsters of Quality," discovers that two of the play's sensible characters are seriously intending to court these women—and that things have proceeded all the way to "love." In a few speeches, the audience has been taken from laughing dismissively at stereotypes to reframing these unlikely characters as the objects of desire. Shift even says that if he and Hunt can "manage matters it may prove lucky" (1.1.193). Lucky? To marry a dwarf and a giantess? To marry Jewish Mexicans? How so?

By implicitly linking the "monsters," the "New World," and the fate of all the women in the play, Behn offers a critique of male, European prerogative, as Heidi Hutner has argued.[13] As in *The Rover*, in this play, women's desires count, though, as will be the case in *The Luckey Chance* as well as in *The Country Wife* and *The Way of the World*, it is largely male homosociality—specifically the competitiveness between men—that drives the plot. The primary dynamic at this point in the century (1681 being the height of the Exclusion Crisis, with James himself in exile) is antagonism between "cit" and courtier. If for no other reason than that, Willmore, who has been wanting a good laugh ever since Fetherfool came on the scene to announce the presence of the monsters, decides to use the bits and pieces of information gleaned ("I am sure *Fetherfool* and *Blunt* have some wise design upon these two Monsters") to set up an "extravagant" joke (1.1.215–17). The first audience had no doubt been wondering how Blunt was to be the source of derisive laughter in this play as he had been in the first *Rover*. What could top a dousing in a gutter better than a ridiculous courtship doubled—Blunt wooing the Dwarf with flowery language, Fetherfool frightened by the role he's agreed to play, and Willmore having his "share of . . . [the] jest"? (1.1.230) Willmore dons the garb of a mountebank, enlists the help of those staples of commedia, Harlequin and Scaramouche, and the farce commences.

Behn not only lets her audience see the "monsters," she gives those characters a good bit to say as well. Act 3, Scene 1, in which the Giant and the Dwarf attended by Shift and Harlequin are courted by Blunt and Fetherfool, is highly entertaining. The two "monsters," however, are not assigned language or business, which would suggest they play their roles for laughs. Indeed, as will be the case in Sturges's *Sullivan's Travels*, expected monstrosity, examined closely, turns out to be humanity, after all. We already have an inkling of the women's characters from what we have heard of them in Act 1 wherein we are informed that it is the *women*, not Shift and Hunt, who wish to be transformed physically into bodies more nearly the size of their potential mates. Shift has agreed to enlist an advertised mountebank's skills for this purpose (and therefore ingratiated himself with the women), but he is quick to agree to Willmore's trick on Blunt—which means no "real" mountebank is ever employed. It would seem, therefore, that Shift and Hunt are very little concerned with the size of their intended spouses. Blunt in Act 3 seems similarly undaunted by the prospect of marriage with the sister he calls "my little diminutive Mistriss, my small Epitome of Womankind" (3.1.53–54), and, later, "my little spark of a Diamond" (3.1.105), but Fetherfool is intimidated: "What, does the Cavalier think I'le devour him?" the Giantess glumly asks (3.1.46).

Shift brings in a ladder so that Fetherfool can run up and kiss his mistress, but the Giantess has a hard time feigning interest in this fop whom she accuses (rightly, as it happens) of "Court[ing] my Fortune, not my Beauty" (3.1.73–4). Shift has to whisper to her, aside, to "dissemble, or you betray your Love for us" (3.1.81)—a rather touching evidence of collusion, although she continues to be "peevish" toward Fetherfool (3.1.87). She complains that she'd rather "meet . . . [her] Match, and keep up the first Race of Man intire," but because that doesn't seem possible, she will "be new Created" by the mountebank's potion—and then "expect a wiser Lover" (3.1.83–86), obviously meaning Shift. Fetherfool pouts, "'tis not done like a Monster of Honour, when a man has set his heart upon you, to cast him off" (3.1.88–90). The Dwarf is a better actress, although Blunt, at least compared to his partner in crime, is gifted with "delicate Speech" and "Concise Wit" (3.1.58–59). Once she determines that religion is not at issue with the suitors (Fetherfool claims that as a nation England "stands . . . little upon Religion" (3.1.99), and Blunt goes even further to say he was "born a Jew" [3/1/105]), she, like her sister, promises to "compleat . . . [her] Beauty . . . to appear the more grateful to you" (3.1.107–8). The Giantess has the last word for both suitors: "Well, Seigniors, since you come with our Uncles liking, we give ye leave to hope, hope—and be happy" (3.1.116–17), and, with that, she, her sister, and Harlequin leave the stage, allowing Willmore (dressed as the mountebank) to negotiate with Blunt and Fetherfool as to the form in which each suitor would like his intended to be recast. They both opt for the look of a fifteen-year-old "Damzel" (3.1.128), although Blunt would prefer the marriage before the transformation just in case, as in Killigrew's *Thomaso*, Behn's source material, his future wife be "boyled away in the "Baths of Reformation" (3.1.129–30). As they dither and postpone the operation, a new gag is introduced in the form of a giant man. "Good Lord!" exclaims Fetherfool. "I wonder what Religion he's of" (3.1.160–61). Willmore is not in on this joke—for it is Hunt, on the shoulders of another man, who is asking to be led to the ladies. When Willmore points out that the door won't accommodate him, the Giant breaks in two—a doublet and a pair of britches—and goes in, he says, "at twice." Willmore is left to explain this enchantment to Blunt and Fetherfool as best he can, grumbling to himself "these damn'd Rascals will spoil it all by too gross an imposition on the fools" (3.1.173–74). For good measure, he assures Fetherfool that the Inquisition will put a stop to any marriage between the Giant and the Giantess "for fear of a Race of Giants" which would be "worse than the Invasion of the *Moors*, or the *French*" (3.1.178–80). With this comment, Blunt and Fetherfool are dismissed, and Willmore, still in disguise, moves on to pursue his own romantic desires (his love of "the slavish mercenary Prostitute," La Nuche [3.1.197]).

The Giantess has another scene in Act 5 where she is discovered "asleep" onstage, waiting for her lover, Shift, to arrive. Confusion abounds, and she winds up leaving the stage with Fetherfool, mistaking him for Shift. Harlequin dances them offstage. When they all reappear, the Lieutenant is with his Giantess and the Ensign, his Dwarf. Blunt and Fetherfool discover, as Willmore puts it, they can be "couzen'd as well as . . . [their] Neighbours" (5.1.550–51). "Who the Devil wou'd have look'd for Jilting in such Hobgoblins?" Blunt muses (5.1.520). Those Hobgoblins, however, have the last laugh, for they are successfully married at play's end to the men they love, and although to be sure this resolution is simply the conclusion of the subplot, it does resonate with the main plot that has Willmore pursuing the "whore" La Nuche, and the two of them deciding at the play's end to live and love without marriage and without money. Willmore pledges allegiance to "Love and Gallantry," whereas Fetherfool vows to return to England, "take the Covenant, get a Sequestrators place, grow rich, and defie all Cavaliering" (5.1.610–11; 604–605). He will dwindle into a full-fledged cit, in other words!

What is praiseworthy about the scenes involving the Jewish heiresses is that in creating the farce, Behn both pays homage to all the comic tricks and devices she has inherited from the conventions and traditions of her craft—including stereotypes that she then manages to subvert—*and* persuades her audience to side with humanity in the form of "monsters" and (in the main plot) in the form of a "whore."[14] That she does so at the expense of another, newer stereotype (the cit) is less praiseworthy, although fully predictable. Comedy works that way, after all. It always has; it always will. A joke needs a butt, but the butt has a way of eventually demanding his due, having his say. It won't be many years before Behn herself is reconsidering the cit who by 1686, as we will see in *The Luckey Chance*, is no laughing matter.

First, however, I want to briefly consider Sturges's similar meditation on stereotype in *Sullivan's Travels*, which, like *The Second Part of the Rover*, parades comic clichés in order to investigate their cultural power and their aesthetic purpose. *Sullivan's Travels* begins by announcing its concern with filmmaking and genre. The opening scene turns out to be a scene in a movie that Sullivan, or Sully, the director, and his producers are watching. The screen shows a fight on the top of a railway car, which Sully interprets for the producers and for us as the camera pulls back to reveal him and the others watching a screen: "You see? You see the symbolism of it? Capital and Labor destroy each other. It teaches a lesson, a moral lesson." The lines are meant to provoke a laugh, and they do.[15] Sullivan (played by the wonderfully earnest Joel McCrea) is known for his lightweight comedies, *Hey Hey in the Hayloft*, *Ants in Your Pants*, but he wants to make a serious film, a film about suffering. He is concerned. He is sincere. And he is determined to pursue his film project, which has the working title of *O, Brother Where Art Thou?* When his producers in an effort to dissuade him point out that he has never experienced hardship (never, in Boethian terms, "been forsaken by Fortune"), he decides to dress as a poor man and go in pursuit of tribulation (an inversion, obviously, of the typical comic pursuit).

For the first third of the film, Sully is stuck with happiness. He hitches a ride and winds up smack back in the middle of Hollywood. He takes on manual labor and finds himself petted and pampered by the woman for whom he works. (He is also pursued a bit too adamantly. He does end up doused in a rain barrel as he makes his escape from her!). Down to his last dime, he meets up with a girl, "The Girl" in the cast list (played by Veronica Lake), who buys him breakfast and becomes his traveling companion. Together in the middle part of the film, they do see a lot of unhappiness and suffer a little themselves, although with the luxury of knowing that when they've had enough, they can go back to Sully's Hollywood mansion—interestingly, and self-reflexively, Joel McCrea's actual home. But Sullivan's sincerity will eventually be punished, after all. In a parting gesture to the tramps and hoboes who let him see what penury and privation are really like, Sullivan decides to give out five-dollar bills. His naïve sanctimoniousness is rewarded with violence, and he is robbed and left for dead; he suffers a concussion that deprives him of his memory for quite some time. While in that state, he attacks an official of the railroad, an act which he considers self-defense, but which the law regards as aggression. The result is that he finds himself in a labor camp in some unspecified part of the South.

Here, he finds true hardship. He is beaten and berated. Sentenced to hard labor, he suffers when he's being treated well. When he fails to toe the line, his punishment is an afternoon in a sweatbox so small, even the viewer feels claustrophobic and parched. It is hard to believe that anyone could survive such heat, thirst, and airlessness, let alone be able to go to the movies afterwards. But, that's what happens. Sully, along with the other prisoners, is treated to a night at the "picture show." It is a scene of remarkable texture and irony in that it chronicles the role of film in the renewal of Sullivan as a character, even as it elaborates the uncomfortable facts of both the film conventions and the social realities that define the times.

Early in the movie, when Sullivan begins his search for trouble, he is followed by an entourage of "handlers" designated to protect the producers' investment in the valuable commodity (the director) who is to their minds unaccountably putting himself at risk by dressing in rags and living a hobo's existence. The staff follows him in a large van to which they refer as a "land-yacht." Sully hitches a ride with a kid in what appears to be a homemade hot-rod which is small and fast and which the bulky land-yacht has trouble tailing. In the chase sequence that follows, a white policeman ends up with mud on his face (blackface), a black cook ends up with vanilla cake batter covering his face (whiteface), and the passengers in the yacht writhe and cavort in an over-the-top effort to seem discombobulated by the speed and the jerkiness of the van in which they ride, calling attention, in other words, to the way film produces its various "special (or not-so-special) effects." The allusions to racist film stereotypes, the pilfering of black culture (blackface) and the erasure of black identity (whiteface) are discomfiting in this scene—and meant to be so, I would argue. They are designed to make us think about film's encoding of ideologies, to make us question the illusory effect of cinematic realism. The later scene, in which Sully and the other prisoners see the movie, recalls the stereotypes and the farcical exaggeration through the choice of film (a Mickey Mouse cartoon, replete with cartoon violence and mayhem) as well as in the contrastive ennoblement of the black characters who host the film screening in their church's sanctuary.

Ella Shohat and Robert Stam describe *Sullivan's Travels* as a "summa of cinematic genres" in which we can observe the "very distinct roles" reserved for blacks in 1940s Hollywood comedy, documentary, and musical genres (all controlled by white producers and directors, of course):

> In the slapstick land-yacht sequences, the Black waiter conforms to the prototype of the happy-go-lucky servant/buffoon; he is sadistically "painted" with whiteface pancake batter, and excluded from the charmed circle of White sociality. In the documentary-inflected sequences showing masses of unemployed, meanwhile, Blacks are present but voiceless, very much in the left-communist tradition of class reductionism; they appear as anonymous victims of economic hard times, with no racial specificity to their oppression.[16]

In the final sequence involving black actors, however, Sturges "complicates conventional representation" (210). He desegregates the black musical and structures the scenes as one in which "Blacks exercise charity toward Whites" (210). In fact, the scene acquires complex resonance "when congregation and prisoners sing 'Let My People Go,'" in that "the music, the images, and the editing forge a triadic link between three oppressed groups: Blacks, the prisoners, and the Biblical Israelites in the times of the Pharaoh, here assimilated to the cruel warden" (210). In this scene, Sturges reflects self-awareness of the way "racial attitudes are generically mediated" (210), and like Aphra Behn in her overdetermined use of "monsters" he subverts stereotype even as he invokes it.

Sturges goes further to momentarily direct our attention to the world offscreen, to cultural practices we may never have witnessed, but practices we know exist. As the pastor and his congregants prepare for the prisoners' entrance, a white sheet is lowered from the ceiling. The preacher announces in his stentorian tone, "Well, brothers and sisters, once again we're going to have a little entertainment. I don't guess I have to tell you what it is. The sheet kind of gives it away." Given the setting and the milieu, sheets could be assumed to mean something quite sinister to the black congregation, a point exploited by the Coen Brothers in their tribute to this film, *O Brother Where Art Thou?* in a layered scene that presents a Klan rally as a choreographed sequence that itself becomes a tribute to classical Hollywood film. The intervention of Ulysses, Delmar, and Pete to save Tommy from the lynch mob is a clear parody of the scene in *The Wizard of Oz* in which the Scarecrow, Tin Man, and Cowardly Lion employ a similar ruse against the Wicked Witch of the West on Dorothy's behalf. In both instances, in the Sturges film as well as in the Coens' movie, the uneasy marriage of homage and critique, comedy and condemnation, is allowed to exist as unresolved and unresolvable.[17]

Sully's attempt to make movies matter is not rejected in the end, although Sully himself has decided to return to a kind of mindless comedy that just aims for laughter. As he says—still earnest, still sincere, but with newfound respect for comic films: "There's a lot to be said for making people laugh! Did you know that's all some people have? It isn't much but it's better than nothing in this cockeyed caravan! Boy!" This pronouncement, the last words spoken in the film, is followed by images of laughing faces, images that recall the faces of the prisoners in the church responding to Mickey Mouse and remind us of Sully's renewal (at the movie, he had turned to his neighbor in astonishment, asking "am I laughing?"). But the images are also over the top, like the flailing passengers in the land-yacht. And the laughers are laughing at nothing, seeming almost demented in their jollity, their mindless and objectless enjoyment.

One way of reading the ending of *Sullivan's Travels* is to conclude that Sully doesn't need to choose between "socially relevant films" and "comic films." As Sturges has so pointedly illustrated in this very film, a movie can serve both ends. It can make us laugh, and it can make us think. It can hold our limitations and wrongs up to ridicule, and it can make us want to do better, to be nobler, to strive for more. But the ending is also an admission that a movie can do only so much in pursuit of justice. At least partly because of the film's stated moral, Schocket sees *Sullivan's Travels* as "politically evasive,"[18] but most commentators find the ending, although problematic, potentially ironic. As Martha Nochimson says, "the film ends on a riptide of laughter, which may or may not trivialize the serious issues it has probed."[19] R. L. Rutsky and Justin Wyatt have noted that "*Sullivan's Travels* . . . is quite critical of the capitalist social system," although it also "recognizes [and celebrates] its own liability to fun"[20] In the end, its main job is to please the audience. So, another way of reading the rather disturbing image of the laughing audience is as Sturges's indictment of filmgoers as the reason for generic limitations and distortions and wrongs. In this gesture, he is very like Aphra Behn who uses her prologue and epilogue to condemn the taste and the politics of the times that have reduced her to providing a farce-laden script full of "fantastic wit" rather than the satire and sense she'd prefer to offer. Nancy Copeland has discussed the Prologue's reference to "*Fantastick Wit*" as signaling a world that is out of kilter and monstrous, although she also notes that the play is "too heterogenous to be read univocally"; if "'freedom from constraints of patrilineal responsibility'" is celebrated in the play's portrayal of exile, it is also true that Willmore's behavior is "more outrageous than ever," suggesting some discomfort with "freedom from responsibility."[21] How is the critic (particularly the critic who has enjoyed the comedies) to respond—not only to these self-reflexive comedies that at least interrogate generic conventions but to more standard fare in which we are not invited to see discordances as generically driven or audience-induced but as artistically embraced?

The intersection of medium and message clearly has moral implications for these two writers, a topic they also address (although without specific focus on larger cultural questions of injustice and prejudice) in two works that can be said to fully participate in the related genres I'm considering in this study. Each of these texts announces a preoccupation with "luck." In *The Lady Eve*,[22] a presumption of luckiness or good fortune naturally attends the affairs of Jean and her cardsharp father (although cheating also helps!), and of course *The Luckey Chance* foregrounds "luck" and "chance" in the most obvious way possible, the title of the play.[23] There is a sense of gambling and risk in all of the texts of each genre, but these two go further than the others to address what philosophers Bernard Williams and Thomas Nagel have termed "moral luck"—a concept that complicates not only the pursuit of moral perfectionism, but also the notion of moral action itself. Further, in both texts there is overt attention to the art of making texts and the limitations and possibilities that define such artistry, a fact that broadens the concern with morality—and moral luck—to the genres themselves.

As human beings, we are capable of moral behavior. But should we be praised or blamed for our choices (including our aesthetic choices) for actions, productions, and consequences beyond our control? After all, luck (good or bad) often intervenes to deprive us of our intended goals (good or bad) or to direct our behavior (good or bad) without our consent. Does that matter morally? Kant thought it did not, but Williams and Nagel disagree. Dana K. Nelkin offers a useful summary of the various kinds of "luck" that according to Thomas Nagel may compromise moral choice or affect a consideration of guilt and innocence:[24]

1 "Resultant luck is luck in the way things turn out." This kind of luck involves the various possible effects of moral choice. So, to take an example from *The Luckey Chance*: Sir Feeble intends that Belmour be executed for murder. He sets the action in motion, but the intended effect does not come to pass. Do we consider Sir Feeble to be as morally culpable as we would had Belmour been executed as intended? In general, our laws suggest otherwise. Attempted murder (via a hitman, for example) is considered a serious crime, but not as serious as murder. Yet in the case of *The Luckey Chance* it was only luck (resultant luck) that kept the would-be murderer's intentions from becoming fact. Another kind of "resultant luck" has to do with a wrong committed in pursuit of a greater good that had the good not been realized would deserve a condemnation that success mitigates. The example given by Nelkin is from Bernard Williams: that of "a somewhat fictionalized" Gauguin who leaves his family to pursue his art. Because he achieved highly in his artistic pursuit, we tend to judge his treatment of family with

more leniency than we would had he failed. In *The Lady Eve*, Jean cons Hopsy into marriage by pretending to be Lady Eve Sidgwick. She teaches Hopsy a much-needed lesson in love and forgiveness, and although he suffers, he learns this important lesson. We forgive her deception because it is necessary for his enlightenment. What if, however, he had learned nothing? Would her masquerade strike us as a valid moral choice? Resultant luck makes it so; resultant luck could have made it otherwise, as well.

2   "Circumstantial luck is luck in the circumstances in which one finds oneself." This kind of luck can also make a difference in our evaluation of moral choice. One might hold racist views, for example, that one has no opportunity to express through action or choice (Nelkin offers as an example Nazis who lived in Argentina in the 1930s and did not participate in the atrocities carried out in Europe). With fictional texts, it is difficult to apply this example of "moral luck," but we can do so to the authors who reflect or reject the prejudices of their times in ways that must be adjudicated for moral evaluation. Is Gayman's insulting analogy "insatiable as a brokering Jew" the result of the circumstances of Behn's existence (casual anti-Semitism being the order of the day) or does it express her own deep-seated prejudice? Is Sturges's solidly white cast in *The Lady Eve* reflective of his own biases or the result of circumstantial luck relating to the date of his birth and the conditions of the industry in which he worked?

3   "Constitutive luck is luck in who one is, or in the traits and dispositions that one has." Here, we can apply the test to fictional characters as the author ascribes traits to them in the beginning of the text and, in the interest of coherence, must not violate the basic template without cause. Is a character to be held responsible for decisions driven by basic personality? Do we fault Hopsy for being so close-minded and prim? Or, do we applaud him for overcoming his basic prudishness and myopia in the end and accepting that there are things he doesn't know—and, more importantly, doesn't want to know? Do we applaud Julia for her decision to remain married and do we understand her choice to be driven by her basic character traits which include a sense of social responsibility, personal dignity, fairness, and the virtue we are told she possesses? Or do we fault her for marrying someone she did not love for his wealth and betraying someone to whom she'd given her vow for his poverty, all in violation of the virtue she is said to possess?

4   Causal luck refers to the way, in the words of Nagel, "'one is determined by antecedent circumstances.'"[25] This category is important because it introduces the notion of "free will" which is, in regard to these texts, the central problem. *The Lady Eve* invokes the notion with its very reference to the originary myth of Eden. Without engaging in theological debate as to whether or not the original "fall" was predestined or even occurred, once Adam and Eve ate the apple, the story goes, they (or more specifically Eve) doomed mankind forevermore to a state of sinfulness. Secular determinisms

ask the same question. Do we really have moral choice in our actions? Aren't we driven by biological, psychological, social, behavioral, etc., forces beyond our control? And by virtue of things beyond our control, aren't we by definition doomed to make the wrong choices most of the time? Even if we make the right choices, are these moral acts or predetermined behavioral patterns? The question (in the Edenic sense) hovers over Sturges's and Behn's texts as well as the milieus in which they produced their works. It is this question, in fact, that is central to *The Luckey Chance* and *The Lady Eve*. Is the Fall fortunate? Is luck a matter of chance, after all?

Moral absolutism, of course, clarifies moral responsibility, as both Behn's Belmour and Sturges's Jean discover to their detriment. Belmour is exiled because in his world, "rigid Laws . . . put no Difference / 'Twixt fairly killing in in my own Defence, / And Murders bred by Drunken Arguments, / Whores, or the mean Revenges of a Coward" (1.1.5–8). And Jean finds herself jilted because Hopsy discovers she's one of (in Mugsy's words) "a gang of sharpies." Hopsy says very little on this discovery, but clearly the knowledge that Jean is less innocent than he assumed her to be causes him to reject her as too guilty to love. Moral absolutism, however, is not condoned by either text—indeed, both genres eschew such oversimplification as antithetical to the kind of relationship (in Cavell's terminology, the pursuit of moral perfectionism) at the heart of the narratives. These two texts are unique, however, in highlighting the problem from the outset of their narratives.

Moral luck exists in each text, but in neither does such luck preclude moral choice. In reviewing the moral decisions of the central characters in each narrative, we can see the negotiations between circumstance, result, character, and cause on the one hand and free will and self-direction on the other. I'll begin with *The Luckey Chance*. This play features two supremely immoral characters—Sir Feeble Fainwou'd (an Alderman) and Sir Cautious Fulbank (a Banker), both old cits who interfere with the course of true love by marrying young women who have exchanged lovers' vows with men of their own age and of their own choice. If that isn't a bad enough crime, both older men consolidate their power over their women by lying, concealing evidence, extorting money, and, in the case of Sir Cautious, actually prostituting his wife for three hundred pounds. Both old men are versions of the "cit," a comic butt familiar to the Restoration stage (and played by two of the foremost comic actors of the time—Antony Leigh and James Nokes, respectively), yet Sir Feeble and Sir Cautious exceed the cit's usual meanness, jealousy, and sexual silliness (we'll see a more typical version in *The Country Wife*'s Jasper Fidget) by manipulating circumstances not only to secure the women in question but to harm irreparably the young men who stand as rivals. Furthermore, these cits are, as Nancy Copeland has put it, "securely in control while the young men are seemingly at their mercy."[26] Indeed, "not only have they stolen the young men's women, but they have also effectively erased the identities of their opponents" (69).

As a consequence, these two old cits are not as easy to combat as is typical in Restoration comedy, and besting them involves moral compromise on the parts of both "genteel libertine[s]," that is, Belmour and Gayman. As a result, Copeland observes, "despite his sexual potency, the genteel libertine no longer offers a vigorous alternative to the embourgeoisement of society, but is contaminated by the values of his opponent" (77).

In the play's prehistory, Belmour killed a man in a duel shortly after the passage of "The Act against Duelling" (he is, he reveals, "the first Transgressor" [1.1.246]), and for that he was exiled. Pardons, as Janet Todd notes, were not easy but were not impossible to come by, and Sir Feeble has seen to it that one is produced.[27] But Feeble's aim is not to license Belmour's return. Instead, he procures and then withholds Belmour's pardon, as he explains to his "nephew" Francis, for purely selfish reasons:

> what dost think 'twas in Kindness to him? no, you Fool, I got his Pardon my self, that no body else should have it, so that if he gets any Body to speak to his Majesty for it, his Majesty crys he has granted it; but for want of my Appearance, he's defunct, trusd up, hang'd *Francis*.
>
> (3.1.67–71)

In an example of "moral luck" (similar to such an example in a later film, *His Girl Friday*), the disguise that Belmour's lack of a pardon has prompted him to assume is that of this very nephew, Francis Fainwou'd, so the dastardly old cit has inadvertently revealed his nefarious plot to the intended victim. We don't have a Mr. Pettibone dropping into the script to thwart city corruption by his comic country simplicity, as in *His Girl Friday*, but we do have a similar nod to the "spirit of comedy," a sobriquet bestowed on Pettibone by Cavell (*PH* 184), in this lucky chance. But it is also a generically motivated detail. After all, cits (even powerful ones) are basically buffoons, so their most threatening gestures are doomed to fail in a comic plot—and laughter is the retribution they suffer, not the direr punishment they would suffer for success. Genre, as well as moral luck, would have it so.

Belmour's moral luck is somewhat less fortunate, as far as his character is concerned. Yes, he can proceed toward happiness with Leticia without true danger of losing his life (as he knows the pardon exists and who has it), but in his trickery and imposture, he loses some of the moral edge his virtuous character should have over his foe. As Kathleen Leicht has observed, Belmour "gets possession of the pardon by resorting to the very tactics Sir Feeble has used against him—deceit and disguise. Behn's play shows the corruption of the established representatives of authority . . . and shows that the younger Belmour will have to match their corruption to be able literally to live in England."[28] And, indeed, all of the virtuous characters in *The Luckey Chance* find themselves somewhat unlucky in that regard, often teetering on a tightrope slung between innocence and guilt. Leticia, for example, truly loves Belmour and considers herself his wife as they have exchanged private vows and have planned to wed prior to his banishment. She has been brought to agree to marry again only because she has been told that Belmour was hanged at the Hague for a crime he committed afterwards. Nevertheless, she accepts moral culpability when she and Belmour meet, and she realizes that she has been deceived in the report of his death. When Belmour complains that she too easily threw their love away, too quickly resolved to marry during a period which should have been devoted to mourning, she concedes, "I will not justify my hated Crime." She does invoke circumstances that perhaps mitigate her culpability: "But Oh remember I was poor and helpless. / And much reduc'd, and much impos'd upon," lines whose poignancy is emphasized by their having been written in blank verse (2.2.48–50). Belmour accepts this answer, weeping, "Want compell'd thee to this wretched Marriage—did it?" (2.2.51) Still, we as readers or theater audience may be left with some discomfort at Leticia's hasty capitulation to pressure—especially as she herself seems eager to take a moral stance as if in restitution. Her current union, she declares, is "not a Marriage, since my *Belmour* lives"; therefore, "the Consummation were Adultery" (2.2.52–3). Although obstacles abound (at this point, neither Belmour nor she knows of the pardon), she is fully determined to avoid consummation of her marriage to Sir Feeble and to share Belmour's life and "humblest Fortune," there or anywhere "o're the World" (2.2.62, 61).

Leticia lives up to her description in the "Dramatis Personae" as "vertuous," but because of the contrastive example of Julia also a virtuous character (described in the "Dramatis Personae" as "honest and generous"), we come to understand that predisposition or constitutive moral luck is not always enough when circumstances press against virtue and morality. In the scene just examined, Belmour asserts that Leticia's "native Modesty" will protect her from Sir Feeble's amorous advances while his "Industry" procures them freedom to live as man and wife (2.2.70), but Leticia herself understands the need for firmer purpose, clarity of vision, and unswerving devotion to a course of action despite its dangers and inconveniences. This determination is not presented as a matter of luck. The only moral luck Leticia has (and it is an important fact to consider) is that Belmour returns and identifies himself to her on the day of her marriage, before evening renders a complicated situation even more complex.

What would she have done had he arrived a day later? As I said earlier, that question is moot, in a sense. She is a character, not a person. Still, as Bernard Williams demonstrates in his discussion of Anna Karenina, although it is not possible to say what a fictional character *would* do in a hypothetical instance, it is quite legitimate to discuss the significance of the choices they *do* make in the text.[29] Leticia's immediate moral decision to regard her vow to Belmour as binding, and to work with him to invalidate her marriage to Sir Feeble, indicates will, volition, desire that are under her own control. Further, in the end, she behaves (as does Julia, as a matter of fact) with compassion and kindness to the old man who has usurped the rightful prerogative of Belmour. When Belmour's "ghost" frightens Sir Feeble into relinquishing his claim on Leticia, the young woman's happiness is tinged with compassion: "Blest be this kind Release, and yet me-thinks it grieves me to consider how the poor Old man is frighted" (5.1.101–2). Indeed, Sir Feeble's transformation following the appearance of the "ghost" is so complete that even Belmour is moved to empathy. The old man forgives the young people for their "couzening" and moreover promises to give Leticia her "Jewels" and Belmour his "Pardon," as he puts it, "so you give me mine" (5.2.350; 352–53). Belmour is touched: "You are so generous Sir, that 'tis almost with grief I receive the Blessing of *Leticia*" (5.2.354–55). This plot ends with redemption all around, the earlier moral taints and (on Sir Feeble's part) worse, absolved in mutual forgiveness.

Julia, like Leticia, conceives of herself as a moral agent. She evidences remorse for her choice to marry a man she did not love, although she may have had compelling reasons. She tells the "vertuous" Diana, designed by her father for the fop Bearjest but in love with Leticia's brother Bredwell: "Let our two Fates [Julia's and Sir Cautious's] warn your approaching one" (4.1.249). Although she acknowledges earlier that her marriage to Sir Cautious was "forc'd," even so, she refuses to blame circumstances (luck) for her fate: "Had I but kept my sacred Vows to *Gayman* / How happy had I been—how prosperous he!" (1.2.31; 33). As Anita Pacheco notes of this speech, "the woman who starts out sounding like a victim ends up sounding like the culprit. Julia appears in this speech to claim that not even forced marriage excuses troth-breaking and disloyalty."[30] The Julia/Gayman plot is, however, more morally problematic than either the plot featuring Leticia or that surrounding Diana. Both Julia and Gayman employ disguises that result in scenes of farcical confusion that are highly theatrical and entertaining, but that also raise serious philosophical questions about identity, responsibility, and justice. Is Gayman disloyal to Julia when he agrees to meet a woman who promises to give him jewels and money in exchange, perhaps, for "a little sex" (to borrow language from *Sullivan's Travels*)? I tend to read the scene as one of coitus interruptus, although many other critics (perhaps following Catherine Gallagher's influential reading) read the encounter as an adulterous one.[31] There are moral questions either way. I will begin by elaborating those emanating from my reading. Although Gayman is interrupted before the encounter can be consummated, had he not been, would he have failed or passed Julia's test? The woman in disguise, after all, is Julia herself. Yet Gayman never perceives that fact. What does it say about identity, knowledge, and love that, at receipt of the invitation, he is convinced the woman is old and haggard, that she has summoned him because her appetites and her decaying form are at odds? Like his landlady, he thinks, this woman must be so unattractive that she resorts to disguise and subterfuge to satisfy desires she can no longer raise in another. For Julia, the fact that Gayman can be so deluded despite having held her in his arms is an affront. Yet her point had been to test his commitment to her. Does his failure to consummate the encounter demonstrate that commitment or does his inability to recognize his partner as the woman he loves controvert the deep emotion and desire he claims to have for her? Or, if he is lying to spare Julia's feelings, is his lie a fault or a virtue? If the couple does, in fact, consummate their relationship at this point, is the consummation a true one given Gayman's ignorance that it was Julia he bedded? Given that the only other person present thought Julia was an old woman and not Sir Cautious's wife (or even a young woman and not Sir Cautious's wife), has anyone been cuckolded by this act? Does Sir Cautious have grounds for complaint?

Julia herself is not so easily gulled when Gayman pretends to be her elderly husband. As Gayman explains, "my Excess of Love—betray'd the Cheat" (5.2.242). "Ay, ay, that was my Fear—" (5.2.243), Sir Cautious abashedly admits. But other questions arise: Is Julia an adulteress, as she weepingly asserts? Or is Gayman correct when he tells her, "You are an innocent Adulteress. / It was the feeble Husband you enjoy'd / In cold Imagination and no more, / Shyly you turn'd away—and faintly resign'd" (5.2.236–40)? Or, does Sir Cautious's remark in aside, "Hum—did she so—[?]," indicate that his addresses are not usually met with such submission (5.2.241)? Are we to think that Julia recognized and accepted her lover on a subconscious level as long as she could maintain the pretense that in doing so she did no wrong (i.e., until "Excess of Love" clearly revealed her bedmate to be someone other than her husband)? Or are her protests signs of remorse for a sin she willingly committed, knowing full well all along who came to her bed that evening? Is there a difference between guilty and innocent adultery? If one thinks one is making love to one's husband, is it adultery if that turns out not to be the case? (This question will arise at the end of *The Lady Eve* as well.) How far does moral culpability or responsibility extend? And, finally, how can one make just decisions in an unjust world?

Interestingly, although Julia, like Leticia, is a sincere lover, she is also a kind wife. Sir Cautious, like his brother cit Sir Feeble, learns a valuable lesson about the difference between youth and age, love and power—and he responds with as generous a gesture as the alderman offered. He says to Gayman: "if I dye, Sir—I bequeath my Lady to you—with my whole Estate" (5.2.386–87). This arrangement may seem out of keeping with the theme of moral perfectionism, but, as Cavell has argued, the texts that treat such themes are concerned most fundamentally with building a perfect society. The moral perfectionism pursued by the couple at the center of the comedies of remarriage, for example, is simply illustrative of foundational attitudes, values, and beliefs that should/will transform American society. Many times (most often, in fact) the texts treat members of the ruling class only—the rich and wellborn and leisured. But in some instances (in *It Happened One Night*, for example), there is a deliberate effort to examine the relationship between classes. We can argue that point with regard to *The Lady Eve*, but *Sullivan's Travels* offers a handier way of accessing Sturges's view—one we have seen already in the disastrous consequences of the lead character's effort to understand those who are not of his class. The usual effect of the comedies of remarriage in terms of class relations is therefore, as Cavell points out, snobbery.

Generally, the treatment of the newly rich merchant class on the Restoration stage is snobbish in the same way—which makes *The Luckey Chance* an interesting exception (almost anticipating the sentimental treatment of the cit in Sheridan—although certainly not the ennoblement as will occur in George Lillo and Richard Cumberland). The cits, although clearly wrong to marry (or seek to marry) young women whose appetites they cannot satisfy and whose curiosities they cannot prevent, are treated in this play less as individually flawed characters than as products of a flawed system in which money equals power and power equals control over women's sexuality and knowledge. But to assert control is not necessarily to have control, and *The Luckey Chance* quite clearly argues for the avidity of woman's desires as well as the efficacy of her designs (especially in the character of Julia, although both Leticia and Diana bolster the argument as well). Playwrighting is another manifestation of desire and design, as Behn makes clear in her Preface, both blurring and heightening gender distinctions as she

> ask[s] . . . the Priviledge [sic] for my Masculine Part the Poet in me (if any such you will allow me) to tread in those successful Paths my Predecessors have so long thriv'd in, to take those Measures that both the Ancient and Modern Writers have set me, and by which they have pleas'd the World so well.[32]

And, she further observes, that she writes not only for profit, but for "Fame," which she "value[s] . . . as much as if I had been born a *Hero*" (217). Accused by the increasingly "moral" age of "Indecency" (215) in the scene in which "*Mr. Leigh* [as Sir Feeble] *opens his Night Gown, when he comes into the Bed-chamber*," Behn defends herself with an interestingly layered argument. First, she says, it was "a Jest of his own making" (216), and, second, "he has his Cloaths on underneath" (216), and, third, this gesture is one familiar to dramatic tradition: "I have seen in that admirable Play of *Oedipus*, the Gown open'd wide" (216).

The comparatively kindly attitude toward the alderman and the banker and the class they represent and the concern about women's desire which is spoken to in the prefatory letter and also in Julia's own "staging" of the devil's appointment seem connected by another reference in the dedicatory letter, addressed to Laurence, Lord Hyde, Earl of Rochester. Here, Behn points out that there is

> No surer Testimony to be given of the flourishing Greatness of a State, than publick Pleasures and Divertisements—for they are . . . the Schools of Vertue, where Vice is always either punish't or disdain'd. They are secret Instructions to the People, in things that 'tis impossible to insinuate into them any other Way.
>
> (213)

And although the reference to the punishing of vice may not seem to apply to *The Luckey Chance*, the newly moneyed will certainly learn the dangers of assuming that wealth can—or should—purchase fidelity in young women for whom more appropriate mates exist. This truth is not one founded in notions of the salacious, unquenchable sexual appetites of women. It is one grounded in nature and common sense. As Julia puts it, "Wise men . . . should not expose their Infirmities, by marrying us young Wenches; who, without Instruction, find out how we are impos'd upon" (2.2.131–32).

Interestingly, the play does not restrict its criticism to old men with decayed sexual prowess. Old women, like Gayman's landlady, are just as likely to use economic power to purchase what they cannot naturally inspire. I think the criticism of the landlady is not particularly gendered criticism; in this play, power to purchase is power to abuse and abase— whether the victim be male or female. And those who have money and power are old. This detail marks the play, to my mind, as a meditation on a shift in society—a new generation emerging from the old. In the "old," marriages were arranged by fathers for daughters or by brothers for sisters. In *The Luckey Chance*, rich older men are in possession of young women without our having seen the family negotiations. And indeed the example of Gayman (and his feminized position—Janet Todd notes that he is like *The Rover*'s Angellica in his willingness to sell himself) renders family a moot point.[33] The world as it has evolved operates according to a new kind of economics. We can structure that world by ascribing primogenitural power to those with the most capital or we can modify the sense of hierarchy by attending to the desires of those to whom the old order never listened. These include young women, the men they love, and even apprentices like Bredwell. It is true that this play marks the foppish character as unworthy of concern; and Jews, for example, still provide the casual epithet for improper attitudes toward capital (although, truly, less often than one might expect in a play centered in a sense on the distribution of wealth). And, yes, there is no scene in which the old landlady receives the kindness (or demonstrates the self-knowledge) afforded to Sir Cautious and Sir Feeble in the end. But the play does ask fundamental questions about moral choice in the structuring of society—and it provides some answers as well.

The myth of Eden is important to both *The Luckey Chance* and *The Lady Eve*. As Cavell has noted, *The Lady Eve* announces its preoccupation in the title sequence; *The Luckey Chance* does so in Gayman's temptation by the "Devil" (i.e. Bredwell in disguise; interestingly Gayman refuses to be tempted by Julia "i'th' Garden" because he won't miss his "Assignation with my Devil" [2.2.228; 197]), which is ironically another assignation with Julia—although he doesn't realize, any more than Hopsy does about Eve, that she is "positively the same dame." Unlike Hopsy, though, Gayman's imagination is warped with presuppositions of the nature and age of the woman to whom the Devil leads him. He would clarify, but Pert, herself disguised as *"an Old woman with a Staff"* reminds him that "too much Curiosity lost Paradice" (3.1.169; 183). Unlike Hopsy, in the end Gayman doesn't acquiesce with an "I don't want to know," because he thinks he *does* know. Consequently, the woman he embraces feels worse than "a canvas Bag of wooden Ladles" (5.2.390–91) because he expects her to be nothing but a decaying carcass over rickety bones. Or does he just say that? And, if so, why? Let's turn to *The Lady Eve* in which a similar confusion occurs for some hints.

Cavell's discussion of *The Lady Eve* emphasizes the remarriage genre's focus on "the creation of woman," the "temptability of men" (*PH*, 48), the fall and forgiveness of both. Jean and her father set out to con the "mug," Hopsy, and they do so quite handily until Jean falls in love. Her father, like all remarriage comedy fathers, is her educator. He guides her and sometimes lectures her; he is always on her side in matters of the heart. But the one signal mistake she makes does have to do with him. After she falls in love with Charles "Hopsy" Pike and vows to quit her life of crime, she expresses the desire for her father and Gerald to quit the racket, "to go straight" as well. "Straight to where?" her father pertinently asks. She's the one, after all, who has "fallen." "The trouble with people who reform is they want to rain on everyone else's parade," her father says, dismissing the entire notion of reformation. As Jean will soon learn, the notion is a romantic fantasy based on a too-idealized version of Hopsy, just as Hopsy's romantic fantasy is based on a too-idealized version of Jean. Once her eyes are opened, she is determined to open Hopsy's eyes too.

"While it is the nature of the erotic to form a stumbling block to a reasonable, civilized existence, call it the political," Cavell observes, "human happiness nevertheless goes on demanding satisfaction in both realms" (*PH*, 64–5). So when Hopsy turns away from romance because he discovers that his "passion may have a past of flesh and blood," he is allowing the "stumbling block" to destroy the possibility for private happiness by an "overtrust in the wrong thing, the public thing" (i.e. Jean's identity as one of a ring of card sharps). Jean's reappearance in "Connecticut" as the Lady Eve is revenge of the purest sort. If Hopsy likes public images, Jean will create one as pristine and pure as his desires dictate. And once she has him fully entranced, she will completely destroy that image. That is her plan, and it works. The honeymoon train revelations of lover upon lover upon lover of the past send Hopsy into a kind of madness. As Cavell notes,

> had he found a sense of humor to outlast his credulity and her anger, he would be able to charge her with stalling on her wedding night by putting up a barrier, between her and her husband, of a thousand and one bawdy tales.
>
> (*PH*, 65)

Cavell's explanation of the way this film and all the remarriage comedies address the problem of public/private or political/personal or societal/individual happiness is lengthy, but worth quoting and contemplating in full as its resonance with Behn's vision is significant:

> It is not news for men to try . . . to walk in the direction of their dreams, to join the thoughts of day and night, of the public and the private, to pursue happiness. Nor is it news that this will require a revolution, of the social or of the individual constitution, or both. What is news is the acknowledgment that a woman might attempt this direction, even that a man and a woman might try it together and call *that* the conjugal . . . . For this we require a new creation of woman, call it a creation of the new woman; and what the problems of identification broached in these films seem to my mind to suggest is that this creation is a metaphysical enterprise, exacting a reconception of the world. How could it not? It is a new step in the creation of the human. The happiness in these comedies is honorable because they raise the right issues; they end in undermining and madcap and in headaches because there is, as yet at least, no envisioned settlement for these issues.
>
> (*PH*, 65)

Hopsy announces his dream in the beginning as he leaves the island on which he has been studying snakes for a year: "I'd like to spend all my time . . . in pursuit of knowledge." Of course, my ellipsis leaves out the delusional part of his initial wish. He claims, at the outset to want to be "in the company of men" exclusively. Once he meets Jean, the knowledge he seeks is very different. One can read the ending of the film, when Hopsy declares "I don't want to know," as a repudiation of his initial fantasy. But as the door shuts on him and Jean in embrace, we should realize he is pursuing knowledge just as he always dreamed of doing.

As he is being led into his secret admirer's room, Gayman hesitates, telling Pert (who is disguised as an old woman), "I wou'd fain ask—a civil Question or two first" (3.1.182). He is no doubt wondering why the devil has led him to this place—and what the significance of the old lady (Pert) "*with a Staff*" might be. But Pert prevails by reminding him of the dangers of curiosity, and he follows her into a chamber in which he is treated to a song and dance involving shepherds and shepherdesses. He remains confused: "Sure I have not liv'd so bad a Life, to gain the dull Reputation of so modest a Coxcomb, but that a Female might down with me, without all this Ceremony," he says (3.1.254–56). That, to Julia, may be the problem. Like Jean who as Eve stages a play that will reveal Hopsy to himself, Julia creates a scene in which Gayman is to experience enlightenment of some kind. Her motives are not fully clear, but there seems to be some sort of test that Gayman fails (by accepting the invitation in the first place? by not recognizing Julia when he embraces her?). Whereas Jean acts out of revenge, Julia seems to act out of doubt—has her own disloyalty rendered Gayman unfaithful? Oddly, she never really finds out.

In his twice-articulated declaration of love, Hopsy gives expression, with "fervor as well as . . . sappy deliberateness" (*PH*, 69) to another dimension of his fantasy: the recovery of lost innocence:

> Every time I've looked at you here on the boat, it wasn't only here I saw you. You seemed to go way back. I know that isn't clear, but I saw you here, and at the same time further away, then still further away; and then very small, like converging perspective lines.

He goes on to describe their imagined shared childhood and adolescence, concluding "what I'm trying to say is . . . only I'm not a poet, I'm an ophiologist . . . I've always loved you. I mean, I've never loved anyone but you." His guilelessness (or triteness—he sounds, as he admits on the boat, "dull as a drugstore novel") seems almost calculated when he says the same words to Eve in the forest; she certainly responds that way, egging him on, supplying words in the speech she seems to have memorized, sneering the second time at her own gullibility as she hears again the words that touched her heart and made her want to be the kind of person he wanted her to be, to recapture her own sense of innocence and discover a new world with him. As the door closes on their final embrace, Jean, newly wise, herself, says to Hopsy: "Don't you know, I've waited all my life for you, you big mug?" She embraces innocence just as Hopsy opts for ignorance even as they both enter the world of sensuality, knowledge of sexual love, for which Eden was "lost" in the first place.

Well lost, both genres argue, but nevertheless a source of longing that fuels dreams of individuals, couples, and societies. Jean/Eve creates herself in a sense as she becomes a woman who can forgive just as Hopsy becomes a man who can agree to forget what he knows in order to move forward. Like Behn's play, *The Lady Eve* highlights the essential role of genre in developing the ability to dream and to acknowledge, to fall and to forgive. Jean's cynical narrative about Hopsy and the ladies of the ship, framed as Cavell notes in a mirror that serves as a director's viewfinder, plus her actual directing of him—"Look over to your left, bookworm. There's a girl pining for you. A little further. Just a little further. There!"—establish, as Cavell says, the "attitude the film begins with . . . [as] one of skepticism" (*PH*, 66), an attitude that also infuses the manipulated circumstances at the beginning of *The Luckey Chance*. Both texts, though, revel in such manipulation, such playacting, such con jobs and deceptions. That's their business after all.

Preston Sturges seems adamant in his effort to "break the fourth wall" (much more difficult in film than in realistic theater). Extras who walk into the frame of the parts of the story set at sea can just as easily be "read" as either film production crew or ship's crew. Eugene Pallette, who plays Hopsy's father, is singled out by Cavell for analysis because of the self-referential

Tudor drinking song that he sings in his wonderfully frog-like voice (it would remind viewers of the time of his recent role as Friar Tuck). He's much more Eugene Pallette in that scene than Mr. Pike—and his comment "nut house" is again as applicable to what he sees on the film set as to what he doesn't see in the Pike foyer. In the scene of Hopsy's sappy speech to Eve (in which he quotes the earlier speech we and Jean took to be heartfelt), a horse intrudes into the frame awkwardly, a commentary by the director (Sturges) as if to draw attention to the fact that he knows that we know that Hopsy is being a horse's ass here—and he thinks so too! Behn's self-referencing occurs not only in the oft-quoted preface to *The Luckey Chance*, as mentioned above, but also in the way Julia attempts to direct and manipulate and control her own fate by manipulating and controlling Gayman's fate. Her artistry is never quite fully in her control, just as Behn's success or failure is always subject to her audience's response even if more threatening events do not intervene. Yet, like their surrogates Julia and Jean, Behn and Sturges continue to create, and like Gayman and Hopsy we agree to their "cons"; we pursue our happiness through a willingness to forget or at least to forgive.

"The over-arching question," one raised by both Restoration stage comedies and Hollywood film comedies, is in Cavell's words "what constitutes a union, what binds, what sanctifies in marriage? When is marriage an honorable estate? . . . In thus questioning the legitimacy of marriage, the question of the legitimacy of society is simultaneously raised, even allegorized" (*PH*, 53). This topic, according to Cavell, is most fully worked out in the remarriage genre in *The Philadelphia Story*, a film I will not be treating in this book. Most similarly to Jean/Eve, the central woman of that film, Tracey Lord, must learn to forgive—to accept human fragility and weaknesses, her own as well as those of others. She is treated to many harsh lectures about her tendency to play the role of a "goddess" to be worshipped rather than a woman to love and be loved. Innocence in these films is not, as Cavell explains, a physical virginity, but a metaphysical recovery of wonder, play, childlike openness—accompanied by a past replete with mistakes, attitudes, and behaviors that yearn for (and receive) forgiveness—on a personal and a national level. In the courtship comedies of the Restoration, the past and present, the real and the ideal also converge.

In *The Luckey Chance*, a reference to the Monument provides the best clue as to Behn's serious intent in her madcap bedroom farce. Belmour's disguise as a ghost prompts reference to the obelisk; Sir Feeble says, "He was as tall as the Monument" (3.1.417)—and with "a Mouth . . . like *London Bridge* at full tide" adds Sir Cautious (3.1.418). Erected in the 1670s to commemorate the people and the properties lost in the fire of London and to celebrate the rebuilding of the city, the Monument also bears an addendum, added in 1681, warning that "Popish frenzy, which wrought such horrors, is not yet quenched." The implication that Popish frenzy caused the fire in 1666 was based on a false rumor circulated at the time and reactivated during the turbulent 1680s as Parliament attempted to force Charles to name a Protestant successor to the throne. With the volatile present in danger

124 *Luck, be a lady*

of repeating the crises of the past, it is significant that a ghost of a forlorn lover should seem to bear the city's own features. Yet even as the comedy progresses toward the lover's restoration and the displacement of usurpers of power, it acknowledges that a new world is being born. I take that to be the reason for the gentle treatment of the alderman and the banker—and for the mutual punishment and for the (at least potential) mutual forgiveness and eventual remarriage of Gayman and Julia (punished in much the same way Hopsy and Jean endure punishments and enjoy forgivenesses for their failings). And as a final note, the genres themselves seem to be asking that we see in them their failings and their weaknesses, but that we also forgive them and move forward in pursuit of the pleasures they bring.

Notes

1 Markley, "'Be Impudent, Be Saucy, Forward, Bold, Touzing, and Leud': The Politics of Masculine Sexuality and Feminine Desire in Behn's Tory Comedies," in *Cultural Readings of Restoration and Eighteenth-Century Theater,* ed. J. Douglas Canfield and Deborah C. Payne (Athens: University of Georgia Press, 1995): 124–25.
2 Schocket, "Undercover Explorations of the 'Other Half,' or the Writer as Class Transvestite," *Representations,* 64 (1998): 127.
3 *Philosophy the Day after Tomorrow* (Cambridge, MA: Harvard University Press, 2005), 70, hereafter *Philosophy*. Subsequent citations to this work are given parenthetically in the text.
4 It is probably at least partly for that reason that both exist somewhat outside the canon of even their marginally canonical respective fields. Markley ("The Politics of Masculine Sexuality," 137) notes of Behn that she "has remained half-outside the canon of English literature." In "*The Lady Eve* and *Sullivan's Travels,*" *Cinéaste* 27, no. 3 (2002), Martha Nochimson notes of Sturges that he "was isolated in Hollywood and blocked in his development" (40).
5 Interestingly, Cavell mentions that the person playing the shoeshine man is an actual shoeshine man—Leroy Daniels, representing here not black dance, but "embodying the fate and genius of black culture" (*Philosophy*, 75).
6 James Thompson, "Sheridan, *The School for Scandal,* and Aggression," *Comparative Drama* 42, no. 1 (2008): 89.
7 *His Girl Friday*, directed by Howard Hawks (1940; Culver City, CA: Columbia Classics, 2000), DVD.
8 Peggy Thompson, *Coyness and Crime in Restoration Comedy: Women's Desire, Deception, and Agency* (Lanham, MD: Rowman and Littlefield; Lewisburg, PA: Bucknell University Press, 2012), 65.
9 Felsenstein, *Anti-Semitic Stereotypes: A Paradigm of Otherness in English Popular Culture, 1660–1830,* Johns Hopkins Jewish Studies (Baltimore: The Johns Hopkins University Press, 1995), 200–1.
10 Aphra Behn, *The Second Part of the Rover* (1681), in *The Works of Aphra Behn,* ed. Janet Todd, vol. 6 of *The Plays, 1678–1682,* ed. by Janet Todd (Columbus: Ohio State University Press, 1996). References are to act, scene, and line numbers.
11 *Sullivan's Travels*, directed by Preston Sturges, Criterion Collection (1941; Universal City, CA: Universal Home Video, 2001), DVD.
12 Cynthia Lowenthal, *Performing Identities on the Restoration Stage* (Carbondale and Edwardsville: Southern Illinois University Press, 2003), 146–47. Lowenthal cites Dennis Todd's *Imagining Monsters: Miscreations of the Self in Eighteenth-Century*

England (Chicago: University of Chicago Press, 1995), 44, for the observation regarding the popularity of giants and dwarfs at Bartholomew Fair.
13 Hutner, "Revisioning the Female Body: *The Rover*, Parts I and II," in *Rereading Aphra Behn: History, Theory, and Criticism*, ed. Heidi Hutner (Charlottesville: University of Virginia Press, 1993), 102–20.
14 Lowenthal, *Performing Identities*, 148. Al Coppola describes Behn's similar use of farce, "slapstick and low humor," in her 1686 *Emperor of the Moon*, in which she employs such techniques to draw in "the viewer's critical gaze" and then "retrain it." "Retraining the Virtuoso's Gaze: Behn's *Emperor of the Moon*, the Royal Society, and the Spectacles of Science and Politics," *Eighteenth-Century Studies* 41, no. 4 (2008): 484. We will see similar strategies in *The Luckey Chance*.
15 My observation is based on student responses over the years. Also, I recently attended a screening of the film at Ciné in Athens, GA, with an audience of around a hundred who laughed at the lines.
16 Shohat and Stam, *Unthinking Eurocentrism: Multiculturalism and the Media* (New York: Routledge, 1994), 210.
17 See Hugh Ruppersburg, "'O, So Many Startlements . . .': History, Race, and Myth in *O Brother, Where Art Thou?*" *Southern Cultures* 9, no. 4 (2003): 5–26.
18 Schocket, "Undercover Explorations," 112, 129n17.
19 Nochimson, "*The Lady Eve* and *Sullivan's Travels*," 41.
20 Rutsky and Wyatt, "Serious Pleasures: Cinematic Pleasure and the Notion of Fun," *Cinema Journal* 30, no. 1 (1990): 16.
21 Copeland, *Staging Gender in Behn and Centlivre: Women's Comedy and the Theatre* (Aldershot: Ashgate, 2004), 34, 44, quoting Markley, "'Be Impudent,'" 124.
22 *The Lady Eve*, directed by Preston Sturges, Criterion Collection (1941; Universal City, CA: Universal Home Video, 2001), DVD.
23 Aphra Behn, *The Luckey Chance* (1686), in *The Works of Aphra Behn*, ed. Janet Todd, vol. 7 *The Plays, 1682–1697*, ed. Janet Todd (Columbus: Ohio State University Press, 1996). References are to act, scene, and line numbers.
24 Dana K. Nelkin, "Moral Luck," in *The Stanford Encyclopedia of Philosophy*, ed. Edward N. Zalta (Winter 2013 Edition), http://plato.stanford.edu/entries/moral-luck/. Quotations in the following list are from this site unless otherwise specified.
25 Nelkin cites Thomas Nagel, "Moral Luck," in *Moral Luck*, ed. Dana Statman (Albany: State University of New York Press, 1993), 60. The chapter is from Nagel's 1979 book, *Moral Questions* (Cambridge: Cambridge University Press).
26 Copeland, *Staging Gender*, 69.
27 Todd, introduction to *The Luckey Chance*, 217.
28 Leicht, "Dialogue and Duelling in Restoration Comedy," *Studies in Philology* 104, no. 2 (2007): 278.
29 Williams, *Moral Luck* (Cambridge: Cambridge University Press, 1981), 26–27.
30 Pacheco, "Reading Toryism in Aphra Behn's Cit Cuckolding Comedies," *Review of English Studies n.s.* 55 (2004): 701–2.
31 Catherine Gallagher, "Who Was That Masked Woman? The Prostitute and the Playwright in the Comedies of Aphra Behn," *Women's Studies* 15 (1988): 23–42.
32 Behn, Preface, *The Luckey Chance* in *The Works of Aphra Behn*, ed. Janet Todd (Columbus: Ohio State University Press), 7: 217.
33 Todd, *The Secret Life of Aphra Behn* (New Brunswick, NJ: Rutgers University Press, 1996), 358.

5 Playing and not playing
William Wycherley's *The Country Wife* and Howard Hawks's *Bringing Up Baby*

The two texts featured in this chapter represent for each of their genres the purest as well as the most challenging version of the pursuit of moral perfectionism. Stanley Cavell calls the film "one of the earliest, say the prehistoric phases, of the myth" of remarriage (*PH*, 114). Although *The Country Wife* offers no invitation to employ that metaphor (nonsensical, for the time in which it was written anyway), in Horner's first speech, we are encouraged to see his ruse of impotence as a service to a "Nature" (1.1.3) that has been abandoned by the affected "pretenders to honour," who populate the London of 1675, at least the London as portrayed in the world of the play (2.1.417).[1] Consequently, the play's central plot seems a fantasy of regression. Horner's scheme is often critically configured as a return to a more primitive, a more innocent, state of natural freedom. Douglas Duncan and Peggy Thompson, for example, both invoke interpretations of Eden, reading Horner's goal as an effort to get back to the state of being before Eve's seduction by Satan transformed what had been uncomplicated love to the messy state of things (appetite, jealousy, lust, longing, etc.) we have to deal with now.[2] W. Gerald Marshall, also thinking in terms of Genesis, goes even further to suggest that "by re-ordering creation and casting human beings into a purely bestial role," Horner instigates "the insane uncreation of creation."[3] In other words, *The Country Wife*, like *Bringing Up Baby*, seems to be delving into the very heart of its genre, both texts driving back as far as they can go to the roots of the issues that preoccupy the genres in which these specific works participate, genres that recognize, as Stanley Cavell has put it, that "something evidently internal to the task of marriage causes trouble in paradise" (*PH*, 31).[4]

Cavell says of *Bringing Up Baby*,

> I think it would be reasonable . . . to regard the cause of this comedy as the need, and the achievement, of laughter at the physical requirements of wedded love, or, at the romance of marriage; laughter at the realization that after more than two millennia of masterpieces on the subject, we still are not clear why, or to what extent, marriage is thought to justify sexual satisfaction.
>
> (*PH*, 126)

H. W. Matalene similarly observes of *The Country Wife*,

> After three centuries, most of us may still claim, with Horner, that our couplings arise from the very needs of our biological "Nature" to survive and to reproduce itself, but . . . were this . . . true, all of us would presumably take quite as much bodily pleasure from feeling ourselves raped as from feeling ourselves loved, or (indeed) even married.[5]

Or, indeed, remarried. The problem each of these texts confronts, and each in its own way, is the problem of sexual desire and, to borrow Cavell's language that so resonates with Wycherley's play, "the impotence" of marriage "to domesticate sexuality without discouraging it" (*PH*, 31). How much of sexual longing is merely appetite or need, equivalent to hunger for food or thirst for water? How much is longing for something more? How can marriage satisfy such basic needs? And what are these needs, really? Although we may be prone to say scientifically that sexual desire is, like hunger for food and thirst for water, a fundamental need, do we really long for sex in the same way? For individual human beings, the answer is clearly "no" (given the long history of the practice of human celibacy, documented and undocumented). For the human species, whose survival in the larger sense depends on procreation, the answer is clearly "yes."

It has been impossible as yet to manufacture a baby without the interaction of sperm and egg, although it has become quite possible to do so without intercourse between man and woman. Still, the survival of the species depends on ejaculation of sperm into some receptacle and the introduction of that sperm by some means into the egg. In a sense, then, that event, conventionally known as "sex," is as necessary as food and water for our survival. The biological facts are so clear and so simple and so unemotional. Why do we, then, so often confuse the need for sex with the longing for love? And, more importantly, which of these desires—that for love or that for sex—is the stronger? Is either desire biologically, sociologically, or philosophically expendable? If so, which one? The survival of the species (or, to introduce the seventeenth-century concern, the family name) may depend on the engendering of offspring, but can we rely on that factual knowledge to ensure a new generation? Will people procreate out of a noble commitment to species perpetuation or property rights? (Will they cease to have sex when and if we decide that species survival is not something we want to endorse or when and if we decide we're happy enough without rights to the family estate?) Don't we require pleasure of some sort in the sexual act even if we engage in it for procreation's sake? Don't we have sex for pleasure even without the notion of engendering anything but our own satisfaction? And, in fact, isn't pleasure the point of all of this activity on every level? Would we agree to propagate the species or provide an heir to land, title, and holdings without the pleasure (physical or emotional or both) involved? And doesn't doing so provide us pleasure of a sort (even without emotional investment) as well? These were vexed issues in the periods of both genre's flourishings.

Although not overtly seeming to address the issue of procreation, *The Country Wife* and *Bringing Up Baby* both allude to fundamental anxieties attending parenthood. The seventeenth-century text does so in its obsessive focus on cuckoldry; the twentieth-century text in its very title, which as Cavell notes, "is . . . that of an education manual, one of those cute ones, written for the millions who find it reassuring to be told that babies are not scary and mysterious" (*PH*, 114). But they are, in fact, scary and mysterious for both ages, if for different reasons. And, for each age, babies seem both the point and beside the point of the scary, mysterious state known as marriage.

The Country Wife and *Bringing Up Baby* can be called beast fables, although in the case of Wycherley's play, perhaps the appropriate term is, following Marshall, "bestial" fable.[6] Horner is the untamed male, who—in order to fulfill his mission to have sex whenever, wherever, and with whomever he wants—must camouflage his desires from the other males of his species (weak, incapable males, in any event). Having successfully achieved camouflage through the ruse of impotence, he is able to help himself to the mates and wards of others while preserving peace in the animal kingdom. The females of the species are also able to enjoy satisfaction of their basic urges without violating their mates' or guardians' sense of proprietary ownership. It is basically, as many more conventional beast fables are, a trickster tale in which the shape-shifting protagonist helps himself to what he wants or needs, usually things that belong to the antagonist (the trickster's less protean enemy). And the moral for that stolid, stable (pun intended) soul is: Don't trust your wives or daughters with a handsome young male, even if he says he's impotent. Or, another moral, for a broader audience, might be: Where there's a will, there's a way (and, when it comes to sex, there's always a will—and always a way). The point is fundamental. Notions of ownership notwithstanding, players will find playmates and sometimes those playmates will be the wives, daughters, and wards of those who do not, will not, or cannot play.

In the beast fable at the heart of *Bringing Up Baby*, a dog buries a brontosaurus bone that a man says is "his," and a leopard that "belongs" to a woman becomes confused with a leopard that "belongs" to a circus. And, as in *The Country Wife*, in the end all this "ownership" turns out to be illusory. *Bringing Up Baby* suggests also that ownership is unimportant. After all, as Susan tells David early in their dispute over whose golf ball she is playing: "It's only a game, anyway." The moral of *Bringing Up Baby*'s beast fable is that playing, not possessing, is—or should be—the serious business of life. Clearly, both beast fables are about the basic drive of sex and the problem that the concept of "ownership" introduces into the natural scheme of things. Yet, at the center of *Bringing Up Baby*, as at the center of *The Country Wife*, is acknowledgment that "belonging to" someone and having someone "belong to us" is part of what we all naturally long for. Very early in the film, in the first scene shared by Grant and Hepburn, the one set at the golf course, David Huxley says to Susan Vance that she is in his car, just as he told her a few moments before that she was playing his golf ball. "*Your* golf ball? *Your* car? Is there anything in the world that doesn't belong to you?" she asks. "Yes, thank heaven. You!" he replies, as though already understanding that he has begun a madcap adventure that will end in the very intimacy he both desires and fears.[7]

Since Eve Kosofsky Sedgwick's groundbreaking discussion of *The Country Wife* in *Between Men*, we have understood that the competition for mates in Wycherley's play is centered on male relations. In this study, Sedgwick first drew our attention to the homosociality that motivates Horner: "If he gives up the friendship and admiration of other men, it is only to come into a more intimate and secret relation to them."[8] Later critics, such as Kathleen Oliver, have refined her insights, particularly with regard to the domestic violence (such as that Margery Pinchwife suffers or is threatened to suffer) that is the "potential/probable by-product of the rake-cuckold dynamic."[9] John Vance also emphasizes the violent outcome of homosocial relations in his observation that Pinchwife comes to know "that only an expression of primitive violence will serve him faithfully against the likes of Horner, Harcourt, and Dorilant, whose motives . . . were not to administer justice but to indulge their power."[10] Sexual possession of the women in the Horner/Fidget/Pinchwife plot is evidence of male power and control and competition. The women—Lady Fidget and Margery Pinchwife, in particular—represent victory over male opponents, not worthy companions or even valued conquests in and of themselves. With regard to the concept of "natural" behavior, it must be said that human males (as described by Sedgwick) do not differ so much from the males of the animal kingdom, that is, the world of apes, with whom we share a common ancestor, as well as the world of territorial cats, such as leopards. Of course, analogies to animals aside, concepts of ownership and dominance pervade Western culture, and both *The Country Wife* and *Bringing Up Baby* reflect those preoccupations in their depictions of marriage, the institution by which human sexual "ownership" is displayed.

Masochism/sadism is the matrix of *The Country Wife*—and that it is so is announced early on, not by Horner, but by the play's true lover Harcourt. Sparkish, the fop, he says, "is fond of me only, I think for abusing him" (1.1.221–22). This sort of attraction to pain also infects Alithea, who has to be talked into a view of marriage as a domain of pleasure and personal fulfillment rather than an act of self-sacrifice and social duty. *Bringing Up Baby* participates in this dyad as well, beginning as it does with David Huxley, man of science, devoted to his brontosaurus and destined for a marriage that will be "purely a dedication to . . . work," according to Alice Swallow, his fiancée. From that point, David goes on to an adventure with Susan that he finds exasperatingly painful on many levels. And the acute and uncomfortable painfulness of his adventure is experienced by many on viewing this film, as noted in the reviews on its debut. Frank

S. Nugent's *New York Times* commentary labeled Hepburn "terribly, terribly fatiguing," Aunt Elizabeth's terrier George (played by Skippy, better known as *The Thin Man*'s beloved Asta) "annoying," and the entire movie as an "ominous tread of deliberative gags."[11] Although other reviews at the time were more positive, audiences did not respond well, and Katharine Hepburn famously continued to suffer the label of "box-office poison" until she redeemed herself in another comedy of remarriage, *The Philadelphia Story*. She, as *Bringing Up Baby*'s madcap, hair-brained Susan, got on people's nerves—and most audience members were not masochistic enough to come back for more.

Wycherley suffered something of the same fate following *The Country Wife*, but not immediately. His play was quite successful when first staged (in 1672 or 1673) and equally successful as a printed text. There were five quartos published during Wycherley's lifetime (he died in 1715), and the play was also issued in octavo in *The Works of the Ingenious Mr. W. W. Collected into One Volume* in 1713.[12] Wycherley's "poisonous period" (instigated, although to little immediate effect, by Jeremy Collier in 1698) was not fully in place until 1766 when David Garrick sanitized *The Country Wife* as *The Country Girl* and drove the original underground until the twentieth century.[13] Elizabeth Inchbald included Garrick's version of the play in her twenty-five volume collection entitled *The British Theatre* (1808), prefacing it with remarks that obliquely highlight the homosocially competitive valence of the parts of the original text that Garrick "expunged" in deference to the "improved taste" of his times. Inchbald describes the relationship between Wycherley and Charles II as one inflected by sexual competition:

> Wycherly [*sic*] lived in the cheerful days of Charles the Second; was the companion of the wits of that period, caressed by his sovereign, and, it is said, beloved by his sovereign's mistress, the beautiful Duchess of Cleveland.
>
> As a wife has too often the power to make her husband conceive a friendship for the very man who is the means of his disgrace, such surely may be the power of a mistress; and the singular partiality, which his Majesty showed for the author of this play, might possibly be derived from the same artful source.[14]

Indeed, Inchbald is so committed to this interpretation that she attributes Wycherley's fall from royal favor to his marriage, which provoked the ire of the Duchess of Cleveland, the mistress he shared with the king. "His majesty," Inchbald speculates, "might require Wycherly's passion to incite his own" and, thus, resents Wycherley's marriage as an event depriving him of pleasure. Inchbald opines that, perhaps, like Sparkish, Charles "could not love a woman, whom other men did not love" (5).

Garrick's revision eliminates the Horner/Fidget plot and retains the Alithea/Harcourt/Sparkish plot. It treats the core of the Pinchwife plot to a revision that punishes Pinchwife (now named Moody and not really a husband) and vindicates Margery (now named Peggy and not a country wife, but a country girl) by rewarding her with the lover who, unlike his prototype Horner, wants to marry the young woman he "tousles and mousles." These revisions make the play much more respectable, to be sure. In a sense, however, they do so by adhering to notions of ownership that *The Country Wife* rejects or at least calls into doubt.

What is mine? What is yours? These are questions at the center of both Wycherley's text and Hawks's film. *Bringing Up Baby*'s Susan Vance finds such quibblings ridiculous. A car is a car and if one can start it up and put it into gear, then one can appropriate it for whatever purpose it serves, knowing always that it can be returned and repaired in the morning. Wycherley's Horner is also unimpressed by notions of ownership—especially of wives owned but not used in the way he supposes wives are meant to be. Like Susan, Horner knows that return (if not repair) is possible. And what needs repairing that doesn't seem damaged? Who can tell what Mrs. Fidget has been up to in the china closet? No one, by looking at her. And as long as her "dear Honour" seems to be intact, for all practical purposes (that is, as far as her husband and her world are concerned), it is intact. Pinchwife's threatened mutilation of his wife (a threat retained by Garrick's Moody) is a much more serious violation of property rights and value than Horner's china closet shenanigans—for it would spoil the surface of things. And, both texts suggest, all this worry about ownership is truly worry about the surface of things—the way things look—rather than about the substance of things—the way things really are.

Any child knows that what is mine is what I can grab from the other children. It's not that adults have forgotten this playground rule; possession is, after all, said to be nine-tenths of the law in the grown-up world as well. For children, however, such an attitude toward property, ownership, and possession is part of the world of play. Consequences of play end when the sun goes down or when recess ends. The games start again tomorrow. For Nietzsche, "rediscovering the seriousness we had towards play when we were children" is the hallmark of maturity.[15] Yet, for many, it does seem to be the price of adulthood and of marriage that we no longer play in the way that children play—seriously and for the highest stakes of all: fun, happiness, joy. But should it be? At the beginning of his analysis of *Bringing Up Baby*, Cavell quotes Freud's final words in *Wit and Its Relation to the Unconscious*, which describe childhood as the time "when we were ignorant of the comic, when we were incapable of jokes and when we had no need of humor to make us feel happy in our life" (*PH*, 113). It is that childlike mood that defines the interplay of David and Susan in Hawks's film, although their interplay is not naively childlike. As Gerald Mast notes, the "improvisation that dominates the playing and shooting of *Bringing Up Baby* could only have been accomplished by an attuned group of professionals exercising their craft and trusting one another to return every surprising serve they send in each other's direction."[16] Successful improvisation of the sort that defines *Bringing Up Baby*, in fact, is a supremely adult activity, although one that does attempt to reclaim the joy and happiness of childhood. The longing for such reclamation of happiness inflects the improvisational behavior featured in *The Country Wife* as well. Horner, Harcourt, and Margery Pinchwife are all characters who excel at invention (improvisation) when it comes to play: Horner by strategy, Margery by instinct, and Harcourt by desire. Of the three, only Harcourt can be said to achieve the happiness he pursues. How he does so, by playing and not playing, links him (and Alithea) to Susan (and David) in commentary on what (re)marriage should—indeed must—be.

Playing and not playing (pleasure and business) are central concerns of *The Country Wife*. In fact, we may even say that in a sense Hawks's film is simply an elaboration at a later date of a cultural tension that emerged in the early modern period as incipient capitalistic enterprise began to redefine class and gender relations and expectations. Although certainly an important part of the audience to whom Wycherley addressed his plays was aristocratic, the world in which the courtiers lived was defined by new realities, new centers of power and influence that were located in the city, not the court. Acts 1 and 2 set up a certain number of motifs having to do with some of these new influences that will reverberate throughout the course of the play.

The first of these motifs has to do with the pseudoauthority of modern science, its prestige as well as its fundamental fallibility. Horner's first words are to us, the audience, as he speaks "aside," giving us his opinion as to the usefulness of the modern physician: "A Quack is as fit for a Pimp, as a Midwife for a Bawd; they are still but in their way both helpers of Nature" (1.1.1–2). If the need to speak to the doctor, Quack (who has entered the stage with him) were not so pressing, Horner might, perhaps, have elaborated this analogy. Or, did the conversation between the two not distract us, we the audience might ponder this odd comparison, as well as the significance of the fact that Horner regards us as appropriate confidantes for this jaded point of view. His verbal "wink" is one that puts us on the side of what he calls "nature," that is, on the side of illicit sexual activities—prostitution, in particular. How—and more importantly why—should nature be associated with bawds and pimps and why should doctors, even quacks, be added to the mix? We are assumed to approve, but do we? The answer is probably yes at this point. Conventionally, the aside defines our perspective in a dramatic work (just as the close-up defines our perspective in a film). And as far as we know, this perspective is not false. It was common knowledge in Wycherley's time and it continues to be common knowledge in our time that sexual intercourse sometimes results in disease, other times in pregnancy, and often in both. An unscrupulous midwife and a compliant doctor are certainly useful acquaintances for a libertine male. The surprise comes when we discover the specific purpose for which Horner has engaged his Quack, for he is depending as much, if not more, on the doctor's cultural authority as on his lack of medical integrity. Horner does not want a quick fix for his sex life; instead he seeks from Quack, paradoxically, a lasting and permanent cure.

The notion of scientific, especially medical, unreliability is perhaps overly familiar to readers of literature produced in the early modern period—so familiar, in fact, that we may assume everyone felt disdainful about the potential to master the world through experiential knowledge and ameliorative practices. However, we should remember that satire on Quacks from Jonson to Fielding exists side by side with ever-increasing cultural investment in medical and other scientific pursuits. As Roy Porter has observed, "Quacks were often assailed as a 'vile race', yet they could easily win favour amongst fashionable patrons."[17] In Wycherley's own time, of course, the Royal Society had elevated experimentation to an all-time high point, and "improving natural knowledge" had royal sanction and, therefore, unprecedented prestige.[18] Horner's plan is fully dependent on the cultural elevation of a man of science whom, significantly, he dubs a "helper of Nature." If Quack's name tells *us* that he's an ineffective physician, the "town" seems to hold him in high regard. After all, it credits his report that Horner is "as bad as an *Eunuch*" (1.1.6). Expert though he might be in venereal matters, however, Quack is less proficient in knowledge of human nature than his patient proves. And, in fact, that is the entire trajectory of the first scene from the moment Quack enters with Horner until he exits over 150 lines later.

Quack's opinion that Horner's scheme is "preposterous" is based on an analogy: "as if we Operators in Physick, shou'd put forth Bills to disparage our Medicaments, with hopes to gain Customers" (1.1.37–39). His reasoning is very straightforward: publicity draws in (or frightens away) potential clients (or lovers). It just makes no sense to Quack that Horner will gain by advertising himself as "a Man unfit for Women" (1.1.33). But Horner knows that human nature is complicated and human relations even more so. And much has to do with timing. After all, he explains, "the wisest Lawyer never discovers the merits of his cause till the tryal; the wealthiest Man conceals his riches, and the cunning Gamster his play" (1.1.43–46). Husbands are wary—and it's the husbands Horner has to draw in first, in order to gain access to their wives: "False friendship will pass now no more than false dice upon 'em, no, not in the City" (1.1.47–48).

A bit of self-abasement solves the problem of access, as Quack sees when Sir Jasper, Lady Fidget, and Mrs. Dainty Fidget show up. Sir Jasper is eager to employ the impotent Horner as an escort for the women of his family, whose diversions he finds tedious. After the Fidgets leave, Horner turns to Quack and explains impatiently to the doctor, who continues to voice his skepticism:

> Thou art an Ass, don't you see already upon the report and my carriage, this grave Man of business leaves his Wife in my lodgings, invites me to his house and wife, who before wou'd not be acquainted with me out of jealousy?
>
> (1.1.131–34)

Quack remains dubious that Horner's ultimate goal—the women—can be brought to endure his company. Horner then gives the doctor (who, he says will "never make a good Chymist, thou are so incredulous and impatient" [1.1.146–47]) a lesson in human nature: "Women of Quality are so civil, you can hardly distinguish love from good breeding, and a Man is often mistaken; but now I can be sure, she that shows an aversion to me loves the sport" (1.1.150–53]). Quack defers and dubs Horner a "Doctor" with a "Process . . . so new, that . . . it may succeed" (1.1.161–62)—and it does.

Of course, Quack is a stand-in, in many ways, for the audience. He is necessary to the plot, and the comic effect of the plot, so that Horner can explain his methods and we can be in possession of more information than the characters have. The creation of viewer superiority is a standard comic strategy, especially useful in farce and slapstick (and the hilarity of the farcical china closet scene is completely driven by our awareness of Horner's secret and our knowledge that Sir Jasper is ignorant thereof). But by employing Quack, as opposed to a male confidante or a bawd, say, Wycherley turns a basic comic joke into satiric cultural commentary regarding trust in so-called authority as well as a nod to the scientific method itself. Horner is the experiential scientist; Quack is a Quack because he is relying on theory alone.

In the scene just examined, another controlling motif is introduced by Sir Jasper Fidget—and that is the competition between business and pleasure—or the conflation of the two in the business of pleasure and the pleasure of business. Identified with the city (a "cit," in other words), Sir Jasper articulates city values: "business must be preferr'd always before Love and Ceremony with the wise Mr. *Horner*" (1.1.108–09).[19] Sir Jasper ends his first scene on stage as Horner begins his—with an aside to the audience, taking us into his confidence, providing us his rationale for his behavior, engaging us in a relationship of trust: "'Tis as much a Husband's prudence to provide innocent diversion for a Wife, as to hinder her unlawful pleasures; and he had better employ her, than let her employ her self" (1.1.117–19).

The aside here is actually Sir Jasper's third. He has been conspiring with the audience since he entered the stage, sharing his glee at Horner's sexual incapacity and letting us know his plans to "play the wag with him" and "plague him" (1.1.68, 72). We, of course, are in Horner's confidence as well, and Sir Jasper's unawareness of that fact makes him appear the buffoon from the outset as we know that he is the butt of the jokes he thinks he's telling at Horner's expense. Both Horner and Sir Jasper keep us apprised of their thoughts, motives, and strategies when they once again appear together in Act 2, having followed the Fidget women to the home of Mr. Pinchwife. In this scene, though, they add whispering to their repertoire, sharing confidences with Lady Fidget, in particular, but confidences we can well understand by the responses of the lady and the knowledge we have of what each man thinks and desires and is.

However, our perspective becomes increasingly troubled. As he crosses the threshold of Pinchwife's home, Sir Jasper greets his wife, who has just uttered the word "Honour," by observing, "thou hast still so much honour in thy mouth—"(2.1.391–92). Horner turns to us and finishes the sentence: "That she has none elsewhere" (2.1.393)—a rather judgmental observation from one who has deliberately taken on a laughable character in order that she be able to have her honor and lose it too (so to speak). Are we still with him? As Sir Jasper whispers we-know-what to his wife, the other women of his family continue to warn Horner to "stand off," "not approach" (2.1.410–11). They are continuing behavior begun in Act 1 based on Horner's reputation as a rake and a libertine. Mrs. Dainty Fidget exclaims, "You are obscenity all over" (2.1.412). And Mrs. Squeamish goes further to invoke the Garden of Eden in explicit allusion to the kind of temptation Horner represents: "I wou'd as soon look upon a Picture of *Adam* and *Eve*, without fig leaves" (2.1.413–14). Horner seems to despise them, harshly explaining to Dorilant that they are nothing but "pretenders to honour," who are trying to get a reputation for virtue by "railing at the Court" (an interesting choice of words) (1.1.417, 420–21). City hypocrisy seems to be the irritant getting on Horner's nerves. And he seems relieved when the supposedly enlightened Lady Fidget (apprised by her husband of Horner's impotence) reveals that her contempt is no longer feigned. She does despise him as a "French Weather" (i.e. wether), even as he disdains her as he would a "Spaniel" who "can fawn, lye down, suffer beating, and fawn the more; barks at your Friends, when they come to see you; makes your bed hard, gives you Fleas, and the mange sometimes," the only difference being that "the Spaniel's the more faithful Animal, and fawns but upon one Master" (2.1.464, 456–60).

Is Horner playing or not playing? Is his combativeness a diversionary prelude to his own whispered confession to Lady Fidget a few lines later—a confession that has her praising him as a "generous . . . Man of honour," who has made a supreme sacrifice for the "Women of honour," whom he knows can now enjoy his "conversation" without shame (2.1.526–27, 530)? Or does he really despise the sexually avid women as much as he disdains the neglectful husbands he plans to cuckold? Is his game a game for fun, his ruse defining a protected secret space in an overly refined and increasingly anti-sensual world? Or is he playing for higher stakes (as is suggested when the gambling metaphor replaces the gamboling—or, fawning—spaniel)? In terms familiar to the seventeenth and eighteenth centuries themselves, does Horner speak his satiric truths (and indeed his comments regarding honor as reputation are truths) with Horatian laughter or with Juvenalian anger?

The end of Act 2 is richly resonant. How can Lady Fidget trust Horner? What if she and he have a "future falling out" (2.1.546)? What's to keep him from revealing his secret (and hers) to everyone? Reputation, itself. What he's sacrificed to protect her reputation is his own reputation. If he denies his impotence, "no body wou'd believe me," he asserts (2.1.550). And she agrees—fully knowing that a lost reputation truly cannot be recovered. She and Horner are, to Sir Jasper's delight, "reconciled" (2.1.555). As Lady Fidget puts it,

> Master *Horner* is a thousand, thousand times a better Man than I thought him . . . I can name him now, truly not long ago . . . I thought his very name obscenity, and I wou'd as soon have lain with him as named him
>
> (2.1.557–61)

which, as we have seen in *It Happened One Night* and *The Rover* is partly what naming signifies anyway. So, as Sir Jasper says, they can now proceed to "to go to . . . [their] business, . . . pleasure; whilst . . . [he] go[es] to [his] pleasure, business" (2.1.567–68). The act ends with Lady Fidget's couplet:

> Who for his business, from his Wife will run;
> Takes the best care, to have her bus'ness done.
> (2.1.573–74)

Sir Jasper's sentiments, or at least his words, exactly—only not what he means exactly; indeed, the opposite of what he intends, the very thing he hopes to prevent.

The movement of the play's action from Sir Jasper's entrance in Act 1 to Lady Fidget's exit in Act 2 is largely about groupings and regroupings. As Joseph Roach has pointed out, "grouping . . . [was] the dominant scenic element" of the Restoration stage, with the asides, soliloquies, prologues, epilogues providing the feel of "public intimacy," the "prevailing . . . fantasy" that the spectators came to experience.[20] Cavell uses different language about *Bringing Up Baby*, emphasizing the way the characters follow or don't follow one another. This motif is present in Wycherley's play as well. Sometimes the following is physical, but in this most shifting of all shifting linguistic environments, the most important following has to do with the mind's ability to grasp another's meaning. James Thompson notes the way language (metaphor in particular) in *The Country Wife*, often "yields two entirely different messages" to those who listen (particularly in the case of Jasper and Lady Fidget).[21] As audience members, we are able to "follow" several characters' habits of mind because we are clued into their motives and desires; the characters have a harder time with each other—especially if motives and desires are blocked by, say, fiancés or husbands. In this case, the trick is making oneself understood while not being exactly clear so that the right one follows and the wrong one is left behind. This technique is increasingly employed as the play progresses. We see it in the conversation between Lady Fidget, Sir Jasper, Horner, and Mrs. Squeamish in the china scene—and, as we have witnessed the formation of the linguistic community of Lady Fidget and Horner and as we have been privy to Sir Jasper's designs, we have little difficulty knowing what everyone means, even though each character, other than Horner, misconstrues or is misled by another at some point in the scene.

Yet the central joke of the china scene—the repeated emphasis on Horner's "coming into you the back way" (4.3.125–26)—raises questions about "following" in a way similar to the first joke in *Bringing Up Baby*. David, newly in possession of the intercostal clavicle bone of a brontosaurus, opines that he should try it in the tail. His fiancée, Alice Swallow, says, "Nonsense. You tried it in the tail yesterday." Are we (as audience) being alerted to a way of reading or following the film that relies on double entendre? And, if so, to what (pardon the pun) end? Cavell acknowledges the difficulty posed by the sexual puns in *Bringing Up Baby*. How far are we to "press such references" as Miss Swallow's comment about "putting it in the tail" or Susan's promise to "open my puss and shoot the works" or David's negligee-clad proclamation that he just "felt *gay* all of a sudden"? Cavell suggests that our uncertainty is "meant to characterize a certain anxiety in our comprehension throughout, an anxiety that our frequent if discontinuous titters may at any moment be found inappropriate" (*PH,* 118). In the film, he concludes,

> if it is undeniable that we are invited by . . . events to read them as sexual allegory, it is equally undeniable that what Hepburn says, as she opens the box and looks inside, is true: "It's just an old bone." . . . The play between the literal and the allegorical determines the course of this narrative, and provides us with contradicting directions in our experience of it.
>
> (*PH,* 118)

I do not mean to suggest, of course, that anyone in the Restoration playhouse would have or could have or should have heard the reference to "coming into you the back way" with the same kind of anxiety as moviegoers of the thirties would have responded audibly to the double entendre of *Bringing Up Baby*. Still, a certain anxiety does attend this scene—and probably did so from its first staging.

The anxiety, however, is not about whether or not to hear the language as sexual language. The situation insists that we do so. Moreover, as Celia R. Daileader has demonstrated, the reference draws on a long and established literary (poetic as well as dramatic) association of "back door sex" with gynosodomy. The connotation of "back door" (in terms of architecture and who would be likely to use such an entrance), as Daileader explains, would range from the surreptitious (secret lovers) to the lowly (servants) to the generally abject.[22] But, in terms of anal sex, the implications were traditionally much more positive. For women, "erotic agency, variety of pleasure, even reproductive freedom—all may be accessed or denied women through the back door" (306). And although, as Daileader carefully acknowledges, "we must resist the temptation to treat [a] . . . male-authored text as a Kinsey Report" (313), it is clear that Lady Fidget expects pleasure from the encounter, be it back door or front door: "Let him come, and welcome, which way he will" (4.3.127).

In her reading of male anxiety in gynosodomical scenes of (primarily) Renaissance literature Daileader links the association of the sexual practices with Italians, in particular, and finds the tension illustrative of xenophobia. Our modern discomfort is more a matter of homophobia and a too-narrow sense of what "back door sex" both connotes and denotes in the early modern period. Her conclusion is very witty—and I quote it partly to pay homage to her ability to strike a highly intellectual pose without losing her sense of humor: "Modern Anglophile scholars need to get real about assholes. Despite the fact that we're obsessed with 'the body' and love to talk about 'sex and gender,' our scholarship is, well, a bit 'anal' when it comes to anal eroticism" (326). Even Queer theorists find themselves confused from time to time as they discuss gynosodomy as girling the boy or boying the girl (the exception is Jonathan Goldberg, whose discussion of anal eroticism in *Romeo and Juliet* treats, Daileader says, "gynosodomy *as* gynosodomy" [326]). Non-Queer theorists/critics are too apt to see sodomy as "inherently abusive"—which problematizes treatment of androsodomy, a common practice in male homosexual love: "are all those happy sodomites out there just confusing the bodily signals of pleasure and pain?" (327).

Although both texts under consideration in this chapter suggest that there is a thin line between pleasure and pain, the anxiety at the heart of the china scene has less to do with that or with the sense that gynosodomy is an exotic and imported sexual practice (although, as Daileader points out, Horner is likened to an Italian castrato, so the veneer of ethnocentrism may gloss the scene). I think the real source of anxiety is whether and/or how to hear the reference to "the back way" as a literal description of what goes on in that closet. Is it just how Horner enters the closet or is it how he enters Lady Fidget or both? Will we (and the members of the first audience) seem unsophisticated and prudish if we *don't* assume a gynosodomical act? Will we seem overly prurient if we do? Or, a third possibility: Will our assuming that a gynosodomical sex act takes place infuse our laughter with a knowingness that actually *lacks* the imagination we'd like to demonstrate?

In *Philosophy the Day After Tomorrow*, Cavell observes:

> It can seem a mystery that on the whole that we do not *have* to accommodate ourselves to one another in speaking—we *are* accommodated, attuned I have said. It is no scandal—it is, I would rather say, a fact—that

this attunement is based on nothing more than our sharing of (and our capacity for imagining) interests, judgments, impressions, needs, inclinations, desires, temptations, compulsions, surprises, moods, tastes, curiosities, qualms, antipathies, attractions, conflicts, perplexities, perceptions, satisfactions, games, proofs, jokes, news, fictions, gossip. It is rather something that sometimes gives us the feeling that the fact of language is like a miracle.

(*Philosophy*, 139)

When we feel we strain to accommodate, as we, the audience of both *The Country Wife* and *Bringing Up Baby*, feel we do, we become anxious—tittering, laughing too loudly, hoping we "get" it, not sure we want to reveal through our reactions that we do—or that we don't. Within the worlds of the film and the play, however, anxiety of that order rarely manifests itself. There are those who are "in the know" and those who are not, but the ones left out seldom feel their exclusion, even when pressed, like Sparkish, to do so (I will return to this scene in a moment).

In fact, the comedy of each work depends on the moments when the audience does *not* strain to accommodate, when we know what all the characters know, therefore, more than some who are involved in the scene. We know Horner is not really impotent, so we laugh at Sir Jasper's glee as Lady Fidget "moils and toils" for china with the man who is secretly cuckolding the cit. Our laughter is more complicated in the case of Pinchwife as we know that Horner is reputedly harmless and that, had Pinchwife heard as much, he would be less anxious about Margery's "crush" or Horner's lust. On the other hand, he does have cause for worry, although no one else in his world (with the exception of Horner and Quack) would agree—so, in a sense, he seems both more paranoid and wiser than anyone else in the play, several times pushing the comedy to the end of violence. He threatens Margery with a penknife twice—a phallic allusion to his own inadequacy and the violent frustration he feels as a result. Interestingly, Margery appropriates the phallus, using her own pen to write to Horner, her own wits to follow her would-be lover and to escape from the prison (or the cage, we might say) of her marriage.

Margery, of course, is this play's cross-dresser. I did not make much of the feature in my discussion of *The Rover*, but the "breeches role" is a common Restoration stage trick, a holdover from the Renaissance stage with different erotic undertones. In *The Rover*, Hellena in boy's garb offers to pimp for Wilmore and for a while anyway Wilmore is taken in, excited by the possibility of yet another woman—and only late in the interchange realizing that his "little gypsie" has tricked him. In *The Country Wife*, Margery's disguise fails to deceive Horner most likely because Margery herself has no desire to do so. Pinchwife, whose scheme to dress his wife as her brother James was specifically designed to keep Horner's attentions at bay, can't intervene in Horner's egregious flirting with the "boy" although he suspects he "knows her" because "she carries it so sillily" (3.2.375–76). But, he can't be sure: "I should be more silly to discover it first" (3.2.376) At one point, Horner observes: "Methinks he is so handsom, he shou'd not be a Man" (3.2.419), teasing Pinchwife with the truth—but taking his "torment [of] this jealous Rogue" further by kissing Margery repeatedly and having Dorilant and Harcourt do so as well (3.2.424). This scene is focused on the tension between the men rather than on Margery's desires. Yet, she is there on the stage dressed as a boy, and she is being kissed and "musl'd" by a man (4.2.37). Spectators may understand that the point is to torment Pinchwife, but what they are witnessing also alludes to various kinds of desire.

Certainly, Margery is transformed by the experience. Seeming perhaps "backward" to the point of imbecility when we first meet her, she reveals herself in Act 4 to be both literate and inventive. Although Pinchwife's mean-spirited misogynistic assessment of her response is objectionable on both grounds, he notes that her awakening, as it were, in the Playhouse and on the Exchange has had a predictable effect: "Why should Women have more invention in love than men? It can only be, because they have more desires, more solliciting passions, more lust, and more of the Devil" (4.2.59–61). There are some in the audience who will agree with Pinchwife, but only those who are predisposed to do so. For the play itself provides ample evidence that men are every bit as inventive as women in pursuit of their desires whatever those desires happen to be. After all, from the beginning we have been watching Horner launch the boldest scheme of seduction ever devised. And Harcourt, whose desires are more specific than those of his friend, is no less inventive than Margery in pursuit of his passion. And he is a good deal more successful.

As James Thompson has pointed out (and as most playgoers and readers agree), "while Alithea and Harcourt do come to represent correct conduct, they are much less vital and interesting than Horner," but if the couple were not in this play amidst such extreme behaviors and confusions and schemes, their romance might be more clearly seen for what it is: the Restoration's *Bringing Up Baby*.[23] Thompson eventually reaches a similar conclusion, noting that the fifth act reveals a "change in Horner" that "we are not entirely prepared for"—and one which disallows a comfortable amusement (72). His "willingness to trifle with Alithea's reputation and happiness," Thompson points out, is a "troublesome" moment at which point "an especially bright and witty comedy of intrigue . . . takes a nasty turn, deliberately disturbing the audience" (71). Alithea and Harcourt in the end represent the true honor of mutual "understanding and trust" in the midst of all kinds of hypocritical uses of "honor" that involve myriad abuses of trust and understanding: "The corrupt society in which these two must live underscores how valuable are these ideals" (91). David Gellineau agrees, noting that in their commitment to "meaning based on faith and trust," Alithea and Harcourt represent "a real reinstitution of an Edenic pair."[24] Deborah Payne's reading of Alithea and Harcourt as overcoming the skepticism of their world through "silence and unreasonable acts" (i.e., faith in one another) accords with these views—and mine.[25]

Harcourt, like Susan Vance, falls in love at first sight. Sparkish, unlike Pinchwife, is not a jealous man. He introduces his betrothed to his friend Harcourt, asking "do you approve my choice?" (2.1.130) Harcourt is smitten: "So infinitely well, that I cou'd wish I had a Mistriss too, that might differ from her in nothing, but her love and engagement to you" (2.1.145–47). He even bluntly tells Alithea that, if he could, he would "break the Match" between her and Sparkish (2.1.176). Sent "into a corner" with her by Sparkish in order to "trye if she has wit," Harcourt, who quips "if a Woman wants wit in a corner, she has it no where," pleads with Alithea not to marry a man who can be so easy with her, so lacking in jealousy "the only infallible sign" of love (2.1.196, 198–99, 220–21). When that fails to move her, he argues that Sparkish marries her only out of interest, whereas he himself would marry her out of love. When that (although the argument does "put a scruple" in Alithea's mind [2.1.229]) also fails to convince, Harcourt points out that her reputation is at stake. She agrees, but they differ, of course, on how she should best protect that reputation—by being true to her promise or by breaking it.

At the end of *Bringing Up Baby*, Susan tells David that everything that happened during their madcap time together (roughly twenty-four hours) happened because she just wanted to be with him: "I was trying to keep you near me, and I just did anything that came into my head." That's partly true. She was also, like Harcourt, facing a deadline. When she met David, he was within a day of being married to Miss Swallow. This fact is not immediately known to Susan, as it is to Harcourt, who is introduced to Alithea by the man who is to marry her. Like Harcourt, however, Susan is determined to prevent the marriage from happening as soon as she learns the facts. In his audio commentary for the DVD of *Bringing Up Baby*, Peter Bogdanovich, whose *What's Up Doc?* (1972) was inspired by Hawks's film, notes that the film's first close-up comes roughly twenty minutes into the narrative.[26] And it is a close-up of Susan reacting to David's announcement that he is to be married the following afternoon. She and he have met and squabbled over golf balls and automobiles. They have endured mutually embarrassing wardrobe malfunctions having to do (significantly) with his tails and her bottom. They have conked Mr. Peabody on the head with a rock—or Susan did as David stood too transfixed to move. The bopping of Boopie, as it were, sends David into such despair that he confides in Susan that his interest in Mr. Peabody was merely as the lawyer for a Mrs. Carleton Random, who plans to donate a million dollars to the museum. Mrs. Carleton Random, of course, turns out to be none other than Susan's Aunt Elizabeth, so the threads of connection are established as Susan (significantly) mends the tails of David's coat.

We know, all along, that the Huxley/Swallow marriage is imminent. We heard about it in the very first scene in which Alice Swallow vowed to

David Huxley that their marriage would "entail" (again significantly) "no domestic entanglements of any kind." We already question the wisdom of David's devotion to Alice. Perhaps we even see the possibility of escape in this chance encounter with Susan. That we are supposed to do so, I think, is clear, but we may also find ourselves uncomfortable with Susan's zaniness and unpredictability. Such anxiety would match David's initial response, articulated as Susan drops David off at his home, after the unfortunate bopping of Boopie, after she has sewn together the rip in the tails of his coat: "Now it isn't that I don't like you, Susan, because, after all, in moments of quiet, I'm strangely drawn towards you, but, well, there haven't been any quiet moments." David falls after this pronouncement as he turns away from Susan—a sure sign in this genre that he will have difficulty leaving her despite his "good-night—and I hope I never lay eyes on you again." As Susan contemplates him we see her, in her second close-up, smile, nod, and turn decisively toward the steering wheel of the car. Without having said a word, Hepburn and Hawks have told film audiences, Susan has a plan.

Wycherley can't use close-ups, of course—and, in Harcourt's case, he opts to avoid using an aside in order for the character to articulate a plan—an interesting choice given the careful use to which that stage convention has been employed for all the other schemes being carried on in the play. Harcourt does speak to Horner about the dilemma presented by the Alithea/Sparkish engagement, a dilemma quite similar to that faced by Susan Vance: "I am in love with *Sparkish*'s Mistriss, whom he is to marry to morrow, now, how shall I get her?" (3.2.48–49). The word "get" suggests something of the primal urge Harcourt feels. He wants her in a very basic way—not to impress another man with his power or to avenge himself on the wrongs done his class by another class nor to wound Sparkish in particular. His desire is more than carnal. Indeed, from the beginning he names his feeling "love"—impetuously, but firmly, insisting that he has a lover's right to interfere in Alithea's match with Sparkish, and that she has an "obligation" to admit that his complaint is just (2.1.217). Susan Vance behaves with similar force and singlemindedness, proclaiming to Aunt Elizabeth that David is "the only man I've ever loved." Harcourt, unlike the typical rake in Restoration comedy, who is driven by both a keen sex drive and a sharp aversion to matrimony, immediately agrees to marry Alithea, "if you take Marriage for a sign of love" (2.1.227–28), but his primary drive is simply to be near her. As in *Bringing Up Baby*, this couple can be read as discovering a definition of marriage through the course of their relationship.

Horner's advice to Harcourt is that he should just rely on Sparkish to provide eventual means of access to Alithea (he himself seems to hope to profit in that regard, as well): "a foolish Rival, and a jealous Husband, assist their Rivals designs; for they are sure to make their Women hate them, which is the first step to their love, for another man" (3.2.52–54). But, it's not enough that Sparkish so evidently offers no hope of happiness in marriage (just as it's not enough that Alice Swallow is so clearly wrong for

David). Alithea is principled. David is inexperienced. And both are proceeding into matrimony half asleep as a result of their individual limitations. Neither Alithea nor David seems to expect happiness from or in marriage. The lesson that happiness can be found in and only in such a union, such a conversation, is the lesson that Harcourt and Susan have to teach.

Alithea, unlike David, does value pleasure, and she knows where to find it—innocently (for now). She loves the plays, the walks, the shops of London, and she finds joy and satisfaction in the town itself. She's seen, in her brother's treatment of her sister-in-law, the primary fate she hopes to avoid: a jealous husband who refuses to allow her the treats London has to offer, who may even insist that she become a "country wife." Sparkish's "want of jealousie" (4.1.44) more than makes up for his lack of wit, Alithea tells her maid Lucy, who cannot understand why any woman, especially one who "intend[s] to be honest" (4.1.47) would marry an "errant Natural" (4.1.42), a "fool" (4.1.46), rather than a "fine Gentleman" of "wit," whom one admits one loves (4.1.42–43). Lucy, like Quack in a sense, is a helper of nature, for she has more worldly wisdom than her young mistress, and she offers some advice regarding both theoretical and practical morality. Alithea's principled stance regarding her engagement to Sparkish, whom "my justice will not suffer to deceive or injure" is countered by Lucy's alternative reading: "Can there be a greater cheat, or wrong done to a Man, than to give him your person, without your heart?" (4.1.17–20). When Alithea opines that she will learn to love Sparkish, Lucy pragmatically dismisses her: "The Woman that marries to love better, will be as much mistaken, as the Wencher that marries to live better" (4.1.23–24). There are facts of human nature that simply cannot be denied; love cannot be manufactured where it does not exist any more than lust can be controlled by institutionalizing (or caging) it, as it were. Marriage does impose limits; it is not a particularly natural state. But given the option, a woman should never marry for honor when she can marry for love, "the life of life" (4.1.34).

The Country Wife, for all its cynicism, has at its core the most adamant defense of the love match of any of the Restoration courtship comedies—and it is significant that this defense is spoken by the servant, who is also given the role of rectifying the various mistakes and misunderstandings to draw the play to a satisfying conclusion. Lucy's primary interest is Alithea, much in the same way that Mugsy's interest in *The Lady Eve* is Hopsy. Both Lucy and Mugsy are servants of the rich whose livelihood and well-being are attached to the young people who are their primary charge, but their devotion exceeds their role. Mugsy's hyperalertness to any potential harm that can come to his naïve master leads him to repeat over and over again a truth that Hopsy and we, the audience, variously accept and reject, care about and are indifferent to, believe and disbelieve, know and don't know and eventually don't want to know: "She's the same dame." He's right, and he's wrong. And Hopsy's growth in the film (as well as our own growth through viewing the film) is realizing just how little and how much it matters in terms of their pleasure and our own. Our pleasure in both Jean and Eve *is* partly a pleasure in Barbara Stanwyck, the actress, whoever that is. (In fact, Barbara Stanwyck was born Ruby Catherine Stevens, had been a Ziegfield girl, was a star of a melodrama, *Stella Dallas*, as well as other genre films, was divorced and married for the second time during the filming of *The Lady Eve*, and was having an affair with her costar, Henry Fonda, to boot—as if any of that tells us anything.) In the end, our pleasure in Jean, Eve, and Barbara Stanwyck in *The Lady Eve* is just that—pleasure. Mugsy notwithstanding, we enjoy their company and we take joy in their presence—however paradoxical that concept is when spoken of film. And, whereas *Bringing Up Baby* has no cynical Mugsy to call attention to sameness and difference, the topic is clearly central to Hawks's film with mix-ups about cars, golf balls, purses, and leopards. References to another of Cary Grant's screen roles ("Jerry the Nipper" in *The Awful Truth*), to his real name ("Archie Leach"), to the movies that Susan has seen and which she imitates in order to escape from jail—none of these self-conscious reminders that the person we are looking at is the "same dame" or the "same mug" that we've seen elsewhere under different names or in different genres interferes with the pleasure we take in their company, which seems so real on the one hand and so insubstantial on the other.

Presence is not a paradoxical concept at all, of course, when spoken of stage performances—witnessed live, that is. But even so, we are asked to believe that actresses and actors are the characters they portray, at least for the duration of the play. And we are expected to believe what we see or what we're told or what's implied about the actions of the characters onstage. Costumes and sets and actions define the identities we witness—and, although we know the character is brought to life by an actor with a completely separate identity, we agree through the conventions of theater to put aside certain kinds of knowledge (to "suspend disbelief" of one sort and embrace belief of another) to enjoy the action, to take pleasure in the events unfolding before us. Throughout *The Country Wife*, this fact of theatrical pleasure is alluded to in various scenes that add to our enjoyment, but that emphasize the essential pain, discomfort, and anxiety at the heart of the question of sameness and difference. Pinchwife's agony in the Exchange as the rakes kiss the "boy" he calls James results from his knowing the "boy" is really his wife in disguise. Alithea's anxiety as Harcourt pretends to be his clergyman "brother" Ned is a more complicated kind of discomfort, born of exasperation that what she sees so clearly is so clearly not seen by Sparkish. She is in a sense in on the joke (or "trick" as Lucy calls it [4.1.91]) that Harcourt is playing, without really wanting to be. She is, moreover, impatient that her husband-to-be cannot see through the ruse. Harcourt's acting is several times in the scene referred to as implausible, inconsistent, unconvincing. Lucy, his most enthusiastic supporter (his manager, perhaps?), tries to enhance his character's believability by describing his affect as authentic: "I'll be sworn he has the Canonical smirk, and the filthy, clammy palm of a Chaplain" (4.1.121–22). But she has to admit a little later that he "forget[s] his Function" as he goes too far in double entendre when he says to Alithea, "no body else shall marry you, by Heavens, I'll die first, for I'm sure I shou'd die after it" (4.1.149, 146–48). Even he admits that he has a difficult time speaking in coherence with the costume he wears: "I had forgot, I must sute my stile to my Coat, or I wear it in vain" (4.1.133–34).

Harcourt's "play," although bad, does deceive and even please Sparkish. Alithea does what she can to open the eyes of her husband-to-be, explaining, Mugsy-like, that the "trick" is just that "Frank goes and puts on a black coat, then tells you he's Ned." Still, Sparkish continues to enjoy himself, hearing even Harcourt's confessions of love as evidence of Ned's honesty. Alithea impatiently and pedantically explains, "Invincible stupidity, I tell you he wou'd marry me, as your Rival, not as your Chaplain" (4.1.158–59), but Sparkish is no more convinced than Sheriff Slocum is by David's warning that Susan is making things up "out of motion pictures she's seen." When Alithea asks "what can you hope, or design by this?" (4.1.164), Harcourt's answer is tellingly like Susan's explanation of her own zany tricks and implausible scripts. He says, "if she will not take mercy on me, and let me marry her, I have at least the Lover's second pleasure, hindring my Rivals enjoyment, though but for a time" (4.1.166–68).

Admittedly, Harcourt does invoke the homosocial dynamic here, but it seems so implausible to think that he really has a point to prove with Sparkish that I choose to read his chaplain-play as the same kind of improvisation (sometimes Chaplin-like, although more often reminiscent of the Marx Brothers or Buster Keaton) that Susan engages in to keep David near her. First Susan writes the "I need to take my leopard to Connecticut, and you have to help me" road movie starring both herself and David, and featuring Baby, the leopard, whose supporting role includes a bit of improvisation as well (the chickens and the ducks). Once in Connecticut, Susan writes another play, this one starring David Bone, the big game hunter friend of Mark, who has had a nervous breakdown and really likes George. Aunt Elizabeth ("George is a perfect little fiend, and you know it!") is this play's intended audience, although Major Applegate, who *is* a big game hunter, gets drawn in as well. David eventually comments on the fact that he has been starring in a dramatic narrative without fully understanding his role or knowing his lines:

> You told your aunt I was crazy, didn't you? You told her my name was Bone, and you didn't tell me. You told her I was a big game hunter, and you didn't tell me. You'd tell anybody anything that comes into your head, and you don't tell me.

But eventually David accepts his role without having it fully explained to him, and when he does so, it is not a matter of playing. At the jail that Susan has successfully escaped, Aunt Elizabeth, Major Applegate, and Fogarty have joined David in lock-up as members of what Sheriff Slocum calls "The Leopard Gang." Amid the pandemonium of their protests, two circus employees enter looking for an escaped and dangerous leopard—one that Susan has earlier released, thinking it was *her* leopard. Just about the same time, her leopard, the tame one, Baby, enters the jail, followed by George. David quickly grasps the significance of the fact that there are two leopards in Connecticut (to echo Cavell): "Oh, my goodness! Susan's out trying to catch the wrong leopard. Oh, poor darling Susan. She's in danger, and she's helpless without me." When, seconds later, Susan appears, dragging the wild leopard, who is slapping and growling at her, David becomes, if not exactly a big game hunter, at least a circus tamer, who can force the dangerous beast (from whom even Baby and George flee) into a jail cell before fainting into Susan's arms.

We can see, of course, that not only is Susan anything but helpless, but that Katharine Hepburn also seems to have more courage than one would expect from the average Hollywood actress. Bogdanovich marvels, "I don't exactly know how they did that. That's really her pulling that leopard." The camera doesn't lie, we assume, and we see, in long shot, Hepburn's full body straining at one end of the rope, and the writhing, snarling animal at the other. Grant, we know from movie lore, was afraid of the leopard, and most shots in which he and the leopard seem to be together are camera "tricks" such as back projection or split screen or puppetry. And the technological manipulation is usually obvious. But Hepburn was quite comfortable, stroking Baby as if she were a housecat at one point. Does it affect our reading of David's heroic gesture that Grant himself does not physically encounter the leopard? I guess the answer depends on whether we ourselves are "playing" or "not playing"—as well as what we are "playing at."

For sometimes we are willing to be deceived in the interest of pleasure or peace of mind; other times, we resent being taken for a mug, a patsy, a fool. Even Sparkish, who had very little interest in Alithea or marriage or anything other than "be[ing] envy'd" (3.2.342) and dining at Whitehall with the King, finds it galling when Lucy "reveals" that she disguised Margery as Alithea in the interest of "breaking off the match, between Mr. *Sparkish* and her, to make way for Mr. *Harcourt*" (5.4.321–22). Given that he has avoided being knighted, as he explains earlier, because of the current penchant for ridiculing knights on the stage, it is a fine irony that Sparkish is the only character who stands at the play's end exposed as a gull and a fool. Pinchwife and Fidget may be cuckolds, but because the ladies silence Margery and thereby protect Horner's secret (and their own), they are not exposed as such. Pinchwife points to the moral of their story in his closing speech:

> For my own sake fain I wou'd all believe.
> Cuckolds, like Lovers, should themselves deceive.
> *But*—[*sighs.*]
> His honour is least safe, (too late I find)
> Who trusts it with a foolish Wife or Friend.
>
> (5.4.410–14)

Playing and not playing 147

He then joins, along with Sir Jasper, "*A Dance of Cuckolds*" that concludes the play. L. J. Morrissey long ago analyzed the entire action of *The Country Wife* as following the elaborate pattern of a country dance in which Wycherley "skillfully arranges his characters in patterns reminiscent of the dances of the period."[27] Horner "opens the dance," which will through the course of the play "expose hypocrisy and lust, his own included" (427). But the dance also celebrates "genuine virtue" in the partnering of Alithea and Harcourt, who "affirm the world of romance and love" (427–28). Morrissey points out that all the women choose their own partners—the city wives and Margery opting for Horner; Alithea at first choosing Sparkish, but in the end led to change partners and join hands with Harcourt. In terms of the country dance, "configurations involving Margery and Lady Fidget have both been resolved in scenes of broad and slightly squalid farce" (428). Morrissey elaborates:

> Horner moves from the formal and sedate set with the city women in Act III to increasingly farcical sets with both the city women and Margery. Alithea and Harcourt, on the other hand, move from the farce rendering of a set in Act II to a stable, formal joining as a couple in the last act of the play.
>
> (428)

This reading assumes that Harcourt does not join in the dance of cuckolds. I am not sure that he never does. The stage directions do not specify that he should or should not.

The courtship of Alithea and Harcourt has been conducted in this world of distorted behaviors and values in which wildness and tameness vie for dominance. Jealousy turns a husband into a "wild beast," who attempts to tame his wife by treating her like "a bird in a cage" and thereby makes her determined to fly. City wives find themselves neglected by potential lovers as well as husbands because they insist on "ceremony" when a man is interested in "falling on briskly" (5.4.87–88). But women like "freedom," Lady Fidget insists: "a person may be as free as he pleases with us, as frolick, as gamesome, as wild as he will" (5.4.90–92). They may say they want a tame, tractable man, but they long for "wildness" (5.4.94). The language points to the basic struggle central not only to the institution of marriage, but to civilization itself. Alithea chides herself for her "over-wise" intent to marry a fool in the interest of preserving her liberty (5.3.77), for she sees, by Act 5, that such a liberty is not really freedom. Further, as Lucy well knows, the compass of Alithea's desire is now defined by the pleasures afforded by the town. Marriage will teach her new appetites. If Lucy fully understands that Alithea will "make no use of [what she cynically terms] her fortune, her blessing" in marrying a fool (i.e., to cuckold him), she also understands that "Master *Sparkish*'s bed" will be no more than "a stinking second-hand-grave" (3.2.235–36; 4.1.4–6). And, thanks to Lucy, both Alithea and Harcourt are "edified" by the lesson provided by the Pinchwifes and articulated by Lucy herself: "any wild thing grows but the more fierce and hungry for being kept up, and more dangerous to the Keeper" (5.4.385–86).

Like *Bringing Up Baby*, *The Country Wife* puzzles over the question of marriage and desire, and like the film, the play offers a tentative solution in the love match. As in any screwball environment, in Wycherley's play the zanies can seem to overwhelm the rational characters. Indeed, sometimes, especially in the film genre, that is exactly what needs to happen to precipitate the remarriage that must occur. We will see a clear example of this phenomenon in *My Man Godfrey*, the subject of the next chapter. Hawks felt that *Bringing Up Baby* actually suffered from the fact that everyone in the movie was a "screwball."[28] No one represents normality—and rationality is invariably misled and misleading in that script. *The Country Wife*, although it has its zanies, does include the normative point of view represented by Alithea and Harcourt. They are the text's optimistic investment in marriage, its hope that, evidence notwithstanding, somehow basic urges and desires can be satisfied in a truly honorable union, that individual liberty can coexist with marital devotion, that the pleasure of business will not make Harcourt neglectful, and that the business of pleasure pursued by Alithea will remain focused on the theater, the shops, and the walks of London rather than the kinds of pleasures pursued by the city wives around her.

Bringing Up Baby represents the prehistoric myth of the remarriage genre, according to Cavell. As such, it makes explicit a few features that are implicit to the other texts in the genre, and that, to my mind, find echoes in the Restoration play with which I have paired Hawks's film. I say "echoes" in the spirit of regarding *Bringing Up Baby* as the prehistoric myth behind the dramatic genre that I am arguing is ancestor to remarriage film comedy. Three features of the myth are particularly important. First, the omnipresence of repetition is not simply coincidental or comedic. It is at the heart of the perception of marriage as a "willingness for repetition"—which is essentially a "willingness for remarriage' (*PH*, 126–27). "Put . . . metaphysically," Cavell says, "only those can genuinely marry who are already married" (*PH*, 127). That insight applies as well to the Restoration couples (meant for each other from the moment they exchange their first witticisms). Cavell's continued meditation cannot be evidenced by the Restoration texts (except, perhaps, *The Way of the World*), largely because of the impossibility of divorce. Cavell continues, "It is as though you know you are married when you come to see that you cannot divorce, that is, when you find that your lives simply will not disentangle." "If your love is lucky," he concludes, "this knowledge will be greeted with laughter" (*PH*, 127). Susan laughs a lot, but as Cavell points out, David (or Grant) "never smiles" (*PH*, 127), yet they cannot divorce as their perpetual and perpetually unsuccessful leave-taking proves. And although in the Restoration the impossibility of divorce made remarriage impossible, it is also true that false marriages are characterized by the kind of separate lives the Fidgets arrange to live. Were they truly married, their story would have a different ending. Their lives are easily disentangled as they were never meshed in the first place.

Pinchwife, of course, will take Margery back to the country. They are in a way remarried at the end of *The Country Wife*, with Margery resigned to her fate, if not happy about it. But their "remarriage" lacks the elements central to true remarriage as suggested by the "prehistoric myth" in *Bringing Up Baby*. The film comedies insist on the creation of a "shared, lost past, to which . . . [the central couple] can wish to remain faithful" (*PH*, 127). Hopsy creates it for Jean (and Eve) in his rhapsody about their growing up together. Susan and David create a shared childhood during their evening's search for the bone George has buried. David, though (or because) subjected to various indignities during the "hunt" (a slide down a hill, a net on his head, a dunking in a "shallow" stream, burnt socks and broken glasses, to name a few), will remember this evening as "the best . . . I ever had in my whole life"—a sentiment he shouts to Susan just before he tells her he loves her and just before she causes the brontosaurus to break apart and crash to the floor. Cavell assigns various meanings to the demise of the dinosaur—the end of virginity, the death of science, the signaling of the parameters of happiness—all of which seem to obtain. It also signals a new game—pick up sticks—which the couple can share.[29] The film ends as it began with Grant in the posture of a Rodin sculpture. The Thinker is now locked in the embrace of a Kiss—a somewhat awkward kiss, but a kiss (along with David's "oh dear") that signifies a willingness to continue, to repeat, and to forgive.

If Margery evokes the notion of childhood—and she does—she does not participate in creating a shared past with her husband. And although she does play games (dress up, in particular), she does not have a willing partner in play. Pinchwife is a father/guardian/tyrant of a husband, who has no sense of fun and who seems incapable of developing such a sense. Margery's true match in terms of play and fun would seem to be, indeed, the one she chooses for herself, but Horner rejects her in the end, preferring to continue his secret and sordid revenge on the cits of London. The childhood moment they experienced in the Exchange will not be repeated, nothing will be broken, and forgiveness will be neither requested nor conferred. Games and play have been invoked by Lady Fidget in her celebration of "wildness," but we don't get the sense that these are games of carefree fun such as Margery seemed to have had as Horner plied her with fruit and kisses. Alithea and Harcourt may not have had frolics, may not have enjoyed innocent play, but the elements of the myth in the play in which their love is posited as ideal resonate interestingly to me.

Childhood, of course, is not fully theorized in the Restoration period as it will be in the post-Romantic age. Yet we will see the theme re-emerge in *The Way of the World*, not integrated into the story of Millamant and Mirabell, but there, nonetheless, as though straining for some basic notion of who and what and why we are and who and what and why we want what and whom we want. *The Country Wife,* like *Bringing Up Baby,* offers no answer, but indicates that the questions are fundamental to human experience. It would be ideal if, like Baby, we could be content with a song about love. But there is in everyone a wild leopard that doesn't particularly respond to the clichés of civilized society. In each of us, there is the desire to find our own path and walk it with the person we desire. In other words, we tend to wish to validate our own marriages—as Harcourt and Susan so well understand, as Alithea and David come to accept, and as Miss Swallow and Sparkish will never know.

The Country Wife can thus be read in light of Cavell's pithy summation of the significance of the plot of *Bringing Up Baby*: "marriage requires its own proof" (*PH*, 127). Some betrothals (e.g., those of Sparkish and Alithea and of David and Miss Swallow) can and should be deemed false and invalidated. By extension, what seems to be marriage may not be true marriage (in the sense these genres privilege), after all. No viewer or reader of the play is meant to spend any time at all worrying about the wrong done to Sir Jasper Fidget and to Mr. Pinchwife by Horner's imposition. No one is supposed to care that Sparkish doesn't get the girl. Neither is any viewer of the film meant to feel wrong or regret on behalf of Miss Swallow. Yet, it must be acknowledged that anxieties provoked by both texts are not restricted to those having to do with the double entendre and sexual suggestiveness of the language of each work, which were discussed earlier. Some anxieties do attend the fates of those we are meant to dismiss. The texts may insist that we not care, but they also provide reason for us to resist their cavalier dismissal of the unlucky in love. *The Country Wife* overtly acknowledges this dimension of its address to the audience by concluding with the "dance of the cuckolds." *Bringing Up Baby* as well shatters our complacence with the dramatic destruction of the "baby" built by David and his former fiancée, the very brontosaurus that had been the focus of a "no-entail" clause in David's first marriage settlement. Does the demise of the dinosaur at the hands (or limbs) of Susan signify entailment now? Is that what the lopsided kiss at the end of the film conveys? Or are we back to square one with the initial problem (entailment) simply left to other hands (or limbs)?

Further, viewer reception of both works tends to feature skepticism to the point that we might suspect an egregious courting of such response. Although it certainly came as an unwelcome surprise to Katharine Hepburn (and Howard Hawks) that this film did nothing to redeem the actress's flailing screen career, it must be acknowledged that Susan is pretty hard to take, even today. She's attractive, certainly. And when we first see her on the golfcourse, she seems the epitome of self-possession and commonsense. The exchange she has with David Huxley regarding the golf ball under dispute, although ludicrous, convinces us that she has reason on her side. She's a necessary tonic for David's earnestness when he explains painstakingly that his golf ball is "Pro-Flight" as opposed to the "PGA" she's playing and that hers has "two black dots" whereas his features a "circle." "I'm not superstitious about things like that," she calmly remarks, and then "sinks a 25-foot putt," according to the screenplay. David, still focused on the *idée fixe* that has driven (so to speak) him to Susan in the first place, runs to collect the ball from the hole: "There, you see, it's a circle," he prosaically remarks, to which she wittily replies, "Well, of course it is. Do you think it would roll if it were square?" David persists: "No. I have reference to a mark on the ball. That proves it's a Pro-Flight and that's my ball." Hepburn delivers the next line with a perfect blend of resignation and exasperation: "I know. . . . Well, what does it matter?" And she concludes with the comment I've referenced already: "It's only a game anyway." I think most viewers are on her side at this point (excepting, perhaps, golfers—and maybe even golfers because David has, after all, left his game "on the first fairway" and it is, as Susan notes, "silly of . . . [him] to be fooling around on the eighteenth green"). But, then, Susan ups the ante. She destroys property. She commits casual acts of violence. She lies. She steals. She creates an ever-increasing cacophonous chaos for which Hepburn's voice (timbre, tone, and accent) seem unusually (and, appropriately, unpleasantly) suited. Whereas Susan becomes an irresistible and ultimately pleasurable problem for David in the film, in that all audience members are not seeking escape from the boredom of a Miss Swallow, Katharine Hepburn proved in 1938 (and regrettably still proves for many first-time viewers of this movie) a burden to surmount. Hepburn's performance is brilliant, but it induced such resistance, such skepticism (of a nonphilosophical order), at the time it appeared and cost her such effort to reclaim her place on the screen, she never trusted herself to perform in this kind of comedy again.[30]

Circles or squares? That is the central problem posed by both Restoration courtship comedy and the Hollywood comedy of remarriage. The problem of other minds is that they are other. We can't always know that our words as spoken will register when heard with our intent, with our purpose, with our desire. *Bringing Up Baby* was initially rejected by the culture it addressed as too other, in a sense. *The Country Wife*, on the other hand, was received well by the audience for whom it was initially written and staged. The dance of the cuckolds truly is a celebration of the mystery of sexual desire, an acknowledgment of the things that we cannot know and probably don't want to know about the secret longings of our partners—an embracing of the fact that we will always have fears and yet we embrace love anyway. Laura Rosenthal reads the dance as nationally significant, as well:

> the cuckolds . . . become finally aligned in this play with national identity and national amnesia. The triumph of the cuckold marks a new phase in English history: embracing one's inner cuckold celebrates . . . a nation recovering from a leveling rebellion that it must, with the help of repeated performances of *The Country Wife* . . . and other sex comedies, remember to forget.[31]

In this sense, the end of *The Country Wife* is very like the ending of *Bringing Up Baby*—an affirmation that sometimes skepticism can be overcome by a simple willingness to forget the past, to embrace the future by kissing the girl or joining the dance. Although Alithea seems unlikely to cuckold Harcourt, I think I would have him join the dance in recognition of the fact that his love makes him vulnerable, his pursuit of happiness in marriage, although a risk worth taking, has no guarantees. To join the dance is to give up the notion of certainty and control, to acknowledge the need to pay attention, to join the human race, in a sense, rather than to exist outside (as Horner does) or above (as Miss Swallow does). For Harcourt, to dance with the cuckolds would be the equivalent of David Huxley's "oh dear."

Although it may be counterintuitive to expect marriage to be the domain of permanent sexual satisfaction, cultural conventions insist that it must serve that purpose despite the fact that desire is, for both men and women, so wayward, so unpredictable. Over and beyond sex itself, marriage with its central notion of "belonging to" seems to militate against fun and play and freedom, things associated more with childhood than maturity. But *The Country Wife* and *Bringing Up Baby* insist that marriage is exactly the condition necessary for adult fun and play and freedom to have full reign. Neither text suggests that marriage automatically confers these favors, but both affirm that marriage, rightly pursued, creates favorable conditions for happiness in a way no other plausible arrangement can do. The Alithea/Harcourt plot in *The Country Wife* resonates with the Susan/David plot in *Bringing Up Baby* to this end. Set against the bestial fable of Horner and his women, the story of the courtship of Harcourt and Alithea prefigures the serious attention that "play" will receive in the classical Hollywood remarriage comedy.

Notes

1 William Wycherley, *The Country Wife*, in *The Plays of William Wycherley*, ed. Arthur Friedman (1675; Oxford: Clarendon Press, 1979). References are to act, scene, and line numbers.
2 Douglas Duncan, "Mythic Parody in *The Country Wife*," *Essays in Criticism* 31 (1981): 299–312; and Peggy Thompson, "The Limits of Parody in *The Country Wife*," *Studies in Philology* 89, no. 1 (1992): 100–114.
3 Marshall, "Wycherley's 'Great Stage of Fools': Madness and Theatricality in *The Country Wife*," *Studies in English Literature* 29, no. 3 (1989): 423–24.
4 Hence, the emphasis on Eden and "the creation of woman and . . . the temptability of man," in the films (*PH*, 48), a notable emphasis in the plays as well.
5 "What Happens in *The Country-Wife*," *Studies in English Literature* 22 (Summer 1982): 411.
6 Marshall, "Madness and Theatricality," 423.
7 David experiences throughout *Bringing Up Baby* what Cavell calls the "riddle of intimacy, which repels where it attracts" (*PH*, 31). *The Country Wife*'s Alithea will be seen to suffer similarly.

8 Sedgwick, *Between Men: English Literature and Male Homosocial Desire* (New York: Columbia University Press, 1985), 56.
9 Oliver, "'I Will Write Whore with This Penknife in Your Face': Female Amatory Letters, the Body, and Violence in Wycherley's *The Country Wife*," *Restoration* 38 (2014): 46.
10 Vance, *William Wycherley and the Comedy of Fear* (Newark: University of Delaware Press, 2000), 92.
11 Review, *New York Times*, March 4, 1938, rptd. in *Bringing Up Baby: Howard Hawks, Director*, ed. Gerald Mast, Rutgers Films in Print Series (1988; New Brunswick, NJ: Rutgers University Press, 1994), 265. Mast also includes the more positive unsigned review from *Variety* (February 16, 1938), which finds Hepburn "invigorating" (266), and Otis Ferguson's *New Republic Review* (March 2, 1938), which characterizes Hepburn's performance as one of "intelligence and mercury" (268).
12 Thomas H. Fujimura reviews the print and production history in his introduction to his edition of *The Country Wife*, Regents Restoration Drama series (Lincoln: University of Nebraska Press, 1965), ix.
13 Fujimura, Introduction, x. He references Emmett L. Avery, "*The Country Wife* in the Eighteenth Century," *Research Studies of the State College of Washington* 10 (1942): 142–58.
14 "Remarks," *The Country Girl; A Comedy, in Five Acts; as Performed at the Theatre Royal*, Drury Lane, alter'd from Wycherly's *The Country Wife*, by David Garrick, in The *British Theatre, or a Collection of Plays ... with Biographical and Critical Remarks by Mrs. Inchbald*, vol. 16 (London: Longman, Hurst, Rees, and Orme, 1808), 5, 3.
15 Friedrich Nietzsche, *Beyond Good and Evil: Prelude to a Philosophy of the Future*, ed. Rolf-Peter Horstmann, trans. Judith Norman, Cambridge Texts in the History of Philosophy (Cambridge: Cambridge University Press, 2002), 62.
16 Mast, Introduction, 8.
17 Porter, "Before the Fringe: Quack Medicine in Georgian England," *History Today* 36 (1986). http://www.historytoday.com.
18 The Royal Charter formally decrees that the body be known as "The Royal Society of London for Improving Natural Knowledge."
19 Samuel L. Macey notes that Sir Jasper, the "City knight," is, like other "men of business ... dominated by the clock." *Patriarchs of Time: Dualism in Saturn-Cronus, Father Time, the Watchmaker God, and Father Christmas* (Athens: University of Georgia Press, 2010), 93.
20 Roach, "The Performance," in *The Cambridge Companion to English Restoration Theatre*, ed. Deborah Payne Fisk (Cambridge: Cambridge University Press, 2000), 27, 25.
21 James Thompson, *Language in Wycherley's Plays*, Seventeenth-Century Language Theory and Drama (Tuscaloosa: University of Alabama Press, 1984), 73.
22 Daileader, "Back-Door Sex: Renaissance Gynosodomy, Aretino, and the Exotic," *ELH* 69 (2002): 306.
23 James Thompson, *Language in Wycherley's Plays*, 71.
24 Gellineau, "*The Country Wife*, Dance of the Cuckolds," *Comparative Drama* 48, no. 3 (2014): 294.
25 Payne, "Reading the Signs in *The Country Wife*," *Studies in English Literature 1500–1900* 26 (1986): 411.
26 Bogdanovich, "Commentary," *Bringing Up Baby*, Disc 1, directed by Howard Hawks (1938; Warner Home Video, 2005), DVD.
27 Morrissey, "Wycherley's Country Dance," *Studies in English Literature 1500–1900* 8 (1968): 429.

28 Richard Schickel, *The Men Who Made the Movies: Howard Hawks*, directed by Richard Schickel, disc 2 of *Bringing Up Baby*, directed by Howard Hawks (1973; Burbank, CA: Warner Home Video, 2005), DVD.
29 As Cavell mentions, the film alludes to many childhood games including pin the tail on the donkey (dinosaur), hide and seek, follow the leader, and squat tag: "[T]he principals' actions consist of, or have the quality of, a series of games" (*PH*, 124).
30 Bogdanovich, "Commentary."
31 Rosenthal, "'All Injury's Forgot': Restoration Sex Comedy and National Amnesia," *Comparative Drama* 42, no. 1 (2008): 26.

6 Forgotten men
William Wycherley's *The Plain Dealer* and Gregory La Cava's *My Man Godfrey*

There is an undeniable melancholy at the heart of each of the genres with which this book is concerned, and the two texts that form the subject of this chapter acknowledge and examine the source of that melancholy without, finally, succumbing to it. Still, it lingers and defines the tone of each work, redeemed only (in both cases, interestingly enough) by a young, passionate female, whose sense of personal romantic destiny overcomes the weary dejection of the man she loves and the society in which she lives.

Each story begins with incongruities so conspicuous that if we were allowed the leisure of reflection we might refuse consent to the worlds represented. But the pace of "Act 1" in each work is so rapid, we are carried along, as it were, drawn in initially by the oddness of the central male character (a misanthrope in the one case, a down-and-out tramp in the other). Our interest is sustained as he comes up against a variety of "others," in conversation with whom he begins to complicate our initial sense of who he is. As each beginning action unfolds, initial incongruities are deepened and seem to become essential to the self-definition of each main male character. It's as though his time is out of joint, and his choices are so bizarrely limited that he does well to retain a sense of self at all, distorted and unbalanced though that self seems to be. In each case, there is a fundamental drive to dignity, in particular, that marks the man as unusual and vulnerable. He is in great need of protection, and paradoxically, he finds his eventual safety (salvation) in the company of one who seems initially to be too weak, incapable, or zany to take care of herself, much less give aid to another.

The most notable incongruity in each text is the "forgotten man" at the center. In both cases, he is a generic paradox. *The Plain Dealer's* Captain Manly, as Robert D. Hume notes, has long proved an interpretative problem. Although "for nearly three centuries, critics almost universally assumed that Manly was the 'hero' and served as spokesman for the author against a corrupt society," in the mid-twentieth century, that consensus was challenged by Alexander H. Chorney, who "offered a radical reinterpretation, arguing that Manly is 'a recognizable comic type, a "humourist," whose plain dealing is a folly to be castigated,' even though his 'social criticism may often be valid.'"[1] As Hume puts it, "in this reading, Manly winds up as a comic butt who is as thoroughly discredited as the corrupt world he denounces so harshly." In light of Chorney's challenge, a definitive reading of Manly for our time has yet to be proffered. Hume concludes, "Critics of the last half century have made little progress toward a resolution. The play itself contains disconcertingly contradictory elements. It can be staged effectively with Manly as either hero or butt" (205–6). So Manly, at the center of a text that contains the familiar fops and wits and that seems bent on pursuing the theme of courtship, love, and marriage, stands as an anomaly, who has only vestiges of the rakishness (and not even vestiges of the charm and desirability) that would link him to Dorimant, Wilmore, Harcourt, or even Horner.

Similarly, Godfrey Parke/Smith is an oddball in the comedy of remarriage genre. It is probably significant that Cavell does not treat *My Man Godfrey* in *Pursuits of Happiness*, although the film does in many ways fit his template of the remarriage comedy. Godfrey and Irene meet, "marry," divorce, and remarry. Godfrey is as hypnotized by her as David is by Susan or Peter by Ellie or Hopsy by Jean/Eve. In the way of the genre, his growth as a human being is fully dependent on his relationship with Irene, but—unusual for this kind of narrative—his growth is also tied to his integration into the Bullock family as a whole. The story line is as much about his following and not following Cornelia as it is about his following and not following Irene. Like Manly, Godfrey is introduced to us through a sequence of encounters with various individuals, each of whom reveals a side of his character and personality. As in Manly's case, however, these various sides fail to yield a coherent character. When Mr. Bullock asks Godfrey midway through the film, "say, who *are* you?" he gives voice to the conundrum around which the script is built. And, as Godfrey's answer, "I'm just a nobody, sir" indicates, Godfrey is a "forgotten man," his identity lost and, in some ways, irrecoverable. It must be rebuilt from the ashes of the dump in which Godfrey Parke died and Godfrey Smith was born.[2]

Manly first appears in *The Plain Dealer* as the speaker of the prologue. After announcing that he is to "*Act . . .* [the] *rough Part*" of the Plain Dealer today, he speaks for the playwright in predicting that few will like the play because it's too honest and forthright (Prologue 1–2).[3] It holds a mirror to members of the audience, who will see themselves, if a "*fine Woman,*" to be none other than a "*mercenary Jilt*"; if "*Men of Wit,*" "*dull Rogues*"; if "*a Friend,*" one who "*break[s] his trust*" (Prologue 34–39). Yet, he ends the prologue with a couplet that appeals to the "*Prosp'rous*" at court to be "*Friends*" with the Plain Dealer (Prologue 49–50). Perhaps the court will develop a taste for bluntness, satire, and misanthropy? There is some contemporary evidence that, at least in their taste for Wycherley's wit, they did so. From this point on, the playwright himself would be known as "Manly Wycherley." And this play along with *The Country Wife* would be considered by his contemporaries to be his finest achievements—and by posterity, as two of the finest plays of the Restoration stage.

Forgotten men 157

The play proper begins in "*Captain* Manly's *Lodging*." The Dramatis Personae list has told us that Manly has, "in the time of the *Dutch War*, . . . procur'd the Command of a Ship, out of Honour, not Interest; and . . . [has chosen] a Sea-life, only to avoid the World." He enters the scene "*surlily*," followed by the "Coxcomb" Lord Plausible and a couple of sailors. Manly and Plausible are in the middle of a conversation—and a serious one, at that—in which somewhat implausibly the foolish fop seems to have been mounting a philosophical justification of the forms of the age, judging from the first words we hear as Manly enters. The sea captain is protesting that such "*Decorums*, supercilious Forms, and slavish Ceremonies" are performed "not out of love or duty, but [from] your servile fear" (1.1.2–5). Plausible begs to differ: "they are the Arts, and Rules, the prudent of the World walk by" (1.1.7–8). Immediately, then, Manly's quarrel with his age is established: he chafes at the demand to follow forms, to dissimulate affection and admiration where he feels none, to say one thing to a person's face and another behind his back. He will "have no Leading-strings": "I can walk alone; I hate a Harness, and will not tug on in a Faction, kissing my Leader behind, that another Slave may do the like to me" (1.1.9–11). Lord Plausible does his best to defend what he calls "pure good manners," but before long, Manly leaves the stage, "*thrusting out my* Lord Plausible" as he exits (1.1.42).

Left on the stage at the exit of the captain and the lord, the two sailors, between them, provide us the story of Manly's sea venture. At sea a mere month, the captain's ship and crew encountered the hostile Dutch, and in an altercation, Manly's ship was sunk. The sailors speculate that the disaster was deliberate: "our Bully *Tar* sunk our Ship: not only that the *Dutch* might not have her, but that the Courtiers, who laugh at wooden Legs, might not make her Prize" (1.1.95–98). His perversity is further elaborated as they note his determination to leave England for good: "He was a weary of this side of the World here . . . [and] had a mind to go live and bask himself on the sunny side of the Globe" (1.1.114–18; 132–34). The second sailor thinks the case more extreme than this explanation of national disaffiliation would suggest. Indeed, he feels the captain naturally pugnacious, incapable of happiness, gratitude, or ease: "after we had tug'd hard the old leaky Long-boat, to save his Life, when I welcom'd him ashore, he gave me a box on the ear, and call'd me fawning Water-dog" (1.1.132–34). We may hear these words as evidence of a misanthropy so deep it has led Manly to crave (and maybe even seek) his own demise, risking the lives of others as well in his despair.

As the act proceeds, Manly's ill-tempered grudge against the world becomes more and more evident, although it begins to seem less and less motivated. In fact, in the third conversation of Act 1, Manly makes a rather surprising revelation to his lieutenant Freeman (described in the Dramatis Personae as "a Gentleman well Educated, but of a broken Fortune, a Complyer with the Age"). It turns out that on his flight to the Indies, Manly has left behind two people, whom he venerates and trusts: his one true friend and, in this true friend's care, his one true love. So, Manly is not, after all, a thorough misanthrope. He simply believes that "a true heart admits but of one friendship, as of one love" (1.1.198–99), and he is spoken for on both counts. Freeman, who would be his friend, and Fidelia, who would be his love, make cases for themselves in scenes that follow—with mixed results. Although Freeman confesses that he is adept at the courtesies and ceremonies despised by the captain, he feels he can meet Manly's standard of friendship. "Try me, at least," he pleads (1.1.299). Manly does so— rejecting as evidence all behaviors that could benefit Freeman. So Freeman would fight for him? That brings him honor and doesn't count for friendship. So he would lend money? Then he would expect to borrow at a later date. So he would say nice things about Manly to Manly's enemies? Well, that just encourages "others to be your Friends, by a shew of gratitude" (1.1.308–09). OK, then, Freeman says: "I wou'd not hear you ill spoken of behind your back, by my Friend." Manly is stumped: "Nay, then, thou'rt a Friend indeed." Interestingly, though, he advises Freeman against such sacrifice: "It were unreasonable to expect it from thee, as the World goes now: when new Friends, like new Mistresses, are got by disparaging old ones" (1.1.310–14).

Whereas in his conversation with Lord Plausible, Manly may seem to be excoriating the individual complier, here with Freeman, the thrust of his critique is clearly aimed toward society. Freeman may be less to blame than Lord Plausible, who presumably, because he is an aristocrat, has some power in setting standards. But far from exulting in his social power, Plausible like Freeman seems to feel the age has a will of its own with tastes, habits, customs, and creeds that no one person or any one class defines. It's an interesting formulation that will find an echo in *My Man Godfrey* when the Park Avenue brat turned bum turned butler tells his old friend Tommy Gray that his family had been puppets for generations. Puppets of whom or what? Weren't the Park Avenue elites the ones pulling the strings in America in the 1930s, just as the aristocracy and court were pulling them in the 1670s? La Cava and Wycherley (or, at least Godfrey, Plausible, Freeman, and even Manly) don't really seem to think so. Societal attitudes, behaviors, and values are more complex than that.

Having reached that insight in his conversation with Freeman, Manly seems almost frantic as he confronts another would-be friend in the young volunteer Fidelia. In fact, when Fidelia enters the stage just as he finishes uttering his concession to Freeman, Manly without skipping a beat immediately turns to challenge the "boy": "Dost not thou love me devilishly too, my little Voluntier, as well as he, or any man can?" (1.1.315–17). Although his tone is mocking, it is significant that Manly is the one introducing the topic of friendship to Fidelia, whereas it was Freeman who brought the subject up in the earlier conversation. Manly almost seems to be inviting the protestations that follow. Fidelia speaks honestly and with irony (given her disguise) when she claims to love Manly "better than any man can love you" (1.1.318). Her love of him equals his own love of "Truth or Honour" (1.1.320). She even says "I cou'd dye for you" (1.1.317), again evoking a double entendre as her sex is clear to the audience and actors, although not to the characters onstage. Fidelia's litany of dedication is punctuated by Manly's accusations that (s)he is no more than a flatterer, who acts like a "Cushion-bearer to some State Hypocrite" (1.1.332). The willingness to die provokes his downright contempt: "Nay, there you lye, Sir; did I not see thee more afraid in the Fight, than the Chaplain of the Ship, or the Purser that bought his place?" (1.1.338–40). Fidelia counters that her very presence on the journey proves her courage, but she admits that in the fight she was afraid. Still, her fear signifies the very friendship Manly questions: "for you I wou'd be afraid again, an hundred times afraid: dying is ceasing to be afraid; and that I cou'd do sure for you, and you'll believe me one day" (1.1.344–47). With these words, she begins to weep.

Freeman is touched and says to Manly, "believe his eyes, if not his tongue: he seems to speak truth with them" (1.1.448–49). Manly, though, is incensed and dismisses the volunteer with the harsh observation that "Cowardice and I cannot dwell together" (1.1.370). When she begs him not to dismiss her "to shame and misery" and friendlessness, he offers her gold—which she refuses, calling him cruel (1.1.372). He counters that his cruelty derives from his pity, and they part. The incoherence of their exchange is highly reminiscent of several conversations between Godfrey and Irene—conversations in which Irene attempts to express her devotion for Godfrey, Godfrey insists on propriety and distance, and Irene bursts into tears. I will look at this shared pattern of exchange in more depth in the following discussion. For now, I simply note that Manly has been pushed or pushed himself to a kind of illogic in his exchange with Fidelia—first teasing her about her devotion to him, and then bluntly dismissing her from his service because of cowardice in facing sea battle. His ship, we remember, is at the bottom of the sea. His fortune is lost as well. How likely is another confrontation with the Dutch? Manly himself puts the case as conditional: "when I go to Sea again, thou shalt venture thy life no more with me" (1.1.354–55). But given the circumstances, this date is surely not in the immediate future. Why the escalation of the conversation to the point that Manly sends Fidelia on her way, and Fidelia exits weepingly saying that the man she'd earlier called "the bravest, worthiest of Mankind" is treating her "cruelly" (1.1.336, 378)? (Irene will use the word "mean" for Godfrey in such situations.) Although a definitive answer is not provided in the text, we can speculate that somehow Manly's version of himself is challenged by Fidelia in ways that it is not challenged by Plausible and Freeman. Fidelia, like Manly, is something of an idealist. Perhaps therein lies the problem. Whereas the sailors blame Manly and Manly alone for the loss of the battle, Manly seems to want to project his own failures onto his young recruit. Does he reject her/him because of his own self-loathing, because Fidelia's belief in his perfection is one that he himself does not share?

Perhaps that is the case, for his next encounter finds him much more self-controlled, again in command of his emotions, again bolstered by his contempt for the ways of the world, not confused by self-doubt. The Widow Blackacre and her son, Jerry, arrive spouting legalese and threatening lawsuits. Manly admits their company because the widow is Olivia's relation and he longs for news of his mistress, the woman he loves. The widow seeks him out because he is her "chief witness" in the lawsuit she pursues (1.1.447). Manly is so unengaged in the talk of this legal action that we never actually hear what it is all about. We do see him, however, toss away a subpoena, clearly indicating his refusal to engage in discourse of this type with this widow. Freeman is more interested—self-interested, that is. He would like to marry the widow for her money, but he has a difficult time engaging her in conversation that would lead to fulfillment of that goal. His efforts will provide the secondary plot in this play. For now, the widow's appearance allows Manly to reassert his self-control, to recover from his altercation with Fidelia.

Act 1 concludes with two conversations focused on Olivia (who has yet to appear). The first is an exchange between Fidelia and Freeman. Fidelia asks Freeman to ameliorate the captain's anger and encourage Manly to take pity, to recant the dismissal from service. Freeman does not answer that request (although he will prove a friend to Fidelia). Instead, he turns the conversation to Olivia. Who is she? What are her attractions for Manly? Fortune? Beauty? No, Fidelia reveals. The attraction is that "he fancies her . . . the onely Woman of Truth and Sincerity in the World" (1.1.519–20). Freeman departs to find out more from Manly himself, leaving Fidelia alone onstage to speak a blank-verse soliloquy in which she meditates on the difference between showing and telling (Olivia "told him she lov'd him; I have shew'd it" [1.1.534]). She also reveals her plan, the strategy she was pursuing in following Manly to the Indies. First, she had planned to do "such convincing Acts / Of loving Friendship for him" that eventually he would "find out both my Sex and Love" (1.1.536–38). Because they would be there together away from the "bright World of artful Beauties" and "amongst the sooty *Indians*," he would look on her with desire and she could "choose there to live his Wife, where Wives are forc'd / To live no longer, when their Husbands dye: / Nay, what's yet worse, to share 'em whil'st they live / With many Rival Wives" (1.1.540–46). Fidelia has written quite the romance for herself and Manly, complete with his adopting of the European's notion of Indian customs, sati and polygamy—sacrifices she is willing to make for love. We will note the presence of an "Indian wife," similarly refracted through Western sensibility, in Godfrey's story as well.[4]

The reference to "Indians" is one of the more curious parallels appearing in *The Plain Dealer* and *My Man Godfrey*; indeed, it may be the oddest coincidental echo in any two texts featured in this study. And perhaps "coincidental" is not exactly correct, although the "Indians" (West Indians) referenced in Wycherley's text are not those (Native Americans) referenced in La Cava's film. Still, for both the "Indian" represents the male's rejection of the role he should play (according to the ultimate resolution of each work) in national life by virtue of his birth and station. Godfrey's ancestors, as far as he knows, have "always been here," as he tells Mrs. Bullock. She herself hails from a family that came over on "not the Mayflower, but the boat after that." It is she who introduces speculation about Godfrey's Indian connections ("You do have rather high cheekbones. . . . Carlo, did you notice his cheekbones?"), and she is the source as well for the speculation that Godfrey's wife (invented by Tommy Gray) is "that Indian woman," whose story drives Irene into a fit of despair and whose ultimately revealed nonexistence "makes a difference." Godfrey does not actually endorse the notion that he is Native American in heritage, nor does he claim the existence of an Indian wife. But he does not deny these associations, either—until the very end of the film. Why? Do these myths represent for Godfrey a means of escape in the same way that different but (at least nominally) related myths represent a means of escape for Manly? Manly's commitment to the West Indies, first motivated by a sense of disgust with English life at home, is renewed by the revelation of Fidelia's love and loyalty: "You deserve the *Indian* World," he tells her; "I would now go thither, out of covetousness for your sake only" (5.3.136–38). He doesn't have to do that, however, because Fidelia herself is in possession of a fortune. Her name, she reveals in the end, is Fidelia Grey.

Perhaps the point of Fidelia's last name (as well as Tommy's) has to do with the moral complexities (the gray areas) of the worlds and the main characters involved. The final scene of *The Plain Dealer*'s Act 1 reveals some contradictions in what Manly seems to regard as his moral purity. James Thompson has pointed out that in a "very curious passage," Manly reveals that although he "seems to trust Olivia, yet he bribes her" and although he "trusts Vernish, . . . [he] talks of 'proof'" (103). The first act ends with Manly conflating his idealism and misanthropy, insisting that he distrusts mankind in general—and therefore would prefer living in the Indies where "honest, downright Barbarity is profest"—and yet maintaining that Olivia is a "miracle of a Woman," whose sincerity only a man of "weak faith" like Freeman can doubt (1.1.595–96, 599).

If we subject the first "act" of *My Man Godfrey* to a similar scene-by-scene analysis, we find that Godfrey, too, reveals a character who is equal parts misanthropist and idealist and who is similarly confused by his contradictory tendency to suspect human motive and to trust human nature. Unlike *The Plain Dealer*, which informs us as a matter of exposition both why Manly has left England and how it happens that he has returned, *My Man Godfrey* simply introduces its central character as one who is living down-and-out in a makeshift community built in and from the refuse of the city dump. We find out about midway through the film that he is actually living there by choice, having suffered a romantic disappointment (perhaps a failed marriage), following which he contemplated suicide-by-drowning in the East River—a fate from which he was rescued by his admiration of the "forgotten men" living at the dump. They taught him, he tells Tommy, that "there are two kinds of people: those who fight the idea of being pushed in the river, and the other kind." But we don't hear this in the beginning. In fact, we are somewhat misled as the scene opens with a bar of music that is easily recognized as the opening riff in the popular Depression-era song "Brother, Can You Spare a Dime." Yip Harburg's lyrics tell the all-too-familiar tale, with reference in the opening verses to "building a dream" and in subsequent verses to building the railroads and tall buildings that make up the American dream specifically and, then, to defending the dream in "khaki suits . . . and boots . . . slogging through Hell." All of these images of male dedication, strength, achievement, prowess, and courage yield to the poignant final lines in which the forgotten man is reduced to begging for his keep:

> Why don't you remember? I'm your pal
> Say buddy, can you spare a dime?

In their study of the "moral and cultural roles" performed by "music and organized sound" Philip Alperson and Noël Carroll cite this song as one that "communicate[s] an accusatory sense of moral indignation that grabs the body as well as the mind" with its "plea for help in a languid, chromatic melody in a minor key."[5] The very short instrumental quotations of this song, briefly introducing and then following the opening credits of *My Man Godfrey* (credits that are accompanied from the short introduction until the end by an upbeat swing score) would have been instantly recognizable to 1936 audiences from the highly popular recordings of the song by Bing Crosby, Rudy Vallee, and Al Jolson, all of which appeared soon after the song debuted in the Broadway Musical Review *Americana* (1932). The shifts from minor to major and back to minor keys would on their own have signaled to audiences an opening mood of anxiety, a dominant mood of joy, and a final return to anxiety or perhaps sadness or at least concern, as they watched the camera move from the title to the neon art deco credits to the opening scene in the "Hooverville" dump. Because this film is a comedy, joy will ultimately prevail, but only after the narrative acknowledges adamantly the hardships of those who don't so easily find happiness in the America of 1936.

So, the setting and the eminently recognizable opening chord make us assume that Godfrey, like the other men in the camp and like the men described in the song, is a victim of the Depression, someone who has given his all, done his part, and reaped no reward—or, even worse than no reward, has reaped poverty and degradation and been unfairly stigmatized by the very country he helped build, the very country for which he fought, the one for which he was willing to sacrifice his life. The opening exchange between Godfrey and Mike reinforces that sense as the two cynically refer to Herbert Hoover's empty promise that "prosperity is just around the corner." "I wish

I knew which corner," Mike says. This comradery in penury and deprivation defines Godfrey as a noble sufferer of sorts. In fact, he is known in the dump as "Duke." His dignity, though, does not set him apart here; it defines him as a denizen of this oddly incongruous environment built on refuse, but sustaining itself with inherent pride and a kind of innate nobility. The two tramps bid each other good night, after all, in French.

Godfrey's next encounter is with the woman who will define one of the "plots" of his story. Cornelia is the instigator of most of Godfrey's troubles once he leaves the dump. Her machinations provide stumbling blocks sometimes, opportunities at other times. She is an active agent in the writing of Godfrey's tale, although as we will see the ending never comes out the way she'd prefer. And it is that way from the beginning. She enters the scene, peremptorily asking Godfrey how he'd like to make five dollars by accompanying her to the Waldorf-Ritz so she can, as she bluntly puts it, "show you to a few people." His response—"May I inquire just why you would want to show me to people at the Waldorf-Ritz?"—provokes Cornelia's impatience: "Well, if you must know, it's a game . . . a scavenger hunt. If I find a forgotten man first, I win. Is that clear?" Her condescension annoys Godfrey to the point that he menaces her physically—striding toward her and causing her to back into a pile of ashes. At this point, her companion, George, intervenes to ask Godfrey if he is in the habit of hitting women; Godfrey offers to hit George, and George and Cornelia promptly leave the dump, mumbling something about the police.

This encounter sets up the antagonism with Cornelia—and the source of Godfrey's irritation is not at all mysterious. Cornelia, after all, appears at the dump in all of her elegance, dressed to the nines (the women in this film are almost always dressed to the nines); she treats Godfrey as the object the scavenger hunt assumes he is. His sense of dignity, already established in the initial conversation, is simply too strong to tolerate such abuse. His violence, however, is a move away from dignity into a more primal emotion. He clearly has distinct problems with whatever it is that Cornelia represents (and we will find out that she, like Fidelia for Manly, suffers here and elsewhere an ire born of self-disappointment and self-critique). Her class, however, is also at fault—and those of that class will be told as much when Godfrey finally gets to the hotel. First, however, he will meet a redemptive agent—one who speaks to Godfrey with openness, curiosity, and respect, instead of the condescension her sister employs, even though she belongs to the same world as Cornelia, and, like Cornelia, also seeks to bring a forgotten man to the Waldorf-Ritz and is herself dressed to the nines (in white, significantly, as opposed to Cornelia's black). The effect on Godfrey is palpable.

It is amusing that while Godfrey faces the truly menacing Cornelia and George alone, as he begins to talk to the zany Irene, Mike appears in the background offering assistance. In a sense, Irene does pose the greater danger to Godfrey's sense of self-possession, especially to his sense of grievance with the world. Their conversation is disjointed in the way that discussion with Irene will always be disjointed, but in the end Godfrey offers to help her "beat Cornelia" by accompanying her, Irene, to the Waldorf-Ritz and being *her* "forgotten man." Godfrey is intrigued, not by the scavenger hunt, as he pretends, but by Irene. William Powell plays the scene as a man somewhat mesmerized by the woman before him. Although he begins to talk to her in the same hostile tone he used for conversation with Cornelia, offering to "push Cornelia's sister in the ash pile" too, his demeanor and tone change once Irene begins to laugh uncontrollably. She always wanted to do that—to push Cornelia in a pile of ashes. She's delighted that Godfrey stood up to her bossy sister. Her laughter is not infectious; Godfrey doesn't smile once. It is, however, mesmerizing to him. Once Irene begins to laugh and prattle, Godfrey can't take his eyes off her. He invites her to sit down. He draws her out in conversation by asking her to explain what a scavenger hunt is. She tells him that it's "exactly like a treasure hunt, except in a treasure hunt you try to find something you want, and in a scavenger hunt you try to find something that nobody wants." "Like a forgotten man." Godfrey says somberly, leading Irene to declare a few moments later that she's not going to play any more games with people as the object: "It's kind of sordid, when you think of it."

The degree to which these two very different individuals begin to modulate speech and behavior in response to each another is quite remarkable. Irene, for example, says that she is curious as to why Godfrey would choose to live in a dump when there are so many other nice places to live. Godfrey sarcastically tells her that his doctor felt it would be good for his asthma. Instead of becoming defensive and calling him "fresh" (and, as we see several times throughout the film, she is capable of recognizing irony and doing just that), she just dreamily informs him that her uncle too has asthma. At the end of their meandering conversation, Godfrey offers to go to the Waldorf-Ritz with Irene out of his own "curiosity"—"See, I've got a sense of curiosity, just the same as you have. I'd really like to see just what a scavenger hunt looks like." Irene illogically wails, "But I *told* you!" to which Godfrey replies, "Yes, uh, I'm still curious." Irene's whine of protest here is somewhat surprising, as she seems genuinely happy that Godfrey is going to help her "beat Cornelia." But she does resist his articulation of his motive, his "curiosity." Why? Perhaps she already knows that she prefers being alone with Godfrey. Perhaps she suspects their conversation has been a catalyst for some kind of action on Godfrey's part that goes beyond his fascination with her. Perhaps his "curiosity" about the people at the Waldorf-Ritz pleases her less than his willingness to entertain her at his "home" amid the ashes and the junk; it is, perhaps she feels, a curiosity that will take her from a newly discovered Eden back to the fallen world. Whatever the case, Irene seems to have accurately sensed that Godfrey's skepticism is something that will have to be overcome. And, as she is soon to discover, that will not be easy.

Godfrey's encounter with the rich scavenger hunters comprises the final "scene" in what I'm calling "Act 1" of *My Man Godfrey*, after which there is a black screen dissolve indicating a shift in time. Although I wouldn't insist too rigidly that each black screen in the film marks the end of an "act," the film does systematically use that device to denote the passage of time and the development of plot, each segment chronicling a change in Godfrey, his identity, and his condition of life. At the Waldorf, he is still a tramp in tattered clothing, unshaven, dirty, and projecting hostility and contempt to all around him except Irene, whom he follows into the ballroom and whom he acknowledges in a formal speech to the crowd as a "young lady" he wanted to "aid." That's one of the reasons he has appeared there before them. The other is to see "how a bunch of empty-headed nitwits conducted themselves." Satisfied, he announces his desire to return to the "society of really important people," his friends at the dump. But he does not. Now Irene is the one who is mesmerized. She rejects her trophy (won for bringing in the first "forgotten man" of the evening) and tells Godfrey that she'd like to do something for him, introducing the theme of reciprocity that will define the relationship between Godfrey and Irene as well as Godfrey and the Bullock family. He says (as will typically be said on these occasions) that he doesn't understand. "Well," Irene explains, "this is the first time I've ever beaten Cornelia at anything, and you helped me do it. . . . I wish I could do something for you." He offers a suggestion: "I could use a job." "Do you butle?" Irene asks in reply.

The Bullocks need a butler, Godfrey needs a job, and a bargain is struck. When Irene's mother, Mrs. Bullock, joins them and protests, it is Godfrey, who instead of contemptuously walking away as we might expect him to do makes the case for himself: "stray cats make the best pets, Madam!" Mrs. Bullock is not convinced, but neither Irene nor Godfrey pay any attention to her or to the very angry Cornelia, who shows up with her own "forgotten man" and who clearly has determined neither to forgive nor to forget Godfrey's earlier affront. The scene ends with Irene sealing the deal by giving Godfrey a few coins that fall through the torn lining of his coat pocket, emphasizing one final time the depth of his penury and the shabbiness of his life. But it is Godfrey who makes sure the bargain will be fulfilled. He is the one, after all, who asks the address of the Bullock home. "Funny, I never thought of that," says Irene dreamily.

Irene, like Fidelia, precipitates a narrative for the man she loves while she pursues a counternarrative of her own. The end of Act 1 has been orchestrated in a sense by the woman, but the ensuing scenes will become increasingly painful to her as the man resists her version of their story—indeed, as the man refuses to admit to himself or to her that they even have a story of their own. In this general characteristic, the narratives are similar, but the specific stories that the men pursue seem on the surface to be quite different—Godfrey, disguising himself as a butler, redeeming himself through work, and helping the Bullocks redeem themselves through capitalistic investment; Manly, disguising his hurt by employing Fidelia to lie for him, pimp for him, and eventually serve as an accessory to a would-be rape for him. Manly does not redeem himself or anyone else; instead, he is the one who has to be redeemed, even as he has been depraved, by friendship and love. Rose A. Zimbardo argues that Manly suffers from "pride which leads to [an] . . . inevitable fall," and Robert D. Hume notes that Manly's alleged moral superiority is called into doubt by his "amazingly bad" judgment of others, as well as his behavior, particularly his egregiously vindictive "desire to rape the duplicitous Olivia by means of a 'bed trick,'" which "has upset some readers (perhaps not unreasonably so)."[6]

It was in his April 7, 1932, campaign radio address that President Franklin D. Roosevelt introduced the "forgotten man" to Depression-era America. Two paragraphs of the speech are particularly noteworthy in the context of the narratives centered on Manly and Godfrey:

> It is said that Napoleon lost the battle of Waterloo because he forgot his infantry—he staked too much upon the more spectacular but less substantial cavalry. The present administration in Washington provides a close parallel. It has either forgotten or it does not want to remember the infantry of our economic army.
>
> These unhappy times call for the building of plans that rest upon the forgotten, the unorganized but the indispensable units of economic power, for plans like those of 1917 that build from the bottom up and not from the top down, that put their faith once more in the forgotten man at the bottom of the economic pyramid.

The speech obviously has more direct pertinence to the film than the play, but *The Plain Dealer* like *My Man Godfrey* is concerned with national stature and the individual's relationship to the country's health. Is there a "flashy cavalry" in *The Plain Dealer*? Of course—its name is Westminster, where relationship is a matter of subpoena, conversation consists of depositions and testimony, and individuals become "*John-a-Stiles*" (1.1.469). As James Thompson points out, "with the Widow, . . . all those at law become a confused mass of indistinguishable claimants."[7] The alternative is the infantry—the choice of Freeman and Fidelia, each a plain dealer in his or her own way, but neither a pure idealist so easily fooled as Manly and so apt as Manly to let despair destroy personal worth.

I use the word "worth" deliberately, for that is exactly what Manly loses and Godfrey has lost in a time prior to the film's "present" as a result of misplaced and disappointed affection. Manly loves Olivia and has staked his entire worth on their plighted troth, leaving jewels and money with her to finance her journey to the Indies when her family finally relents and allows her to follow him. The remainder of his fortune is lost at sea, so his discovery in Act 2 of her treachery toward him is the discovery of his absolute material ruin. His response is to degrade himself in continued pursuit of something he has lost irrevocably, even to the moral low point of plotting against Olivia's "honour" in Act 4 (4.2.255). Fidelia very astutely observes that as Olivia "has no honour," an act against her honor is no real revenge (4.2.256–57). But that is really a secondary point. Fidelia tries repeatedly to bring Manly to a sense of his own self-worth: "reflect . . . how she hates and loaths you" (4.2.258)—evidence of which has been provided aplenty in various derisive remarks uttered by Olivia and overheard by Manly, from Act 2's disdainful reference to "boisterous Sea-love" and rough manners to Act 4's admission that "his Money" was her true interest all along (2.1.518; 4.2.238). Olivia goes so far as to reveal her cynical manipulation of Manly in a speech to Fidelia that Manly once again overhears:

> I knew he lov'd his own singular moroseness so well, as to dote upon any Copy of it; wherefore I feign'd an hatred to the World too, that he might love me in earnest: but, if it had been hard to deceive him, I'm sure 'twere much harder to love him.
>
> (4.2.206–09)

Fidelia suspects that Manly's determination to shame Olivia by making love to her is motivated as much by continued passion as by revenge, and her role in the ruse is decidedly uncomfortable to her. But she continues to play the part Manly requires of her, although she herself begins to tread dangerously close to despair: her final soliloquy in Act 4 confessing her sense that she is being punished by heaven for "loving well," for attempting "to find a Heaven here" in a world that offers her only the cruelty and hopelessness of an "unmerciful" life (4.2.279, 282, 289).

Of course, Act 5 reverses her fortunes—and Manly's fortunes as well. The ending, as well as the ending of *My Man Godfrey*, deserves and will receive full treatment as I examine the way each "forgotten man" is reintegrated into his society, remembered by others, and, as—if not more—significantly, by himself. For now, though, I want to note another shared pattern in the two texts—a chiastic pattern of self-definition that the central couple undergoes. These texts, like all the members of their genres, play around with the question of who is following whom. Fidelia follows Manly to sea, but Manly follows Fidelia on the various expeditions to Olivia's home. Godfrey follows Irene to the Waldorf and to her Fifth Avenue home, but she follows Godfrey into his bedroom, around the Bullock home, and eventually back to the dump. Conversation between the central pairs in these works is more difficult than usual. Godfrey "has trouble following" Irene sometimes. Manly hears Fidelia's vows of friendship as sycophancy, her revelations of Olivia's treachery as betrayal. These couples, though, experience a radical "following" of status and identity that sets them apart from those in the other texts. Just as Manly has been an inadvertent pimp (bringing Olivia and Vernish, as well as Olivia and Fidelia, together), he insists that Fidelia "Pimp for" him (3.1.90)—and he, in fact, uses that shockingly harsh language, which is all the more startling given that he has rejected the notion of a "Sea-Pimp" in Act 1, calling those such as the sailor, who would be introducing women to him, "the strangest Monster[s] she [presumably the sea] has" (1.1.155). So, in asking Fidelia to take on this role, he is placing her in a role he himself finds contemptible, not so much as a mark of dishonor bestowed on the "volunteer," as a sign of self-contempt. If Fidelia wants to serve him, he now finds himself in such a lowly state that the only service she can provide is that of a pimp.

My Man Godfrey is informed by a happier version of this chiastic exchange. Godfrey recovers his sense of self and human dignity by taking on the role of a servant. As he explains to Mr. Bullock, he is "proud of being a good butler," serving the family that gave him a chance to escape the poverty of the dump. Of course, as we learn immediately following this expression of gratitude, Godfrey has other options—a wealthy family. We are given no true explanation as to why returning to this family is not a possibility. The failed love affair (or even marriage) in Boston seems to have had something to do with Godfrey's estrangement, but the family has invented a story about his pursuing business in South America (an exotic and remote locale—somewhat like the West Indies). They don't seem to be pretending that he is happy and in love with the woman he "gave everything he had." And it is also unclear why "working" for the Bullocks is such a redemptive activity for Godfrey. His job is one that only rank and privilege would define as "work." The rest of us can get our own drinks, make our own beds, and nurse our own hangovers. In Irene's response to Godfrey, however, we may see the value of his role-playing. She begins to want to "help" with the menial chores of housekeeping—preparing the food, wiping the dishes. She bonds with Molly, the housekeeper, in sorrow over their shared unrequited love for Godfrey. Early in the film, Molly had called Irene "insidious." By the end, Molly embraces Irene as they both mourn Godfrey's departure, after which Molly, significantly, calls the car for Irene, who announces, "he's not going to get away from me." We know that Godfrey isn't going to marry Molly. He's a Parke, after all, not a butler. Molly knows it too. But for a while she and Irene were in the same position, longing for and loving a man who did not and could not long and love in return.

As film critic Bob Gilpin says on the Criterion collection commentary of *My Man Godfrey*, Godfrey is a stickler for propriety.[8] Although it is her complete disregard for such that attracts him to Irene in the first place, Godfrey finds himself nonplussed by her relentless insistence on breaking social boundaries. When he brings her breakfast the first morning of his employment, she asks him to sit on her bed and talk with her. He obeys, as is his duty (as he defines it), but he is clearly ill at ease. A few hours later, Godfrey lectures Irene on the topic of appropriate behavior. She has followed him into his room to which he has fled for sanctuary after she surprised him with a kiss on the lips. Here, she wants to have another talk while sitting on the bed. Exasperated, he tells her a story of a "little girl" who did a good thing by helping a man, but who then became a nuisance who has to be told that she must never, ever, under any circumstances enter the butler's room again. "When can we talk?" she wails. "When I'm serving breakfast in the morning, I can say 'good morning, Miss Irene,' and you can say 'good morning, Godfrey.'" As he ushers her from his room, Godfrey tells Irene that she should find someone of her own class to marry. And, of course, she does.

Irene refers to Godfrey as her "protégé." He is her "responsibility," she tells him, and she will "sponsor" him, the way her mother "sponsors" Carlo. Of course, just how her mother does sponsor Carlo is open to debate. Who is Carlo to Mrs. Bullock? Does she simply want him around to sing "Ochi Chernye" and accompany her to concerts and other social events that her husband, Alexander, may not wish to attend? Or does she keep him around to do his gorilla impression for Irene when she needs cheering up? Or is he her lover? Of course, post-Hays Code, any definitive suggestion that he was such would have been censored. Thus Carlo remains a cypher, who indicates that something is awry in the Bullock marriage, but not exactly what that something may be. At one point, Alexander Bullock says, "either Carlo is or I am," prompting Mrs. Bullock to ask, "Am what?"

Irene explains Carlo's presence in the home as evidence of her mother's commitment to art. Mrs. Bullock's sponsorship makes it possible for Carlo to devote his time to practicing, "but then, he never does." Irene hasn't fully thought through her own sponsorship of Godfrey at this point, having gotten only so far as "if Cornelia got mean, you wouldn't have to do anything about it. . . . I'm your sponsor, and I'd just take a sock at her." And Godfrey himself is quite confused as to what his duties as a protégé might entail. As no clear job description in that regard is forthcoming when he asks the question, Godfrey takes on the vaguely defined duty of making Irene proud of him. "I know how you feel about things," he says late in the film. Perhaps he interprets her parting words as he leaves her bedroom the first morning of his employment as an injunction to moral behavior, whatever mixed signs the household provides of the duties of protégés and the behavior of sponsors. She says, "See you in church." Perhaps it's her own fault that she finds herself being lectured to later in the day about propriety, bedrooms, and marriage with men of her own class.

Manly, too, is concerned with propriety. Usually, as in Act 1, he rails against ceremony and courtesy as evidence of hypocrisy; nevertheless, there are some codes of behavior he does regard as evidence of sincerity and truth. Indeed, like Godfrey, it is from his young "sponsor" that he especially demands propriety. All along, Manly has found Fidelia's behavior and demeanor confusing and inappropriate. The youth's devotion to him is not like Freeman's devotion (Freeman is his lieutenant, next-in-command). Fidelia might have been convincing in the role of a young seaman had (s)he not been such a coward during the battle. Manly is flummoxed by the paradox of fear in a crisis and fierce devotion to him in general. He is also reluctant to take the "boy" on as a protégé, although (s)he begs him for a lesson in courage, responding to his declaration "I ever hated a Coward's company" with the plea,

> Let me follow you till I am none then; for you, I'm sure, will through such Worlds of dangers, that I shall be inur'd to 'em; nay, I shall be afraid of your anger more than the danger, and so turn valiant out of fear.
>
> (3.1.44–48)

Gilpin points out that Irene has a way of "unmanning" Godfrey, causing him to cast her off time and again. The same can be said of Fidelia's effect on Manly. In both texts, the man's focus on propriety leads to a kind of perverse definition of his relationship to the woman. Granted, Manly at this point has no idea that Fidelia *is* a woman, but he does recognize, as Godfrey recognizes of Irene, that the young volunteer is devoted to him. He also seems he understand at least subliminally the source of that devotion: "thou art as hard to shake off, as that flattering effeminating mischief, Love" (3.1.63–64). Fidelia assumes he is talking about his continuing love for Olivia, and once she says so, he believes it, as well. Yet, isn't his decision to take Fidelia into his confidence a bit intense? Consider the way he words it as he speaks in an aside to the audience:

> I had almost discover'd my Love and Shame; well, if I had? that thing cou'd not think the worse of me:—or if he did?—no—yes, he shall know it—he shall—but then I must never leave him, for they are such secrets that make Parasites and Pimps Lords of their Masters; for any slavery or tyranny is easier than Love's.
>
> (3.1.68–72)

Manly's "I must never leave him" is very interesting considering that every speech directed toward Fidelia since the play began has included some version of the phrase "leave me." He's said it four or five times, in fact, in this particular conversation with Fidelia. Now all of a sudden he hatches a scheme that will bind him to the volunteer forever, while not particularly advancing his love for Olivia (although it may serve his purported thirst for revenge). Interestingly, too, he feels shame for his inability to cast off his feelings for Olivia, a shame he has confessed in the soliloquy that directly precedes his conversation with Fidelia and one that he feels particular chagrin about with regard to Freeman's potential discovery ("lest he contemn me") and resulting "scorn" (3.1.32–33). It is interesting to note Manly's concern with the opinions of both Freeman and Fidelia, although certainly his treatment of the young volunteer seems as motivated by contempt as by regard.

Godfrey's change in different although similar circumstances is almost immediate. Upon entering the Bullock home, he finds himself feeling compassion for the elder Bullocks in particular. Mrs. Bullock's pixie-infused hangovers evoke in Godfrey (as Powell plays the scene) a sudden tenderness. The scene in which he serves her Worchestershire-laden tomato juice (a "pixie remover" he tells her) is remarkable for its fusion of Godfrey's and Angellica's points of view. The camera seems to be an observer as we switch from Godfrey's perspective climbing the stairs with the tray to an angle of vision from within the room as Godfrey enters. A strange "music" plays, and Angellica comments, "Why do they keep playing that same tune over and over?" "Why *do* they?" Godfrey asks tentatively, looking around, clearly not hearing what we and Mrs. Bullock hear except for the tinkling of crystals that hang from a lamp—part of the music we hear, but clearly not enough to be called a "tune" as Godfrey hears it. We look around the room as he does, the camera once more adopting his perspective, and then as the tune is stilled the camera moves back for a long shot of Godfrey and Mrs. Bullock: she, happy and still partly inebriated; he, solicitous, careful, and calm.

Godfrey's treatment of Mr. Bullock is just as delicate and decorous. Godfrey is discreet and kind from the moment he dons the role of butler, his lesson (that the rich can be forgiven and redeemed) apparently learned quite effortlessly and almost instantaneously. His reconciliation with Cornelia will take longer as she actively antagonizes him, pursuing several hostile maneuvers, including an attempt to accuse him of theft. In turn, Godfrey's treatment of Cornelia is often harsh. Whereas he maintains decorum in public, in private, when she forces his hand, he is quite blunt with her, calling her a "Park Avenue brat" and describing her as "a spoiled child who's grown up in ease and luxury, who's always had her own way, and whose misdirected energies are so childish, they hardly deserve the comment even of a butler on his off Thursday." In the end, he is proud of her for having the courage to admit that she tried to frame him, and he compliments her on her growth as an individual in that regard. When she asks if he has seen any good in her at all, he is just as forthright as ever, but this time he can speak both honestly and kindly. And, interestingly, the portrait he paints of her is by his own admission a self-portrait: "Miss Cornelia, there have been other spoiled children in the world. I happen to be one of them myself." When he tells her that her high spirits can be employed constructively, he is describing the trajectory of his own development—from spoiled brat to a productive citizen, who can play the market intelligently to the benefit of the elite as well as the downtrodden.

The ensuing acts of *The Plain Dealer* offer the problematic spectacle of Manly's sinking further and further into the depravity of revenge. Not only does he plot the rape of Olivia, he also threatens to kill Fidelia if she "breathe[s] the least murmuring Accent" to warn his mistress (4.2.266). But, perhaps worst of all, Manly, the plain dealer, begins to lie. He informs Vernish that he has "lay'n with" Olivia (5.2.124). At this point, he does not know that Vernish is Olivia's husband. He still purports to think of him as his one true friend. Why, then, does he lie? Is it simply evidence of the degradation to which he has sunk? Or, although he does not know the identity of Olivia's husband, does Manly suspect Vernish at this point? Is he taunting his former friend in revenge for the disloyalty he suspects? We can't be sure. The scene could be played either way—with Manly knowingly torturing his former friend by repeated allusions to Olivia's infidelity or with Manly obsessively spinning a tale that will underscore her infamy, which he will expose later that evening in front of many witnesses. He does not "invite" Vernish, which may be a significant piece of evidence that he suspects he will not have to do so. Instead, he sends Vernish on a quest for money while he makes his own way to Olivia's home. When Vernish asks "don't you apprehend the Husband?" Manly laughs: "He! sniveling Gull! he a thing to be fear'd! a Husband, the tamest of creatures!" (5.2.327–29). A slap across the face with a glove would have been less effective.

Interestingly, although Vernish does react to Manly's taunting as though it were a direct challenge, he articulates his deep confusion. Knowing Manly as a plain dealer, a truth teller, deepens his concern. He must be telling the truth about his affair with Olivia ("he does not use to lye" [5.2.337]). Still, if one is going to lie, it would be about something of this sort ("belying a Woman, when she won't be kind is the onely lye a brave Man will least scruple" [5.2.338–39]). Or maybe the plot is deeper and thicker:

> Perhaps, she is his Wench, of an old date, and I am his Cully, whil'st I think him mine; and he has seem'd to make his Wench rich, only that I might take her off his hands: or if he has but lately lay'n with her, he must needs discover, by her my treachery to him; which I'm sure he will revenge with my death, and which I must prevent with his, if it were only but for fear of his too just reproaches.
>
> (5.2.349–55)

The truth is really simpler. Manly departed England for the Indies, leaving behind the woman he loved in the care of the man he trusted. He returned and found them both unfriendly and unfaithful. His shock was such that his own nature seemed to turn on itself, his idealism perverted and his virtue transmuted into vice. Redeemed in the end by the loyalty of Freeman and Fidelia, Manly has also been instrumental in their education.

What does Fidelia learn? She learns that love is not rational. Manly's feelings for Olivia persist long after reason should dictate their demise. But so do hers. She learns that love will demand sacrifices, sometimes humiliating ones. It turned her into a pimp and maybe worse. It caused her to lie all along (she does, after all, spend very nearly the entire play in disguise), and it demanded that she lie to support the falsehood she was living as well as to protect the man she was lying for and to in the first place. But most significantly she does learn to fight courageously. She is wounded in the battle with Vernish, and it is her wound that finally permits her to reveal the fact that she is a woman as well as the truth that she is in love with Manly. And, finally, she learns that Manly is capable of renouncing a false love and embracing a true one. Manly's reaction to the revelation of Fidelia's identity is to understand immediately that she has "been my Volunteer in love" (5.3.91–92). His next response is chagrin: he admits that although he "deserv'd not from her [Olivia] the treatment she gave . . . [he] does from you" (5.3.107–08).

What does Freeman learn? He too employs a "pimp" to forward his aims—marriage with the wealthy Widow Blackacre. But what he finds is a protégé, Jerry, whose sense of self-worth and personal dignity he first bolsters by advice and then assures by law. His "pimp," as he puts it, is "justice," and what justice provides Freeman is a living (an annuity from the widow to which she agrees in order to avoid a defamation lawsuit brought by her "minor"). In that way, therefore, I suppose it does "pimp" for him. In another way, however, law secures justice for Jerry as the settlement stipulates "you must say no more he is the Son of a Whore"—and obviates the need for a "pimp" as the Widow also agrees that her "minor" should have "free ingress, egress, and regress to and from your Maids Garret" (5.2.471, 474–75). Certainly the "justness" of this arrangement from the maids' point of view is questionable, but I think we need not press that point too earnestly, for Wycherley has been playing around with the notion of "pimping" for the entire play. And it is generous in Freeman to try to provide for Jerry so that he is not forced into either playing the role or seeking the service of such a creature!

Still, when we think about it, what *is* a pimp? In the Restoration period, as now, the term denoted a go-between, one who arranged sexual encounters. In providing opportunities for a social superior to indulge his illicit appetites, the pimp was certainly tainted by association with the nature of the behavior, but given the period and the manners and mores of the court, it was surely the case that many higher servants and even courtiers found themselves playing the role of "pimp" from time to time. Why did they do it? No doubt from the desire to serve power in many cases. But sometimes I imagine loyalty and devotion played a role, as it does in Fidelia's case. Pimping is a way to try to help Manly—not to the woman, whom he says he desires, but to clarity of vision, the knowledge of Olivia that Fidelia feels sure will (and that eventually does) "alter" his perception of her and, therefore, relieve him of a responsibility that his "constancy" would otherwise insist he maintain. In other words, to "pimp" for him, is to serve him, to care for him. In exchange, she hopes Manly will care for her.

The play ends with a gesture toward mutuality in this regard and in a broader sense as well. In the confusion of the evening, Olivia has mistakenly given Manly's chest of jewels and money back to him. When all identities are revealed, Manly transfers the chest to Fidelia, who as Olivia's would-be lover, was to have been its recipient in the first place. As he hands the chest to Fidelia, however, Manly takes some jewels and offers them to Olivia. His words are demeaning ("I never yet left my Wench unpaid" [5.3.116]) but, given the way she has treated him, not uncalled for. And the jewels are sincerely meant for her possession, although she strikes them down and they end up in the hands of Novel and Lord Plausible. Manly does not protest; instead, he expresses regret for Vernish's loss: "I would have return'd part of your Wives portion; for 'twere hard to take all from thee, since thou hast paid so dear for't, in being such a Rascal" (5.2.128–30).

174 *Forgotten men*

Although other interpretations are possible, I like to think of Manly by Act 5 as a Godfrey-like figure, who has returned to the world he has left in order to be reconciled with it. The reconciliation must be effected by himself, through actions that speak both to his clear-sighted judgment of the world for its good and its evil and his willingness to again become a part of that world, and even participate in its redemption. Just like Godfrey at the end of his text, Manly disposes wealth and, therefore, justice. In his case, however, Fidelia's portion of two thousand pounds a year is an additional bonus, one that obviates the need to seek further wealth abroad, an adventure Manly is glad enough to forgo now that Fidelia and Freeman have "reconcil'd" him to the world:

> *I will believe there are now in the* World
> *Good-natur'd Friends, who are not Prostitutes,*
> *And handsom Women worthy to be Friends.*
> (5.3.158, 168–70)

For Manly, as for Godfrey, there came a time in life when he needed help. And help was provided by friends willing to take a chance on him despite alienating behavior, demeanor, and discourse. Manly's pursuit of redemption is similar to Godfrey's in one sense. He, like Alithea in *The Country Wife*, has to be convinced that Olivia has truly forfeited his loyalty and love, and that Vernish has somehow failed to fulfill the office of friendship (which should have prevented Olivia's marriage). At the end of Act 2, we and Fidelia may feel he has evidence enough, but he has not seen Vernish at that point, and until he does he remains perplexed and uncertain. His employing Fidelia to "pimp for him" can be read as a kind of ruse; he dons the habit of a vengeful rapist as convincingly (and with a similar kind of exaggeration) as Godfrey dons the "monkey suit" of a butler. They are both "forgotten men" in the beginning of their narratives. In the middle, they are men in disguise. And by the end, they are men redeemed by love and friendship, men restored to a sense of their own integrity and worth.

This chapter has treated the central texts so far without reference to Cavell. Part of the reason for that lacuna is that much of what I've said echoes the conversations we have had ("Cavell" and I) about the parallels between the Restoration courtship comedies and Hollywood remarriage comedies featured earlier in this book. But it is also true, as I state in the beginning of this chapter, that these two texts are such generic oddballs that I doubt Cavell (the actual Stanley Cavell) would agree to include *My Man Godfrey* in his remarriage canon. Similarly, I can barely bring myself to think of *The Plain Dealer* as participating in the Restoration canon, despite its inclusion by Nettleton, Case, and Stone in their long-dominant anthology, the one I've suggested may have spurred the very creation of the Hollywood remarriage comedy (particularly the brilliant couple at the center of the movies). In a sense, though, both works offer such poignant reflections on the genres to which I have assigned them by focusing primarily on the male's education rather than the female's that I find I need to include them in my own understanding of the work of both canons. Irene and Fidelia are the teachers in these films. Godfrey and Manly are the ones seeking knowledge, the ones attempting to overcome the skepticism and melancholy that challenge the comic vision of each text in both genres.

Godfrey and Manly both see themselves as outsiders, and indeed they *are* outsiders. We may see them as self-defined outsiders who have bullheadedly and misanthropically checked out. Or we may grant them their self-definitions as inhabitants of worlds they do not and cannot understand. Either way, the fact remains that both have doubts about what they know, and, when they come to resolve those doubts, they have further doubts about what to do about what they know. They are both creatures caught in a philosophical nightmare—a world in which knowledge does not provide guidance in terms of moral action.

It is with regard to this dilemma that we can call on Cavell for insight, for the situation of both Manly and Godfrey can be read as a one posed by philosophical skepticism. In the last two sections of his book *The Claim of Reason*, sections entitled "Knowledge and the Concept of Morality" and "Skepticism and the Problem of Others," Cavell confronts the basic questions that seem to me to be at the center of Wycherley's and La Cava's texts, particularly the conception of the central character of each text. "Historically as well as dialectically," Cavell begins, "the concept of reason or knowledge . . . raises two major problems for the moral philosopher."[9] These questions are of two different sorts. The first is about what should be done regarding knowledge. So, for example, once Manly comes to discover that Olivia has been unfaithful to him, what should he do? Leaving aside for the moment what he does do, we will acknowledge that there are several possible courses of action, all of which can be comprehended under the notion of "justice": he can publicly expose her; he can privately break with her; and, as she is already married to another, he can simply walk away without confronting her at all. What he chooses to do is the second of Cavell's examples of the way knowledge poses problems for moral philosophers: why, given various alternatives and in full knowledge that the course of action we determine to pursue is wrong, do we often choose to do that wrong? The example Cavell gives is Medea, who says what we presume everyone committed to such a course of action says: "'I know what crimes I am about to commit, but my anger is stronger'" (*CR*, 247). Cavell is drawing on Bruno Snell's discussion of Socrates's notion that "as long as a man knows the good, he will do it. . . . Nobody commits a crime voluntarily." This is indeed a criticism of Euripides, but one to which the modern philosopher no longer subscribes, for it is a moral truth that sometimes we choose the wrong, as a response to knowledge, although we know our choice to be wrong.[10] Manly can indeed be read as an individual so shocked by knowledge that he deliberately pursues what he knows to be morally wrong. He becomes a kind of monster.

Godfrey recounts that he too was brought to such a pass by romantic disappointment. Suicide as a response to such betrayal is a moral wrong. We are given too few details about "that business," and the "bitterness" that Godfrey experienced as a result to speculate as to what proper moral choices Godfrey had, but we know that the course of action he had temporarily chosen was wrong. His ultimate choice, to become a "forgotten man," is a thornier moral problem—arguably wrong, but perhaps not. Godfrey himself adamantly thinks not, as he makes perfectly clear in conversations with his old friend Tommy Gray, with whom he unexpectedly reconnects at the Bullocks' home. We, however, are free to question his choices, as Tommy does. Even so, we must admit that Godfrey neither eschews community nor seeks isolation, although he chooses to identify with the forgotten, to make common cause with those who have been rejected. We also must recognize (especially in the context of the Depression) that there is a valid sense in which some moral responses stand as an indictment of society's failings. As Cavell says, "a philosopher struck with the fact of men's divided opinions is likely to concentrate on methods which can lead to the settlement of social conflict and to develop a theory of the good society and a mode of criticizing existing institutions" (CR, 248). In that sense, Godfrey's turning away from moral wrong to form community outside society's sanctioned borders, making a choice that others might debate, suggests a concern in this text with a "theory of the good society, and a mode of criticizing existing institutions" (CR, 248). Manly, on the other hand, is an example of "man's divided nature," as he actively chooses to pursue a crime of violence and thereby focuses our attention on basic questions regarding "the nature of society's authority, what it is that makes its deliverances binding upon us" (CR, 248).

In a sense, the moral agents—the ones for whom knowledge actually "provide[s] a basis for morality" (CR, 248)—in both of these texts are the women, Fidelia and Irene. As much as Manly and Godfrey do, each in their own way, set themselves up as exemplars of plain dealing and propriety (Manly places greater emphasis on the former and Godfrey on the latter, although their emphases are intertwined), they cannot be said to truly exemplify moral behavior in the sense that Cavell discusses it: "What is required in confronting another person is not your liking him or her but your being willing, from whatever cause, to take his or her position into account and bear the consequences" (CR, 326). Perhaps this observation strikes with less force regarding Irene than Fidelia, but, in fact, the film text demonstrates over and over again that Irene, screwball though she is, is determined to restore Godfrey to a rightful sense of his own dignity. Ed Sikov argues that

> an appreciation of Lombard's performance ... is essential to one's acceptance of the story.... You have to believe that not only is Godfrey attracted to Irene, but also that there is an immutable reason for the attraction, a sense that something of great value lurks beneath her imbecilic words.[11]

Sikov, however, is apparently immune to Lombard's charms, as he calls the couple "one of screwball comedy's worst" (138). But viewers of the time responded positively as do many today. Besides, as is the case with *Bringing Up Baby*'s Susan Vance, the important thing is not that we like Irene, but that Godfrey finds something in her that is necessary to his moral growth. Irene must improvise constantly in her mission to do so because she has an opponent in Cornelia, who is every bit as determined to humiliate and disgrace Godfrey as Irene is to redeem him.

Gilpin points out the way that Irene manipulates her entire family when Cornelia begins her attack of insinuations the first day of Godfrey's servitude in the Bullock household. Mr. Bullock is quite ready to dismiss Godfrey based on what Cornelia has to say about his lack of references and the dangers of employing unknown men by whom "we might all be stabbed in the back and robbed." Irene has to feign a fit, which throws everything into confusion. She almost exemplifies Cavell's definition of the moralist as "the human being who best grasps the human position" and teaches us to do so "in ways that we cannot escape but through distraction and muddle" (*CR*, 326). Granted, the "distraction and muddle" actually provide the escape in this scene, but it is just such an escape as is necessary for Godfrey's confrontation of the human position to occur. He is prepared to stay and confront that position in one sense, that is, serving the Bullocks, including Cornelia, and thereby rescuing them from the degraded positions they now inhabit as frivolous wastrels of American wealth. He is not, however, prepared to confront the human position in the sense conveyed by Irene's kiss (the kiss that ends this scene). It is her kiss that prompts Godfrey's lecture on propriety and that temporarily halts the progress of their story.

Irene's response to Godfrey's erecting of boundaries doesn't strike us as particularly mature. She parades in a posture of grief and throws out none-too-subtle hints in Godfrey's presence that "some people will be sorry someday." When Tommy Gray (old friend of Godfrey Parke, surprised to discover him playing butler under the name of Godfrey Smith) ad libs a story about a wife and five children to protect Godfrey's cover, Irene impetuously announces her engagement to the bemused and hapless Charlie Van Rumple. She almost immediately breaks that engagement and departs for a European tour with Cornelia—again, not a particularly admirable response to a situation she herself has created. Godfrey, meanwhile, continues to impress us and the Bullocks with his responses to various trials, particularly the one in which Cornelia tries to frame him for the theft of her pearls. Godfrey evades the "frame-up" and invests the pearls, making enough money to bail out the Bullock finances as well as to start an entrepreneurial enterprise to benefit his friends down at the city dump. But Godfrey is in moral peril similar to that exemplified, in Cavell's view, by Othello—the peril of "one of purity, of a perfect soul" (*CR*, 485). In Othello, Cavell argues, Desdemona sees "a romantic hero," for that is how he sees himself: "in entering his life, hence in entering the story of his life, [she] enters as a fit companion for such a hero; his perfection is now opened toward hers" (*CR*, 485). But purity is a sticking point for Othello. "Surprised . . . to find that [Desdemona] is flesh and blood," Othello "sacrifice[s] her . . . to his image of himself and of her, to keep his image intact, uncontaminated" (*CR*, 491–92). For Othello, moreover, it is awareness of Desdemona as "other" that tortures him by rendering his sense of his own existence as "partial" (*CR*, 493). Such knowledge, though, does not have to be greeted with "pity and terror"; it can be met with "rue and laughter" (*CR*, 494). One can accept "humanity"—one's own and that of others—rather than "thinking to escape" (*CR*, 494).

Godfrey, like Othello, is confronted with Irene's otherness when she, out of jealousy of her sister, feigns a fit and faints to keep him from meeting Cornelia "around the corner"—the place of prosperity, as we recall. Although he has no more intention than he has ever had of falling victim to Cornelia's attempts to manipulate him into a compromising position, Godfrey almost indicates the opposite to Irene when she begs him not to yield to Cornelia's demands: "I think I should decide these things for myself." Faced with his posture of all knowingness, Irene improvises a reason for him to stay, but the response she elicits goes beyond that. Godfrey allows her ruse to move him past propriety into the human condition ("that foolish feeling"); he picks Irene up and carries her, caveman style over his shoulder, to her bedroom (a highly compromising action, given that he is no longer employed by the Bullocks at this point). He proceeds to lose his temper when he discovers she's been faking her fit all along. Irene, wisely, understands exactly what this behavior means. He loves her, not as an idea that completes his ennobled sense of self (in fact, she is absent for the revelation of his magnanimity toward her family), but as someone who can make him feel foolish, without also making him want to kill himself. He does not overcome his skepticism by remaking the world in his own image. He overcomes it, as is always the case in the texts at the center of my concern, by accepting that he cannot do so. For all his "somber and isolating eloquence" (*CR*, 494) in the scene in which he reveals his heroic behavior to the Bullocks, leaving them all in tears, Godfrey's finest moment is his silent resignation in the last scene of the film as Irene positions him to exchange marriage vows: "Stand still, Godfrey; it'll all be over in a minute." Fittingly, the last sound we hear before the music signals the film's end is Irene's lilting giggle.

In his 1984 monograph, *Language in Wycherley's Plays*, James Thompson focuses his interpretation of *The Plain Dealer* on Wycherley's language, without once citing Cavell, whose pertinent work was contemporary and therefore was not really available for citation even had Thompson somehow envisioned a significance of that work for literary studies that Cavell himself had yet to claim. Thompson presents a proto-Cavellian reading of Wycherley's play, a reading very much in keeping with the themes, concerns, and consequences I have described as preoccupying La Cava in *My Man Godfrey*.[12] Manly, he notes, "rails against the world's failures because he believes so passionately that it should be better" (93). In this sense, Manly is a hypocrite in that his "cynicism is a . . . 'cloak' for his idealism" (93). Far from being the plain dealer he wants to be, Manly is the play's most egregious liar. Further, the second plot of this "split-plot play" hones in on "a central question": "the application of justice, perfection, and idealism in an imperfect world" (93–94). Freeman is at the center of this concern. Thompson invokes Northrop Frye's observation that law governs tragedy whereas liberty directs comedy: "The characters of Manly and Freeman, their actions, and the plots which follow them pose this generic or legal choice: will the play affirm or overcome the law?" (94)

Of course, the play overcomes the law. Thompson makes the interesting point that although Manly is a hypocrite in attitude, he is true in language. He "exemplifies the correct use of words in contrast to the lawyers [in the play] who represent the abuse of the art of persuasion" (99). Yet, of course, Manly falls linguistically as he falls morally. Stunned and scarred by Olivia's betrayal, he begins, like everyone else in his world, to misuse language. "Honor" becomes "revenge," and somehow the word allows for attempted rape. Manly has fallen, "descend[ing] to the level of Vernish and Olivia" (101). But Fidelia is on hand to point out "that honor and revenge are not at all the same"; it is "injury" and "revenge" that are equal because "'they both have the same end which is anothers harme'" (101).[13] One can hear the echoes of Fidelia's position when Irene rejects making people part of a scavenger hunt: "It's kind of sordid, if you know what I mean." These naïve, uncomplicated women phrase their moral insights so clearly that the complicated is unmasked as pure deception—of self and other.

These childlike women also employ a shared strategy in the face of moral outrage. They cry and faint. What else can they do when language fails? Fidelia has argued with Manly, delineating Olivia's treachery as clearly as she can. Plain language has had no effect. Already in disguise in terms of her gender, Fidelia is forced to assume a more serious subterfuge—disguise as the worst version of the man she loves—and the effort reduces her to tears, thoughts of suicide (if only she could), and pretended fainting fits. She is very much the ancestress of Irene Bullock. Neither can use language as effectively as she understands it. Because both texts end in the fulfillment of the female's desire, it seems that each genre pays homage at least once to the power of listening. What Manly says may not matter to anyone else, but it does matter to Fidelia, who listens not only for the meaning he tries to convey but for the desires he has so fully sublimated that he himself does not know how to articulate his need. Irene listens in the same way. At the end of each text, the women abruptly achieve their desires and audiences are left wondering: "Can we say what we mean and mean what we say?" And, if we can, should we, given how often we have no idea what we want?

180 *Forgotten men*

Notes

1 See Robert D. Hume, "The Socio-Politics of London Comedy from Jonson to Steele," *Huntington Library Quarterly* 74 (2011): 187–217. Hume is referencing Alexander H. Chorney's "Wycherley's Manly Reinterpreted," in *Essays Critical and Historical Dedicated to Lily B. Campbell* (Berkeley: University of California Press, 1950), 161–69.
2 *My Man Godfrey*, directed by Gregory La Cava (1936; Universal City, CA: Universal Home Video, 2001), Criterion Collection DVD.
3 William Wycherley, *The Plain Dealer* (1676), in *The Plays of William Wycherley*, ed. Arthur Friedman (Oxford: Clarendon Press, 1979). References are to act, scene, and line numbers.
4 For a cogent discussion of matters of national identity (though without reference to Native Americans) in the comedy of remarriage genre, see Cavell's treatment of *The Philadelphia Story* in *Pursuits of Happiness*, 135–60. Jean Marsden's "Performing the West Indies: Comedy, Feeling, and National Identity," *Comparative Drama* 42 (2008): 73–88, tracks eighteenth-century drama's engagement with the figure of the "Indian" in the staging of national identity.
5 Alperson and Carroll, "Music, Mind, and Morality: Arousing the Body Politic," *Journal of Aesthetic Education* 42, no. 1 (2008): 4, 12.
6 Zimbardo, *Wycherley's Drama: A Link in the Development of English Satire* (New Haven, CT: Yale University Press, 1965), 141; Hume "Socio-Politics of London Comedy," 205.
7 James Thompson, *Language in Wycherley's Plays*, 96.
8 Bob Gilpin, "Commentary," *My Man Godfrey*, directed by Gregory La Cava (Universal City, CA: Universal Home Video, 2001), Criterion Collection DVD.
9 Cavell, *The Claim of Reason: Wittgenstein, Skepticism, Morality, and Tragedy* (Oxford: Oxford University Press, 1979), 247, hereafter *CR*. Subsequent citations to this work are given parenthetically in the text.
10 Snell's observation is in his *Discovery of the Mind* (Cambridge, MA: Harvard University Press, 1953), 182.
11 Ed Sikov, *Screwball: Hollywood's Madcap Romantic Comedies* (New York: Crown, 1989), 136.
12 James Thompson, like Cavell, is dedicated to an examination of ordinary language as used in the plays. Indeed, though Cavell makes no appearance in his bibliography, J. L. Austin, Cavell's inspiration, does.
13 James Thompson is quoting Guillaume du Vair, *The Moral Philosophy of the Stoics*, trans. Charles Cotton (London, 1667), 83, in summarizing Fidelia's moral position (137n21).

7 Provisos and reprieves
William Congreve's *The Way of the World* and Howard Hawks's *His Girl Friday*

William Congreve's Millamant and Howard Hawks's Hildy Johnson enter their respective comedies with confidence and self-possession. Mirabell describes Millamant as she approaches him in St. James's Park: "Here she comes i'faith full sail, with her Fan spread and her Streamers out, and a shoal of Fools for Tenders" (2.1.323–24).[1] Although Mrs. Fainall revises the portrait with regard to the "shoal of Fools" ("I see but one poor empty Sculler; and he tows her Woman after him" [2.1.326–27]), we nevertheless get the impression that Millamant moves through life with confidence, aplomb, and style. She toys with Mirabell throughout the scene, always one step ahead of him, eventually leaving him feeling as though he "lives in a Windmill" or a "Whirlwind" or some other "whimsical Dwelling" (2.1.494, 491, 494). Yet, a few scenes later, Millamant has agreed to "dwindle into a Wife" (4.1.227).

Hildy, too, arrives in "full sail." A tracking shot follows her through the outer offices of *The Morning Post* as she exchanges greetings and pleasantries with the staff, until she reaches the office of the paper's editor and her former husband, Walter Burns. As Marilyn Fabe notes, the "dialogue in conjunction with editing and dynamic camera movements work together to create a highly sophisticated and delightful mélange of mixed messages," although whatever Hildy says in this scene, we know from the way it is presented that Bruce "is not the right man for her and Walter, her ex-husband, is."[2] Her chin tilts upwards, her gait is confident, and her tone is cheerful. In Walter's office, she retains control. He is her fast-talking match, but she more than holds her own in each exchange until she "gets out" what she came to tell him: she is going to marry Bruce Baldwin and quit her life as a "newspaperman."[3] She is determined, and there is nothing Walter can do about it. He even tells her, "you kind of took the wind out of my sails." Yet, by the end of the film, she has agreed to remarry her former husband, to come back to *The Morning Post*, and to spend her honeymoon covering a strike in Albany. The last image we see is Hildy, head and shoulders bowed, straining under the weight of a suitcase, following Walter, who walks breezily down the stairs, calling to her, over his shoulder "say, why don't you carry that in your hand?" She, too, seems to have "dwindled." He's the one "sailing" in the end.

Of all the women in the two genres of concern to me, Millamant and Hildy (and the women with whom they share their stories) offer the bleakest critique of what marriage means to a wife. Their narrative arcs highlight the cost and compromise demanded even when the woman marries the man of her choice, one who matches her wit, treats her as an equal, and values her as a friend as well as a lover. And whereas other texts in each canon argue that it is the husband or husband-to-be who feels himself most restricted by the demands and duties of marriage, in these two works, it is the male who adamantly pursues and who benefits most decidedly from legal union.

In a 1985 essay entitled "Why Didn't Mirabell Marry the Widow Languish?" I considered the odd relationship between Mirabell and his former mistress, who had been a rich widow during their love affair, but who had been "married off" by Mirabell to another man (Fainall) when the widow feared that, in Mirabell's decorous words, "the familiarities of our Loves had produc'd... Consequence." "Where could you have fixed a Father's Name with Credit, but on a Husband?" he asks Mrs. Fainall, a question he appears to consider rhetorical (2.1.267–69). His logic may have made sense to his mistress, but it certainly lays bare in the bluntest of ways the famous double standard of sexual behavior that, in some quarters, persists today:

> I knew *Fainall* to be a Man lavish of his Morals, an interested and professing Friend, a false and designing Lover; yet one whose Wit and outward fair Behaviour have gain'd a Reputation with the Town, enough to make that Woman stand excus'd who has suffer'd herself to be won by his Addresses. A better Man ought not to have been sacrific'd to the Occasion; a worse had not answer'd to the Purpose.
>
> (2.1.269–76)

The play, I argued, initially presents women as a formidable force that was challenging male social and economic authority through control of both inheritance rights and sexuality. Satiric Amazonian imagery, in particular, suggests that Congreve's dramatic narrative is focused on the reestablishment of a homosocial order imperiled by the cabalists in Lady Wishfort's circle. Mrs. Fainall's role is to provide evidence of the power as well as the ultimate rectitude of Mirabell's judgment and authority. He does protect her fortune, as well as her fame, and that he does so without damage to his own marks him as an enlightened patriarchal figure by the standards of the time. Although these standards have been thoroughly deconstructed since 1700, we can still recognize them as having had positive valence in their own day.[4]

My question in this study has shifted from a focus on whom Mirabell does *not* choose to marry to a focus on the woman he *does* choose. As with the Widow Languish, my question is why. Likewise, I want to know why Walter remarries Hildy. In the course of examining these questions,

I will consider the motives of the women as well, but it is the nature of the happiness pursued by these particular males in their pursuits of these particular women that intrigues me. What do the men see in these women and why do they pursue them through what Scott R. MacKenzie has called "squabbling courtships"?[5] Are they attracted solely by their self-confidence, intelligence, and wit or is the draw primarily fortune (in Millamant's case) or talent (in Hildy's case)? Does the man desire to control (or even profit from) the woman or to provide an environment for her growth and self-fulfillment? Why does each man seem to feel that his union with the particular woman constitutes, not only his personal happiness, but also, and perhaps even more importantly, the restitution of justice? Richard Braverman sees Mirabell as an example of the *honnête homme*, who comes to replace the attractive rake as comic hero in the comedies of the English stage, beginning in 1690, and who is paired with a villain to whom the "rakish" qualities are attributed.[6] Is this honest man's sense of his own significance and the significance of his marriage self-serving or self-seeking? Is it socially responsible? Is it ethical? Is it moral? If so, why do the women seem to "dwindle"? Why does a feeling of heaviness attend the fate of each of these women, who "sailed" into view in the beginning, only to be tethered in the end?

In the first scene of *The Way of the World*, Mirabell is fairly forthcoming as to what he wants from Millamant, and in his comments to Fainall, we also begin to understand why and how she in particular, of all the women in the play, has captured his attention and become the sole focus of his romantic efforts. Indeed, Mirabell has always struck critics as a reformed rake, who has given up the pursuit of women in general to actively seek marriage with Millamant in particular. Of course, this play, unlike the ones I discussed in my previous chapters, was written and performed after Jeremy Collier published his *Short View of the Immorality and Profaneness of the English Stage*. In that essay, Collier charged that from the drama of the age one would glean that "a fine Gentleman, is a fine Whoring, Swearing, Smutty, Atheistical Man."[7] But if Mirabell seems less "fine" than Dorimant or Horner in meeting Collier's definition, he is more fine than Harcourt or Manly (or anything we know about them besides the company they keep or have kept), in that he has had a documented affair with Mrs. Fainall. That he maintains such a reputation is evidenced by the fact that both Marwood and Wishfort have harbored hopes of dalliances with him. In other words, if Mirabell has left behind a mode of behavior, his reform seems, like Collier's demands themselves, to be following rather than leading the taste of the times. As Michael Cordner has said, "whatever his tactical innovations [and those were significant], Collier was swimming with the tide in mounting an attack on the contemporary drama," a point that can be applied with equal force to the moral reform movement that led to the adoption of the "Hays Code" or the Motion Picture Production Code in the mid-1930s.[8] Robert D. Hume sees Congreve's *The Way of the World* as "a kind of answer to Collier," and although he feels that post-Collier stage comedies would not have pleased the clergyman any more than those that provoked his ire in the first place, it is a fact that the (mis)behavior of gentlemen, in particular, will soon become the focus of much cultural attention.[9] The problem of redefining a "manly" yet moral code of conduct will preoccupy writers and social reformers from Addison and Steele through Samuel Richardson. Mirabell will not find a place in the pantheon that will include Steele's Belvile, Jr., or Richardson's Sir Charles Grandison, but compared to his immediate predecessors, he seems in some ways to be a prototype of heroes to come.

The play begins with Mirabell's pique at Millamant. What has so upset him that he cannot enjoy a game of cards with his archrival, Fainall? What has "put him out of Humour" and made him "grave"? (1.1.13–15). The answer seems perfectly clear to Fainall:

> Confess, *Millamant* and you quarrell'd last Night, after I left you; my fair Cousin has some Humours, that wou'd tempt the patience of a Stoick. What, some Coxcomb came in, and was well receiv'd by her, while you were by.
>
> (1.1.17–21)

This description of Millamant will prove not far from Mirabell's own view of her and his own experience of her the evening before. In Act 2, when he and Millamant speak alone for the first time, he upbraids her for having "the Tyranny to deny me last Night; tho' you knew I came to impart a Secret to you, that concern'd my Love" (2.1.429–31). Her excuse? "You saw I was engag'd" (2.1.432). Mirabell is provoked further by this comment, accusing her of "entertain[ing] a Herd of Fools" (2.1.433–34) and going on to chastise her for doing so in terms of taste and self-respect and morality:

> How can you find delight in such Society? It is impossible they should admire you, they are not capable: Or if they were, it shou'd be to you as a Mortification; for sure to please a Fool is some degree of Folly.
>
> (2.1.436–40)

Millamant maintains her position, declaring, "I please my self" and asserting that she finds "convers[ing] with Fools" a healthful antidote to "the Vapours" (2.1.441–42, 445). Mirabell persists, but Millamant wins the point. Threatening to break off their understanding if he does not cease the "offensive Freedom" with which he critiques her social life, she forces Mirabell to concede that they will simply disagree on the point of the company of fools (2.1.447).

Fainall, it seems, is right. Mirabell is out of sorts because of Millamant's evening preference for Witwoud and Petulant, although he apparently has other cause for concern. As he reveals to Fainall, Lady Wishfort "came in" and, following her lead, the company became "grave" and "fell into a profound Silence," making it clear that Mirabell was not welcome (1.1.24, 30–32).

Therefore, he explains to Fainall, "I resolv'd not to stir." He was perhaps assuming that eventually he would be able to speak to Millamant and convey the secret he had come to tell her (1.1.34). However, Lady Wishfort's "Invective against long Visits" produced an expression of agreement from Millamant, at which Mirabell was so hurt or offended that he rose to leave, delivering an icy comment to Millamant that made her blush (1.1.36). Fainall defends his cousin-in-law, telling Mirabell that he was "to blame to resent what she spoke only in Compliance with her Aunt" (1.1.41–42). But Mirabell insists that "she is more Mistress of her self than to be under the necessity of such a resignation" (1.1.43–44). Even though he knows that Millamant's fortune is tied to Lady Wishfort's approval, he had "been better pleas'd if she had been less discreet" (1.1.47–48).

The causes of Mirabell's frustration with Millamant and his attraction to her seem to be one and the same. He, like Fainall, finds her a character of "some Humours" (1.1.18), meaning, of course, that she is capricious sometimes, following her various emotions or impulses or mental dispositions without much concern for the way her behavior affects others.[10] Fainall does not find the trait attractive, but Mirabell (having once agreed with Fainall) is now drawn to Millamant's "faults," that is, her vagaries (1.1.159). Perhaps they seem challenges to him. He longs to order and control her fate as well as his own (and everyone else's). In the beginning, as we hear about Millamant only through the description offered by Mirabell, we might also be inclined to agree that she is on the wrong course and in need of guidance. When we meet Lady Wishfort, we may feel even more strongly that such is the case. But is speaking in compliance with a foolish older relative the serious infraction against love that Mirabell paints it? He interprets Millamant's blush as admission of that fact, but it is also possible that she reddens out of embarrassment at Mirabell's breach of civility—his own offensiveness. She does, after all, love him, and he has lost control of himself. Has he shamed himself in trying to shame her? Can we postulate that he is attracted to her partly because of the way she calibrates the delicate divide between social and individual ethical demands or is he genuinely annoyed that she has impeded his purpose—not just the purpose of revealing a secret, but, more significantly, the purpose of reforming his world?

Mirabell is a man on a mission from the beginning of the play until the very end. He (as is also the case with Walter Burns) is a contriver of plots meant to get money or power (or both) out of the wrong hands (his rival's) and into the right hands (his). The world he lives in is a world of frivolity and corruption, and, by God, he plans to do something about it. Millamant, too, lives in this world. Her approach is not that of a reformer. She (as does Hildy Johnson) accepts the fact that the world in which she finds herself is the only world she's got. All she wants is to have some say in how she positions herself within that world vis-à-vis the man she loves. While he is plotting and scheming and controlling, she is trying to get him to talk to her and to listen to her. It is significant to the highest degree that in their first scene alone together, Millamant and Mirabell discuss the power of words, with Mirabell insisting that women owe their beauty to men's "Commendation" and Millamant countering that "they could not commend one, if one was not handsome" (2.1.396, 401–02). Still, she does immediately claim that she and other women have the same creative power:

> Lord, what is a Lover, that it can give? Why one makes Lovers as fast as one pleases, and they live as long as one pleases: And they die as soon as one pleases, and then if one pleases, one makes more.
>
> (2.1.403–06)

If Mirabell is going to take this approach to language, appropriating it for power and position, Millamant can do that, too—and better. She exhibits the same quality in her exchange with Witwoud in the beginning of the scene. Responding to the fop's metaphorical excess, Millamant impatiently cries "truce with your Similitudes" (2.1.337), but then she turns right around and employs the same figure of speech, telling Mrs. Fainall, "I have enquir'd after you, as after a new Fashion" (2.1.354). Pat Gill complains of Millamant that she never speaks her desire, that whereas the other women in the play make "known their passion for Mirabell, ... Millamant sends up smoke screens on which Mirabell can read only his own desire."[11] I think Millamant's approach to language is a bit more complicated than this description suggests. As Gill notes, Millamant is unique in the Restoration canon in that, "unlike ... other Restoration heroines ..., but presumably like most Restoration women, Millamant worries about life after marriage" (118). That worry is clear in her extended simile regarding Mrs. Fainall and in her response to Mirabell's claim that he creates her beauty by noticing it. Her desire funds that worry because it is a desire defined not as temporary sexual gratification but as love, marriage, and conversation that will last a lifetime. If only someone were listening! As there appears to be no one doing so in this particular scene, however, despite the clarity of her own remarks as to what "displease[s]" and offends her (she will have more luck in the proviso scene), Millamant redefines her role as listener in the conversation she would like to have: "Well," she asks Mirabell, "what do you say to me?" (2.1.448, 462–63). Disappointingly, to her, he responds with a similitude: "I say that a Man may as soon make a Friend by his Wit, or a Fortune by his Honesty, as win a Woman with plain Dealing and Sincerity" (2.1.464–66). Oh, good grief; he's on his high horse again, and Millamant calls him on it: "Sententious *Mirabell*! Prithee don't look with that violent and inflexible wise Face, like *Solomon* at the dividing of the Child in an old Tapestry-hanging" (2.1.467–69). She goes even further to try to get him to stop being the savior of the world and pay attention to the happiness in front of his face: "If ever you will win me, woe [i.e. woo] me now" (2.1.477–78). How much clearer can you get?

Frustrated in her first attempt to clarify matters between them, Millamant succeeds in her second scene with Mirabell. It begins, more auspiciously, with an exchange of poetic verses, during which Mirabell completes the couplet she has begun quoting from Waller, thus indicating that he is willing to be led by her in this conversation. They banter about Daphne and Phoebus, chasing and flying, pursuing and being pursued, but eventually, Millamant gets out what she has come there to say, to paraphrase not her, but her twentieth-century counterpart Hildy Johnson. What Hildy has "come to say" when she utters that line initiates her journey back to Walter, indicating that she needs pursuing (even rescuing) from the false happiness represented by her portended marriage to Bruce Baldwin. What Millamant has "come to say" signals the end of her journey to Mirabell. Her articulation of her "will and pleasure" (4.1.181) and Mirabell's agreement to "Conditions" (4.1.229) prompt a quid pro quo. Mirabell asks permission to enter his own stipulations. "Speak and spare not," Millamant replies (4.1.232–33). To his credit, Mirabell does just that. He speaks of sexual jealousy, concern for progeny, worries about intimacy lost, and fears of desire soured by bad habits and behaviors. And although she calls his provisos "horrid" and "odious," Millamant agrees to them (4.1.278–79). Although she first says, "well—I think—I'll endure you," when pressed by Mrs. Fainall to "have him, and tell him so in plain terms," Millamant does just that, stating clearly, "I'll have you." As though staving off any other possible conclusion to the exchange, she adds, "Hold your tongue now, and don't say a word" (4.1.289–92, 296–97). There is no need for further language; they have come to the terms on which their happiness can be pursued.

Although he has, to his credit, temporarily suspended his concerns with the way of the world, Mirabell does have wrongs to rectify and grievances to settle. The world in which he lives is characterized by a concentration of power in the hands of Lady Wishfort, and that is unacceptable to him (and, implicitly, to the viewers/readers of the play). What does it mean that Lady Wishfort is the one in charge? Fainall is correct that Millamant's security, if not her survival, depends on her complaisance to her aunt. Mirabell's annoyance is rooted in his desire to supplant Lady Wishfort in the hierarchy of social and economic power, to reassert masculine authority in a world that is dominated by women. Interestingly, one can read the general plotline as an allegory of the Collier controversy, with Mirabell as "reformer" and Lady Wishfort as representative of the offending playwrights. Certainly, she evidences many of the tendencies identified by Collier as "Disorders of Liberty" (12). She drinks, she lusts, she speaks, if not "smuttily," then with too much vehemence, when she is alone with Foible, and with sexual suggestiveness, when she is with "Sir Rowland." Braverman notes the association of Lady Wishfort with the offending values of the Restoration. He describes her as one "obsessed with romantic illusions that keep the ideal of the old libertine alive," one still taken with "the Stuart mystique," which she must come to see as a sham in order for Mirabell to introduce a new kind of leadership that is more appropriate to the "new sociopolitical circumstances" of the nation. Braverman goes on to cite compromise, such as that Mirabell and Millmant achieve in the proviso scene, as the hallmark of this new governance.[12] Still, although Lady Wishfort is an object of satire, she is also, we must admit, the center of the play's most enjoyable scenes.

Lady Wishfort is, like the Restoration stage repertoire itself, a flouter of convention. Her inner circle is composed of women who have sworn their hatred of men. Only fops and fools of the male gender are welcome on cabal nights, and they are there just to "avoid Scandal" (1.1.56). This "scandal," presumably, would include gossip about what John Dennis, in his *Defense of the Stage*, calls "unnatural sins," one of the "moral vices" that characterize the age. The others are "Love of Women," "Drinking," and "Gaming," all of which are male vices, in Dennis's view.[13] But we've seen in *The Country Wife* how women of a certain age begin to adopt some of these vices—gaming and drinking and sexual excess, in particular. Why not the "unnatural sins," especially after "breeding" is no longer an issue? Lady Wishfort has at least toyed with the idea of a world without men, as we discover in her description of her daughter's upbringing. She "made it . . . [her] Care" to teach her daughter "a Young *Odium* and *Aversion* to the very sight of Men," by shielding her from an awareness of their existence as a separate gender (5.1.183–86):

> She was never suffer'd to play with a Male Child, tho' but in Coats; Nay, her very Babies were of the *Feminine Gender*,—O, she never look'd a Man in the Face but her own Father, or the Chaplain, and him we made a shift to put upon her for a Woman, by the help of his long Garments, and his Sleek-face, till she was going in her fifteen.
>
> (5.1.187–94)

When Mrs. Marwood expresses wonder that "she shou'd have been deceiv'd so long" (5.1.195), Lady Wishfort elaborates, painting a very curious picture of Mrs. Fainall's education by the family chaplain, who provided, in addition to a religious education (catechism), a thorough critique of the modern sins of "Singing and Dancing . . . and going to filthy *Plays*, and Profane *Musick-meetings*, where the Leud Trebles squeak nothing but Bawdy, and the Bases roar *Blasphemy*" (5.1.209–12). After such indoctrination, "she would have swooned at the sight or name of an obscene playbook!" (5.1.198–201).

It sounds suspiciously as though Jeremy Collier himself must have been Mrs. Fainall's tutor! Even without the instruction provided by dramatic narrative, however, Lady Wishfort's daughter has discovered sex—both lawful concupiscence and illicit desire. She has also learned to disguise her motives and feelings and to play her part in the dramas of her world (to act, in other words). The primary effect of her education, however, seems to have been to deprive her of agency. Unlike all the other women, Mrs. Fainall perpetually reacts to situations created by others or acts in the service of others' desires. Strict moralists might argue that her long-preserved ignorance at least saves Mrs. Fainall from the manipulative impulses of a Marwood, but I would counter that it also renders her bland and somewhat enervated, incapable of defining and pursuing the object of her own desire—whether that desire be focused negatively on Fainall or positively on Mirabell.

In Act 2's very odd, but symptomatic, private exchange between Mrs. Fainall and Mirabell, one can observe her lack of focus and definition. She begins well enough, evidently wishing the conversation to center on her and desiring that Mirabell pay some attention to his former mistress, who, as she tells him, has moved from hating her husband to despising him. Mirabell's response ("O you should Hate with Prudence" [2.1.256]), although probably not what she had hoped for, does give her the opportunity to steer the conversation toward a more intimate topic: "Yes, for I have Lov'd with Indiscretion" (2.1.257). Mirabell chooses to respond in an ambiguous way, telling her that she should indulge "just so much disgust" for Fainall "as may be sufficient to make you relish your Lover" (2.1.258–60). Is he speaking of himself in the third person and therefore indicating his willingness to go further and explore their mutual and abiding attraction or is he assuming she has taken another lover? Mrs. Fainall's next remark seems calculated to seek clarity on this score: "You have been the cause I have lov'd without Bounds, and wou'd you set Limits to that Aversion, of which you have been the occasion?" (2.1.261–63). Briefly put, Mirabell's answer is "yes."

Mrs. Fainall apparently realizes the need to change direction, especially after Mirabell reviews their past and alludes to the "Remedy" he has arranged when she is ready to leave her marriage (2.1.277). It is almost as though his explicitness sobers her, and she shifts tack as a result: "I ought to stand in some degree of Credit with you, *Mirabell*" (2.1.278–79). He agrees, replying, "In Justice to you, I have made you privy to my whole Design, and put it in your Power to ruin or advance my Fortune" (2.1.280–82). From that point on, their discussion is centered on that "design," which, by the way, Mrs. Fainall does almost "ruin," albeit inadvertently. She is committed to advancing Mirabell's fortune, although, truth to tell, she does so at her own expense. The entire plan is designed to forward the marriage of Mirabell and Millamant without forfeiture of the half of Millamant's fortune that is under Lady Wishfort's control. At this point, Lady Wishfort is furious with Mirabell, who took a peculiar path into what he hoped would be her good graces, that is, he flirted with her in behaviors that Marwood revealed to be "sham addresses." Lady Wishfort's pique and chagrin insure that she would not be likely to consent willingly to the marriage of her former "beau" and her niece. Mirabell's "design" is, essentially, a plan to blackmail Lady Wishfort into agreeing to the marriage, thereby assuring the young couple of Millamant's entire £12,000. If his plan fails and he and Millamant marry anyway, as Fainall knows, the £6,000 in Lady Wishfort's power will become part of Mrs. Fainall's estate. Even though, by the laws of the times, a wife's fortune is her husband's to spend (or not) as he so desires, it would nevertheless make more sense (or at least as much) for Mrs. Fainall to oppose Mirabell's scheme, if she were acting in her own self-interest. The credit she stands in with her former lover is credit seemingly based on loyalty to him.

What is the significance of the linguistic register in which these two speak? Both employ morally valenced terms. Mirabell invokes "prudence" and "justice," two of the four cardinal virtues, and Mrs. Fainall accuses herself of "indiscretion," a violation of a virtue that is, perhaps in her mind, equivalent to intemperance. At the least, it is the opposite of "prudence." By the time she invokes "credit," Mrs. Fainall has yielded the point that prudence, justice, and discretion are points of concern in their affairs, as well as in the affair Mirabell currently pursues. As justice, in particular, is also at stake in *His Girl Friday* and is similarly problematized, it is useful to ponder the following question: How is it an example of "justice" that Mirabell has trusted Mrs. Fainall and given her the power to help or harm him? In other words, given his treatment of her, how can he expect (and what does it mean that he *does* expect) her to help forward his love affair with another woman? The easy answer, of course, is that he has earned her gratitude by protecting her wealth, which she has signed over to him prior to her marriage and which he will endorse over to her if she chooses to leave Fainall. This very odd arrangement raises more questions than it answers if we think about it too carefully, particularly if we examine the "justice" of the arrangement.

Certainly, from Fainall's point of view, a grave injustice has been committed. Indeed, in reviewing a case that "anticipates the plot of Congreve's *The Way of the World*," Susan Staves notes that "Restoration courts held that a widow's attempts to convey to trustees before marriage were fraud against the marital rights of the husband and void."[14] Fainall refers to the discovery of the affair between Mirabell and his wife as a peculiar act of cuckoldry. He is, he says memorably, "a Cuckold in Embrio" (3.1.632). When he was "born" as a husband, he was already cuckolded, his rights violated before he enjoyed them himself (3.1.632). We must also remember that when Fainall makes this observation, he doesn't know the half of it. He is referring merely to his rights to his wife's person, not her fortune, and he is ignorant as to her suspected pregnancy, which had it been confirmed would have resulted in additional insults to his property, name, and fortune. If we manage to convince ourselves that Fainall's affair with Marwood, which also predates his marriage, somehow designates him as more morally corrupt than the others of his world, we can revel, unconcerned, in the machinations that have trod on and will continue to tread on his rights as a husband and a human being. He bears more similarity to Mirabell, however, than is often acknowledged. For example, he has been trusted by his mistress with her fame and fortune, just as Mrs. Fainall trusted Mirabell. How did Mirabell protect Mrs. Fainall's fame? By marrying her to Fainall. Her fortune? By taking it, but not spending it. Here, it is true that Fainall has been a less effective steward, for he has spent his mistress's fortune "as the prodigality of . . . [her] Love would have it" (2.1.199–200). Marwood's fortune may be depleted, but there's more money to be had. In fact, as he reminds her, he married "to make a lawful Prize of a rich Widow's Wealth," so that he could "squander it on Love" and her (2.1.206–07). He's also doing his damnedest to get hold of even more money—that hotly contested £6,000.

Sure, these doings are all rather sordid, but is there truly a great moral distinction between marrying your pregnant mistress off to an unsuspecting friend, as Mirabell does, and marrying a woman you don't love in order to spend her money on one you do love, as Fainall does? In either case, is justice served? Both men think so. Just as Mirabell claims that justice is behind his use of Mrs. Fainall in forwarding a plot that, basically, will require financial and emotional sacrifice on her part, so does Fainall attempt to make up for the "wrong" he has done Marwood (that is, in suspecting that she loves Mirabell, which indeed she does) by hating his wife more and offering to "part with her [and] rob her of all she's worth" (2.1.244–45). The way of justice in this world is clearly not a well-lit, straight, and narrow path. Although we are surely intended to agree with Mirabell that his marrying Millamant is a better outcome than her marrying Sir Wilful, it is difficult to look closely at the play and find that justice in any pure sense of the term has been served.

Katherine Mannheimer has recently argued that conventional distinctions between Fainall and Mirabell as "wits" will not withstand close scrutiny.[15] In fact, she focuses on Fainall's "Cuckold in Embrio" speech as a paradigmatic use of language that alerts us to a leitmotif within the play in which language barely contains the chaotic impulses of passion. Even in Mirabell's document protecting Mrs. Fainall's wealth, language is used to address erotic consequence and to make space for further play. Unlike many Restoration comedies, the various speeches of various characters do not so much create a hierarchy of true wit and false wit, as they demonstrate that language is almost interchangeable in its inventiveness, crispness, energy. The pleasure we take in all of the speeches by all of the characters is the same. Even Petulant and Sir Wilful, the least regarded of the characters, are capable of extraordinarily apt observations. Petulant is particularly eloquent when drunk, calling Witwoud "one half of an Ass" (Sir Wilful being the other half): "A *gemini* of Asses split, would make just four of you" (4.1.350–52). Again, Witwoud forgoes personal pique at the pleasure of a good similitude: "Thou dost bite, my dear Mustard-seed; kiss me for that" (4.1.353–54). Although Sir Wilful's metaphors are not so refined, they can be surprisingly literate. A song celebrating "*Apollo*'s Example" of being "drunk every Night" produces this gloss from the inebriated country bumpkin: "The sun's a good Pimple, an honest Soaker; he has a Cellar at your *Antipodes*. If I travel Aunt, I touch at your *Antipodes*—your *Antipodes* are a good rascally sort of topsy-turvy Fellows" (4.1.418–19.422–25). Perhaps, however, Sir Wilful's true forte is his bluntness, his tendency to voice what everyone else is thinking. My favorite example is his addressing Millamant as "cousin with the hard name," words reminiscent of my students' response (and my own, truth to tell, when I first encountered this play) (4.1.427). Who can, on first reading, keep Mirabell and Millamant straight?

Language in the play creates, in Mannheimer's words, a sense of "sublime disorder" that is barely contained, if that, by the ending in which all troubles are supposedly "resolved." In fact, the ending overtly suggests that matters are left hanging that will need further attention, as most Restoration plays do. In *The Plain Dealer*, for example, the Widow Blackacre leaves the stage threatening a lawsuit; similarly, at the end of *The Way of the World*, Mirabell promises Lady Wishfort that he will figure out a way to reconcile the Fainalls. One wishes Congreve had written that play as a remarriage comedy in which the couple discovers a "shared childhood," the fun of whatever they do together, and such fascination with one another's personalities that, like Hildy and Walter, they find "they simply *appreciate* one another more than either of them appreciates anyone else, and they would rather be appreciated by one another more than by anyone else" (*PH*, 167). Although it is difficult to imagine the Fainalls as candidates for a remarriage of this sort, the play does allow us to imagine a special kind of marriage for Mirabell and Millamant. It is one ordered by provisos, but one that emerges from and honors, in a sense, the exuberant disorder of the world these characters inhabit—a disorder against which they fight and in which they delight.

The problem with people who decide to reform, as Jean's father points out in *The Lady Eve*, is that they want everyone else to reform, too. He is speaking of the personal choice Jean has made, at that point in the film, to be what Charles (Hopsy) wants her to be. The same can be said, of course, of those who wish to reform, not themselves, but the world in which they live. People like Jeremy Collier, whose strictures may seem easy enough to employ (no smut, no double entendre, no demeaning depictions of clergymen), propose not merely cosmetic changes, but also a true restructuring of society on principles that depend on a fundamental change in our very nature as human beings. As Congreve and other playwrights knew, the entire fabric of the comic stage is intimately woven with awareness of our sexual nature and the way our body's demands, urges, and desires sometimes conflict with our higher aspirations, and, at other times, confound our hypocrisies. There are darker urges as well that are part of the human experience. Sometimes they are the stuff of tragedy, but it is also possible to speak of them comically—to acknowledge them and yet continue to live and love. There is an interesting resonance between *The Way of the World* and *His Girl Friday*, in that both contain themes typical of tragic plots (adultery in the first case and murder in the second), which form the nucleus around which a comic vision is articulated. In both cases, it's a legal document—a deed in *The Way of the World* and a reprieve in *His Girl Friday*—that allows for the (qualified) happy ending. But it is another kind of writing that provides the means for shaping a sense of the realities at issue, not by law but by public perception.

In neither *His Girl Friday* nor *The Way of the World* do newspapers have much to do with the truth. Mirabell has employed the world of print to circulate rumors of his supposed infatuation with Lady Wishfort. His means have been both flattering—"a Song in her Commendation"—and scandalous—"a Lampoon . . . [which] complement[ed] her with the Imputation of an Affair with a young Fellow" (1.1.70–72). In keeping with Mannheimer's identification of the play's leitmotif, we note that these bits of popular ephemera give rise to rumors of pregnancy: "when she lay in of a Dropsie . . . she was reported to be in Labour" (1.1.75–76). Mirabell considers his use of writing in this case to have been a great success; an "old woman" should be "flatter'd" by such rumors of vitality and fecundity, especially as he had not really "debauch[ed] her" (his "Virtue forbad" him, he says) (1.1.76–79). And, indeed, she seems to have been quite pleased, until Marwood revealed that Mirabell's were "sham Addresses" (1.1.64). Fainall is censorious: "Had you dissembl'd better, Things might have continu'd in the state of Nature" (1.1.66–67).

Although this line can be read as an indication of just how unnatural the world has become, closer attention to the comment as well as the situation reveals the truth of what Fainall says. What he refers to as "the state of nature" is Mirabell's attraction to Millamant. Their "separation" is unnatural, and it has come about because facts (rather than truths) have been revealed. Did Lady Wishfort truly want to marry Mirabell? Did she think he was courting her in earnest? (Her Act 4 description of Mirabell's romantic protestations seems an exaggerated portrait painted for the benefit of "Sir Rowland.") Might she not have been simply enjoying the flirtation and casual flattery, which, given time, would secure Mirabell a place in her family? That seems to have been Mirabell's plan (although Fainall was banking on its failure), and although it has certainly backfired by the time we meet the characters, it has done so solely at the intervention of Marwood. In fact, in the play's present, everyone, including the lady herself, accepts the view that Wishfort is actively seeking a husband and that her vows of misandry and her all-female cabals are simply hypocritical ruses. Even her daughter says that her mother "will do anything to get a Husband" (2.1.308). By this time, Mirabell agrees that "the good Lady wou'd marry any Thing that resembled a Man, tho' 'twere no more than what a Butler could pinch out of a Napkin" (2.1.311–13). Her desire makes her vulnerable, and Mirabell's scheme will exploit (and then rescue her from) the nature of an old woman's longing: "the craving of a false Appetite when the true is decay'd"; "the Green Sickness of a second Childhood . . . [that] serves but to usher in the Fall; and withers in an affected Bloom" (2.1.315–20).

Although Mirabell's first scheme was designed to sate that appetite with the flattering illusions of print, he has now been driven to concoct a different scheme—a play, in which Lady Wishfort will act the part she wishes to be perceived as playing. There will be inevitable humiliation and exposure, but Mirabell's plan prevents the worst that could happen, that is, the pilfering of her estate by an unscrupulous imposter (it happened often enough to rich widows in these times and in other times, too, for that matter). It's an elaborate plan designed, at least partly, to teach Lady Wishfort a harsh lesson. And why does she need that lesson? Perhaps her library offers a clue. She has been reading Collier's *Short View*. No longer content with the pleasing illusion of flirtatious dalliance, despite the pleasure of hearing herself spoken of in songs and lampoons, Lady Wishfort demands serious intent. Her anxiety as she readies herself for Sir Rowland's visit is one of the comic highlights of the play—indeed, of the dramatic repertoire in general. But it is also an indication of just how traumatic the prospect of sex and/or marriage is to her.

In an interesting (and significant) juxtaposition, Mirabell's comment to Mrs. Fainall regarding the life cycle of women's desire, from the "depraved" appetites of a girl to the "sickness" of a "second childhood," is followed immediately by the announcement of Millamant's first appearance on stage. "Here's your Mistress," Mrs. Fainall says, as though pointing out to her former lover that Millamant, too, is a woman and she, too, is subject to "Female Frailty" and she, too, will age and feel cravings and so forth (2.1.321, 314). Mirabell is not blind to this fact. He is censorious in this scene, as noted previously, criticizing Millamant for frivolity, unkindness, and insincerity. But somehow he cannot help loving her. Perhaps it is because she resists being written into a script, unlike the other women of her world. One could say of Millamant the very words Hildy's then-fiancé, Bruce Baldwin, utters about her: "Everybody else I've ever known, well, you could always tell ahead of time what they were gonna say or do, but Hildy's not like that." Bruce will not always appreciate this trait of hers, but he is right about its being the source of Hildy's specialness, and it is the source of Millamant's charm, as well.

Women are particularly susceptible to the threat posed by circulating stories in *The Way of the World*. In fact, that is the way Marwood persuades Lady Wishfort to capitulate to Fainall's demands for a legal document transferring all of Mrs. Fainall's assets as well as Millamant's half-fortune to him. Lady Wishfort is so angry at everyone at the beginning of Act 5 that she momentarily considers taking Fainall to court for blasphemy against her daughter: "Let him prove it, let him prove it," she cries (5.1.206–07). But Marwood begins to describe the likely effect of such a course of action. First, she predicts, Lady Wishfort would be "prostituted in court" and her "Daughters reputation" would be "worry'd at the Barr by a pack of Bawling Lawyers" (5.1.209–11). Then, the "Young *Revellers* of the *Temple*" would start in, discussing the case "again in Commons, or before Drawers in an *Eating-house*" (5.1.224–27). If those two consequences are not bad enough, the final insult would be dealt by "the publick Press" (5.1.231). The case will be transferr'd to the hands, nay into the Throats and Lungs of Hawkers, with Voices more Licentious than the loud *Flounder-man's*, or the *Woman* that crys *Grey-peas*. And this you must hear till you are stunn'd; Nay, you must hear nothing else for some days.

(5.1.232–36)

Such is the power of the press that Lady Wishfort agrees to capitulate, to "give up all, myself and my all, my *Niece* and her all—any thing, everything" (5.1.238–40).

In the end, of course, Mirabell produces the piece of paper that saves Lady Wishfort from Fainall's rigid control, but she is obliged now to Mirabell. Her reign as queen of the world of Amazons and fops has come to an end. Indeed, several readings of this play (including my own reading of 1989) suggest that Congreve's serious purpose in the play is to restore an order through the reestablishment of masculine authority or, as Braverman suggests, through the establishment of a new order defined by legal authority.[16] The new order, of course, is gendered masculine, as opposed to having less stable mechanisms of social control such as gossip, which are gendered feminine, or pamphlets like Collier's *Short View* that present an alternate masculinity, one that suppresses natural behaviors entirely. Everything that happens in the end is of a piece with various exchanges throughout the play. The legal document does indeed restore Mrs. Fainall's fortune to her own hands, but considering Mirabell's closing comment to his former mistress that he hopes the deed will "be a means well manag'd, to make you live Easily together" with Mr. Fainall, we might be forgiven the sense that nothing has actually changed, except that now Fainall really does have access to the fortune he only thought he was spending before (5.1.618–19).

In another way, though, the deed functions as Mirabell intends, that is, as a version of the provisos he and Millamant exchange. That scene, with its legal language, has been discussed by Mannheimer as an exchange that "transforms the seeming certainties of law and print-culture into what I see as a free-flowing phantasia." What Mirabell and Millamant demonstrate in this scene is the ability to improvise and imagine, to revel in what is and what may be, but without false promises or on false premises. Their linguistic agility bodes well for their adaptability, and that boding is vindicated in the end by Millamant's playacting (pretending to have accepted Sir Wilful's proposals) and, of course, by Mirabell's deed-producing. Both stop short of providing an answer to the world's ills (or the family's troubles), but each offers a momentary reprieve, time to breathe, regroup, and begin the pursuit of happiness again. In this world, as in *His Girl Friday*, that pursuit may never be fully successful, but in this world, as in Hawks's film, there are at least two people who dwell in the here and now, preferring the journey over the journey's end, the pursuit of happiness to happiness itself.

At the end of *His Girl Friday*, just as at the end of *The Way of the World*, a document arrives to solve the problem of what we have come to feel is an unjust situation. The execution of Earl Williams, like the fractured Fainall marriage, has been at the center of all the activities of the film, and we, the audience, have come to think of his scheduled hanging as an act of grave injustice. Just as we root for Mirabell in his fight with Fainall, so, too, do we root for Earl Williams. Why? He has indeed shot a policeman. Even today such a crime carries the death penalty in states that have it. And the rationale, advanced in the film, that the policeman's race is the cause for extreme measures ("the colored vote's very important in this town"), resonates uncomfortably today as it may imply that race should be a mitigating factor in determining Williams's guilt. These factors notwithstanding, we take the side of Earl Williams because *The Morning Post* takes his side. And the *Post* is on his side because the mayor and the sheriff, whom the paper designates representatives of corrupt, self-serving government, are against him. Indeed, the mayor and the sheriff have egregiously undermined Mr. Pettibone's earlier effort to deliver a reprieve by bribing the messenger with a job offer in the City Sealer's office, sending him on his way, and tearing up the Governor's order to call the hanging off. Certainly what they do is wrong, and when the simpleminded Mr. Pettibone finally realizes that, he steps into the final scene to expose the chicanery of the city officials. Suddenly, Hildy and Walter, handcuffed and facing ten years in jail for harboring a criminal, find themselves, too, reprieved as the mayor and sheriff now face charges of corruption.

But what has really changed? Earl Williams has not been found innocent. We learned earlier in the film that he has been reprieved twice already, the hanging postponed and rescheduled repeatedly to serve one political agenda or another. The fact is that Hildy and Walter *were* harboring an escaped criminal, not to save his life, but to advance the reputation of the newspaper. Walter doesn't save the front page for a human interest story, but for what he thinks of as real news: "Earl Williams Captured by the *Morning Post*: Exclusive." When Hildy reads him her first draft, Walter chastises her for failing to mention the *Post* until the second paragraph: "Who's gonna read the second paragraph? Listen, honey, for ten years I've been telling you how to write a newspaper story, and this is what I get?" Mumbling apologetic assent, Hildy goes back to work.

It is as difficult to make the case for Walter's moral superiority to the forces he combats as it is to make the argument that Mirabell somehow stands for a greater rectitude than we find in Fainall. Cary Grant is certainly a more appealing screen presence than Gene Lockhart and Clarence Kolb, who play the sheriff and the mayor, respectively, but photogenic appeal is not the same thing as moral worth. Bruce Baldwin, were he to realize the source of his many troubles in the city, would certainly have a thing or two to say about Walter's code of ethics. Is it right to entrap an innocent man in charges of robbery, mashing, and counterfeiting? And how are we to regard Walter's reaction to Mollie Malloy's plunge from the upper floor window of the press room in the Criminal Courts building? Sure, she seems to have survived the fall ("she's moving" one of the newsmen exclaims), but there is no question that she has been harmed in myriad ways by the press during their coverage of the Earl Williams case. *The Morning Post,* of all the newspapers, may have treated her most kindly up until the moment she jumped, but the fact is that her action was the direct result of the news frenzy surrounding Williams, and the *Post* is every bit as involved in that as all the other print venues. After Mollie's jump, when Walter enters the pressroom, now deserted except for Hildy (all the other reporters have scurried to the street below, not out of compassion, but in pursuit of the next installment in the Williams "saga"), he barely even responds to Hildy's concern for the girl. When, shaken, she asks him, "Did you see that?" Walter, focused on Williams, snaps, "where is he?" Hildy, distracted and upset, says softly: "She jumped out of the window." Walter, impatient with her, loudly insists: "I know that! I said where is he?" Walter understands that the big story is not on the pavement below, but hidden somewhere in the room. Finally, Hildy tells him where Earl Williams is hiding: in Benzinger's rolltop desk.

Although, earlier in the film, Walter does stop short of ordering Duffy to dynamite the train that is to carry Hildy and Bruce to Albany, he balks at little else to keep her with him and to focus her attention on whatever news story is breaking. The speed with which the dialogue is uttered throughout the film keeps us from pausing to question his stratagems, just as the complications of plot and extravagance of language in *The Way of the World* bedazzle and distract us from any worries we might have as Mirabell pursues his goal of securing Millamant. Cavell argues that Walter's "amorality" is a version of improvisation. Although he "seems to lack altogether the concept of his actions as having moral consequences," we would be wrong to "consign him to moral idiocy" (*PH,* 179). As Earl Williams says of himself, "I'm not guilty. It's the world," a "heartless yet not quite hopeless world," as Cavell puts it (*PH,* 179).

What keeps the world from hopelessness is not a hero free from corruption, but one who, although deeply involved with the most sordid (or frivolous) aspects of his world, has not succumbed to bitterness, ennui, or despair. Walter's capacity for self-reform may be limited in the extreme, but his ability to improvise seems boundless. He knows from the second scene in the film (the restaurant scene, which Cavell dubs, "satisfying beyond praise" [*PH,* 166]) that "Hildy's coming back," but what he hasn't yet figured out is exactly how to make that happen. Cavell makes the point that Hildy's appearance at the *Post* on the day before she is to marry Bruce seems obviously enough to be a gesture of uncertainty. She doesn't have to tell Walter about her marriage in person. They are divorced already. Besides, she gives two reasons for appearing in his office—first, to tell him to quit calling and sending telegrams, and second, to tell him about her forthcoming marriage. But Walter seems to understand that she has really come back in order to "escape not from unhappiness . . . but from a counterfeit happiness, anyway from something decisively less for her than something else" (*PH,* 165).

Cavell makes the point that the life Bruce represents is not a bad life in and of itself. It is a life of domestic pursuits, a life many women in America in 1940 would have agreed is the life they want, one of in which they "have babies and take care of them, and feed them cod liver oil and watch their teeth grow," as Hildy almost tearfully describes it to her former newsroom colleagues. They present a less glowing portrait: "Can ya picture Hildy singing lullabies, hanging out didies, swapping lies over the back fence?" But they themselves are susceptible to such dreams—a job in publicity, a desk and a blonde secretary with big . . . brown eyes. It is not just Hildy who is chafing at the calling of journalism. All the reporters seem trapped, not only in a life they can't control, but in personae they despise but must inhabit. Hildy wants to be a woman, she tells Walter (and anyone else who will listen), but when a fire alarm sounds, a prisoner escapes, a story needs writing against a deadline, she's quick to declare, "You can't change me! I'm a newspaperman." The "gentlemen of the press" are duly chastened after Hildy leads the weeping Mollie from their heckling presence; yet, when they confront the girl again, they go right back to their jeers and taunts. Why? That's the way they will get their stories, the way they will provoke disclosures, or, as in this instance, prompt action that becomes its own story.

Mollie's leap, though, is a false lead. As Cavell points out, it is deliberately so. He notes that Mollie jumps to divert attention from Hildy, who is being grilled as to what she knows about Earl Williams's whereabouts, referencing as evidence Mollie's declaration that "'she don't know; only I know . . . and now you'll never find out.'" Cavell sees Mollie's act as a kind of improvisation that links her to Walter—a gesture of contempt toward the same men that Walter is attempting to defeat. It is also a link to Hildy, who told Walter earlier that she "jumped out that window a long time ago," that is, the window in which, he says, "a lamp" has been "burning" for her. Cavell sees Hildy as linked to Earl by a need for escape, and Walter as linked to Mollie through a talent for improvisation. But Mollie's improvisation is way too costly, and if it "purifies" Walter in a sense, by suggesting that even he is capable of self-sacrifice, it also demonstrates that some escapes are deadly. Hildy's jump from the window of her marriage is potentially as harmful to her as Mollie's plunge is to the girl twitching on the pavement.

Maria DiBattista notes that, "by connecting Mollie's literal jump and Hildy's metaphorical one . . . [Hawks] alert[s] us to the possibility that Walter may pose a real danger to Hildy." [17] On the other hand, it is the jumping out the window (the reckless refusal of the specific kind of happiness Walter represents for her) that has endangered Hildy, even as Mollie has needlessly risked her life. Had she waited a moment, Walter, himself, would have provided the distraction Mollie sought. I think Cavell is absolutely correct that Walter's choice to ignore the fact of Mollie's gesture is both a tribute to her successful diversion of attention from the real story at hand and a commitment to the living rather than to the dead (or dying), a signal characteristic of Walter's personality. This trait is most firmly attested to by his response to Bruce's prosaically paradoxical description of the insurance business as "a business that really helps people, but we don't help you much while you're alive, only afterwards." Walter smiles agreeably at first, but then he frowns and barks, "I don't get it." His "this-worldly" focus is what distinguishes Walter, and it is also what keeps him from dwelling on consequences. He knows, it is his business to know, that every minute can change the shape of circumstance. His job as a newspaperman is to be able to move forward when the story changes. A pre-scripted life is not of interest to him, nor is it truly possible—insurance or no insurance.

Hildy is not the improviser that Walter is, but she, too, is more focused on what is than what should or could be. She has not been made happy by that focus, and she is pursuing, as we meet her, the counterfeit happiness of a conventional narrative, an insured future, as if such a thing could truly be. Her true forte is in constructing unique narratives that speak to the human experience with compassion and insight. The story she writes about Earl Williams and "production for use" is, in Cavell's words, a "piece of nonsense," but so are all the stories being written about the trial. At least in Hildy's story, Earl Williams is "victimized . . . for his own good" (*PH*, 174). At this point, as Cavell says, we are also awarded a glimpse of Hildy that shows her in profile, "turned equally from Earl and from us, private to the universe of news . . . [and] alive to herself, to her reality, . . . but not necessarily in possession of a name for what is going on in her" (*PH*, 174). I would name that reality *compassion*. Cavell uses different language, but, in my view, he, too, emphasizes fellow feeling when he glosses Hildy's parting remark to Earl ("Good-bye Earl. Good luck") as follows:

> I know you Earl and if you could know anything you would know me. We are both victims of a heartless world, and condemned to know it. The best the likes of you and me can hope for is a reprieve from it, on grounds of insanity. Good luck to us both.
>
> (*PH*, 174)

Hildy's true gift is to have retained the ability to see herself in the plight of others and to be able to express that sense of common humanity in the stories she writes. She can also turn a phrase when speaking of the corruptions that surround her: "Can I call the mayor a 'bird of prey?'" she asks Walter eagerly as she types up the news release of "Earl Williams Captured by the *Morning Post*." But it is her "woman's touch" that Walter says he needs in the beginning, and although we don't necessarily believe anything Walter says, it seems that she does have a gift for reaching the hardened hearts of readers. Think of the newspapermen as they surround the typewriter in which Hildy's half-written story is threaded, all the others falling silent as Schwartz intones the words,

But the State has a production for use plan, too. It has a gallows and at seven a.m., unless a miracle occurs, that gallows will be used to separate the soul of Earl Williams from his body. And out of Mollie Malloy's life will go the one kindly soul she ever knew.

"Can that girl write an interview?" "She'll do 'til somebody else comes along." And these are the guys who were laughing at Mollie earlier, teasing her about the state "fixing up a pain in the neck for [her] boyfriend."

If *The Way of the World* abounds with metaphor-lovers that range from the sententious (as Millamant says of Mirabell) to the wildly fanciful, *His Girl Friday* also celebrates colorful language—slang ("more slop on the hanging"), sobriquets ("Stairway Sam"), and jargon ("policies," "beneficiaries," "Sold, American!"), as well as suggestive euphemisms ("shot him right in the classified ads," "in your hat"). The language derives from a recognizable world that coheres in its preoccupations and prejudices, marked by a lively lingo. We may find some of it quaint or even offensive today ("red menace," "colored," "pickaninny"), but it nonetheless suggests a world alive with communication. There are also the metaphors, generally produced by Hildy and Walter as they parry verbal attacks and trade satirical barbs. Any given conversation that includes those two will be a rapid-fire piling of image on image as they move in and out of various characters, envisioning different scenarios, altering emotions with head-spinning speed—and all for each other's benefit, entertainment, and sometimes exasperation. Walter's gambit as he pretends to mistake the old man in the waiting room for Bruce is a case in point. Hildy watches with a look of wry amusement on her face, not speaking or moving to intervene, letting Bruce himself badger Walter until Walter finally pays attention and realizes his mistake (which he has known all along). Why doesn't Hildy step in? Obviously, she knows he is acting for her benefit. She is, quite simply, enjoying the show.

There is a sense, too, that all the newsmen are acting parts, some more effectively than others. The treatment of Mollie, again, is instructive, as the men are quite rough with her the first time she shows up in the newsroom, but when they encounter her again, after Williams escapes, they are casual and noncombative: "Hello, Mollie, how are you?" "Can I get you anything?" At this point, they seem willing to fold her into the community of writer and story, treating her with the same rough affection they reserve for Pinky Hartwell, the sheriff, and one another. Her leap from the window, in a sense, confirms their judgment that she is "one of them." And for all her whining in the first scene, the last time we see her, Mollie does seem able to hold her own, taking in the situation, acting a part, going to extreme lengths to get the story she wants.

There are, however, those who cannot keep up, slow talkers, in a sense, Bruce Baldwin most notably. Unlike Sir Wilful, who is brought into the community of *The Way of the World*, however, Bruce is expelled at the end.

He just does not belong. For one thing, he lacks the imagination necessary to survive let alone thrive in the city environment. Even Hildy becomes weary of his propensity to land himself in jail. The first time, she goes running to his rescue. The second time, she tries to send Louie to bail him out and send him back to her. The third time, she tells him to wait because there is something more important happening. The fourth time, she gives up: "Send Louie down with some honest money . . . and send him [Bruce] back to Albany, where he belongs." Bruce's complacent optimism and naïve romanticism, are reflected in his deliberate drawl and in his bankrupt range of references. Whereas Hildy, Walter, the newsmen, and even the sheriff and the mayor (I love his complaint about the pinochle-playing man, who, when elected governor, suddenly becomes a Tarzan) have a vocabulary and store of images and levels of diction and reference that mark them as fully involved in the world, Bruce seems almost speechless, barely alive. When his wallet is stolen, he bemoans the loss of "that picture of us in Bermuda," which sounds about as static as it probably was. When Walter reminisces with Hildy, he paints a different kind of "picture"—of the mayor coming into their hotel room just as he emerged from the shower ("She didn't know I was in town."). When Hildy thinks of her past life with Walter, she does so in moving pictures, like the time "we stole Old Lady Haggerty's stomach off the Coroner's physician"—an adventure the thought of which makes her smile—or when they spent their honeymoon in the mine with John Kropsky, a less pleasant memory, juxtaposed as it is with the memory she feels she should have had (of a week in Atlantic City). Still, by the end of the film, given the choice between life in Albany with Bruce and a honeymoon with Walter covering the strike in Albany on the way to Niagara Falls (a destination she seems to feel certain they will never reach), she chooses the latter. Although it must be said she does so more with resignation than with delight, it is also the only choice that makes sense.

Cavell has remarked that "*His Girl Friday*, notably among the comedies of remarriage, does not end, even by implication, with a request for forgiveness by the man and woman of one another" (*PH*, 182). He sees this fact as "a way of understanding the terrible darkness of this comedy" (*PH*, 182). For all of its examination of selfish human motivation, *The Way of the World* cannot be said to end on such a note or to qualify at any point between the prologue and the epilogue as an example of "terrible darkness." Yet, as Brian Corman has noted, the play does exhibit a greater "moral seriousness" than earlier Restoration comedies. He writes that consequently, "Mirabell and Millamant's ultimate triumph over the folly and malice that are so much a part of their world gains a special significance."[18] Still, the folly and malice of their world don't quite reach the level of graft and corruption that permeates the world of *His Girl Friday*. Perhaps, therefore, the joint emphasis on language that I believe unites these texts will seem too slight a point of comparison to serve as the basis for any further conclusions regarding the pursuit of "moral perfectionism" in the two texts. It may be time to say, as Millamant does to Witwoud (and Witwoud to her), "a truce with your similitude." The societies and situations are so different, the analogy simply cannot be sustained.

To such an observation, I will reply "fair enough," as far as the comparison goes. But my purpose in bringing these texts together is not to direct our attention away from one thing to another thing (which is, in a sense, what similitude does), but to indicate through juxtaposition what Cavell has described as his own purpose in the pairing of philosophical texts and films: "to show the persistence of a family of articulations of the moral life in modern thought" (*CW*, 5). Therefore, I will not call a truce with similitude before I note that, inasmuch as metaphor occupies a central place in these two texts, we should recognize that the figure of speech is kin to skepticism as Cavell sees it. Both metaphor and skepticism, he explains, are "unnatural," but in different ways. Whereas skepticism leads to a repudiation of the world and a turn toward the private, metaphor attempts to transcend the world in creation of the personal.[19] Moreover, both skepticism and metaphor are unnatural in ways that are "natural to the human being; parts of the nature or fate of a creature complex enough for, or fated to, language."[20] What unites the texts at the heart of this chapter is the fluent, skeptical woman, who, although "knowing the falseness of the ... world" (false in different ways in each text, but false just the same), nonetheless understands "the real value of things" (*PH*, 177). Millamant and Hildy, in the end, opt for neither repudiation nor transcendence, neither skepticism nor metaphor. For they, of all the characters in their respective texts, are the ones who most clearly understand that there are no guarantees of happiness in the world. There are only provisos and reprieves, and when those come your way, the only thing to do is to sign the contract or the court order and step as lightly as you can, carrying the burden of what you know, into the uncertain, unknowable future. Why does Mirabell marry Millamant? Why does Walter remarry Hildy? Conventions of genre demand it, for one thing. But for another, each man, driven by dreams of control and visions of reform, desperately needs a partner who understands the world for what it is and who accepts the limitations (finitude) of human possibility without succumbing to despair or resorting to fantasy.

Notes

1 William Congreve, *The Way of the World* (1700), in *The Complete Plays of William Congreve*, ed. Herbert Davis (Chicago: University of Chicago Press, 1967). References are to act, scene, and line numbers.
2 Fabe, *Closely Watched Films: An Introduction to the Art of Narrative Film Technique* (2004; Berkeley, CA: University of California Press, 2014), 65.
3 The fast-talking of this pair is achieved by the technique of overlapping dialogue and speed of delivery. For a close analysis of this technique in this film and in *The Front Page* (the 1928 play by Ben Hecht and Charles MacArthur on which Hawks's film was based), see Lea Jacobs, "Keeping Up with Hawks," *Style* 32, no. 3 (1998): 402–26, especially 405–17.

4 Kraft, "Why Didn't Mirabell Marry the Widow Languish?" *Restoration: Studies in English Literary Culture, 1660–1700* 13 (1989): 26–34.
5 MacKenzie, "Sexual Arithmetic: Appetite and Consumption in *The Way of the World*," *Eighteenth-Century Studies* 47 (2014): 261.
6 Braverman, "The Rake's Progress Revisited: Politics and Comedy in the Restoration," in *Cultural Readings of Restoration and Eighteenth-Century Theater*, ed. J. Douglas Canfield and Deborah C. Payne (Athens: University of Georgia Press, 1995), 159–63. Walter Burns does not receive such high praise, even from Cavell, though he values Walter for his "capacity for adventure" (*PH*, 185). Cary Grant's role in *The Philadelphia Story* is the most akin to the *honnête homme*, the man who has rejected excess (self-indulgence) for value (love of the woman he pursues) and whose decision is one of national import. See Cavell's discussion of *The Philadelphia Story* (*PH*, 161–88).
7 Collier, *A Short View of the Immorality and Profaneness of the English Stage*, 2nd ed. (London, 1698), 143.
8 Cordner, "Playwright versus Priest: Profanity and the Wit of Restoration Comedy," in *The Cambridge Companion to Restoration English Theatre*, ed. Deborah Payne Fisk (Cambridge: Cambridge University Press, 2000), 210; and Gregory D. Black, "Hollywood Censored: The Production Code Administration and the Hollywood Film Industry, 1930–1940," *Film History*, 3 (1989): 167–89.
9 Hume, "Jeremy Collier and the Future of the London Theater in 1698," *Studies in Philology* 96 (1999): 502.
10 This meaning of "humourous," now rare and archaic, was current in the period and often applied to actions and sometimes things as well as people. The *OED* cites Thomas Kyd's *Spanish Tragedy* in illustration: "You know that women oft are humorous." s.v. "humourous," *adj.* and *n.*
11 Gill, *Interpreting Ladies: Women, Wit, and Morality in the Restoration Comedy of Manners* (Athens: University of Georgia Press, 1994), 129.
12 Braverman, "The Rake's Progress," 161–63.
13 Dennis, *The Usefulness of the Stage, to the Happiness of Mankind, to Government, and to Religion* (London, 1698), 23.
14 Staves, *Married Women's Separate Property in England, 1660–1833* (Cambridge, MA: Harvard University Press, 1990), 50.
15 Mannheimer, "Cuckolds in Embryo: Congreve and the Phantasmagoric Sublime" (paper delivered at the annual conference of the American Society for Eighteenth-Century Studies, San Antonio, TX, March 2012).
16 Kraft, "Why Didn't Mirabell?" 31; Braverman, "The Rake's Progress," 159–63.
17 DiBattista, *Fast-Talking Dames*, 276.
18 Corman, "Comedy," 67.
19 Cavell, *In Quest of the Ordinary: Lines of Skepticism and Romanticism* (Chicago: University of Chicago Press, 1988), 148. See Garrett Stewart's discussion of this passage in his "Self-Relayance: Emerson to Poe," in *Stanley Cavell Literature and Film: The Idea of America*, ed. Andrew Taylor and Áine Kelly (New York: Routledge, 2013), 75.
20 Cavell, *In Quest of the Ordinary*, 148.

8 Happily ever after?
The awful truth about careless husbands

In Colley Cibber's 1704 comedy *The Careless Husband*, Lord Foppington puts the dilemma of marriage crudely, but clearly: "women of virtue are now grown such idiots in love, they expect of a man, just as they do of a coach-horse, that one's appetite, like t'other's flesh, should increase by feeding" (2.2.192–95).[1] There, you have it: the whole problem of marriage (and remarriage) in a nutshell, "a simple story for simple people," as Peter Warne would say, and a rephrasing of Doralice's opening observation in *Marriage à la Mode*: "*Why should a foolish Marriage Vow / Which long ago was made / Oblige us to each other now / When Passion is decay'd?*" (1.1.4–7). Indeed, a few years later Cibber would premiere his reworking of Dryden's text into a play he initially advertised as *Marriage-a-la-Mode*, but subtitled *The Comical Lovers*, by which it became known. Therein he combined the comic plot involving Doralice, Melantha, Rhodophil, and Palamede with scenes from *Secret Love* and *The Mock Astrologer*. *Marriage a la Mode; or The Comical Lovers* was first staged on Tuesday, February 4, 1707, at the Queen's Theatre in the Haymarket, with an all-star cast: Robert Wilks as Palamede, Colley Cibber as Celadon (from *Secret Love*), Barton Booth as Rhodophil, Anne Bracegirdle as Melantha, and Anne Oldfield as Florimel (from *Secret Love*).[2] It is safe to assume that by then Cibber had long been familiar with Doralice's complaint, her wonderment that marriage demands the willingness, even eagerness, for repetition after passion has been spent. Doralice marvels at first, and later accepts, that marriage is always, to borrow Cavell's language, "remarriage." And this is the awful truth that preoccupies Cibber in his first comedy *Love's Last Shift* (1696), as well as in his most successful comedy, *The Careless Husband*. In both plays, Cibber is concerned to demonstrate (rather than simply assert, as Dryden had done in *Marriage à la Mode*) the means by which marriages remain vital. Indeed, Gary A. Richardson's remark that in *Love's Last Shift*, Cibber "treats marriage with a seriousness rarely seen in the era," applies with equal, if not greater, force to *The Careless Husband*.[3] In *Love's Last Shift*, Cibber hedges his bets, in a sense, with a bed trick, a plot device guaranteed to evoke some cynical response, as Vanbrugh demonstrated hilariously in *The Relapse* (1696). Without taking offense (he did, after all, play Lord Foppington in

Vanbrugh's play), Cibber seems to have been led as a result to rethink the central problem of marriage as well as its solution. Whereas in *Love's Last Shift*, Amanda's courtesan-act causes Loveless to look at his wife again and anew, in *The Careless Husband*, Lady Easy accomplishes the more difficult task of arousing her husband's desire to talk to her.

Of course, conversation between a man and a woman in the genres central to this study is both a literal subject of contemplation and a metaphor for sexual intercourse. The central couples in the Restoration courtship comedies as well as in the Hollywood comedies of remarriage intrigue us and each other by their ready wit, their verbal virtuosity, their obvious love of language, and their care to communicate. They call attention to themselves as unique in their dramatic worlds by their concern to make themselves, in Stanley Cavell's words, "intelligible to themselves" (*CW*, 263)—a goal that needs a partner who will listen and respond with equal wit, virtuosity, love, and care. Just how rare a thing it is to find such a partner is often highlighted by the texts. Think of Dorimant in the opening scene of Etherege's *Man of Mode*—quoting verses, reveling in the language and sentiments of Waller, significantly a poet of a bygone age, as if to say (as Peter Warne *does* say in *It Happened One Night*), "they don't make 'em like that anymore." Peter, too, is introduced as a lover of poetry—his own poetry, the free verse with which he writes the article that provokes his editor to fire him. Both Dorimant and Peter are surrounded by admiring individuals in their first scenes. There is no lack of chatter in their lives. Certainly, in terms of exposition, that chatter is useful to the audience, if less than fulfilling to the central character. But when Dorimant meets Harriet and Peter encounters Ellie, talk becomes conversation. The heightened level of attentiveness necessary to engage and respond to the comments of these women snaps the men out of their ennui and challenges their sense of solipsistic mastery.

This focus and intensity is characteristic of all the central couples in the plays and films examined thus far. Even in *Marriage à la Mode* and *The Shop around the Corner*, texts that I have discussed as precursors to the genres with which I am concerned, there is a clear sense of residual (in *Marriage*) and incipient (in *Shop*) engagement between the central couple, the nature and texture of which endorses the view of (re)marriage as the kind of conversation more thoroughly investigated by the other works under consideration. Indeed, we remember, Rhodophil describes his early married life as one of lively, fulfilling, mutually enjoyable intercourse (pun intended), which lasted until the couple became self-conscious about their specialness and yielded to the pressure to be (or seem) like most other married couples of their time: as indifferent and inattentive to one another as they are aware of and compliant with the dictates of society's forms and modes. Significantly, one of the insights of the Restoration comedy of courtship will be the damage social pressure can bring to bear on private happiness. Inevitably, the female half of the witty pair will deal with that pressure by flouting it and superseding fashion with her own rules.

For the film comedies of remarriage, the insight is different. Rather than the forms and modes and fashions of public life posing threats to individual happiness, it is the private fantasy, the internalized romance, that proves most damaging. Klara's reading a novel about the actress in the Comédie Française, who used her devoted lover "like a dog," provides a template for the way she acts toward Kralik, to whom she feels "very attracted" when she first begins employment at the shop around the corner. By the end of the film, she has come to understand the gap between her fantasy and her reality: "You see, she was an actress in the Comédie Française, and I was a clerk at Matuschek and Company." Although Klara's way of expressing her insight may suggest that a real actress would be romantically successful in her tactics of disdain and hostility, the fact is that Margaret Sullavan herself is an actress. As she utters these words of humility, she is more disarmingly appealing than she has been since the scene in which she first appeared on the screen to charm a middle-aged woman into purchasing a cheap "Ochi Chernye"-playing cigar box, capitalizing on the woman's hope (fantasy) of controlling candy consumption and thereby restoring a girlish figure.

We know that it is Miss Novak, not Margaret Sullavan, who is shyly admitting (to herself and to Mr. Kralik) her true feelings. But, in a curious way, she speaks as well for the members of the audience. At this point in the film, they are beginning to relinquish their own investment in fantasy, with perhaps the same combination of wistfulness and hope Sullavan conveys as Klara turns from the fantasies of literature to the story of her own life. It is worth noting that there was a perceived intensity in the James Stewart/Margaret Sullavan relationship, although shy revelations (according to trade sources and industry gossip) were more likely to have come from him than her. Lawrence J. Quirk's observation of their first meeting is typical of the stories that abound regarding this pair: "for Stewart, it was love at first sight, and was to remain love for all the years that followed."[4] In the genre proper, it will often be the male half of the central pair (Peter Warne, Hopsy Pike, Godfrey Parke) whose indulgence in narratives of romantic fantasy impedes his recognition of the one with whom he can pursue, not a cherished dream, but more importantly, an enjoyable and significant conversation. But in *His Girl Friday*, as we have seen, the role reverts to the female, Hildy, who, like Klara, has been seduced by fiction. Also like Klara, she finally realizes that the life she has been living and the man with whom she has been living it are much more interesting than the stories she has been taught to prefer. In *His Girl Friday*, the point is brought home nicely as Hildy's articulation of her fantasized happiness so clearly exposes its inadequacy: "I'm going to get married and have babies and feed them cod liver oil and watch their teeth grow." The last phrase, in particular, sounds like a metaphor for boredom.

Yet the appeal of steadiness, regularity, predictability, and even boredom is never treated disdainfully by either genre. The central couple does take a risk in ultimately choosing a life of conversation that challenges each member of the pair and that demands attentiveness and attention at such an exhausting and even dangerous level. It is no wayward detail that Klara reads *Anna Karenina* during the course of *The Shop around the Corner*, nor is it simply incidental that she takes the novel to her long-anticipated meeting with her "dear friend." The novel's central theme, like that of the song "Ochi Chernye," which plays in the background of the restaurant scene, is the seductive danger of romantic love. The third and fourth lines of that passionate song are, after all, "How I fear you, / How I love you," which seems true of Klara and Kralik as they spar in the restaurant wherein fear on both sides temporarily prevails.[5] Eventually, of course, when they embark on their journey together, they must do so in the state of vulnerability and openness to each other that makes the pursuit of happiness and moral perfectionism possible, but that also involves risk, uncertainty, and sometimes danger. The Matuschek marriage figures danger as infidelity, but the invocation of *Madame Bovary* alerts us to another possibility: that marriage may confer an ennui so desperate that it leads to self-annihilation.

The Restoration courtship comedies figure dullness more positively, presenting, as foils to the risk-taking witty pair, the true lovers, whose genuine affection for each another is based on a mutual attraction that is asserted rather than demonstrated. It is a fact of their narratives that Young Bellair and Emilia and Florinda and Belvile are "in love"; they must overcome the resistance of guardians and the threat of rivals to realize their love, and that struggle drives the arc of their story. Their verbal exchanges on the stage are heartfelt and sincere, but neither sparkling nor lively. We know they wish to marry, and we accept it as a fact and root for them, but we also feel that there is a possibility that the appeal of a Dorimant or a Wilmore (or a Harriet or a Hellena) some years down the line may cause one or the other of the couple to repeat Doralice's dirge concerning the decay of passion and the foolishness of the marriage vow. Steadiness, regularity, predictability, and dependability are what we long for when we do not have them and what we chafe against when we do.

In a sense, genre itself embodies the ambiguities of the natural human tendency to crave stability and long for change. Indeed, film genre theorists have regularly featured meditations on the various appeals of the typical Hollywood genres, including the one generally referred to as "screwball comedy." Westerns, film noir, romantic comedies, melodramas, horror films, action films, and so forth have been analyzed as both myth and ritual, serving basic psychological or even religious needs for the society that developed an interest in the basic formulae of each type of film and that sustains interest in many of the genres to this day.[6] Serious stage genres are typically talked of in Aristotelian terms, with broader genres (comedy, tragedy, farce, and romance) supplying the general rubrics. But, as in the world of film criticism, both artistic and marketing forces often drive creative choices and influence both audience reaction and critical evaluation. Occasionally, in both theater and film, an author will come to define his or (less commonly so far) her own niche market—we look forward to the next David Mamet play or Wes Anderson film, for example, as a subgenre of its own. What we want in genre (even genre that is auteur based) is both repetition and novelty—our pleasure is derived from the interplay of the familiar and the new. It is, in other words, our craving for something different but the same that drives us to seek fulfillment from the stage, the screen, and, truth to tell, from other experiences as well—television series, theme parks, city hop-on-and-off bus tours, community life-cycle ceremonies, annual holiday celebrations, to name a few. That urges so fundamental should be the foundation of, and perhaps the challenge to, the fundamental social pact, marriage, is not surprising. It is the one relationship that we continue to enter by choice and, at least theoretically, for keeps. We demand much of marriage, but often we fail to understand that marriage demands much of us, not to mention *what* it demands of us. For all his reputation in his own time and through the ages as one of literature's least philosophical playwrights, Colley Cibber does seem to have been gifted with a profound philosophical insight: what is needed in marriage, first and foremost, is that we pay attention.

Even the most ridiculed aspects of Cibber's first comedy, *Love's Last Shift*, reveal a surprising philosophical sophistication when representative scenes are placed side-by-side with those from the equally philosophical and equally sophisticated Hollywood comedies that Cavell explores. To take one example—and probably the most (in)famous: in the play we learn that Amanda is unrecognizable to Loveless, not only because he has not seen her for ten years, but also because she has suffered from smallpox, and the disease has enhanced her beauty. This detail has provoked much ridicule, and, given the devastating effects of smallpox, could even seem cruel as a plot device (although the opposite argument could be made as well). Still, to focus on the challenge to realism is to miss the adjudication of two philosophical puzzles introduced by Amanda's altered appearance. First, what constitutes moral action? And, second, what determines knowledge? Or, put another way, what does it mean to be known? Amanda plans to entice Loveless to her bed, but she can do so only if he does not know she is his wife. Before she pursues her plan, she experiences certain doubts that she expresses to her friend and confidante Hillaria. Amanda wants to know, "What think you of it?" Hillaria is supportive for interesting reasons: "Oh, I admire it," she says. "Next to forgetting your husband, 'tis the best counsel was ever given you, for under the disguise of mistress you may now take a fair advantage of indulging your love" (3.1.6–11).[7] One might expect the pious Amanda to object to this less-than-subtle reference to sexual appetite (and, indeed, Vanbrugh's Amanda no doubt would do so), but, although she chides Hillaria for her "mad humor," Cibber's Amanda does not deny the fact of desire. Indeed, she remarks thoughtfully, "I don't think the worse of you for what you say" (3.1.14, 20–21). Amanda, it turns out, can discriminate between true modesty and an affectation that would have you "run from all you see"; there must be a way to "converse with men" without being or seeming "an ill woman" (3.1.27, 30, 28). Aparna Gollapudi argues that Cibber's project in this play is precisely "to reconcile virtue and sexuality by evoking rational self-control rather than fear of scandal" through "dramatizing the virtuous constancy as well as the sexual pleasures . . . a wife [such as Amanda] offers."[8]

Amanda asserts that "the rules of virtue have been ever sacred" to her, and she is "loath to break 'em by an unadvised understanding" (3.1.33–35). So, what does Hillaria think? Can Amanda "justify" her "intended design" (3.1.36–37)? "Why, if I court and conquer him as a mistress," she asks,

> am not I accessary to his violating the bonds of marriage? For though I am his wife, yet while he loves me not as such, I encourage an unlawful passion. And though the act be safe, yet his intent is criminal. How can I answer this?
>
> (3.1.39–44)

In *The Luckey Chance*, Behn asks the same question, as does Sturges in *The Lady Eve*. Their answers are less clear than those provided by Hillaria, who initially advises Amanda to think selfishly: "If he don't intrigue with you, he will with somebody else in the meantime, and I think you have as much right to his remains as any one" (3.1.45–47). Fair enough, Amanda admits. Still, to pursue her scheme is, without doubt, to encourage Loveless's vice. And it won't necessarily "prevent his doing worse elsewhere" (3.1.49–50). Hillaria concedes the moral truth of Amanda's observation and goes even further to express it in an epigram: "a certain ill ought not to be done for an uncertain good" (3.1.51–52). Another epigram, however, expresses another moral truth: "of two evils, choose the least": "sure 'tis less criminal to let him love you as a mistress than to let him hate you as a wife" (3.1.52–55). Finally, moral luck will decide the extent and nature of guilt: "If you succeed, I suppose you will easily forgive your guilt in the undertaking" (3.1.55–56). Amanda acknowledges the truth of Hillaria's observation: "I find no argument yet strong enough to conquer my inclination to it" (3.1.57–58).

Moral qualms adjudicated and the act determined upon, Amanda moves on to another philosophical conundrum: "is there no danger, think you, of his knowing me?" (3.1.58–59). Hillaria's answer, "not in the least" (3.1.60), is based on a complex set of criteria that taken in aggregate amounts to a theory of knowledge. First, Loveless's own psychological predisposition will determine the extent to which he can perceive what (or who) is before him. He won't know you, Hillaria tells Amanda, because "he confidently believes you are dead" (3.1.60–61). We remember Gayman's experience of the "bag of bones" he encounters in the form of his beloved (and nonskeletal) Julia, an experience completely determined by his expectation of meeting with an old, undesirable bedmate as opposed to the young, attractive woman he had been yearning for and pursuing. We remember Hopsy's inability to recognize Jean and Jean's admitted difficulty in seeing Charles at the Pikes's manor as the same Hopsy she loved on the ship:

You see, on the boat we had an awful yen for each other, so I saw him as very tall and very handsome. He probably thought I had big melting eyes and a rosebud mouth . . . and a figure like Miss Long Beach, the dream of the fleet.

"Sir" Alfred McGlennan Keith has also "taken the precaution" of telling Hopsy the story of Cecilia, the Coachman's Daughter—a "gaslight melodrama"—predisposing the gullible "mug" to accept whatever odd coincidences might otherwise lead to knowledge (acknowledgment).

No one has to resort to melodrama to ensure Loveless's blindness. Time and chance have done enough to supplement his all-too-complacent reaction to the news of Amanda's death. For one thing, Hillaria points out, "he has not seen you these eight or ten years. . . . [and] besides, you were not above sixteen when he left you" (3.1.61–62; 62–63). She notes further, there is "the alteration the smallpox have made in you (though not for the worse)" (3.1.63–64). These are "sufficient disguises," but Amanda herself finds two more: "the considerable amendment of my fortune, for when he left me, I had only my bare jointure for a subsistence," as well as her "strange manner of receiving him" (3.1.65; 66–70). Something, in other words, has changed in Amanda's perception of herself. She feels the weight of the task at hand, but she accepts not only the burden of its portent for her own personal happiness, but its cultural significance as well. Her final speech to Hillaria reflects these thoughts:

> I can't help a little concern in a business of such moment. For though my reason tells me my design must prosper, yet my fears say 'twere happiness too great. Oh! to reclaim the man I'm bound by Heaven to love, to expose the folly of a roving mind in pleasing him with what he seemed to loathe were such a sweet revenge for slighted love, so vast a triumph of rewarded constancy, as might persuade the looser part of womankind ev'n to forsake themselves and fall in love with virtue.
>
> (3.1.87–96)

Amanda's goal, indeed, becomes that of much of the literature of the early to mid-eighteenth century, evidenced most adamantly in Addison and Steele's *Tatler* and *Spectator* essays, which aimed "to make morality fashionable," as Taine famously put it.[9]

Addison, himself, referred to his project as a philosophical one. Where Socrates "brought Philosophy down from Heaven, to inhabit among Men," Addison designs to bring "Philosophy out of Closets and Libraries, Schools and Colleges, to dwell in Clubs and Assemblies, at Tea-Tables and in Coffee-Houses."[10] Discuss these papers, he is advising. Talk over the notions, think about the ideas, ponder the morality, debate the ethics, scrutinize the behavior revealed in the vignettes or expositions I provide. In a sense, Addison is the first "ordinary language" philosopher, emphasizing the need to pay

Happily ever after? 211

attention to common experience, to live and speak carefully, to mull over what we really mean when we say (or do) something, just as Amanda does in the scene discussed above. But, if Amanda's approach to circumstance is philosophical in a way recognizable by us today as well as by her near-contemporary Joseph Addison, the term "philosophy" and what it signifies in the context of the play itself is one that the play disavows. In *Love's Last Shift* as well as in Vanbrugh's send-up, "philosophy" means the opposite of paying attention, living and speaking carefully, or thinking about what we really mean when we say (or do) something. Indeed, it means removing oneself from experience and letting thought substitute for action, feeling, and impulse.

In *Love's Last Shift*, it is Sir William Wisewoud who is the "philosopher" or at least the one who, as defined in the Dramatis Personae, "fancies himself a great master of his passion, which he is only in trivial matters." This dismissive description suggests, as indeed is the case, that Sir William is the play's comic butt, the dupe whom we do not take seriously, despite (or because of) his own tendency to regard and govern himself with deliberation and care. If we ignore the description of his character, however, it is difficult not to admire him, even if we do chuckle at his dilemmas and his blindnesses. After all, he maintains his composure in some challenging moments that speak to the shift in the comic enterprise, as does the fact that Sir Novelty Fashion, the play's fop, is not the source and end of the play's laughter. In fact, Sir Novelty is this play's Dorimant/Willmore/Horner rolled into one, complete with a mistress, Flareit, whom he is attempting to cast off and who, although she breaks china instead of tearing fans or wielding pistols, is every bit as violent as Mrs. Loveit or Angellica Bianca. "This woman is certainly the Devil," Sir Novelty says, in aside; "Her jealousy is implacable. I must get rid of her, though I give her more for a separate maintenance than her conscience demanded for a settlement before enjoyment" (2.1.390–94).

Sir Novelty, indeed, plays straight man to Sir William when he tries to break the older man's composure by offering himself as husband to Narcissa, an offer Sir William coolly declines as he has already settled on the Elder Worthy for Narcissa's mate. Whereas the fop is correct in pointing out that Young Worthy is a threat to this arrangement, the philosopher is also correct in pointing out that the fop is an unworthy mate for his child. Why? Sir William tells Sir Novelty, "my daughter is disposed of to a gentleman that she and I like very well. . . . [and besides], you have too great a passion for your own person to have any for your wife's" (3.1.160–62, 173–5). Sir William Wisewoud may be the play's fool, but his sense of what will make his daughter happy is not foolish in the slightest, and the play itself endorses his view that mutual desire must underwrite the state of matrimony.

Sir William has been lied to by Narcissa about her feelings for the man he intends her to marry as well as by the Elder Worthy with regard to his intent (the Elder Worthy is in love with Hillaria, but he has allowed Sir William to believe he is courting Narcissa, partly in an effort to forward his younger brother's desire to marry her). Sir William does place emphasis on the wealth of the elder brother, but at no point in the play prior to the announcement of the marriage between Young Worthy and Narcissa is he confronted with her love for the younger brother and called upon to react or act accordingly. The choice to distance Sir William from what had been a staple of the Restoration courtship comedy plot (i.e., the role of the blocking agent committed to codes of behavior that undervalue young love) is an interesting move on Cibber's part, as is his staging of a comic scene involving two bullies and the philosopher. The bullies try repeatedly to provoke Sir William to anger, drawing on the stereotypical insults that the comic stage of the preceding half-century had worked to such effect. One cannot imagine Blunt, for example, reacting with anything but explosive anger at the suggestion of cowardice or Pinchwife turning aside the remark that he is nothing but a "sniveling old cuckold" with the observation that his wife told him otherwise: "and I believe her too" (4.1.59, 68).

Sir William does become angry, predictably, in the final scene—the scene that would seem to justify the description of his character in the "dramatis personae." He has been fooled, after all, into legally committing a dowry of five thousand pounds upon the marriage of his daughter to a younger brother of no estate and little fortune, when he meant to sign off on the dowry at her marriage to a man of great estate and fortune. He chafes and blusters and threatens, but very quickly both Loveless (the newly reclaimed husband of Amanda) and the Elder Worthy vouchsafe for the marriage between Young Worthy and Narcissa. Loveless pledges, "I here promise to return you your five thousand pound, if after the expiration of one year, you are then dissatisfied in his being your son-in-law" (5.4.228–31), and the older brother chimes in, "Mr. Loveless, you have been beforehand with me, but you must give me leave to offer Sir William my joint security for what you have promised him" (5.4.233–35). Then Young Worthy, the groom, offers to return the fortune he earlier in the play claimed to be pursuing in this marriage with Narcissa. Perhaps they are all cynically "working" the old philosopher, but if so, his reaction redeems them.

The concluding comments of all and sundry celebrate marriage as a domain of mutual happiness. Most importantly, the speeches of Sir William, Loveless, and Amanda, all of whom comment on the turn of events, feature "happiness": Sir William wishes his daughter and new son-in-law "the happiness of a bridal bed" (5.4.249); Loveless compliments Sir William for relieving Narcissa of "the usual consequence of a stolen marriage, a parent's curse" and, instead, providing her the chance to "be happy in her love, while you have such a tender care on't" (5.4.255–57); and Amanda ends the discussion with the reflection, "this is indeed a happy meeting" (5.4.258). Interestingly, Cibber follows those comments with a tableau that features Love "on a throne attended with a chorus" composed of Fame, Reason, Honor, and Marriage. For all his reputation as a relatively superficial writer, Cibber's masque articulates the tensions and troubles as well as the hopes and dreams of marriage: Is it a road to misery or a path to happiness? Moreover, under the guise of Reason, the masque posits another road to happiness through philosophy, suggesting that the playwright, like other philosophical writers, including Cibber's nemesis Alexander Pope and, in our time, Stanley Cavell, is celebrating the pursuit of moral perfectionism, a "flourishing . . . inseparable from ethics."[11]

Reason insists that "Love gives you but a short-lived bliss, / But I bestow immortal happiness" (5.4.276–77). Love does not explicitly disagree but notes that "thou . . . dost strive in vain / To free the lover from a pleasing chain" (5.4.280–81). Lovers will love despite the knowledge that pleasure is fleeting. Honor weighs in to argue that a man's route to fame is best pursued through valor and the art of war. Love's answer to this argument is that "soft desire" "swells" the breast every bit as much as the "glowing fire" of "war-like" sentiments (5.4.287–89). Honor turns the argument over to Marriage, who appears "*with his yoke*," complaining that Love had misled him with promises of "an eternal round of happiness" when all he got was "this galling yoke—the emblem of a wife" (5.4.295, 297). Love's response is to point to "raptures in the bridal bed" (5.4.299), but Marriage counters by pointing out that those raptures had long since given way to "wand'ring flames" that have destroyed his "peace of mind" (5.4.301, 304). Love advises that the best remedy is to "go home . . . and mourn / For all thy guilty passion past" (5.4.307–308); joy and a "happy life" are to be found just where Love said they would be found: "in a virtuous wife" (5.4.305–306). Loveless rapturously approves the masque, commenting in the last speech of the play:

> 'Twas generously designed, and all my life to come shall show how I approve the moral. Oh Amanda! once more receive me to thy arms, and while I am there, let all the world confess my happiness. By my example taught, let every man whose fate has bound him to a married life beware of letting loose his wild desires. For if experience may be allowed to judge, I must proclaim the folly of a wandering passion. The greatest happiness we can hope on earth,
> And sure the nearest to the joys above,
> Is the chaste rapture of a virtuous love.
>
> (5.4.311–22)

The problem is, of course, that Loveless's experience illustrates no such thing. He has rediscovered his passion for Amanda because he has experienced her anew. She has stimulated and then satisfied his "wild desires." There is no indication that Loveless's experience of Edenic bliss in his renunion with Amanda will continue to satisfy his sexual appetite for "all sorts of fruit" (1.1.52). As he complains in the beginning, "a wife is an eternal apple tree. After a pull or two, you are sure to set your teeth on edge" (1.1.53–55), a sentiment the masque endorses rather than challenges, unless one can develop a taste for virtue.[12]

That's the design of the argument, of course, however unconvincing it may have been to some of Cibber's contemporaries. In *Love's Last Shift*, the point is driven home by Loveless's own recognition that female virtue does not signify the absence of desire, "the defect of unperforming nature," but a victory of "conscience and ... force of reason" that "curb[s] her warm desires when opportunity would raise 'em" (5.2.139–46). Once he realizes that Amanda is not cold, that she too has a sexual nature, Lovelace is willing to regard her as a model for his own behavior, his own use of Reason—not to justify his waywardness, but to support his faithfulness. Insofar as it goes, this argument is effective, although Vanbrugh's criticism, implicit in *his* Loveless's opening speech, is powerful. Invoking "philosophy" as the opposite of "roving pleasures," this Loveless begins where his prototype ended, that is, celebrating the "peace" he has achieved through fidelity (1.1.1, 3, 9).[13] As his speech unfolds, however, "peace" begins to sound a lot like boredom. If life with Amanda has stilled "the raging flame of wild destructive lust," it has also "reduced" his passion to "a warm pleasing fire of lawful love" in the glow of which "life glides on" (1.1.15–17). When he greets Amanda as the "cause of my content" (1.1.18), we cannot help but hear, as Vanbrugh no doubt intends, a restlessness that he will soon act on.

In a sense, *The Awful Truth*, Leo McCarey's 1937 comedy, which Stanley Cavell deemed to be "the best, or the deepest, of the comedies of remarriage" (*PH*, 231), would be better titled *The Awful Truism*, for it is a truism, not a truth, that calls the marriage of the central couple into question and precipitates their divorce: "Marriage is based on faith. When that's gone, everything's gone," says Jerry. He has returned from a fake trip to Florida to find that his wife, Lucy, has spent at least part of a night away from home in the company of her voice instructor, Armand. A suave European who invokes stereotypes of libertine—or as the film has it "continental"—manners and, more significantly, mores, Armand compliments Jerry on his "continental mind," which is "free from all mean suspicions." The situation quickly deteriorates, however, when he leaves and we see Jerry nursing those "mean suspicions" he is supposedly free of and Lucy holding the gift he brought her from "Florida," an orange stamped "California." As he lay in the tanning bed at the opening of the film, acquiring the bronzed look that would attest to two weeks in Florida (had it not been raining the whole time), Jerry told his squash partner, "Well, I'm going to be tanned, and Lucy's not going to be embarrassed. And what wives don't know won't hurt them." But, of course, what they do know or inadvertently discover may. Still, it is not what Lucy concludes based on weather reports and stamps on oranges—that is, based on what she knows—that catapults this couple to court. After all, she has observed that, "you can't have a happy married life if you are always going to be suspicious of each other." The evidence she holds in her hand does not even provoke her to make accusations or voice doubt. It is what Jerry *doesn't* know but suspects that leads *him* to utter that sententious declaration about faith and marriage, after which, tacitly agreeing, we suppose, Lucy picks up the phone and calls their lawyer to initiate the divorce proceedings.

"Tragedy is the necessity of having your own experience and learning from it; comedy is the possibility of having it in good time," according to Cavell (*PH*, 238). And, indeed, this film illustrates the point. Lucy has something to learn, and she does learn that necessary lesson in good time. After her divorce, she entertains the notion of marrying the oh-so-wrong-for-her Dan Leeson. He is, as Cavell points out, tone deaf with regard to Lucy. He doesn't understand her harmony on "Home on the Range"—in the idiom of the film, that means he doesn't understand how to make a home with her. He cannot hear her voice. But, neither can Jerry, in the beginning. Armand can; indeed, he helps her develop her voice. So why isn't he the appropriate match for Lucy?

It turns out that "voice" is a complicated matter. It involves paying attention, which Jerry is so clearly not doing at the beginning of the film. But it also involves joint experience, laughter especially. As Cavell notes, there are situations in an ailing marriage for which, as the broken marriage of Lucy and Jerry suggests, "the right laugh would be the right cure": "Not one laugh at life—that would be a laugh of cynicism. But a run of laughs, within life: finding occasions in the way we are together" (*PH*, 246). For Lucy, Jerry "is the one with whom that is possible, crazy as he is; that is the awful truth" (*PH*, 239). This kind of laughter, this kind of hearing, involves appreciating and learning to perceive anew what was long ago felt to have been processed and categorized and filed under cultural stereotypes of "wife," and "husband," with all the deadening implications of those terms. This kind of laughter, this kind of hearing, this kind of conversation, means remembering, indeed rediscovering, what you looked for and found in this person you married. When Jerry and Lucy do begin to hear and laugh and talk again, they find they simply must remarry.

Remarriage, as Cavell conceives it, "is not a matter of the reception of new experience but a matter of a new reception of your own experience, an acceptance of its authority as your own" (*PH*, 240). Sometimes, it takes a radical defamiliarization to awaken the inattentive spouse to the joys of his (or her) own marriage. Many of the texts under consideration in this study glance at, and some fully examine, this point. In some, such as *The Shop around the Corner* and *It Happened One Night*, the radical revelation of love comes as a shock to the man, who is confronted with the image of his heart's desire in the very woman he has long regarded as inimical, a peevish underling, a spoiled brat. In *Bringing Up Baby*, Susan serves to radically estrange David from himself, showing him, in the process, that there is a part of him that enjoys playfulness, fun, and adventure. In *My Man Godfrey*, the vantage point of butler defamiliarizes Godfrey's view of his own social class to the extent that he learns to feel compassion, even for the idle rich, and learns to channel his contempt for luxury into a program by which the luxurious taste of the upper class can benefit the lives of those less fortunate (in an almost Mandevillian way).

216 *Happily ever after?*

In the Restoration texts, defamiliarization often comes in the guise of breeches roles, which tend to clarify desires and expose hypocrisies. In *The Luckey Chance*, however, defamiliarization backfires on both Gayman and Julia, leading us to ponder the power of mind over matter as Gayman seems to truly find the lovely Julia repulsive when he believes her to be an old woman, and as Julia seems to truly believe Gayman to be impotent when she believes him to be her old husband. Wilmore and Horner are more astute when confronted with the objects of their desire in disguise—but not at the same pace. In conversing with the "breeched" Hellena, Wilmore reveals his lust for a new and as-yet-unseen mistress before realizing that the page who claims to be her emissary is none other than his "little gypsie," to whom he had sworn fidelity a few hours earlier. Horner's response to the "defamiliarized" Margery comes closest in philosophical content to the use of that device in *The Awful Truth*, in that his reaction to the young brother of the country wife to whom he took a shine at the theater the day before shows that he recognizes no impediments to arousal in the mere fact of gender. Indeed, Horner seems as content to "mousle and tousle" a lovely boy as he is to "moil and toil" with the wives of his friends.

It is in her rendition of "My Dreams Are Gone with the Wind" that Lucy recaptures Jerry's attention. And how does she do so? By pretending to be his "sister" and imitating one of her soon-to-be ex-husband's recent "dates": a girl with a provocative club act, a phony Southern drawl, and a trashy personal demeanor. Lucy appropriates the drawl and the act, and she exaggerates the trashiness, first confusing and then appalling Jerry's fiancée, who is described as a "madcap heiress," but who, as Cavell notes, is actually "humorless, conventional, all but nonexistent" (*PH*, 243). Jerry himself is surprised and delighted, not only because he is "forced to leave this house" but also because he "rejoice[s] in . . . having a way out" (*PH*, 251). Lucy "proposes herself as a field on which . . . [Jerry] may weave passion and tenderness, so that he might desire where he loves" (*PH*, 253). Cavell is more explicit than usual in his explanation of the kind of desire, the acknowledgment of which will make it possible for this couple to remarry, in a sense to reclaim their "incestuous . . . past"—the combination of "familiarity and eroticism" that defines the intimacy, the "sexual depth," of marriage (*PH*, 252). That both genres regularly tread so closely and with such gleeful abandon to the edge of taboo behaviors—incest, adultery, sadomasochism, bestiality (and examples of all of these can be readily cited in a mental survey of the texts we have considered)—lends credence to Cavell's summary of the significance of Lucy's performance, not only to *The Awful Truth*, but also to the comedy of remarriage in general:

> Her therapeutic move . . . is to demonstrate that what is . . . [Jerry's] sister in her is not her ladylike accomplishments, as for example her trained voice and her ability to dance; his sister in her is what she shares with Dixie Belle, her willingness to lend her talents and training to the

expression of what Dixie Belle expresses, her recognition of their capacity to incorporate those improprieties. Her incorporation of familiarity and eroticism redeems both. And . . . she thereby redeems the fact of incorporation itself, that we live off one another, that we are cannibals. Thus she uses her sophistication, her civilization, to break through civilization to its conditions.

(*PH*, 252)

Elaine M. McGirr makes a similar observation regarding Amanda's courtesan "act" in Cibber's *Love's Last Shift*: "In other words, the virtuous woman has to really be as libidinous as the abandoned . . . [woman] she impersonates."[14]

"What is necessary" for remarriage, according to Cavell, "is not to estrange ourselves but to recognize, without denying our natural intimacy, that we are also strangers, separate, different; to keep our incestuousness symbolic, tropic, so that it joins us, not letting it lapse into literality, which will enjoin us" (*PH*, 260). It is also necessary for the man to admit, as Jerry seems to admit at the end of *The Awful Truth*, that the "sexual imbalance" in marriage is not tacitly "the woman's fault" (*PH*, 259). Jane M. Greene has examined four versions of *The Awful Truth*, a 1922 theatrical version, two silent films from 1925 and 1929, and Leo McCarey's 1937 film. She finds that the 1937 comedy of remarriage differs from the three previous versions in that the earlier versions feature preoccupation with Lucy's innocence or guilt. In contrast, the 1937 film emphasizes "symmetry . . . between husband and wife": "Jerry is a worthy opponent for his wife, in part, because he may be guilty, just as she may be. And this Lucy, in a role that is neither unambiguously innocent nor guilty, neither completely passive nor sexually aggressive, is made to take his measure as foil and counterweight."[15] This insight is also one that Loveless comes to understand in his recognition of the fact of women's desire and the fact that virtue is not an easy task for women. Rather, it is one to which they commit for the sake of their own integrity and for the sake of the depths of intimacy available only to those who explore faithful and virtuous love, not in a spirit of anger, repression, and revenge, but with the innocence of play and childlike delight. Cavell makes the point that at the end of *The Awful Truth*, that "vision of becoming a child and overcoming revenge is tied up with the achievement of a new vision of time, or a new stance toward it, an acceptance of Eternal Recurrence," symbolized by those "childlike figures" that come in and out of the clock on every quarter hour (*PH*, 263).

If, as Plato suggests and Cavell invokes, the beginning of philosophy is in sexual attraction, then intercourse is philosophy's goal. Obviously, I refer not to sexual intercourse alone, although sexual intercourse can and should, in the case of marriage, be a part of the conversation. It is attentiveness in all realms of engagement between spouses and lovers that raises satisfaction of a basic need to the heights of knowledge and pleasure. This point has been central to all the texts examined, focused as they are on the chattering witty pair whose hyperaware verbal interchanges seem to be metaphors for sexual compatibility in both. In the Restoration texts, however, we are not fully convinced that the intense verbal playfulness will outlast the first week of marriage. And, indeed, individual texts—*Marriage à la Mode*, *The Man of Mode*, and *The Rover*, in particular—give voice to that anxiety in various ways. The *Way of the World* attempts to allay such fears by attesting, not only to the ever-compelling vitality of wit, but also to the attention-focusing power of contract! In *The Careless Husband*, Cibber takes another tack.

Cibber's *The Careless Husband* was first performed in December 1704, with Cibber himself reprising his twice-played role as Lord Foppington, that is, Sir Novelty Fashion, who had been elevated to a peerage by Vanbrugh. Cibber's popularity as the fop in his own play, *Love's Last Shift*, had been eclipsed by his even greater triumph in the play of his parodist. Vanbrugh's Lord Foppington has been critically acclaimed as the best of the Restoration fops, in Robert D. Hume's words, "smart, tough, and dangerous."[16] That these characteristics emerged in *Love's Last Shift* and that they persist in *The Careless Husband* suggests that this greatest fop owes much (probably most) to Cibber's writing and acting, although Vanbrugh may get the credit for placing this paragon of foppishness in a play that pays homage to the Restoration ethos. In *The Careless Husband*, however, Cibber goes one step further to portray his fop as one who is neither foolish and lovable like Etherege's Sir Fopling Flutter nor vain and self-defeating like Wycherley's Sparkish nor effeminate and superfluous like Congreve's Witwoud and Petulant. Cibber's Lord Foppington, conversely, represents an ideology and a viable portrait of a type of effective masculinity for the audience of the time.

Stephen Szilagyi, in fact, argues that different forms of "easiness" are offered for our consideration in *The Careless Husband*. Whereas Lady Easy is "easy" because of feminine self-control and restrained desire, Lord Foppington is "cross-gendered ease"—a combination of feminine self-governance and masculine, aristocratic selfishness. This combination results in a kind of studied indifference, the absence of desire, that does not necessarily betoken the absence of appetite.[17] Indeed, Foppington has a boundless capacity for self-satisfaction, but no capacity for marriage of the kind our genres privilege. Emma Katherine Atwood's description of Foppington accords with Szilagyi's reading of the way the fop's presentism renders marriage "antithetical to . . . [his] philosophy because marriage always ends the comedy, and the fop never wants the fun to end."[18] Still, he's not a fool. Charles's "easiness," on the other hand, is a discrediting of Stuart or libertine "ease," as his crude and callous treatment of both Edging and Lady Graveairs evinces little true relish of the sensual, no pleasure in the discovery of new physical delights or even relish of intrigue, such as we see in Dorimant or Willmore, for example. Along with Lady Betty, Charles has an "ease" that comes from an inherited right of rule and that "performs a kind of violence upon its object" in an almost perfunctory way.[19] Both Charles and Lady Betty must be corrected by the end of the play.

But we begin with Lady Easy's dilemma: How is she to reform her husband without alienating him? She expresses righteous indignation that her husband has "wrong[ed]" her with her "very servant," yet she knows that "patience" is her "only remedy": "for to reproach him with my wrongs, is taking on myself the means of a redress, bidding defiance to his falsehood, and naturally but provokes him to undo me" (1.1.3–9). Although we may question the justice of such a response, we must recognize that Lady Easy, like Lucy Warriner, knows something about psychology when she determines not to confront her husband directly with evidence of his misbehavior. Lady Easy will bide her time "till by some gross apparent proof of his misdoing, he forces me to see—and to forgive it" (1.1.17–18).

Stanley Cavell, no doubt, would argue that one problem with seeing *The Careless Husband* as a comedy of remarriage is the impossibility of divorce. Yet, as witnessed by the Fainalls (as well as by the Sullens in Farquhar's *The Beaux' Stratagem*, a play I do not include in this study), the late seventeenth and early eighteenth centuries did have legal provisions for separate maintenance as well as a host of other measures by which estranged married couples could acknowledge and accommodate divisions and incompatibilities.[20] Lady Easy is determined not to go that route, though, as her husband points out, his wife's lack of jealousy and suspicion seem in a sense to be tacit approval of his need for other women. Oddly, though, he refers to his dalliances as being "intolerably easy" (1.1.332). Indeed, in Act 1, Charles's consistent complaint is of ennui and weariness: "When I was stinted in my fortune almost everything was a pleasure to me, because, most things then being out of my reach, I had always the pleasure of hoping for 'em" (1.1.82–85). Possession, of money, wife, other women—all have dulled Charles's appetite. Although he knows intellectually their value, he simply finds no joy in any of them.

Lady Easy, however, turns out to be less "easy" than Charles thinks she is, and his bringing his "follies" into her home has violated their domestic contract. One way of reading her determination at the end of her opening soliloquy is that she will not simply wait for the "proof" she needs, but that she will actually seek that proof in order to engineer a sincere affirmation of their contract through the forgiveness that ratifies remarriage. Whereas Charles is blithely going through the rote behavior of the privileged aristocratic male, Lady Easy is witnessing the effects, in the girl's jealous and insubordinate behavior, of his dalliance with her servant Edging. Although Charles rightly chastens Edging for haughtily upbraiding him for "us[ing] everybody [meaning herself] as . . . you do your wife," his logic leaves a lot to be desired: "look you, child, you are not *her* strumpet, but *mine*, therefore I only give you leave to be saucy with me" (1.1.134–35; 142–43). Still, skewed thinking or not, Charles at least recognizes here that sexual intercourse with a woman does bespeak a kind of equality, which is the same insight that Lady Easy has had to her chagrin: "this odious thing's jealous of him herself" (1.1.53–54).

Charles is in the process of breaking off his affair with Lady Graveairs, the mistress who has provoked Edging's resentment. She is no real threat to Edging, however, because at this point, Sir Charles considers her more trouble than she is worth. His ennui has deprived him of the energy needed for true intercourse, for true conversation: "Your young fops may talk of their women of quality, but to me now, there's a strange agreeable convenience in a creature one is not obliged to say much to upon these occasions" (5.2.31–34). He finds, however, that Edging has a different notion of lovemaking: "can't you sit still and talk with one? I am sure there's ten times more love in that, and fifty times the satisfaction, people may say what they will" (5.2.54–56). Of course, as we know, conversation begins only when the right partner enters the room.

She does just that in Scene 5, which "*opens and discovers* Sir Charles *without his periwig, and* Edging *by him, both asleep in two easy chairs.*" Lady Easy enters, "*starts and trembles*" and is "*unable to speak.*" But she finally does speak, in blank verse, no less, for this is the momentous occasion for which she has waited. Forgetting her earlier plan to forgive immediately upon having incontrovertible proof that her husband's misdoings have violated her home, she at first thinks to "wake him in his guilt, / And barefaced front him with my wrongs" (5.5.8–9). But, she decides, "duty . . . forbids me to insult / Where I have vowed obedience" (5.5.14–15). Besides, she notes, "Perhaps / The fault's in me, and nature has not formed / Me with the thousand little requisites / That warm the heart to love" (5.5.15–18). "Somewhere there is a fault—" her voice trails off (5.5.19). From what we know of Charles's behavior, we might be inclined to cringe at Lady Easy's propensity for self-blame, but philosophically she is correct. A sexual imbalance is not the fault of one partner alone, as Jerry Warriner comes to realize. Perhaps Lady Easy is on the wrong track in faulting her appearance, which by all accounts, even her husband's, is pleasing. Yet, her "easiness" has left him feeling no compunction about the "easy" opportunities for misbehavior that have come his way. Perhaps she does bear some of the blame. As a consequence, she puts her steinkirk on his bare head. If he gets angry at her "too busy care," she can plead "patience, duty, and . . . fond affection"; after all, he might catch cold (5.5.28–29). Sir Charles, however, has the opposite reaction. Awareness that she has seen him in his baldpated postcoital exhaustion is an immediate source of chagrin: "the thought has made me despicable ev'n to myself" (5.5.48–49). It also produces an energetic resolve. Sir Charles rushes to his wife and says, significantly, "I came to talk with you" (5.6.56–57). And talk they do. Sir Charles has the most pressing question, phrased in the most telling way:

> How could a woman of your restraint in principles, sedateness, sense, and tender disposition, propose to see a happy life with one (now I reflect) that hardly took an hour's pains, ev'n before marriage, to appear

but what I am?—a loose, unheeding wretch, absent in all I do, civil, and as often rude without design, unseasonably thoughtful, easy to a fault, and, in my best of praise, but carelessly good natured. How shall I reconcile your temper with having made so strange a choice?

(5.6.73–82)

It is significant that Charles assumes marriage to be a proposition involving happiness. He also realizes that inattention, absentness, and carelessness are impediments to happiness. But Lady Easy has an answer:

your having never seemed to be but what you really were; and through that carelessness of temper there still shone forth to me an undesigning honesty. . . . I have often thought that such a temper could never be deliberately unkind, or, at the worst, I knew that errors from want of thinking might be borne, at least when probably one moment's serious thought would end 'em.

(5.6.83–93)

And, she's right. One moment's serious thought is all it takes.

Sir Charles acknowledges the truth of what Lady Easy says with a blush, a feminized response that we have seen often in the Hollywood comedies of remarriage—Peter Warne's domesticity, Nick Charles's curling into a fetal position, Walter Burns's fastidious dressing and grooming, David Huxley's negligee, and even Jerry Warriner's nightshirt. This kind of gender-bending is antithetical to the fop's blending of male and female qualities, because in a way that blending speaks to totalitarianism (the aristocratic male absorbing all energies in creation into himself). Sir Charles's blush is a gesture of opposite import: the admission of a feminine side that he keeps from others, but which he is willing to reveal to his wife. In doing so, he acknowledges, he is remarrying her:

Come, I will not shock your softness by my untimely blush for what is past, but rather soothe you to a pleasure at my sense of joy for my recovered happiness to come. Give then to my new-born love what name you please, it cannot, shall not be too kind. O! it cannot be too soft for what my soul swells up with emulation to deserve. Receive me then entire at last, and take what yet no woman ever truly had, my conquered heart.

(5.6.135–44)

"Receive me then entire at last" is the sense of all remarriage endings. And Lady Easy's reply, "to have you mine is something more than happiness, 'tis double life, and madness of abounding joy" (5.6.148–51), expresses what our couples feel as the blanket falls, the dinosaur crumbles, the dog hides his eyes on the top bunk of the bed, and, especially, as the little figurines go into the same door on the clock, for the first time—or maybe just the first time in the hour, to be repeated on the hour every hour for days and days and months and months and years and years to come.

Notes

1 Cibber, *The Careless Husband, A Comedy* (1704), in *British Dramatists from Dryden to Sheridan*, ed. George H. Nettleton and Arthur E. Case, rev. by George Winchester Stone, Jr. (Carbondale: Southern Illinois University Press, 1969). References are to act, scene, and line numbers.
2 Helene Koon, *Colley Cibber: A Biography* (Lexington: University Press of Kentucky, 1986), 53.
3 Richardson, introduction to Colley Cibber, *Love's Last Shift; or, The Fool in Fashion*, ed. Gary A. Richardson, in *The Broadview Anthology of Restoration and Early Eighteenth-Century Drama*, ed. J. Douglas Canfield (Peterborough, ON: Broadview Press, 2001), 710.
4 Quirk, *James Stewart: Behind the Scenes of a Wonderful Life* (New York: Applause Books, 1997), 18.
5 Translation by Alaina Lemon in her *Between Two Fires: Gypsy Performance and Romani Memory from Pushkin to Post-Socialism* (Durham, NC: Duke University Press, 2000), 71. As Lemon notes, "Ochi Chernye" is "a song exalting dangerous, sensual magnetism (although to some it has the flavor of kitsch)."
6 See Rick Altman, "A Semantic/Syntactic Approach to Film Genre," *Cinema Journal* 23, no. 3 (1984): 6–18; and Thomas Schatz, "Film Genre and the Genre Film," in *Hollywood Genres: Formulas, Filmmaking, and the Studio System*, ed. Thomas Schatz (Boston: McGraw-Hill, 1981), 14–41.
7 Cibber, *Love's Last Shift; or, The Fool in Fashion* (1696), ed. Gary A. Richardson, in *The Broadview Anthology of Restoration and Early Eighteenth-Century Drama*, ed. J. Douglas Canfield (Peterborough, ON: Broadview Press, 2001). References are to act, scene, and line numbers.
8 Gollapudi, *Moral Reform in Comedy and Culture, 1696–1747*, Performance in the Long Eighteenth Century: Theatre, Music, Dance (Farnham, UK: Ashgate Publishing, 2011), 35.
9 Hippolyte Adolphe Taine, *History of English Literature*, trans. H. Van Laun, 2 vols. (Edinburgh: Edmonston and Douglas, 1871), 2: 103.
10 *The Spectator*, March 12, 1711, in *The Spectator*, ed. Donald F. Bond, 5 vols. (Oxford: Clarendon Press, 1965), 1: 44.
11 These are Adam Potkay's words describing the Enlightenment notion of happiness, which "does not refer only to a feeling or subjective state, but designates as well an *evaluation* of a life or the narrative of a life" (526, 523). He opposes this concept to "unhappiness" and "joy" as depicted in the novel. "Narrative Possibilities of Happiness, Unhappiness, and Joy," *Social Research* 77, no. 2 (2010): 526.
12 Gollapudi's reading of the masque as endorsing the relationship between spectacle and morality that lies at the heart of the reunion between Loveless and Amanda is germane. She argues that, "just as Loveless's newly-elevated moral stature is affirmed by his approving response to the moral entertainment, so too the audience are skillfully manipulated into the flattering position of the morally enlightened who cannot but approve of the salutary fable dramatized on stage" (*Moral Reform in Comedy and Culture*, 36).

13 Vanbrugh, *The Relapse; or, Virtue in Danger, Being the Sequel of The Fool in Fashion* (1696), ed. James E. Gill, in *The Broadview Anthology of Restoration and Early Eighteenth-Century Drama*, ed. J. Douglas Canfield (Peterborough, ON: Broadview Press, 2001). References are to act, scene, and line numbers.
14 McGirr, "Rethinking Reform Comedies: Colley Cibber's Desiring Women," *Eighteenth-Century Studies* 46, no. 3 (2013): 393.
15 Greene, "The Road to Reno: *The Awful Truth* and the Hollywood Comedy of Remarriage," *Film History* 13, no. 4 (2001): 357.
16 Hume, *The Rakish Stage: Studies in English Drama, 1660–1800* (Carbondale: Southern Illinois University Press, 1983), 166–67.
17 Szilagyi, "The Importance of Being Easy: Desire and Cibber's *The Careless Husband*," *Texas Studies in Literature and Language* 41, no. 2 (1999): 143.
18 Atwood, "Fashionably Late: Queer Temporality and the Restoration Fop," *Comparative Drama* 47, no. 1 (2013): 100.
19 Szilagyi, "The Importance of Being Easy," 146.
20 See also p. 14, wherein I discuss, following Gellert Spencer Alleman, legal options, short of divorce, of invalidating marriage in this period.

Epilogue
Hope springs eternal

The immediate inheritor of the courtship plot adumbrated by Restoration comedy was the courtship novel, perfected by Jane Austen. Like the witty pair of the Restoration repertoire, her central couples are unique in their worlds, distinguished by repartee, and determined to chart a course of happiness and moral perfectionism together. Samuel Richardson's *Sir Charles Grandison*, an important inspiration for Austen, more immediately took up the Restoration plot, cleansing it of its libertine excesses and marrying it to melodrama, the shadow genre, focused on the "unknown woman"— that is, a woman who does not, in the end, find a partner with whom to pursue self-knowledge and intelligibility but stalwartly embraces a fate that few women of her time would have chosen. Alexander Pope's "Eloisa to Abelard" lies behind the story of *Grandison*'s Clementina, and the dramatic genre known as "she-tragedy" lies behind both.[1] Carol Houlihan Flynn notes that Clementina "would be more comfortable in a melodrama than in Sir Charles's drawing-room comedy."[2] Yet, Clementina has also struck critics from Jocelyn Harris on as a version of Shakespeare's Ophelia, who, as Jean I. Marsden has demonstrated, was an influence on the heroines of the she-tragedies of the 1690s.[3] That "Eloisa to Abelard" partakes of the same kind of interest in female suffering that drove the taste for she-tragedies has not garnered much comment. Perhaps this is because its 1720 publication date places it at the end of the cycle of she-tragedy composition (although the plays "remained a standard part of the English repertoire") or because it has seemed more significant to eighteenth-century critics as a precursor of Gothic psychology than as the dramatic monologue it clearly is.[4] As this epilogue will note, filmmaker Charlie Kaufman did not miss the dramatic force of the poem, nor its shadow relationship to courtship/remarriage comedy.

In his first book, *Must We Mean What We Say?*, Stanley Cavell reminds us that "we learn language and learn the world *together*."[5] In the remarriage comedies, the central focus is on the woman who is educated by learning language and the world through conversation with the man who acknowledges her and responds to her (and requires that she acknowledge and respond to him, as well). Stephen Mulhall discusses how both comedies of remarriage and melodramas are focused on the woman's relationship to language and the world. Whereas the comedies feature, Mulhall says, a "meet and happy conversation," "the emblematic linguistic mode of the melodramas is irony—a mode in which communication and interaction are systematically negated."[6] The melodrama is the remarriage comedy's "inevitable shadow," in the way that Cavell has said that "skepticism . . . [is] philosophy's inevitable shadow" (CT, 152). It is a genre centered on "unknownness," that is, on the central woman's "recognition that the terms of . . . [her] intelligibility are not welcome to others—at least not as the basis for romantic investment in any present other whom those terms nominate as eligible" (CT, 12). This state of unknownness leads to her transcendence through "a state of isolation so extreme as to portray and partake of madness, a state of utter incommunicability" (CT, 16). She is not different in kind from her comic sisters in that they too must have the "experience of being unknown" before they can open themselves to knowledge and remarriage (CT, 22). It is just the good fortune of the comic heroines to find another, who will "see . . . [her] separate existence . . . [and] acknowledge its separateness" as a "condition for a ceremony of union" (CT, 22). Cavell describes the battle-of-the-sexes banter, the repartee, and the "amatory wars" that characterize the comedies as "struggles for acknowledgment" (CT, 30). In the melodramas, such a struggle is "avoided or renounced" (CT, 30). He elaborates as follows:

> The man's struggle there is, on the contrary, a struggle against recognition. The woman's struggle is to understand why recognition by the man has not happened or has been denied or has become irrelevant, hence may be thought of as a struggle or argument (with herself) over her gender.
>
> (CT, 30)

The unknown woman, ultimately, has no choice but to try to transcend the world, to escape the ordinary that has excluded her for some inexplicable reason.

We see the same generic phenomenon—the existence of a shadow genre—in the Restoration and early-eighteenth-century dramatic repertoire. Pat Gill has observed that "as the brittle, irreverent, and promiscuous comedies give way to dramas exploring the effects of conscience and moral convictions, the relation of gender, sexuality, and marriage is reconfigured and the categories are revised. The banter and appeal of a witty, well-meaning beauty seem more the stuff of tragedy than comedy as the eighteenth century begins, leading not to marriage but disgrace and death."[7] As is clear from the quotation, Gill reads the generic relationship between courtship comedies and she-tragedies as a linear narrative wherein the former is replaced with the latter. Still, considering the resilience of the earlier comedies on the eighteenth-century stage, I find it more productive to ponder the relationship between the tragic (or the sentimental/pathetic) heroine and her witty counterpart. What renders one tragic or pathetic as opposed to witty and happy? As in the Hollywood generic world, it seems to come down to intelligibility, finding the right partner—or not, as the case may be. Gill suggests as much, too, when she notes that the rake-hero is replaced on the eighteenth-century stage by "kinder, gentler males who succeed by moral persuasion" (207). But her description of the effect of kindness and gentleness on the female characters gives me pause: "the sharp, seductive heroine succumbs to repentant or innocent distress, or hardens into depravity" (207). Acknowledgment, recognition, and forgiveness seem much kinder and gentler even if (indeed, especially if) they are offered by one who needs the same in return.

Jean Marsden and Brett Wilson have also argued that the she-tragedy's suffering women were designed as commentary on the cultural, social, and political nature of late seventeenth-century and early eighteenth-century British society. Marsden is particularly interested in the spectacle of female suffering and the construction of the female spectator in the she-tragedies. Arguing that "sociopolitical stability was dependent on patrilinear control of female sexuality," Marsden finds the plays important evidence of how and why that control was deployed (5). Interestingly, she turns to feminist film theory focused on the "women's film," that is, the Hollywood melodrama, to investigate the "'codes that construct woman as image'" and to "probe the workings of these codes and the ways in which they affect the spectator."[8] Although Marsden acknowledges that much of the theory of spectatorship as it applies to film will not serve for constructions on the Restoration and early-eighteenth-century English stage, she nevertheless finds feminist film theory to be helpful in exploring "the connection between sight and desire" (8). Wilson is less interested in the spectacle of women's suffering than in the way "female centered dramas" of the period "became crucial vehicles for the elaboration of a distinctive brand of civic virtue."[9] Still, his sense that the plays "are preoccupied with virtue in distress . . . and with the bonds of sympathy that join and sustain victims and spectators alike" (viii) clearly acknowledges the relationship between civic virtue and the feelings that link actor and viewer in the playhouse, creating emotions and notions that extend beyond. Wilson clarifies as follows: "These works remind their audiences habitually that British subjects feel for one another, and that impassiveness and insensibility are hallmarks of tyranny, making pity and tenderness buttresses of 'Revolution Principles'" (x). These principles feature "ideas of government by the consent of the governed and of limited monarchial prerogative" (11). And in doing so, they reflect the impact of John Locke, whose emphasis on "life, liberty, and property" underwrites the sympathy and tears with which the she-tragedy heroines were received by audiences (11).

Given that the she-tragedies in general tend to paint absolute power as the source of the heroine's sufferings, it is easy to see how scholars have tended to regard them as a repudiation of the supposedly aristocratic biases of the Restoration comedies. However, the central couples of those comedies always achieve their fragile happiness (or fragile chance for happiness) by consent, the very hallmark of Locke's philosophy. In that sense, the she-tragedies function, not as a means to replace one philosophy with another, so much as a way to shift the focus from light to shadow, in the same way the Hollywood melodrama of the unknown woman negatively shores up the ideals at the center of the comedies of remarriage. In the comedies, Cavell explains, the remarriage is of "national importance" precisely because it is "chosen out of experience" and therefore becomes

> understandable as a favored expression of consent for this democracy, ... showing that ... one hundred and sixty four years after the Declaration of Independence [in the case of the film *The Philadelphia Story*], our political society continued to find attestation that it exists.
> (CW, 75)

With regard to the melodramas, the point is the same: Although the women do not consent to marriage, the conditions in which they remake themselves are conditions of their own choosing. In discussing the choice made by Charlotte (played by Bette Davis) in *Now, Voyager* (1942), Cavell hears a "direct specification" of Locke as Charlotte renounces her mother's authority over her, describing "the maternal instinct" as "tyranny" (*CT*, 147). That she turns right around and chooses a maternal role for herself in relation to the daughter of a man she loves and cannot marry signifies to Cavell that "[i]n Locke's *Second Treatise* ... the existence of consent, hence of the social order, may be no easier to be clear about and establish than, as in Descartes's *Meditations*, the existence of a finite order proved to be" (*CT*, 147).

In other words, the women of the Hollywood melodramas, like those of the she-tragedies, demonstrate both the perils of individual existence under tyranny and the need for a social order emergent from "the constitution of consent" (*CT*, 147). Further, both sets of texts offer in their focus on women, as Cavell says of the films, "a sort of explanation about why we remain studiedly unclear" about the nature of the social contract (*CT*, 147). These women, who can find no conversational partner with whom to enact the consent of social contract and the pursuit of moral perfectionism, nonetheless have choices: transcendence, fantasy, bitterness, or despair (in which I include death by suicide). But, it must be asked, if these are the only choices she has, is she not being forced into a position of self-abnegation? And, if so, doesn't she thereby call into question the whole idea of consent, contract, happiness, and moral perfectionism? Of course, she does. And she has been doing so all along. She is the shadow that causes the dinosaur to collapse at the end of *Bringing Up Baby* and Harriet to start squawking like a crow at the end of *Man of Mode*. She is the weight under which Hildy labors down the stairs at the end of *His Girl Friday* and the sense of dread that causes Millamant to speak of marriage as a "dwindling." She is the skepticism that must be overcome, not by denying her presence, but by walking into the future right on past her—not arrogantly or too confidently, however, for any day a shadow can fall and the known can become unknown, forgotten, or renounced And, although it takes divorce to discover that you are truly married, divorce can also reveal that you truly never were.

We learn language and the world at the same time, and in marriage or courtship we create a new language as we learn each another. Through doing so we also create a new world to inhabit and explore together. This is why, *pace* Richard Rorty, Cavell is right to go back to Descartes in his effort to locate the "truth of skepticism" (*CR*, 241).[10] "Everything which we conceive very clearly and very distinctly is wholly true," Descartes avers, opening up a path for skepticism with regard to the many things we sense, know, feel, and believe without clarity, although with confidence even if it is a confidence that can be shaken. Along with skepticism comes controversy about the conclusion he is soon to reach (i.e., that God exists).[11] Perception is part of how we learn the world. Expression is the rest. Between the two is a vast sea of uncertainty in terms of our relationship to others, especially others with whom we have created a world that perhaps has become uninhabitable for one reason or another, for one or the other, or both. Restoration courtship comedies celebrate the dawning of the new world. Hollywood remarriage comedies record its dissolution and rediscovery. Restoration she-tragedies and Hollywood melodramas document the failure to create and/or re-create. Charlie Kaufman's *Eternal Sunshine of the Spotless Mind* and Alexander Pope's poem "Eloisa to Abelard," the source of Kaufman's title, do the work of all four genres.

In a 2011 essay, William Day notes that from the beginning, *Eternal Sunshine of the Spotless Mind* provoked comparison with Hollywood remarriage comedies in reviews and trade publications.[12] He makes the case persuasively by bringing Kaufman's film into conversation with Cavell. Defining the remarriage comedy, following Cavell, as "finding a way back together . . .[that] requires a conversation that is about, and so enacts, the particular fault lines and glories and misconstruals and transfigurative possibilities of this pair's particular relationship," Day goes on to observe that, in a twist on the remarriage formula, Clementine and Joel "learn how to travel together through memory" (137–39). Two tropes of the remarriage genre— the retreat to a green space and the invention of a shared childhood—are the focus of Joel and Clem's journey through memory. But, most importantly, as Day reads the film, the two learn to work together in preserving a sense of a shared past, even as Joel's memory-purge is about to render him as innocent of knowledge of Clementine as she is of him. Of course, technically, these are Joel's memories alone. In his ability to make Clementine participate in the effort to turn back or thwart the process, however, he is revealing how deeply embedded she is in his life. We can assume from her post-erasure behavior that the same is true for her. She seems, for example, to have residual memory of Joel's words at the lake, and when Patrick says them, she reacts immediately and negatively to the appropriation. *Eternal Sunshine*, Day remarks, "is a tale of [the principal pair's] coming to discover what it means to have memories together" (150). These memories become "their way of learning how to be together again" (150).

Three additional critics treat *Eternal Sunshine*'s meditation on the way the memory of others functions in our and their self-definitions. C. D. C. Reeve notes that after the erasure we find that "[i]t isn't only Clementine that has been erased from Joel's memory, we see a chunk of his childhood is gone too," particularly memory of his Huckleberry Hound doll.[13] Julia Diver considers the film's central question to be, "what [do] we owe people we used to love in terms of memory[?]"[14] For George Toles, Joel's intense determination to remember Clementine is tied to the fact that "memory and love are the most vital agents of continuity in our lives.... Memory makes our world visible, and the assurance or hope of love... makes it inhabitable. If there is no answering "you" for our "I," we no longer *belong* to the world."[15] In that sense, Joel's struggle is for survival.

Joel's success in "remarrying" Clem through his memory provides ballast against the taped revelations both he and Clem listen to at the end of the second of their "first" days together. The effect of the recordings—the bitter words and harsh descriptions—on each character is profound; nevertheless, Joel stops Clementine in the hallway outside his apartment, asking her to wait. "What do you want, Joel?" She asks. "Just wait. I don't know. I want you to wait... just a while." Day counts ten seconds as the two look at each other. In these ten seconds, we, the viewers, replay the scenes of the memory-sequence, scenes that we hope portend a brighter future should they decide to go forward. After the pause, Clementine says "Okay," but she goes on to remind us and to tell Joel, for the first time for all he knows and for the second (or, actually, third) as we know, that she "is not a concept... just a fucked-up girl who is looking for... [her] own peace of mind. I'm not perfect." Joel responds, "I can't think of anything I don't like about you right now." Her answer takes us back to the end of the relationship; we, who have seen the whole thing unravel, know she's telling the truth when she says, "but you will. You will think of things. And I'll get bored with you and feel trapped because that's what happens to me." Of course, she knows herself and she's heard Joel's litany of things he didn't like about her the first time around. And he's heard what she didn't like about him, as well. Nevertheless, giving her his trademark puppy-dog look, Joel says, "Okay." And part laughing, part sobbing, Clementine says, "Okay." As Day reads the film (and I agree), these "okays" signify that the two "can, with eyes open, begin to imagine a life together again" (150), one that, as Lucy Warriner would say, is different, but the same.

In describing the significance of Joel's narrative, Day also has occasion to reference one of the Hollywood melodramas discussed by Cavell in *Contesting Tears*, Max Ophüls's *Letter from an Unknown Woman*.

His point has to do with the treatment of memory in the ending of *Letter* (a montage of images that we see Stefan review as he reads the letter), as opposed to the ten-second pause at the end of *Eternal Sunshine*, wherein we can only surmise what the characters might be thinking, although we ourselves are likely reviewing images drawn from earlier in the film. Day stops short of acknowledging that encased within Kaufman's remarriage narrative is the melodrama of the unknown woman, Mary Svevo, whose transcendent awakening is the catalyst for the tentative, melancholic, but still affirming decision of Joel and Clementine to remarry (signified by "okay"). They do this in the full knowledge that they will likely turn into the people they have heard on all the tapes, to their distress, saying things they can't imagine they will ever feel (again) about each other. Mary, however, has no such option. She transcends and departs. Her story is poignant in that she is, throughout the film narrative proper, partnered by an appropriate, loving man (Stan, played by Mark Ruffalo). But in the end, Mary's inability to erase Howard is the same as Joel's inability to erase Clementine and signifies, to modify Cavell's formula, that she knows she's bound to Howard Mierzwiak because she has not been able to fully erase him from her memory or to "disentangle" her life from his (*PH*, 127). Even though she may have been happy during her affair or, as Stan puts it, "happy, with a secret," upon discovering that her lover has colluded in—or perhaps even coerced—her erasure of their past, Mary Svevo determines to bring about justice for others, although she cannot procure it for herself. Remarriage is only possible if you know the past; by sending Joel and Clementine (and the rest of Howard's patients) their taped indictments of each other, Mary offers them the chance, not to start over, but to begin again.

Interestingly, Kaufman early on envisioned having scenes with Mary bookend the film; in other words, Mary's story was actually planned, at one point, as the narrative that would encase the story of Joel and Clementine.[16] In this version, the film begins with an old woman at a publisher's office holding a manuscript: "She's apparently been to this office before.... And she's this insane old lady and the publisher won't see her."[17] She is then shown in a subway, holding the manuscript on her lap, "which she looks at, and it's called *Eternal Sunshine of the Spotless Mind*, and that's the end of the opening sequence" (142). The closing sequence reveals that Mary has "remained working for Howard for all these years, reading all the transcripts, or listening to the tapes, and making them her memories" (142). Now, having reached the end of her life, she wants to publish these memories "so that the world has a record of the stuff that's been eradicated" (142), but she dies before that happens. In this much bleaker version of the story, we also see Clementine as "an old woman" coming "into Lacuna to get this man erased, and it's revealed through the process that it's Joel, and that they've done this however many times over the years" (142–43). The eventual ending takes a less defined view of what will happen now that Clementine and Joel have discovered the truth about their past. "I never wanted to be happy that they got together at the end," Kaufman says, although he also notes, "I didn't necessarily want it to be sad," either. In other words, Kaufman provides his audiences with the typical headache-inducing ending characteristic of both Restoration courtship plays and Hollywood remarriage films (143). The alternate version, focused on Mary, is not indeterminate. In the bookended version, the skepticism that Joel and Clem agree to overcome with their shared "okays" is skepticism that is transcended by the invocation of justice and compassion in the way of the melodrama and the she-tragedy. As Leger Grindon has observed,

> *Eternal Sunshine* uses its subsidiary romantic couples [Carrie and Rob, Mary and Mierzwiak] to develop irony and skepticism toward love. . . . The move of Joel and Clem toward reconciliation offers only a glimmer of love in contrast to the pervasive skepticism.[18]

Most of the published essays on this film make something of Mary's habit of quotation. Troy Jollimore explores the significance of her two quotations from Nietzsche,[19] and David Smith suggests that quotation is a pervasive trope in the film that points to life itself as repetition, "for all the ways we use the past and are constrained by it."[20] But no one seriously tries to deal directly with the elephant in the room, interestingly announced by an elephant on the screen. (I could not resist the joke, but, as Charlie Kaufman himself points out, the circus scene was not planned. The film crew came upon the parade by serendipity and the footage was used as visual accompaniment to Mary's quotation of Pope's "Eloisa to Abelard," which is the source of the film's title.[21]) In an otherwise insightful article about the movie, Smith here misses the significance of the allusion to Pope; he says that Pope's "Eloisa yearns to erase her past—and Abelard in particular—by withdrawing into a convent." But that isn't Eloisa's point in "Eloisa to Abelard." She doesn't want to be in a convent; she much prefers loving Abelard. Her tragedy is not about his betrayal, but about his incontrovertible, irreversible alteration. Eloisa takes us through the early days of her dawning love for Abelard. As in Restoration courtship comedies and Hollywood remarriage comedies, two notable features are freedom of choice in love and the meeting of souls and minds in a shared language that constitutes a true marriage, if not a legal union:

> Oh happy state! when souls each other draw,
> When love is liberty, and nature, law:
> All then is full, possessing, and possest,
> No craving Void left aking in the breast:
> Ev'n thought meets thought ere from the lips it part,
> And each warm wish springs mutual from the heart.[22]

As she leads us through her remembered happiness, we also learn that Eloisa has been educated by the man she loves ("*He was her Preceptor in*

Philosophy and Divinity," Pope explains [254n66])—a more notable feature in the Hollywood canon, but one that is also present in the Restoration works. But in the poem's present, this man, her lover and teacher and heart-chosen husband, has been transformed by violence done to him by her family, and, as a consequence, he is "cold . . . unmov'd, and silent grown" while she has "not yet forgot . . . [herself] to stone" (ll.23–24). She finds herself in a genre she did not choose—the she-tragedy or melodrama of the left and bereaved. She was known, but, because of the violence done her lover, she has become unknown. Remarriage is not an option.

The passage quoted by Mary, however, is one that Eloisa ultimately does not endorse. Sure, given her emotional distress and the impossibility of retrieving the happiness she's known, Eloisa's momentary attraction to the "blameless Vestal's lot / The world forgetting, by the world forgot" is understandable (ll. 207–208), but the "eternal sun-shine of the spotless mind" is not for those who have lived and loved (l.209). As Eloisa says both earlier and later, she cannot regret knowing and loving Abelard despite her current pain:

> I ought to grieve, but cannot what I ought;
> I mourn the lover, not lament the fault;
> I view my crime, but kindle at the view,
> Repent old pleasures, and solicit new.
> (ll.183–86)

> When at the close of each sad, sorrowing day,
> Fancy restores what vengeance snatch'd away,
> Then conscience sleeps, and leaving nature free,
> All my loose soul unbounded springs to thee.
> (ll.225–28)

Ultimately, though, Eloisa realizes that the only union with Abelard she can hope for is union in death. Like Mary, she finally embraces transcendence—a focus on the afterlife or other lives—in place of the conversation she would have liked to have had. As in Mary's case, Eloisa's isolation and suffering become catalysts for human connection in eliciting compassion for and from others similarly bereaved. The poem ends with Eloisa's reaching out to the reader touched by her story, envisioning that reader as moved to sympathetic tears. The poet, of course, is moved beyond tears to leave a record for posterity of the "sad . . . tender story" of Eloisa and Abelard (l.364).

"Eloisa to Abelard" is one of three poems written by Pope around this time. He wrote an epilogue to Nicholas Rowe's she-tragedy *Jane Shore* in 1713, "Eloisa to Abelard" in 1716, and "Elegy to the Memory of an Unfortunate Lady" in 1717. All of these works train our attention on the unknown woman, who, although her passion and wit are equal to those of her comic counterpart, either cannot locate or loses the conversational partner that would make the pursuit of happiness, of moral perfectionism, possible. Charlie Kaufman reworks the remarriage comedy plot in a text imbued with the melancholy provided by allusion to Eloisa and through Eloisa to the unknown women of both the she-tragedies and the Hollywood melodramas. In doing so, he both affirms that hope springs eternal and pays tribute to the doubts and fears that undermine such hope at the same time that they make such hope meaningful. In the end, Restoration courtship comedies and Hollywood comedies of remarriage insist that when the right partner enters or re-enters the room, one must say "okay" to the conversation. One must somehow overcome the skepticism bred by the disappointments, disillusionments, and difficulties that attend knowing and loving. Forgetting is not the path to overcoming skepticism. In fact, the very opposite is true. To enter and maintain a conversation, one must pay attention. It's what Joel finally begins to do as he relives each memory of Clem. He thus joins the cast of characters in both of the genres central to this study, as one half of a couple whose stories and whose conversations matter—to them, to us, to their worlds, and to ours.

Notes

1 On the relationship between *Sir Charles Grandison* and "Eloisa to Abelard," see Jocelyn Harris, introduction to *Sir Charles Grandison*, by Samuel Richardson, 3 vols. (Oxford: Oxford University Press, 1972), 1: xvii.
2 Flynn, *Samuel Richardson: A Man of Letters* (Princeton, NJ: Princeton University Press, 1982), 287–88.
3 Marsden, *Fatal Desire: Women, Sexuality, and the English Stage, 1660–1720* (Ithaca, NY: Cornell University Press, 2006), 90-91.
4 Marsden, *Fatal Desire*, 192–93.
5 Cavell, *Must We Mean What We Say?* 2nd ed. (Cambridge: Cambridge University Press, 2002), 19.
6 Mulhall, *Stanley Cavell: Philosophy's Recounting of the Ordinary* (Oxford: Oxford University Press, 1994), 238.
7 Gill, "Gender, Sexuality, and Marriage," 206–7.
8 *Fatal Desire*, 7. Marsden quotes Teresa de Lauretis, *Technologies of Gender: Essays on Theory, Film, and Fiction* (Bloomington: Indiana University Press, 1987), 13.
9 Wilson, *A Race of Female Patriots: Women and Public Spirit on the British Stage, 1688–1745*, Transits: Literature, Thought and Culture 1650-1850 (Lewisburg, PA: Bucknell University Press, 2012), vii.
10 See above, p. 6.
11 René Descartes, *Meditations concerning First Philosophy*, in *Discourse on Method and Meditations*, by René Descartes, trans. Laurence J. Lafleur (Indianapolis: Bobbs-Merrill, 1960), Third Meditation, 92.
12 Day, "I Don't Know, Just Wait: Remembering Remarriage in *Eternal Sunshine of the Spotless Mind*," in *The Philosophy of Charlie Kaufman*, ed. David LaRocca, The Philosophy of Popular Culture (Lexington: University Press of Kentucky, 2011): 134. Day cites David Edelstein's March 18, 2004, review in *Slate* and A. O. Scott's April 4, 2004 *New York Times* review.
13 Reeve, "Two Blue Ruins: Love and Memory in *Eternal Sunshine of the Spotless Mind*," in *Eternal Sunshine of the Spotless Mind*, ed. Christopher Grau, Philosophers on Film (Abingdon, UK: Routledge, 2009), 17.

Epilogue

14 Diver, "Memory, Desire, and Value in *Eternal Sunshine of the Spotless Mind*," in *Eternal Sunshine of the Spotless Mind*, ed. Christopher Grau, Philosophers on Film (Abingdon, UK: Routledge, 2009), 81.
15 Toles, "Trying to Remember Clementine," in *Eternal Sunshine of the Spotless Mind*, ed. Christopher Grau, Philosophers on Film (Abingdon, UK: Routledge, 2009), 134.
16 "Q & A with Charlie Kaufman," by Rob Feld, in Charlie Kaufman, *The Eternal Sunshine of the Spotless Mind* (New York: Newmarket Press, 2004), 142, hereafter "Q & A." Subsequent citations to this work are given parenthetically in the text.
17 "Q & A," 142.
18 Grindon, "Taking Romantic Comedy Seriously in *Eternal Sunshine of the Spotless Mind* (2004) and *Before Sunset* (2004)," in *A Companion to Film Comedy*, ed. Andrew Horton and Joanna Rapf (Chichester, UK: Wiley-Blackwell, 2013), 209.
19 Jollimore "Miserably Ever After: Forgetting, Repeating and Affirming Love," in *Eternal Sunshine of the Spotless Mind*, ed. Christopher Grau, Philosophers on Film (Abingdon, UK: Routledge, 2009), 31–61. See Day for a response to this reading ("I Don't Know," 146, 153n32). Toles also references the Nietzschean concept of "eternal recurrence" as reflected in the film ("Trying to Remember," 123–25).
20 Smith, "*Eternal Sunshine of the Spotless Mind* and the Question of Transcendence," *Journal of Religion and Film*, vol. 9, no. 1 (2005): n.p., http://www.unomaha.edu/jrf/Vol9No1/SmithSunshine.htm
21 See "Stills, Including Commentary by Charlie Kaufman," in *The Shooting Script*, p. 152.
22 "Eloisa to Abelard," in *The Poems of Alexander Pope*, A one-volume edition of the Twickenham text, ed. John Butt (New Haven, CT: Yale University Press, 1963): 254–55, ll. 91–96.

Bibliography

Alleman, Gellert Spencer. "Matrimonial Law and the Materials of Restoration Comedy." PhD diss., University of Pennsylvania Press, 1942.

[Allestree, Richard]. *The Ladies Calling. In Two Parts.* Oxford, 1705.

Alperson, Philip, and Noël Carroll. "Music, Mind, and Morality: Arousing the Body Politic." *Journal of Aesthetic Education* 42, no. 1 (2008): 1–15.

Altman, Rick. *Film/Genre.* London: British Film Institute, 1999.

——. "A Semantic/Syntactic Approach to Film Genre." *Cinema Journal* 23, no. 3 (1984): 6–18.

Atwood, Emma Katherine. "Fashionably Late: Queer Temporality and the Restoration Fop." *Comparative Drama* 47, no. 1 (2013): 85–116.

Avery, Emmett L. "*The Country Wife* in the Eighteenth Century." *Research Studies of the State College of Washington* 10 (1942): 141–72.

The Awful Truth. DVD. Directed by Leo McCarey. 1937. Culver City, CA: Columbia TriStar Home Entertainment, 2003.

Backscheider, Paula R. "'Endless Aversion Rooted in the Soul': Divorce in the 1690–1730 Theater." *The Eighteenth Century: Theory and Interpretation* 37 (1996): 99–135.

Barnard, Rita, and Barbara Ching. "From Screwballs to Cheeseballs: Comic Narrative and Ideology in Capra and Reiner." *New Orleans Review* 17, no. 3 (1990): 52–59.

Barton, Anne. Introduction to *Much Ado about Nothing*. Edited by Anne Barton. In *The Riverside Shakespeare*. 2nd ed. Boston: Houghton Mifflin, 1997.

Beach, Christopher. *Class, Language, and American Film Comedy.* Cambridge: Cambridge University Press, 2002.

Beauclerk, Charles. *Nell Gwyn: Mistress to a King.* New York, Grove Press, 2006.

Behn, Aphra. Letter "To the Right Honourable *Laurence,* Lord *Hyde,* Earl of Rochester." Edited by Janet Todd, *The Plays, 1682–1696*. Vol. 7 of *The Works of Aphra Behn*, edited by Janet Todd, 213–14. Columbus: Ohio State University Press, 1996.

——. *The Luckey Chance* (1686). Edited by Janet Todd. *The Plays, 1682–1696*. Vol. 7 of *The Works of Aphra Behn*, edited by Janet Todd. Columbus: Ohio State University Press, 1996.

——. *The Rover* (1677). Edited by Janet Todd. *The Plays, 1671–1677*. Vol. 5 of *The Works of Aphra Behn*, edited by Janet Todd. Columbus: Ohio State University Press, 1996.

——.*The Second Part of the Rover* (1681). Edited by Janet Todd. *The Plays, 1678–1682*. Vol. 6 of *The Works of Aphra Behn*, edited by Janet Todd. Columbus: Ohio State University Press, 1996.

Berglund, Lisa. "The Language of the Libertines: Subversive Morality in *The Man of Mode*." *Studies in English Literature, 1500–1900*, 30, no. 3 (1990): 369–86.

Berkowitz, Edward D. *Mass Appeal: The Formative Age of Movies, Radio, and TV.* Cambridge: Cambridge University Press, 2010.

Bevis, Richard. "Canon, Pedagogy, Prospectus: Redesigning 'Restoration and Eighteenth-Century English Drama.'" *Comparative Drama* 31, no. 1 (1997): 178–91.

Black, Gregory D. "Hollywood Censored: The Production Code Administration and the Hollywood Film Industry, 1930–1940." *Film History*, 3 (1989): 167–89.

Bogdanovich, Peter. "Commentary." Disc 1. *Bringing Up Baby*, special ed. DVD. Directed by Howard Hawks. Burbank, CA: Warner Home Video, 2005.

Boose, Lynda E. "Scolding Brides and Bridling Scolds: Taming the Woman's Unruly Member." *Shakespeare Quarterly* 42, no. 2 (1991): 179–213.

Boswell, James. *Life of Johnson*. Edited by R. W. Chapman and J. D. Fleeman. Oxford: Oxford World's Classics, 1980.

Braudy, Leo. *Native Informant: Essays on Film, Fiction, and Popular Culture.* Oxford: Oxford University Press, 1991.

Braverman, Richard. "The Rake's Progress Revisited: Politics and Comedy in the Restoration." In *Cultural Readings of Restoration and Eighteenth-Century Theater*, edited by J. Douglas Canfield and Deborah C. Payne, 141–68. Athens: University of Georgia Press, 1995.

Bringing Up Baby, special ed. DVD. Directed by Howard Hawks. 1938. Warner Brothers. Burbank, CA: Warner Home Video, 2005.

Brown, Richard E. "The Fops in Cibber's Comedies." *Essays in Literature* 9, no. 1 (1982): 31–41.

Bryant, Roger. *William Powell: The Life and Films*. Jefferson, NC: McFarland, 2006.

Canfield, J. Douglas. "The Ideology of Restoration Tragicomedy." *ELH* 51 (1984): 447–64.

——.Introduction to *The Broadview Anthology of Restoration and Early Eighteenth-Century Drama*. Edited by Douglas J. Canfield. Peterborough, ON: Broadview Press, 2001.

——, Ed. *The Broadview Anthology of Restoration and Early Eighteenth-Century Drama*. Peterborough, ON: Broadview Press, 2001.

Castiglione, Baldesar. *The Book of the Courtier*. Edited by Daniel Javitch. Translated by Charles S. Singleton. New York: Norton Critical Editions, 2002.

Cavell, Stanley. *Cities of Words: Pedagogical Letters on a Register of a Moral Life.* Cambridge, MA: Harvard University Press, 2005.

——.*The Claim of Reason: Wittgenstein, Skepticism, Morality, and Tragedy.* Oxford: Oxford University Press, 1979.

——.*Disowning Knowledge: In Seven Plays of Shakespeare*, rev. ed. Cambridge: Cambridge University Press, 2003.

——.*In Quest of the Ordinary: Lines of Skepticism and Romanticism.* Chicago: University of Chicago Press, 1988.

——.*Must We Mean What We Say?* 2nd ed. Cambridge: Cambridge University Press, 2002.

———.*Philosophy the Day after Tomorrow*. Cambridge, MA: Harvard University Press, 2005.

———.*Pursuits of Happiness: The Hollywood Comedy of Remarriage*. Cambridge, MA: Harvard University Press, 1984.

———.*The World Viewed: Reflections on the Ontology of Film*, enl. ed. Cambridge, MA: Harvard University Press, 1971.

Chorney, Alexander H. "Wycherley's Manly Reinterpreted." In *Essays Critical and Historical Dedicated to Lily B. Campbell*, 161–69. Berkeley: University of California Press, 1950.

Christensen, Jerome. "*Critical Response II*: Taking It to the Next Level: *You've Got Mail*, Havholm and Sandifer." *Critical Inquiry* 30, no. 1 (2003): 198–215.

Cibber, Colley. *Love's Last Shift; Or, The Fool in Fashion* (1696). Edited by Gary A. Richardson. In *The Broadview Anthology of Restoration and Early Eighteenth-Century Drama*, edited by J. Douglas Canfield, 710–59. Peterborough, ON: Broadview Press, 2001.

———. *The Careless Husband, A Comedy* (1704). In *British Dramatists from Dryden to Sheridan*, edited by George H. Nettleton and Arthur E. Case and revised by George Winchester Stone, Jr., 397–434. Carbondale: Southern Illinois University Press, 1969.

Collier, Jeremy. *A Short View of the Immorality and Profaneness of the English Stage*. 2nd ed. London, 1698.

Collington, Philip D. "'Stuffed with All Honourable Virtues': *Much Ado about Nothing* and *The Book of the Courtier*." *Studies in Philology* 103 (2006): 281–312.

Congreve, William. *The Way of the World* (1700). Edited by Herbert Davis. In *The Complete Plays of William Congreve*, edited by Herbert Davis, 386–479. Chicago: University of Chicago Press, 1967.

Copeland, Nancy. "'Once a Whore and Ever?': Whore and Virgin in *The Rover* and Its Antecedents." *Restoration* 16 (1992): 20–27.

———.*Staging Gender in Behn and Centlivre: Women's Comedy and the Theatre*. Aldershot: Ashgate, 2004.

Coppola, Al. "Retraining the Virtuoso's Gaze: Behn's *Emperor of the Moon*, the Royal Society, and the Spectacles of Science and Politics." *Eighteenth-Century Studies* 41, no. 4 (2008): 481–506.

Cordner, Michael, Ed. *Four Restoration Marriage Plays*. Oxford: Oxford World's Classics, 1995.

———."Playwright versus Priest: Profanity and the Wit of Restoration Comedy." In *The Cambridge Companion to Restoration English Theatre*, edited by Deborah Payne Fisk, 209–25. Cambridge: Cambridge University Press, 2000.

Corman, Brian. "Comedy." In *The Cambridge Companion to Restoration Theatre*, edited by Deborah Payne Fisk, 52–69. Cambridge: Cambridge University Press, 2000.

Cox, John F. Introduction to *Much Ado about Nothing*, by William Shakespeare. Edited by John F. Cox. Shakespeare in Production, 1–85. Cambridge: Cambridge University Press, 1997.

Daileader, Celia R. "Back-Door Sex: Renaissance Gynosodomy, Aretino, and the Exotic." *ELH* 69 (2002): 303–34.

Dashiell Hammett. Detective. Writer. DVD. *American Masters*, season 3, ep. 6. Directed by Joshua Waletzky. New York: Winstar TV and Video, 1999.

Davenant, William. *The Law against Lovers*, 1673. Adaptations of Shakespeare's Plays. London: Cornmarket Press, 1970.

Day, William. "I Don't Know, Just Wait: Remembering Remarriage in *Eternal Sunshine of the Spotless Mind*." In *The Philosophy of Charlie Kaufman*, edited by David LaRocca, 132–54. The Philosophy of Popular Culture. Lexington: University Press of Kentucky, 2011.

Denman, Jason. "'Too Hasty to Stay': Erotic and Political Timing in *Marriage à la Mode*." *Restoration* 32, no. 2 (2008): 1–23.

Dennis, John. "A Defense of *Sir Fopling Flutter*." In *1711–1729*. Vol. 2 of *The Critical Works of John Dennis*, edited by Edward Niles Hooker. Quoted in *The London Stage*, pt 1 (1660–1700), 11 March 1676, from "A Defense of *Sir Fopling Fluttter*" in *The Critical Works of John Dennis*, edited by E. N. Hooker, 242–50. Baltimore: Johns Hopkins University Press, 1943.

——.*The Usefulness of the Stage, to the Happiness of Mankind. to Government, and to Religion*. London, 1698.

DeRitter, Jones. "The Gypsy, *The Rover*, and the Wanderer: Aphra Behn's Revision of Thomas Killigrew." *Restoration* 10 (1986): 82–92.

Descartes, René. *Meditations Concerning First Philosophy*. In *Discourse on Method and Meditations*. Translated by Laurence J. Lafleur. Indianapolis: Bobbs-Merrill, 1960.

Detmer, Emily. "Civilizing Subordination: Domestic Violence and *The Taming of the Shrew*." *Shakespeare Quarterly* 48, no. 3 (1997): 273–94.

DiBattista, Maria. *Fast-Talking Dames*. New Haven, CT: Yale University Press, 2003.

Diver, Julia. "Memory, Desire, and Value in *Eternal Sunshine of the Spotless Mind*." In *Eternal Sunshine of the Spotless Mind*, edited by Christopher Grau, 80–93. Philosophers on Film. Abingdon, UK: Routledge, 2009.

Dooley, Dennis. *Dashiell Hammett*. New York: Frederick Ungar Publishing, 1984.

Dryden, John. *Absalom and Achitophel*. In *Poems, 1681–1684*. Edited by H. T. Swedenberg, 3–36. Vol. 2 of *The Works of John Dryden*, edited by Alan Roper and H. T. Swedenberg. Berkeley: University of California Press, 1972.

——."An Essay of Dramatick Poesie." In *Prose, 1668–1691*. Edited by Samuel H. Monk and A. E. Wallace Maurer, 3–82. Vol. 17 of *The Works of John Dryden*, edited by Alan Roper and H. T. Swedenberg. Berkeley: University of California Press, 1972.

——.*The Hind and the Panther*. In *Poems, 1685–1692*. Edited by Earl Miner and Vinton A. Dearing, 119–200. Vol. 3 of *The Works of John Dryden*, edited by Alan Roper and H. T. Swedenberg. Berkeley: University of California Press, 1969.

——. *Marriage à la Mode*. Edited by John Loftis, David Stuart Rhodes, and Vinton A. Dearing, 221–316. Vol. 11 of *The Works of John Dryden*, edited by Alan Roper and H. T. Swedenberg. Berkeley and Los Angeles: University of California Press, 1978.

——.Preface to *A Dialogue Concerning Women, Being a Defence of the Sex Written to Eugenia*, by [William Walsh]. London: R. Bentley, 1691.

——.*Secret Love, or The Maiden Queen*. Edited by John Loftis and Vinton A. Dearing, 114–203. Vol. 9 of *The Works of John Dryden*, edited by Alan Roper and H. T. Swedenberg. Berkeley and Los Angeles: University of California Press, 1966.

Duncan, Douglas. "Mythic Parody in *The Country Wife*." *Essays in Criticism* 31 (1981): 299–312.

Eldridge, Richard, and Bernard Rhie, eds. *Stanley Cavell and Literary Studies: Consequences of Skepticism.* New York: Continuum, 2011.

Eternal Sunshine of the Spotless Mind. collector's ed. DVD. Directed by Michael Gondry. 2004. Universal City, CA: Focus Features, 2004.

Etherege, George. *The Man of Mode; or Sir Fopling Flutter* (1676). In *The Plays of Sir George Etherege.* Edited by Michael Cordner, 209–333. Cambridge: Cambridge University Press, 1982.

Evans, James. "Teaching Willmore." *ABO: Interactive Journal for Women and the Arts, 1649–1830* 4, no. 1 (2014): 1–10.

Fabe, Marilyn. *Closely Watched Films: An Introduction to the Art of Narrative Film Technique.* Berkeley: University of California Press, 2014.

Fawell, John. *The Hidden Art of Hollywood: In Defense of the Studio Era Film.* Westport, CT: Greenwood Publishing, 2008.

Felsenstein, Frank. *Anti-Semitic Stereotypes: A Paradigm of Otherness in English Popular Culture, 1660–1830.* Johns Hopkins Jewish Studies. Baltimore: Johns Hopkins University Press, 1995.

Ferguson, Otis. Review of *Bringing Up Baby*, March 2, 1938, *New Republic Review.* Repr. in *Bringing Up Baby: Howard Hawks, Director*, edited by Gerald Mast, 268. New Brunswick, NJ: Rutgers University Press, 1988.

Flynn, Carol Houlihan. *Samuel Richardson: A Man of Letters.* Princeton, NJ: Princeton University Press, 1982.

Fujimura, Thomas H. Introduction to *The Country Wife*, by William Wycherley. Edited by Thomas H. Fujimura. Regents Restoration Drama, ix-xvii. Lincoln: University of Nebraska Press, 1965.

Gallagher, Catherine. "Who Was That Masked Woman? The Prostitute and the Playwright in the Comedies of Aphra Behn." *Women's Studies* 15 (1988): 23–42.

Gelber, Michael Werth. *The Just and the Lively: The Literary Criticism of John Dryden.* Manchester, UK: Manchester University Press, 1999.

Gellineau, David. "*The Country Wife*, Dance of the Cuckolds." *Comparative Drama* 48, no. 3 (2014): 277–305.

Gill, Pat. "Gender, Sexuality, and Marriage." In *The Cambridge Companion to English Restoration Theatre*, edited by Deborah Payne Fisk, 191–208. Cambridge: Cambridge University Press, 2000.

———.*Interpreting Ladies: Women, Wit, and Morality in the Restoration Comedy of Manners.* Athens: University of Georgia Press, 1994.

Gilpin, Bob. "Commentary." Disc 1. *My Man Godfrey.* Criterion Collection DVD. Directed by Gregory La Cava. 1936. Universal City, CA: Universal Home Video, 2001.

Glitre, Kathrina. *Hollywood Romantic Comedy: States of the Union, 1934–65.* Manchester, UK: Manchester University Press, 2006.

Gollapudi, Aparna. *Moral Reform in Comedy and Culture, 1696–1747.* Performance in the Long Eighteenth Century: Theatre, Music, Dance. Farnham, UK: Ashgate Publishing, 2011.

Gonda, Caroline. *Reading Daughters' Fictions 1709–1834: Novels and Society from Manley to Edgeworth.* Cambridge: Cambridge University Press, 1996.

Gould, Timothy. "Comedy." In the *Oxford Handbook of Philosophy and Literature*, edited by Richard Eldridge, 95–116. Oxford: Oxford Handbooks Online, 2009.

Greenblatt, Stephen. *Shakespearean Negotiations: The Circulation of Social Energy in Renaissance England.* Berkeley: University of California Press, 1988.

Greene, Jane M. "The Road to Reno: *The Awful Truth* and the Hollywood Comedy of Remarriage." *Film History* 13, no. 4 (2001): 337–58.

Griffin, Dustin. *Authorship in the Long Eighteenth Century*. Lanham, MD: Rowman and Littlefield/Newark, DE: University of Delaware Press, 2014.

Grindon, Leger. "Taking Romantic Comedy Seriously in *Eternal Sunshine of the Spotless Mind* (2004) and *Before Sunset* (2004)." In *A Companion to Film Comedy*, edited by Andrew Horton and Joanna E. Rapf, 196–216. Chichester, UK: Wiley-Blackwell, 2013.

Habermas, Jürgen. *The Structural Transformation of the Public Sphere: An Inquiry into a Category of Bourgeois Society*. Cambridge, MA: MIT Press, 1991.

Harris, Jocelyn. Introduction to *Sir Charles Grandison*, by Samuel Richardson, Vol. 1, vii-xxiv. Edited by Jocelyn Harris. 3 vols. Oxford: Oxford University Press, 1972.

Harth, Phillip. "Political Interpretations of *Venice Preserv'd*." *Modern Philology* 85 (1988): 345–62.

Harvey, James. *Romantic Comedy in Hollywood: From Lubitsch to Sturges*. New York: Alfred Knopf, 1987.

Heilman, Robert B. "Some Fops and Versions of Foppery." *ELH* 49, no. 2 (1982): 363–95.

His Girl Friday. DVD. Directed by Howard Hawks. 1940. Culver City, CA: Columbia Classics, 2000.

Holland, Peter. "Restoration Drama in the Twentieth Century." In *The Continuum Companion to Twentieth-Century Theatre*, edited by Colin Chambers, 643–45. London: Continuum, 2002.

Howard, James. *All Mistaken, or, The Mad Couple, a Comedy*. London: H. Brugis, 1672.

Howe, Elizabeth. *The First English Actresses: Women and Drama, 1660–1700*. Cambridge: Cambridge University Press, 1992.

Hume, Robert D. "Construction and Legitimation in Literary History." *The Review of English Studies*, New Series 56 (2005): 632–61.

———. "Jeremy Collier and the Future of the London Theater in 1698." *Studies in Philology* 96 (1999): 480–511.

———. "Marital Discord in English Comedy from Dryden to Fielding." *Modern Philology* 74 (1977): 248–72.

———. *The Rakish Stage: Studies in English Drama, 1660–1800*. Carbondale: Southern Illinois University Press, 1983.

———. "The Socio-Politics of London Comedy from Jonson to Steele." *Huntington Library Quarterly* 74 (2011): 187–217.

———. "Theatres and Repertory." In *1660–1896*. Edited by Joseph Donohue, 53–70. Vol. 2 of *The Cambridge History of British Theatre*, edited by Peter Thomson. Cambridge: Cambridge University Press, 2004.

Hutner, Heidi. "Revisioning the Female Body: *The Rover*, Parts I and II." In *Rereading Aphra Behn: History, Theory, and Criticism*, edited by Heidi Hutner, 102–20. Charlottesville: University of Virginia Press, 1993.

Inchbald, Elizabeth. "Remarks." *The Country Girl; A Comedy, in Five Acts; as Performed at the Theatre Royal, Drury Lane, alter'd from Wycherley's The Country Wife*, by David Garrick. In Vol. 16 of *The British Theatre, or a Collection of Plays . . . with Biographical and Critical Remarks by Mrs. Inchbald*. 25 vols. London: Longman, Hurst, Rees, and Orme, 1808.

It Happened One Night. DVD. Directed by Frank Capra. 1934. Culver City, CA: Columbia Classics, 1999.

Jacobs, Lea. "Keeping Up with Hawks." *Style* 32, no. 3 (1998): 402–26.
Jacobson, Alan. "The Great Marriage Debate of 1924: Lubitsch's Masterful Silent on DVD." *Bright Lights Film Journal* (April 30, 2004). http://brightlightsfilm.com/the-great-marriage-debate-of-1924-lubitschs-masterful-silent-on-dvd/.
Johnson, Samuel. *Dictionary of the English Language.* 2 vols. London: W. Strahan, 1755.
——, "Milton." Edited by Stephen Fix. In *Samuel Johnson: The Lives of the Poets*, edited by John H. Middendorf, 99–205. Vol. 21 of *The Yale Edition of the Works of Samuel Johnson*. New Haven, CT: Yale University Press, 2010.
——. Preface to *Johnson on Shakespeare*. Edited by Arthur Sherbo, 59–116. Vol. 7 of *The Yale Edition of the Works of Samuel Johnson*. New Haven: Yale, 1968.
——. *The Rambler*, May 19, 1750, no. 18. In *Samuel Johnson: The Rambler*. Edited by W. J. Bate and Albrecht J. Strauss, 97–103. Vol. 3 of *The Yale Edition of the Works of Samuel Johnson*. New Haven: Yale, 1969.
Jollimore, Troy. "Miserably Ever After: Forgetting, Repeating and Affirming Love in *Eternal Sunshine of the Spotless Mind*." In *Eternal Sunshine of the Spotless Mind*, edited by Christopher Grau, 31–61. Philosophers on Film. Abingdon, UK: Routledge, 2009.
Kahn, Coppélia. "'The Taming of the Shrew': Shakespeare's Mirror of Marriage." *Modern Language Studies* 5 (1975): 88–102.
Kaufman, Charlie. *Eternal Sunshine of the Spotless Mind: The Shooting Script.* New York: Newmarket Press, 2004.
Kendall, Elizabeth. *The Runaway Bride: Hollywood Romantic Comedy of the 1930s.* New York: Knopf, 1990.
Killigrew, Thomas. *Thomaso, Or, The Wanderer, A Comedy.* London: J. M. for Henry Herringman, 1663.
King, Thomas A. "'As if (She) Were Made on Purpose to Put the Whole World into Good Humour': Reconstructing the First English Actresses." *The Drama Review* 36, no. 3 (1992): 78–102.
Koon, Helene. *Colley Cibber: A Biography.* Lexington: University Press of Kentucky, 1986.
Kotsilibas-Davis, James, and Myrna Loy. *Myrna Loy: Being and Becoming.* New York: Knopf, 1987.
Kraft, Elizabeth. "Ethics, Politics, and Heterosexual Desire in Aphra Behn's *The Rover*." *Essays in Theatre / Études thétrâles* 19, no. 2 (2001): 111–25.
——. "Why Didn't Mirabell Marry the Widow Languish?" *Restoration: Studies in English Literary Culture, 1660–1700* 13 (1989): 26–34.
The Lady Eve. Criterion Collection DVD. Directed by Preston Sturges. 1941. Universal City, CA: Universal Home Video, 2001.
Langhans, Edward A. "The Theatre." In *The Cambridge Companion to English Restoration Theatre*, edited by Deborah Payne Fisk, 1–18. Cambridge: Cambridge University Press, 2000.
Lauretis, Teresa de. *Technologies of Gender: Essays on Theory, Film, and Fiction.* Bloomington: Indiana University Press, 1987.
Leicht, Kathleen. "Dialogue and Duelling in Restoration Comedy." *Studies in Philology* 104, no. 2 (2007): 267–80.
Leider, Emily W. *Myrna Loy: The Only Good Girl in Hollywood.* Berkeley: University of California Press, 2011.
Lemon, Alaina. *Between Two Fires: Gypsy Performance and Romani Memory from Pushkin to Post-Socialism.* Durham, NC: Duke University Press, 2000.

Levine, Lawrence. "Frank Capra's America: Part Three, Capra's Fundamental Values." *Journal for MultiMedia History* 2 (1999). http://www.albany.edu/jmmh/vol2no1/Levine3.html.

———."Frank Capra's America: Part Four, Pessimism in Capra's Cultural Politics." *Journal for MultiMedia History* 2 (1999). http://www.albany.edu/jmmh/vol2no1/Levine4.html.

Lowenthal, Cynthia. *Performing Identities on the Restoration Stage*. Carbondale and Edwardsville: Southern Illinois University Press, 2003.

Macey, Samuel L. *Patriarchs of Time: Dualism in Saturn-Cronus, Father Time, the Watchmaker God, and Father Christmas*. Athens: University of Georgia Press, 2010.

MacKenzie, Scott R. "Sexual Arithmetic: Appetite and Consumption in *The Way of the World*." *Eighteenth-Century Studies* 47, no. 3 (2014): 261–76.

Mannheimer, Katherine. "Cuckolds in Embryo: Congreve and the Phantasmagoric Sublime." Paper delivered at the Annual Conference of the American Society for Eighteenth-Century Studies, San Antonio, TX, March 2012.

Marcus, Steven. Introduction to *The Continental Op*, by Dashiell Hammett, vii–xxix. New York: Vintage, 1974.

Markley, Robert. "'Be Impudent, Be Saucy, Forward, Bold, Touzing, and Leud': The Politics of Masculine Sexuality and Feminine Desire in Behn's Tory Comedies." In *Cultural Readings of Restoration and Eighteenth-Century Theater*, edited by J. Douglas Canfield and Deborah C. Payne, 114–40. Athens: University of Georgia Press, 1995.

The Marriage Circle. DVD. Directed by Ernst Lubitsch. 1924. Chatsworth, CA: Image Entertainment, 2000.

Marsden, Jean I. *Fatal Desire: Women, Sexuality, and the English Stage, 1660–1720*. Ithaca, NY: Cornell University Press, 2006.

———."Performing the West Indies: Comedy, Feeling, and National Identity." *Comparative Drama* 42 (2008): 73–88.

Marshall, W. Gerald. "Wycherley's 'Great Stage of Fools': Madness and Theatricality in *The Country Wife*." *Studies in English Literature* 29, no. 3 (1989): 409–29.

Matalene, H. W. "What Happens in *The Country-Wife*." *Studies in English Literature* 22 (Summer 1982): 395–411.

Mast, Gerald. Introduction to *Bringing Up Baby: Howard Hawks, Director*, edited by Gerald Mast. Rutgers Films in Print Series, 3–16. 1988; New Brunswick, NJ: Rutgers University Press, 1994.

Maus, Katharine Eisaman. "'Playhouse Flesh and Blood': Sexual Ideology and the Restoration Actress." *ELH* 46, no. 4 (1979): 595–617.

McBride, Joseph. *Frank Capra: The Catastrophe of Success*. New York: Simon and Schuster, 1992.

McGirr, Elaine M. "Rethinking Reform Comedies: Colley Cibber's Desiring Women." *Eighteenth-Century Studies* 46, no. 3 (2013): 385–97.

Milhous, Judith. "Theatre Companies and Regulation." In *1660–1895* (108–25). Edited by Joseph Donohue. Vol. 2 of *The Cambridge History of British Theatre*, edited by Peter Thomson. Cambridge: Cambridge University Press, 2004.

Mizejewski, Linda. *It Happened One Night*. Wiley-Blackwell Studies in Film and Television. Oxford: Blackwell, 2010.

Moi, Toril. "The Adventure of Reading: Cavell and Beauvoir." In *Stanley Cavell and Literary Studies: Consequences of Skepticism*, edited by Richard Eldridge and Bernard Rhie, 17–29. New York: Continuum, 2011.

Morrissey, L. J. "Wycherley's Country Dance." *Studies in English Literature 1500–1900* 8, no. 3 (1968): 415–29.
Mulhall, Stephen. *Stanley Cavell: Philosophy's Recounting of the Ordinary*. Oxford: Oxford University Press, 1994.
My Man Godfrey. Criterion Collection DVD. Directed by Gregory La Cava. 1936. Universal City, CA: Universal Home Video, 2001.
Nagel, Thomas. "Moral Luck." In *Moral Luck*, edited by Dana Statman, 57–72. Albany: State University of New York Press, 1993.
Nash, Julie. "'The Sight on't Would Beget a Strong Desire': Visual Pleasure in Aphra Behn's *The Rover*." *Restoration* 18 (1994): 77–87.
Nelkin, Dana K. "Moral Luck." In *The Stanford Encyclopedia of Philosophy*, edited by Edward N. Zalta. http://plato.stanford.edu/entries/moral-luck/.
Nettleton, George H., and Arthur E. Case, eds. *British Dramatists from Dryden to Sheridan*. Rev. ed. by George Winchester Stone. Carbondale: Southern Illinois University Press, 1975.
Nietzsche, Friedrich. *Beyond Good and Evil: Prelude to a Philosophy of the Future*. Edited by Rolf-Peter Horstmann. Translated by Judith Norman. Cambridge Texts in the History of Philosophy. Cambridge: Cambridge University Press, 2002.
Nochimson, Martha. "*The Lady Eve* and *Sullivan's Travels*." *Cinéaste* 27, no. 3 (2002): 40–42.
Nugent, Frank S. Review of *Bringing Up Baby*. *New York Times* March 4, 1938. Repr. in *Bringing Up Baby: Howard Hawks, Director*, edited by Gerald Mast, 265. New Brunswick, NJ: Rutgers University Press, 1988.
Oliver, Kathleen. "'I Will Write Whore with This Penknife in Your Face': Female Amatory Letters, the Body, and Violence in Wycherley's *The Country Wife*." *Restoration* 38 (2014): 41–60.
Osborne, Francis. *Advice to a Son in Two Parts*. In *The Works of Francis Osborn [sic] Esq*. London, 1689.
Pacheco, Anita. "Rape and the Female Subject in Aphra Behn's *The Rover*." *ELH* 65, no. 2 (1998): 323–45.
———. "Reading Toryism in Aphra Behn's Cit Cuckolding Comedies." *Review of English Studies, n.s.* 55 (2004): 690–708.
Palmer, John. *The Comedy of Manners*. London: G. Bell and Sons, 1913.
Parker, Derek. *Nell Gwyn*. Stroud, UK: Sutton, 2000.
Payne, Deborah. "Reading the Signs in *The Country Wife*." *Studies in English Literature 1500–1900* 26 (1986): 403–19.
Pepys, Samuel. *The Diary of Samuel Pepys*. Edited by R. C. Latham and W. Matthews. 11 vols. London: HarperCollins, 1995.
Perry, Ruth. *Novel Relations: The Transformation of Kinship in English Literature and Culture 1748–1818*. Cambridge: Cambridge University Press, 2004.
Pope, Alexander. "Eloisa to Abelard." In *The Poems of Alexander Pope*. A one-volume edition of the Twickenham text, edited by John Butt, 252–61. New Haven, CT: Yale University Press, 1963.
Porter, Roy. "Before the Fringe: Quack Medicine in Georgian England." *History Today* 36 (1986). http://www.historytoday.com.
Potkay, Adam. "Narrative Possibilities of Happiness, Unhappiness, and Joy." *Social Research* 77, no. 2 (2010): 523–44.
Quirk, Lawrence J. *James Stewart: Behind the Scenes of a Wonderful Life*. New York: Applause Books, 1997.

Reeve, C. D. C. "Two Blue Ruins: Love and Memory in *Eternal Sunshine of the Spotless Mind*." In *Eternal Sunshine of the Spotless Mind*, edited by Christopher Grau, 15–30. Philosophers on Film. Abingdon, UK: Routledge, 2009.

Richardson, Gary A. Introduction to *Love's Last Shift; or, The Fool in Fashion*, by Colley Cibber. Edited by Gary A. Richardson. In *The Broadview Anthology of Restoration and Early Eighteenth-Century Drama*, edited by J. Douglas Canfield, 710. Peterborough, Ontario: Broadview, 2001.

Riskin, Robert. Shooting Draft of *It Happened One Night*. 1934. http://www.daily-script.com/index.html.

Roach, Joseph. *It*. Ann Arbor: University of Michigan Press, 2007.

———."The Performance." In *The Cambridge Companion to English Restoration Theatre*, edited by Deborah Payne Fisk, 19–39. Cambridge: Cambridge University Press, 2000.

Roberts, David. *Thomas Betterton: The Greatest Actor of the Restoration Stage*. Cambridge: Cambridge University Press, 2010.

Rorty, Richard. "From Epistemology to Romance: Cavell on Skepticism." *The Review of Metaphysics* 34, no. 4 (1981): 759–74.

Rosenfeld, Nancy. *The Human Satan in Seventeenth-Century English Literature: From Milton to Rochester*. Aldershot, UK, and Burlington, VT: Ashgate, 2008.

Rosenthal, Laura J. "'All Injury's Forgot': Restoration Sex Comedy and National Amnesia." *Comparative Drama* 42, no. 1 (2008): 7–28.

Ruppersburg, Hugh. "'O, So Many Startlements . . .': History, Race, and Myth in *O Brother, Where Art Thou?*" *Southern Cultures* 9, no. 4 (2003): 5–26.

Rutsky, R. L., and Justin Wyatt. "Serious Pleasures: Cinematic Pleasure and the Notion of Fun." *Cinema Journal* 30, no. 1 (1990): 3–19.

Savile, George. Marquis of Hallifax. *The Lady's New-Year Gift: Or Advice to a Daughter*. 2nd ed. London: Matt. Gillyflower and James Partridge, 1688.

Schatz, Thomas. "Film Genre and the Genre Film." In *Hollywood Genres: Formulas, Filmmaking, and the Studio System*, edited by Thomas Schatz, 14–41. Boston: McGraw-Hill, 1981.

———.*The Genius of the System: Hollywood Filmmaking in the Studio Era*. New York: Henry Holt, 1988.

Scheil, Katherine West. "Sir William Davenant's Use of Shakespeare in *The Law Against Lovers* (1662)." *Philological Quarterly* 76 (1997): 369–86.

Schickel, Richard. The Men Who Made the Movies: Howard Hawks, "Bringing Up Baby." Directed by Richard Schickel. 1973. Disc 2. *Bringing Up Baby*, special ed. DVD. Directed by Howard Hawks. Burbank, CA: Warner Home Video, 2005.

Schocket, Eric. "Undercover Explorations of the 'Other Half,' or the Writer as Class Transvestite." *Representations* 64 (Fall 1998): 109–33.

Scott, Mary Augusta. "*The Book of the Courtyer*: A Possible Source of Benedick and Beatrice." *PMLA* 16 (1901): 475–502.

Sedgwick, Eve Kosofsky. *Between Men: English Literature and Male Homosocial Desire*. New York: Columbia University Press, 1985.

Sennett, Richard. *The Fall of Public Man*. Cambridge: Cambridge University Press, 1974.

Shakespeare, William. *Much Ado about Nothing*. Folger Digital Texts. www.folgerdigitaltexts.org

Shohat, Ella, and Robert Stam. *Unthinking Eurocentrism: Multiculturalism and the Media*. New York: Routledge, 1994.

The Shop around the Corner. DVD. Directed by Ernst Lubitsch. 1940. Burbank, CA: Warner Home Video, 2002.

Shuger, Debora Kuller. *The Renaissance Bible: Scholarship, Sacrifice, and Subjectivity.* Berkeley and Los Angeles: University of California Press, 1998.
Shumway, David R. *Modern Love: Romance, Intimacy, and the Marriage Crisis.* New York: NYU Press, 2003.
Sikov, Ed. *Screwball: Hollywood's Madcap Romantic Comedies.* New York: Crown, 1989.
Sklar, Robert. *Movie-Made America: A Cultural History of American Movies.* Rev. ed. New York: Vintage Books, 1994.
Smith, David. "*Eternal Sunshine of the Spotless Mind* and the Question of Transcendence." *Journal of Religion and Film* 9, no. 1 (2005). http://www.unomaha.edu/jrf/Vol9No1/SmithSunshine.htm
Smith, John Harrington. *The Gay Couple in Restoration Comedy.* Cambridge, MA: Harvard University Press, 1948.
Snell, Bruno. *The Discovery of the Mind.* Cambridge, MA: Harvard University Press, 1953.
The Spectator. Edited with an introduction and notes by Donald F. Bond. 5 vols. Oxford: Clarendon Press, 1965.
Staves, Susan. "A Few Kind Words for the Fop." *Studies in English Literature* 22 (1982): 413–28.
——. "Jeptha's Vow Reconsidered." *Huntington Library Quarterly* 71 (2008): 651–69.
——. *Married Women's Separate Property in England, 1660–1833.* Cambridge, MA: Harvard University Press, 1990.
——. *Players' Scepters: Fictions of Authority in the Restoration.* Lincoln: University of Nebraska Press, 1979.
Stewart, Garrett. "Self-Relayance: Emerson to Poe." In *Stanley Cavell Literature and Film: The Idea of America*, edited by Andrew Taylor and Áine Kelly, 57–79. New York: Routledge, 2013.
Stone, Lawrence. *The Family, Sex, and Marriage in England: 1500–1800.* New York: Harper and Row, 1977.
Styan, J. L. *Restoration Comedy in Performance.* Cambridge: Cambridge University Press, 1986.
Sullivan's Travels. Criterion Collection DVD. Directed by Preston Sturges. 1941. Universal City, CA: Universal Home Video, 2001.
Szilagyi, Stephen. "The Importance of Being Easy: Desire and Cibber's *The Careless Husband.*" *Texas Studies in Literature and Language* 41, no. 2 (1999): 142–59.
——. "The Sexual Politics of Behn's *Rover*: After Patriarchy." *Studies in Philology* 95, no. 4 (1998): 435–55.
Taine, Hippolyte Adolphe. *History of English Literature.* Translated by H. Van Laun. 2 vols. Edinburgh: Edmonston and Douglas, 1871.
The Thin Man. DVD. Directed by W. S. Van Dyke. 1934. Burbank, CA: Warner Home Video, 2005.
Thompson, James. *Language in Wycherley's Plays.* Seventeenth-Century Language Theory and Drama. Tuscaloosa: University of Alabama Press, 1984.
——. "Sheridan, *The School for Scandal*, and Aggression." *Comparative Drama* 42, no. 1 (2008): 89–98.
Thompson, Kristen, and David Bordwell. *Film History: An Introduction.* New York: McGraw-Hill, 1994.
Thompson, Peggy. *Coyness and Crime in Restoration Comedy: Women's Desire, Deception, and Agency.* Lanham, MD: Rowman and Littlefield; Lewisburg, PA: Bucknell University Press, 2012.

——. "The Limits of Parody in *The Country Wife*." *Studies in Philology* 89, no. 1 (1992): 100–114.
Thorpe, Vanessa. "My Unforgettable Father, Roy." *The Observer*, February 11, 2007. http://www.theguardian.com/artanddesign/2007/feb/11/art.vanessathorpe
Tilley, Oliver. "American Movies' 'Closest Equivalent to Restoration Comedy.'" *Kinema: A Journal for Film and Audiovisual Media* (Fall 2009). http://www.kinema.uwaterloo.ca/article.php?id=460&feature
Todd, Dennis. *Imagining Monsters: Miscreations of the Self in Eighteenth-Century England*. Chicago: University of Chicago Press, 1995.
Todd, Janet. *The Secret Life of Aphra Behn*. New Brunswick, NJ: Rutgers University Press, 1996.
Toles, George. "Trying to Remember Clementine." In *Eternal Sunshine of the Spotless Mind*, edited by Christopher Grau, 111–57. Philosophers on Film. Abingdon, UK: Routledge, 2009.
Vair, Guillaume, du. *The Moral Philosophy of the Stoics*. Translated by Charles Cotton. London, 1667.
Vanbrugh, John. *The Relapse* (1696). Edited by James E. Gill. In *The Broadview Anthology of Restoration and Early Eighteenth-Century Drama*, edited by J. Douglas Canfield, 1480–1544. Peterborough, ON: Broadview Press, 2001.
Vance, John. *William Wycherley and the Comedy of Fear*. Newark: University of Delaware Press, 2000.
Vernon, P. F. "Marriage of Convenience and the Mode of Restoration Comedy." *Essays in Criticism* 12 (1962): 370–87.
Viefhues-Bailey, Ludger H. *Beyond the Philosopher's Fear: A Cavellian Reading of Gender, Origin and Religion in Modern Skepticism*. Aldershot, UK: Ashgate, 2012.
[Villiers, George]. *Plays, Poems, and Miscellaneous Writings associated with George Villiers, Second Duke of Buckingham*. Edited by Robert D. Hume and Harold Love. Oxford: Oxford University Press, 2007.
Wilkinson, D. R. M. *The Comedy of Habit: An Essay on the Use of Courtesy Literature in a Study of Restoration Comic Drama*. Leiden: Universitaire Pers, 1964.
Williams, Bernard. *Moral Luck*. Cambridge: Cambridge University Press, 1981.
Williams, Gordon. *A Dictionary of Sexual Language and Imagery in Shakespearean and Stuart Literature*. London: Athlone Press, 1994.
Wilson, Brett. *A Race of Female Patriots: Women and Public Spirit on the British Stage, 1688–1745*. Transits: Literature, Thought and Culture 1650–1850. Lewisburg, PA: Bucknell University Press, 2012.
Wilson, Derek. *All the King's Women: Love, Sex, and Politics in the Life of Charles II*. London: Pimlico, 2004.
Wycherley, William. *The Country Wife* (1675). Edited by Arthur Friedman. In *The Plays of William Wycherley*, edited by Arthur Friedman, 245–354. Oxford: Clarendon Press, 1979.
——. *The Plain Dealer* (1676). In *The Plays of William Wycherley*, edited by Arthur Friedman, 357–511. Oxford: Clarendon Press, 1979.
Young, Kay. "Hollywood 1934: Inventing Romantic Comedy." In *Look Who's Laughing: Gender and Comedy*, edited by Gail Finney, 257–74. Studies in Humor and Gender 1. Langhorne, PA: Gordon and Breach Science Publishers, 1994.
Zimbardo, Rose A. *Wycherley's Drama: A Link in the Development of English Satire*. New Haven, CT: Yale University Press, 1965.

Index

actress(es): Hollywood 2–3, 13; Restoration 2–3, 54, 83; *see also* individual names, e.g. Gwyn, Nell; Loy, Myrna
Addison, Joseph 184, 210–11
All Mistaken (Howard) 17–18
Alleman, Gellert Spencer 14, 223n20
Allestree, Richard 27
Alperson, Philip 162
Altman, Rick 4, 22n9
Anna Karenina (Leo Tolstoy) 43, 115, 207
Aristotle 9, 32, 54
Asta (Skippy, George, Mr. Smith) 57, 62, 70, 130, 145–6, 149
Astaire, Fred 101–2, 103
Astree (D'Urfey) 12
Atwood, Emma Katherine 72, 218
audience 18, 27, 42, 51, 53, 56, 69, 71, 73, 128, 142, 145, 150, 159, 162, 170, 205, 206; anxiety in 136–40, 162; comparison of Hollywood film and Restoration theater 5, 7, 8–9, 77; composition of 132; interest in genre 4, 110–11, 207; reactions of 104–5, 107, 115,123, 130, 132, 134, 143, 150–1, 156, 179, 196, 222n12, 226, 231; taste of 1930s American 86; taste of Restoration 29, 218
Austen, Jane 25, 47n5, 224
Awful Truth (McCarey) 14, 39, 57, 94, 144; ending of 222; knowledge in 214–15; remarriage in 215–17

Backscheider, Paula 14,
Barry, Elizabeth 69
Beach, Christopher 85–6
Beaux Stratagem, The (Farquhar) 219
Behn, Aphra 26, 52, 77, 82, 99, 100, 110, 112, 118, 124n4, 125n14, 209; *see also Luckey Chance, Rover,* and *Second Part of the Rover*
Bergland, Lisa 64–5
Berkowitz, Edward 53
Best Years of Our Lives, The (William Wyler): marriage as remarriage in 17
Betterton, Thomas 72
Bogdanovich, Peter 141, 146
Book of the Courtier, The (Castiglione) 26–7, 30–31
Booth, Barton 204
Bracegirdle, Anne 204
Braudy, Leo 42
Braverman, Richard 183, 187–8, 195
breeches roles 8, 139, 216; *see also* cross-dressing, gender
Bringing Up Baby (Hawks) 8, 22n23, 50, 52, 57, 76–7, 126, 128–9, 131, 136, 140, 141–2, 148, 149–52, 177, 215, 221, 227; anxiety attending language in 137–9; as beast fable 128–9; masochism/sadism in 129–30; as prehistoric myth of marriage 148–9; screwballs in 148
Broadview Anthology of Restoration and Early Eighteenth-Century Drama 51
"Brother, Can You Spare a Dime" 162
Brown, Richard 72
Bryant, Roger 16

Canfield, J. Douglas 37, 51, 74n14
canonical texts: of Restoration courtship comedy and Hollywood remarriage film 3, 6, 7, 11, 13, 20–1, 46, 50–2 74n4, 100, 124n4, 174–5, 182, 186, 232
Capra, Frank 7, 77, 85–6; *see also It Happened One Night*

Careless Husband, The (Cibber) 4; marriage in 204–5, 218–21
Carroll, Noël 162
Case, Arthur E. 50–1, 52, 174
Castiglione, Baldesar 30
Catherine, of Braganza, Queen of England 14, 19
Cavell, Stanley 8, 156, 174–5; and literary criticism 35–6, 100–2; and philosophical skepticism 6, 175–8, 202, 225, 228; on film 8–10; on knowledge and transgression 78–80, 83–4; on language 138–9, 202, 224; on marriage 1, 24, 93, 148, 150, 152n7, 204; on pairings of texts 7, 20, 76, 202; on remarriage comedy 2, 5–6, 27, 29, 30, 37, 38–9, 50, 54, 57, 58, 59, 63, 68–9, 83, 88, 119–23, 126–8, 131, 136–7, 148–50, 201, 205, 214–17, 225, 227; on the pursuit of moral perfectionism 54, 56–7, 113, 117, 213; on the melodrama of the unknown woman 5, 40, 73, 225, 227, 229–30; works: *Cities of Words* 20, 54, 57, 69, 73, 76, 202, 205, 227; *Claim of Reason* 6, 175–8, 227; *Contesting Tears* 225, 227, 229; *Philosophy the Day After Tomorrow* 100–2, 103, 138–9; *Pursuits of Happiness* 1–2, 6, 7, 8, 24, 27, 29, 30, 35, 37, 39, 50, 53, 57, 59, 61, 63, 78–80, 83–4, 88–9, 93, 114, 120–3, 126–8, 131, 136–7, 148–50, 152n4, 152n7, 154n29, 192, 197–201, 202, 203n6, 214–17, 230; *Must We Mean What We Say?* 224; *The World Viewed* 8–10
central couple 3, 5, 6, 20; Beatrice and Benedick models for 28–30; *Book of the Courtier* and 27; conversation of 27, 51, 68, 205–6, 218, 224; Gwyn and Hart models of 17–20; happiness and 69, 224, 227; Loy and Powell models of 14–17; "sex antagonism" in 11–12; skepticism and 28; smugness of 69–70; specialness of 54, 56; transformative implications of 28, 80, 167
Charles I, King of England 12, 28
Charles II, King of England 2, 14, 28, 123, 130
childhood 131–2, 152, 154n29, 193–4; invention of shared 58, 122, 149–50, 192, 228–9

Chorney, Alexander H. 155–6
Cibber, Colley 4, 51, 72, 204–5, 208–9, 212–13, 218; *see also Careless Husband* and *Love's Last Shift*
class conflict, reflected in genre 83–4, 86–7, 89–90, 99, 103, 109, 117–18, 132, 163, 169, 215
Coen, Ethan and Joel (the Coen Brothers) 109–10
Colbert, Claudette 16, 77, 83–4
Collier, Jeremy 130, 183–4, 187, 188, 192, 194, 195
Collington, Philip D. 26–7, 47n14
comedy of manners 42, 50, 51–52, 73n1
Congreve, William 26, 52, 182–3, 192, 195, 218; *see also Way of the World*
contract, *see* social contract
conversation 29, 34, 62–5, 73, 80, 88–9, 92–4, 155, 157–60, 163–4, 167–8, 205, 224–5, 232–3; between texts 7, 8, 14, 20–1, 174, 228; in *His Girl Friday* 200; in *It Happened One Night* 87–8; in *Marriage à la Mode* 42, 46; in *The Careless Husband* 220; in *The Man of Mode* 65, 68, 71–3; in *The Rover* 90–1, 93–5; in *The Shop around the Corner* 45–6; in *The Thin Man* 55–6, 62–4, 70, 73; in *The Way of the World* 186–7, 189; literary criticism as 35–7; sexual intercourse as 135, 205, 217; *see also* marriage, as conversation
Copeland, Nancy 81, 110, 113–14
Cordner, Michael 51, 183
Corman, Brian 51, 53–4, 201
Country Girl, The (Garrick) 130–1
Country Wife, The (Wycherley) 105, 113, 126, 127, 134–6, 146–51; anxiety and 137–9; beast fable and 128; homosociality and 129; improvisation in 132, 144–5; as marriage play 51; masochism/sadism in 129–30; medical/scientific authority and 132–4; overcoming skepticism in 140–1, 142–4, 152; reputation of 130–1, 156, 174, 188, 216; as subversive comedy 51
Coward, Noel 7
Cox, John F. 28–9
criticism, literary 30, 34–7, 100–2
cross-dressing 8, 85
cuckoldry 12, 28, 38, 117, 128–9, 135, 139, 146–7, 151–2, 190–1, 212

Index

Daileader, Celia R. 137–8
Davenant, William: *The Law Against Lovers* 28–30
Davies, Moll 19
Davies, Thomas 72
Day, William 228–30
Denman, Jason 41–2
Dennis, John 71, 188
DeRitter, Jones 82, 91
Descartes 6, 227, 228
Dialogue Concerning Women, Being a Defense of the Female Sex (Walsh) 31–2, 34
DiBattista, Maria 13, 198
Diver, Julia 229
divorce 228; Hollywood remarriage films and 6, 13–14, 21, 57, 80, 85, 148, 156, 197, 214–15; Restoration versions of and alternatives to 14, 23n28, 38, 74n14, 148–9, 219; *see also Doctrine and Discipline of Divorce*
Doctrine and Discipline of Divorce, The (Milton) 24
Dryden, John 26, 30–1, 35–6, 51, 71, 204; as critic 30, 34–7; works: *Absalom and Achitophel* 33–4; *Essay of Dramatic Poesy* 36–7; *Hind and the Panther* 34; *Secret Love* 18–20, 204; *see also Marriage á la Mode*
Duncan, Douglas 126
D'Urfey, Thomas 12

Eden, motif of 61, 64, 112–13, 119–20, 122, 126, 135, 140, 152n4, 164, 213
Eldridge, Richard 36
Elizabeth I, Queen of England 32
"Eloisa to Abelard" (Pope) 224, 228, 231–3
Eternal Sunshine of the Spotless Mind (Kaufman) 228–33
Etherege, George 26, 218; *see also Man of Mode*
Evans, Edith 52–3
Evelyn Prentice (William K. Howard) 16, 23n32
Exclusion Crisis 99, 105, 123

Fabe, Marilyn 181
fantasy: as impediment to marriage 28, 79–80, 82, 85, 120–2, 126, 202, 206, 227
Farquhar, George: *The Beaux' Stratagem* 219

Fawell, John 3
Felsenstein, Frank 103
Flynn, Carol Houlihan 224
Fonda, Henry 144
forgotten men 155–6, 161–2, 163–5, 166–7, 174, 176
Freud, Sigmund 42, 131
Frye, Northrop 59, 179

Gable, Clark 15–16, 87
Gallagher, Catherine 116
Garrick, David 130–1
"gay couple" 11–12, 14, 17–18, 19, 26, 28–30; *see also* central couple
Gelber, Michael Werth 30, 34–5
Gellineau, David 140
gender 34, 44, 89, 195, 216, 225; disguised 179, 188; fluidity 8, 44, 118–9, 138, 216, 218, 221; relations 3, 132
genre 4, 22n9, 80, 122, 124, 144, 202, 207–8; and canon 50–1; comedic 3, 101, 114; cultural work of 6–8 10–11, 13, 20–1, 22n9, 37, 46; stereotypes and 102–11
Gill, Pat 186, 225–6
Gilpin, Bob 168, 170, 177
Glyn, Elinor 2–3
Gollapudi, Aparna 208–9
Grant, Cary 1, 8, 10, 39, 97n10, 128–9, 144, 148, 149, 196, 203n6
green space (world) 41, 50, 57, 60–1, 68, 228
Greenblatt, Stephen 25
Greene, Jane M. 217
Grindon, Leger 231
Gwyn, Nell 20, 97n6; and Charles Hart 14, 17–19, 28

Habermas, Jürgen 9
Hammett, Dashiell 16, 66, 69
happiness 5, 11, 12, 55, 59, 61–2, 81, 87, 108, 114, 123, 132, 142–3, 222n11; false 187, 197–9, 206; impediments to 82, 120, 157, 162, 205–6, 231–2; justice and 183, 195, 210; marriage and 14, 20, 24, 28, 30, 43, 53, 121, 131, 152, 212–3, 221; moral perfectionism and 54, 79, 207, 224, 233; parameters to 149; sacrifice of 40, 55, 227; social contract and 68–9, 80, 79, 202
Harbage, Alfred 82
Harburg, Yip 162

Hart, Charles: and Nell Gwyn 14, 17–19, 28
Harth, Phillip 4
Harvey, James 56, 63, 65–6, 70
Hawks, Howard 7, 142, 148, 150, 198; *see also* Bringing Up Baby and His Girl Friday
Hays Code 97n10, 169, 183
Heilman, Robert B. 72
Henrietta Maria, Queen of England 12
Hepburn, Katharine 8, 10, 128–9, 130, 137, 142, 146, 150–1, 153n11
High Society 10
His Girl Friday (Hawks) 1, 50, 195–200; casual racism in 102–3, darkness of 192–3, 201, 227; false happiness in 206; fast-talking in 181, 202n3; language in 200; moral luck in 114
Hobbes, Thomas 34, 66, 67, 68
Holland, Peter 52–3
homosociality 105, 129
Hoover, Herbert 162
Howard, James 17
Howe, Elizabeth 17
Hume, Robert D. 74n4, 155–6, 166, 183–4, 218
humors characters 53, 185; *see also* zanies
Hutner, Heidi 105

improvisation 15, 45, 56, 88, 93, 132, 145, 177, 178, 195, 197, 198–9
Inchbald, Elizabeth 130
Indians 160–1
It Happened One Night (Capra) 1, 16, 76, 205; antimaterialist ethic of 78, 96; boundaries and transgression in 78; class tension in 86, 89, 101–2, 117; conversation in 87–8; darkness of 77–8, 85–6; doubleness of woman's character in 83, 86–7; light in 77–8; naming moment in 84–5, 136; theme of knowledge in 79–80, 215; Walls of Jericho as controlling metaphor in 79, 83, 84, 94–5

Jacobson, Alan 42
jactitation 14
James II, King of England 34, 105
Jane Shore (Nicholas Rowe) 232
Jephthah's daughter 95–6
Jericho, walls of 94–5
Johnson, Samuel 24, 25, 94
Jollimore, Troy 231

Kael, Pauline 52
Kahn, Coppélia 86
Kant, Emmanuel 111
Kaufman, Charlie 21, 224, 228, 230–31, 233; *see also* Eternal Sunshine of the Spotless Mind
Killigrew, Thomas: *Thomaso* 82, 89–90, 97n6, 106
King, Thomas A. 82–3
Kinnear, Rory 72
knowledge 5, 8, 93, 116, 133; acceptance of 178, 213, 217; control of 118; desire for 64, 121–2, 175; and language 84; and moral action 175–6, 208–10; as transgression 78–81
Kraft, Elizabeth 182

La Cava, Gregory 158, 179; *see also* My Man Godfrey
Lady Eve, The (Sturges) 83, 99, 143–4, 192, 209; causal luck in 112–13; circumstantial luck in 112; class conflict in 117; constitutive luck in 112; genre in 122; knowledge in 117, 121; motif of Eden in 113, 119–22; resultant luck in 112
Lake, Veronica 108
Langhans, Edward A. 2
language 64–5, 71, 139; anxiety about 137–9, 150; as a way to take an interest in one's own life 80, 84, 87, 91, 101; barrage of in remarriage films 1; demeaning or shocking language 103–4, 167–8; elaborate in Platonic love tradition 12; failure of 179; just and lively in Dryden 35; learning to speak (or already speaking) the same as characteristic of the central couple in Hollywood film and on the Restoration stage 27, 41, 56, 57, 62, 65, 73, 88, 93, 187, 205, 228, 231; ordinary (and ordinary language philosophy) 35, 52–3, 178–9, 200, 202, 210–11, 224; *see also* metaphor
Law Against Lovers, The (Davenant) 28–30
Leicht, Kathleen 114
Leigh, Antony 113, 118
Letter from an Unknown Woman (Max Ophüls) 229–30
Levine, Lawrence 86
Locke, John 5, 7, 68–9; *Two Treatises of Government* 33–4, 226–7
Lombard, Carole 176–7

Love's Last Shift (Cibber) 214, 217, 218; marriage in 204–5, 213; philosophical sophistication of 208–9, 211–12
Loy, Myrna 14, 17, 19, 23n33; and William Powell 15–17
Lubitsch, Ernst 42–3, 44, 46; *Marriage Circle* 42; *see also* Shop around the Corner, The
Luck 148, 199; moral 111–13, 114, 115, 148, 209
Luckey Chance, The (Behn) 105, 111, 112, 114–21, 123–4, 209, 216; anti-Semitism in 112; causal luck in 112–13; circumstantial luck in 112; class conflict in 107, 113–14, 117–19; constitutive luck in 112; circumstantial luck in 112; constitutive luck in 112; as corrective satire 51; homosociality in 105; forgiveness and 118–19, 123–4; as marriage play 51; moral compromise in 113–17; motif of Eden in 113, 119–20; resultant luck in 113

McCrea, Joel 107, 108
McGirr, Elaine M. 217
MacKenzie, Scott R. 183
Madame Bovary (Gustave Flaubert) 207
Man of Mode, The (Etherege) 1, 8, 26, 218, 227; Fopling Flutter in 71–3; heroine's desire in 53, 55, 59–61; language in 62, 64–5, 205; motif of Eden in 61, 64; mutual fascination of central couple in 56, 58–9, 63–5, 70; smugness of central couple of 69; as social comedy 51; social contract and 66, 67–9
Manhattan Melodrama (Van Dyke) 15–16, 19
Mannheimer, Katherine 191–2, 193, 195
Marcus, Steven 66
Markley, Robert 99, 124n4
marriage 4, 7, 42, 54, 74, 143, 150–2, 204–6, 212–14, 221; companionate 3–4; as conversation 5–6, 24–32, 40, 63, 94, 228; definition of in remarriage films 1–2, 17, 39, 54, 57, 84, 93–4, 121, 123, 126, 149, 192, 215–18; dissolution of 13–14; as meditation on state or nation 8, 33–4, 37–8, 68–9; in Restoration period 10–13, 50, 89, 99, 190; sex and 17, 126–9, 147–8, 152

Marriage à la Mode (Dryden) 20, 63, 204, 205, 218; tragicomic plot of 37–42, 46–7
Marsden, Jean I. 180n4, 224, 226
Marshall, W. Gerald 126, 128
Mary II, Queen of England 32
Mast, Gerald 131–2
Matalene, H. W. 127
Maus, Katharine 3
melancholy 155–6, 175, 233
melodrama 5, 20, 40, 58, 73, 82, 144, 207, 210, 224–33
metaphor 136–7; in *The Way of the World* 186, 191–2, 200–2, 228
Milton, John 7, 24, 68, 94
Moi, Toril 36
moral perfectionism: marriage and 117, 207, 213, 224, 227, 232–3; moral luck and 111, 113; the pursuit of happiness and 54–5, 79, 224, 227
Motion Picture Production Code *see* Hays Code
Mulhall, Stephan 224–5
My Man Godfrey (La Cava) 21, 148, 158, 206, 215; conversation between central couple in 159, 164, 167–70; Godfrey's character in 161–5, 166, 175–9; Indians in 160–1; propriety in 168–9; redemption in 171; relationship to remarriage film genre 156, 174

Nagel, Thomas 111, 112
naming 84–85, 136
Nash, Julie 81
Nelkin, Dana K. 111–12
Nettleton, George H. 50–1, 52, 174
news 57, 59, 64, 84, 88, 104, 139, 193–7, 199; *see also* scandal
Nietzsche, Friedrich 131, 231, 234n19
Nochimson, Martha 110, 124n4
Nokes, James 113
Now, Voyager (Irving Rapper) 40, 227
Nugent, Frank S. 129–30

O Brother Where Art Thou? (Joel and Ethan Coen) 109–10
"Ochi Chernye" 43–4, 169, 206, 207, 222n5
Old Comedy 53, 59–60
Oldfield, Anne 204
Oliver, Kathleen 129
Osborne, Francis 27–8

Index

Pacheco, Anita 97n3, 116
Pallette, Eugene 122–3
Panofsky, Erwin 10
Payne, Deborah 140–1
Pepys, Samuel 10–11, 18–19, 22n22, 28
Perry, Ruth 3–4, 22n8
Philadelphia Story, The (George Cukor) 10, 21, 123, 130, 203n6, 227
philosophy 1–2, 7, 35, 36, 208, 210–11, 213–14, 217–18, 225, 227
Phoenix Society 52
Plain Dealer, The (Wycherley) 21, 51, 192; conversation between central couple in 158–9, 170; depravity in 171–2; Indians in 160–1; Manly's character in 156–160, 166–7, 175–6, 179; as marriage play 51; propriety in 169–70; redemption in 174; relationship to courtship comedy genre 155–6, 174
Platonic love 12, 74n3
Pope, Alexander 213, 224, 228, 231–2; "Elegy to the Memory of an Unfortunate Lady" 232; *see also* "Eloisa to Abelard"
Porter, Roy 133
Powell, William 66, 73, 164, 170; and Myrna Loy 15–17, 23n33
prejudice: reflected in genres 99–111, 112, 200
propriety 159, 168–9, 170, 176, 177, 178

Quirk, Lawrence J. 206

Rambler, The (Johnson) 24
Reeve, C. D. C. 229
repartee 1, 25, 29, 41–2, 55, 224, 225
repertory companies 3, 21n4
Rhie, Bernard 36
Richardson, Gary A. 204
Richardson, Samuel 25, 184, 224
Roach, Joseph 2, 22n22, 52, 136
Roberts, David 67, 75n34
Roosevelt, Franklin Delano 11, 166
Rorty, Richard 6, 228
Rosenthal, Laura J. 38, 151
Rover, The (Behn) 27, 76, 102–3, 105, 119, 218; angel/harlot in 82–3, 91–2; antimaterialist ethic of 78, 96; anti-Semitic language in 102–3; boundaries in 81; breeches role in 139; class tension in 89–91; darkness of 77–8; language in 92–4;

light in 77–8; Jephtha's daughter as controlling metaphor in 95–6; naming moment in 85, 136; quest for knowledge in 80–1; rape in 97n3; as social comedy 51; treatment of wealth and class in 89–90
Rowe, Nicholas 232
Rutsky, R. L. 110

scandal 57, 64, 188, 193, 209
Scheil, Katherine West 29
Schocket, Eric 99, 110
Scott, Mary Augusta 47n14
screwball comedy 42, 43, 52–3, 207; characters in 148, 176–7; features of 15
Second Part of the Rover, The (Behn) 76, 103–7; prejudice reflected and subverted in 103, 105, 107, 109; treatment of class in 99–100
Sedgwick, Eve Kosofsky 129
Sennett, Richard 9
Shakespeare, William 7, 25, 54–5, 100; *As You Like It* 55; green space in 60; *Hamlet* 224; *Measure for Measure* 28–9; *Much Ado About Nothing* 25–30, 55; *Othello* 10, 177–8; *Taming of the Shrew* 86; *Twelfth Night* 55
she-tragedy 5, 20, 21, 40, 224–8, 231–2
Shohat, Ella 109
Shop around the Corner, The (Lubitsch) 20, 205, 206–7, 215; tragicomic plot of 37–8, 40, 43–6
Shumway, David 6
Sikov, Ed 176–7
skepticism 5–6, 38, 47, 80, 122, 150–1 231, 233; knowledge and 175–9, 225, 228; metaphor and 202; overcoming 140–1, 152, 164, 231, 233
Sklar, Robert 53
Smith, David 231
Smith, John Harrington 11–13, 30
Snell, Bruno 175
Spectator, The (Addison and Steele) 210
social contract 5, 57, 66–9, 227
sound technology in motion pictures 55–6
Stage Society 52
Stam, Robert 109
Stanwyck, Babara 144
Staves, Susan 12–13, 22n24, 72, 190
Steele, Richard 184, 210
stereotypes 101, 103, 105, 107–10, 214–15; *see also* prejudice

Stewart, James (Jimmy) 10, 206
Stone, George Winchester, Jr. 50–1, 52, 174
Stone, Lawrence 3–4, 21n8
Sturges, Preston 99, 100, 103, 107, 109–10, 112, 117, 122–3, 124n4, 209; *see also The Lady Eve* and *Sullivan's Travels*
Styan, J. L. 29, 67, 74n9
Sullavan, Margaret 206
Sullivan's Travels (Sturges) 99, 117; self-reflexivity of 107, 110; treatment of stereotype in 103, 105, 108–10
Summers, Montagu 52
Szilagyi, Stephen 81, 91, 218

Tatler, The (Addison and Steele) 210
Thin Man, The (Van Dyke) 16, 102, 130, 221; conversation in 55–6, 62–3; heroine's desire for knowledge in 60; language in 62, 65, 73; melodrama in 58–9, 73; mutual fascination of central couple in 57, 63–4; portrayal of marriage in 17, 21; smugness of central couple of 69–70; social contract in 66–7
Thompson, James 102, 136, 140, 161, 166, 178–9, 180n12
Thompson, Peggy 103, 126
Thurber, James 13
Tilley, Oliver 52
Todd, Janet 114, 119
Toles, George 229, 234n19
tragicomedy 20, 37, 42
transgression 78–81, 86
transvestism 8; and class 99; *see also* breeches roles; cross-dressing

Van Dyke, W. S. (Woody) 15, 16–17, 19, 97n10; *see also Manhattan Melodrama* and *Thin Man*
Vanbrugh, John 51; *The Relapse* 204–5, 208, 211, 214, 218
Vance, John 129
violence 76, 77, 80, 82, 99, 108–9, 129, 139, 151, 163, 176, 218
voice 2, 5, 16, 34–5, 54, 65, 69, 72, 83, 88, 91, 101, 123, 151, 214–17

Walsh, William 30–2
Way of the World, The (Congreve) 1, 26, 52, 64, 89, 105, 148, 218; character of Millamant in 181–2, 185; character of Mirabell 183–5; childhood in 149–50; conversation in 187; justice in 188–91; language in 186, 191–3; as marriage play 51; print culture in 193–5; skepticism in 202; as social comedy 51; *see also* metaphor
Wilkinson, D. R. M. 27
Wilks, Robert 204
William III, King of England 32
Williams, Bernard 111–12, 115
Wilson, Brett 226
Woodward, Henry 72
Wyatt, Justin 110
Wycherley, William 130, 132, 134, 142, 147, 156, 158, 173, 175; *see also Country Wife* and *Plain Dealer*

Young, Kay 62–4, 66, 220, 233

zanies 54, 145, 148, 155, 163
Zimbardo, Rose A. 166

Taylor & Francis eBooks

Helping you to choose the right eBooks for your Library

Add Routledge titles to your library's digital collection today. Taylor and Francis ebooks contains over 50,000 titles in the Humanities, Social Sciences, Behavioural Sciences, Built Environment and Law.

Choose from a range of subject packages or create your own!

Benefits for you
- Free MARC records
- COUNTER-compliant usage statistics
- Flexible purchase and pricing options
- All titles DRM-free.

Benefits for your user
- Off-site, anytime access via Athens or referring URL
- Print or copy pages or chapters
- Full content search
- Bookmark, highlight and annotate text
- Access to thousands of pages of quality research at the click of a button.

REQUEST YOUR FREE INSTITUTIONAL TRIAL TODAY

Free Trials Available
We offer free trials to qualifying academic, corporate and government customers.

eCollections – Choose from over 30 subject eCollections, including:

Archaeology	Language Learning
Architecture	Law
Asian Studies	Literature
Business & Management	Media & Communication
Classical Studies	Middle East Studies
Construction	Music
Creative & Media Arts	Philosophy
Criminology & Criminal Justice	Planning
Economics	Politics
Education	Psychology & Mental Health
Energy	Religion
Engineering	Security
English Language & Linguistics	Social Work
Environment & Sustainability	Sociology
Geography	Sport
Health Studies	Theatre & Performance
History	Tourism, Hospitality & Events

For more information, pricing enquiries or to order a free trial, please contact your local sales team:
www.tandfebooks.com/page/sales

Routledge — Taylor & Francis Group
The home of Routledge books

www.tandfebooks.com